FOSTERING STUDENT SUCCESS

IN THE

CAMPUS COMMUNITY

FOSTERING
STUDENT
SUCCESS
IN THE
CAMPUS
COMMUNITY

GARY L. KRAMER
AND ASSOCIATES

JOSSEY-BASS
A Wiley Imprint
www.josseybass.com

Published by Jossey-Bass
A Wiley Imprint
989 Market Street, San Francisco, CA 94103–1741   www.josseybass.com

Jossey-Bass books and products are available through most bookstores. To contact Jossey-Bass directly call our Customer Care Department within the U.S. at 800-956-7739, outside the U.S. at 317-572-3986, or fax 317-572-4002.

Jossey-Bass also publishes its books in a variety of electronic formats. Some content that appears in print may not be available in electronic books.

Library of Congress Cataloging-in-Publication Data

Kramer, Gary L., 1945-
    Fostering student success in the campus community / Gary L. Kramer and Associates.
— 1st ed.
        p. cm.
    Includes bibliographical references and index.
    ISBN 978-1-933371-24-5 (cloth : alk. paper)
    1. Student affairs services—United States. 2. College student development programs—United States. 3. Universities and colleges—United States. I. Title.
    LB2342.92.K73 2007
    378.1'97—dc22   2007028920

Printed in the United States of America
FIRST EDITION
HB Printing 10 9 8 7 6 5 4 3 2 1

TABLE OF CONTENTS

ABOUT THE AUTHORS

Joe Bagnoli, a graduate of Berea College (1988), earned an M.A. (1992) in student personnel services for higher education from Eastern Kentucky University and is a Phi Kappa Phi scholar. He served as director of admissions and financial aid at Concord University in West Virginia before returning to Berea College as director of admissions in 1997. In 2003 he was appointed to his current position as associate provost for enrollment management at Berea. Called on regularly to consult with colleges and universities on enrollment-related matters, he has served on the executive council of the Kentucky Association of Secondary and College Admission Counselors, earning the president's award for service to the organization in 2000 and the human relations award in 2002. He is a member of the National Association for College Admission Counseling and the American Association of Collegiate Registrars and Admissions Officers.

Jennifer L. Bloom is associate professor and head of the master's program in student development at the University of South Carolina. She received her bachelor's degree (1988) from Illinois State University in physical education teaching (K–12), her master's degree (1990) in athletic administration from the University of Illinois at Urbana-Champaign, and her Ed.D. (1995) in higher education administration. She received the National Academic Advising Association's Outstanding Advising Administrators Award in 2005 and was elected to the organization's board of directors (2005–2008). She has taught a graduate-level class on academic advising at the University of Illinois and the University of Louisville. In addition, she has presented her work at national conferences and at college campuses on numerous topics, including academic advising, appreciative inquiry, and higher education career paths. She is coauthor of the book *Career Aspirations and Expeditions: Advancing Your Career in Higher Education Administration* (Stipes, 2003).

Janice Burdette Blythe has been a professional in higher education for 30 years. She was awarded a B.S. (1972) in administrative dietetics from Eastern Kentucky University, an M.S. (1974) in clinical nutrition from the University of Kentucky, and a Ph.D. (1987) in animal science with an emphasis in nutrition from the University of Kentucky. After serving as a clinical practitioner for a few years, she returned to her undergraduate alma mater, teaching and advising graduates and undergraduates for nearly a decade. For the past two decades at Berea College, she has served as an academic department chair, a full-time teaching faculty member in general education and human nutrition, and a midlevel administrator. At Berea she has been involved extensively in academic advising as an elected faculty representative in the governance system and as chair of the executive council. She currently holds the rank of full professor and serves as associate provost for advising and academic success. Her memberships in professional organizations include the National Academic Advising Association and the National Association of Student Personnel Administrators.

Tom Brown has served as an educator in academic and student affairs for 35 years and was the dean of advising services/special programs at Saint Mary's College of California (1977–1997). In addition to developing and administering Saint Mary's nationally recognized faculty-based academic advising program, he was responsible for new-student and new-family orientation programs; academic support and achievement (e.g., tutoring and services for students with disabilities); and the offices for Asian Pacific American, Black, Hispanic/Latino, and international student programs and for pre-law advising. Tom developed the High Potential Program at Saint Mary's, which provides access and support to first-generation students from disadvantaged backgrounds. Graduation rates for High Potential students grew to exceed those for all other cohorts at the college. When he left Saint Mary's, the students and faculty established the Dean Thomas Brown Advising Award, which is presented each year to a faculty member at the college. He has served in numerous elected and appointed roles in the National Academic Advising Association (NACADA), including member of the board of directors and vice president. He cochaired the 1990 National Conference on Academic Advising and has served since 1987 on the faculty of the NACADA Academic Advising Summer Institute. He has presented and published extensively on academic advising, supporting multicultural students and at-risk cohorts, and international educational exchange. He is currently the managing principal of a consulting network, Thomas Brown & Associates (www.tbrownassociates.com), and he has assessed, developed, or facilitated academic advisor development programs at more than 250 colleges and universities in the United States and abroad.

Emily E. Bullock is an assistant professor in the College of Education and Psychology at the University of Southern Mississippi. She maintains research interests in vocational psychology and assessment, personality, career counseling and academic advising, and work environments. Her work has appeared in the *Journal of College Student Development* and the *NACADA Journal,* and she has presented at the National Career Development Association on issues relevant to career and academic advising. At both the University of Southern Mississippi and Florida State University career centers, she was employed as a career advisor. She taught an undergraduate career development course and plans to teach graduate-level vocational-psychology courses. She received her bachelor's degree in psychology and her master's degree in counseling psychology from the University of Southern Mississippi and her Ph.D. in counseling psychology and school psychology from Florida State University.

Peter B. DeBlois is director of programs and media relations for EDUCAUSE, the nonprofit association for information technology in higher education. He coordinates member programs—including special interest constituent and discussion groups, advisory committee volunteers, board elections, and annual awards—and manages association press releases and media relations. Before his work with EDUCAUSE, he was university registrar, director of registration and records, and assistant director of freshman English at Syracuse University. He helped found the Registrars' Summer Institute at Aspen and the American Association of University Registrars. He has presented at conferences for the American Association of Collegiate Registrars and Admissions Officers, the Middle States Association of Collegiate Registrars and Officers of Admission, the Conference on the Freshman Year Experience, the College and University Machine Records Conference, and EDUCAUSE. He holds a doctor of arts in rhetoric and composition and an M.A. in English from Syracuse University and a B.A. from St. Lawrence University. He has taught composition, literature, and honors seminars at Illinois State University, the Metropolitan State College of Denver, Onondaga Community College, and Syracuse University. He coauthored *Composition and Literature: A Rhetoric for Critical Writing* (Prentice Hall, 1984), has written for *EDUCAUSE Quarterly* and *EDUCAUSE Review,* and is responsible for the annual EDUCAUSE Current Issues Survey.

Rusty N. Fox is vice president for student development services at Tarrant County College's southeast campus and is that campus's chief student affairs officer. Active in his profession, he presents at national and regional conferences and serves as a member of the National Academic Advising Association (NACADA) Consultants Bureau. He has been on the faculty at the NACADA Academic Advising Summer Institute and the Academic Advising Administrators' Institute. As a past board member, he served twice as the association's national commission chair for two-year colleges. Likewise, he is involved in community and educational organizations and currently serves on the board for the Martin Luther King Jr. Celebration Committee for the city of Arlington, Texas. He served as dean of student development and director of counseling/advising at Oklahoma City Community College and as coordinator of academic advising at Brookhaven College. He holds a B.A. in speech communications from Texas A&M University and an M.S. in counseling from Texas A&M–Commerce, where he was named an outstanding alumnus. He is currently a Ph.D. candidate in higher education at Capella University.

Virginia N. Gordon is assistant dean emeritus and adjunct associate professor at the Ohio State University. She has extensive experience in teaching, administration, advising, and counseling in higher education settings. Her bibliography includes many books, monographs, book chapters, and journal articles on advising administration, career counseling, working with undecided students, and advisor training. She is past president of the National Academic Advising Association (NACADA) and the founder and first director of the National Clearinghouse on Academic Advising. Virginia has received national acclaim and numerous awards for her contributions to the field. NACADA named its award for outstanding contributions to the field of academic advising the Virginia N. Gordon Award.

Thomas J. Grites has served as director of academic advising, interim director of teacher education, interim dean of social and behavioral sciences, assistant to the vice president for academic affairs, and currently as assistant to the provost in his 28 years at the Richard Stockton College of New Jersey. He currently has responsibilities related to academic orientation programming, first-year experience efforts, the Banner Student implementation team, and various other projects. He also teaches regularly, most recently piloting a seminar course for new transfer students. He was one of the founding members of the National Academic Advising Association (NACADA) and served as its president for two terms. He currently serves as a senior editor of the

NACADA Journal and regularly provides other services to the organization. Thomas has written more than 50 journal articles, book chapters, and professional reports; he has delivered more than 70 conference presentations; and he has conducted faculty development workshops and academic advising program reviews on more than 100 campuses. He has served on the Absecon Board of Education for more than 20 years. He earned his B.S. and M.S. from Illinois State University and his Ph.D. from the University of Maryland. Both institutions have awarded him distinguished alumni awards.

Wesley R. Habley is a principal associate and coordinator of ACT's Office of State Organizations. He received his B.S. in music education and M.Ed. in student personnel from the University of Illinois at Urbana-Champaign and his Ed.D. from Illinois State University in educational administration. Before joining ACT, Wes directed advising programs at Illinois State University and the University of Wisconsin–Eau Claire. His recent coauthored publications are *What Works in Student Retention? Four-Year Public Colleges* (ACT, 2004) and *Academic Advising: A Comprehensive Handbook* (Jossey-Bass, 2000). He is the author of monographs on four of ACT's National Surveys of Academic Advising. He contributed chapters to *Developmental Academic Advising Foundations: A College Reader* and *Faculty Advising Examined: Enhancing the Potential of College Faculty as Advisors,* as well as numerous journal articles and chapters in monographs published by Jossey-Bass, the National Resource Center for The First-Year Experience and Students in Transition, and the National Academic Advising Association (NACADA). He is a charter member of NACADA and has served the association in numerous roles, including president and treasurer. He founded the NACADA Academic Advising Summer Institute in 1987 and continues to serve on the faculty. He is the recipient of NACADA's awards for outstanding contributions to the field of academic advising and service to NACADA. Wes has served as a consultant at more than 125 colleges in the United States, Middle East, and Canada.

Michael A. Haynes is director of academic advising and interim dean of University College at Ball State University. He received a B.A. in English from Taylor University and an M.A. and a Ph.D. in English from Ball State University. He is a 20-year member of the National Academic Advising Association (NACADA) and has served on the board of the *NACADA Journal.* He served as editor of *Academic Advising News* and was part of the development team for a NACADA faculty advising training video. He has given numerous presentations on issues related to advising and learning communities at regional and national conferences.

Don Hossler is professor of educational leadership and policy studies at Indiana University Bloomington and director of the Project on Academic Success. He has served as the vice chancellor for enrollment services for Indiana University Bloomington, the associate vice president for enrollment services for the Indiana University system, the executive associate dean for the School of Education, and chair of the Department of Educational Leadership and Policy Studies. His areas of specialization include college choice, student financial aid policy, enrollment management, and higher education finance. He served in administrative positions at California Lutheran University from 1972–1981. He taught at Loyola University of Chicago from 1981–1985 and joined the faculty at Indiana University in 1985. He has consulted with more than 50 colleges, universities, and related educational organizations. He has presented more than 130 scholarly papers and invited lectures in the United States, Canada, and China and has lived in Russia and conducted research on higher education reform there. He currently directs research funded by the Lumina Foundation and the College Board on the topics of postsecondary access, student transfer, and retention. He is the author or coauthor of 12 books and monographs and more than 70 articles and book chapters. He is coeditor of the recent book *Incentive-Based Budgeting Systems in Public Universities* (Edward Elgar, 2003). He has received national awards for his research and scholarship from the American College Personnel Association and the National Association of Student Personnel Administrators.

Donald Hudson's career at Berea College has spanned 40 years, during which time he has advanced to the rank of professor of technology. He has taught courses in quality control, manufacturing, and general studies. He served as chair of the Department of Technology for 19 years and held the position of associate provost for advising and academic success for 3 years, during which time he developed GST 101, Strategies for Academic Success, a course for students on academic probation. He holds a B.S. from Berea College, an M.A. from Eastern Kentucky University, and an Ed.D. from the University of Missouri. He has been actively involved in the International Technology Education Association, the Kentucky Applied Technology Education Association, the American Society for Quality, and Phi Kappa Phi. He received the Seabury Award, Berea's highest recognition for teaching, and has been recognized for excellence in advising with the Paul C. Hager Award. He currently holds the William J. Hutchins Alumni Chair in Technology and Industrial Arts.

Margaret C. King is associate dean for student development at Schenectady County Community College in New York, where she provides leadership for the Division of Student Affairs as one of a team of three associate deans reporting directly to the president. In her position she directs the Academic Advisement Center and supervises counseling and career and employment services. Before her work at Schenectady County Community College, she was assistant director of counseling at New Jersey's Ocean County College. She received her B.A. in history from Ursinus College and her M.S. and Ed.D. from the State University of New York at Albany. A founding member of the National Academic Advising Association (NACADA), she was president from 1991–1993. She has been a faculty member of the Academic Advising Summer Institute since its inception in 1987, served on the faculty of the first Academic Advising Administrators' Institute, and serves as a consultant on academic advising and student affairs for both two- and four-year colleges and universities. In her consulting role she has delivered numerous keynote speeches, facilitated many workshops, and spent several days at institutions helping assess and revise services for students. Peggy was editor of the New Directions for Community Colleges publication *Academic Advising: Organizing and Delivering Services for Student Success* (Jossey-Bass, 1993). In addition, she has authored numerous chapters and articles on academic advising in the two-year college, on advisor training, and on organizational models and delivery systems for advising. She is a recipient of the State University of New York Chancellor's Award for Excellence in Professional Service, the NACADA Award for Service to NACADA, and the NACADA Virginia N. Gordon Award for Excellence in the Field of Advising.

Jillian Kinzie is associate director of the NSSE Institute for Effective Educational Practice at the Indiana University Center for Postsecondary Research. She earned her Ph.D. in higher education with a minor in women's studies at Indiana University Bloomington. Before that, she held a visiting faculty appointment in the Department of Higher Education and Student Affairs at Indiana University, worked as assistant dean in the School of Interdisciplinary Studies at the Western College Program at Miami University, and served as an administrator in student affairs for several years. In 2001 she was awarded a Student Choice Award for Outstanding Faculty at Indiana University and received the Professional and Organizational Development

Network's Robert J. Menges Research Presentation Award in 2005. She has coauthored a monograph on theories of teaching and learning and the Lumina Foundation monograph *Continuity and Change in College Choice: National Policy, Institutional Practices and Student Decision Making.* She has also conducted research on women in undergraduate science and the retention of underrepresented students. She is coauthor of *Student Success in College: Creating Conditions that Matter* (Jossey-Bass, 2005) and *One Size Does Not Fit All: Traditional and Innovative Models of Student Affairs Practice* (Routledge, 2006).

Gary L. Kramer is professor of counseling psychology and special education at Brigham Young University and research faculty for the Center for the Improvement of Teacher Education and Schooling in the David O. McKay School of Education. A former dean of students and director of student services on three campuses, he received his Ph.D. from Oregon State University. A past president of the National Academic Advising Association (NACADA) and its editorial board, Gary has written extensively about academic advising, assessment, student academic services, institutional improvement, and student information systems. His research contributions have been recognized by the National Association of Student Personnel Administrators, NACADA, IBM Best Practices, and the National Resource Center for The First-Year Experience and Students in Transition. Gary has published 70 referred journal articles, book chapters, book reviews, monographs, grant proposals, ERIC articles, and institutional reports; has published more than 50 articles and chapters in 12 different referred journals; has edited four monographs and two books; has authored 10 monograph chapters and chapters in books published by Jossey-Bass, Anker, and the Society for College and University Planning; and has delivered more than 130 professional papers, including keynote addresses for 10 different professional organizations. He is the recipient of national and institutional awards for research, distinguished service, and excellence in the field.

George D. Kuh is chancellor's professor of higher education at Indiana University Bloomington, where he directs the Center for Postsecondary Research, home to the National Survey of Student Engagement and related initiatives. A past president of the Association for the Study of Higher Education (ASHE), George has written extensively about student engagement, assessment, institutional improvement, and college and university cultures and has consulted with more than 175 educational institutions and agencies in the United States and abroad. His research contributions have been recognized by the American College Personnel Association, the

Association for Institutional Research, ASHE, and the National Association of Student Personnel Administrators. He received the Academic Leadership Award from the Council of Independent Colleges and the Virginia B. Smith Award for Innovative Leadership from the National Center for Public Policy in Higher Education and the Council for Adult and Experiential Learning. The recipient of three honorary degrees, George is a member of the board of regents of his alma mater, Luther College. In 2001 he received Indiana University's prestigious Tracy Sonneborn Award for his distinguished career of teaching and research. He most recently coauthored the book *Student Success in College: Creating Conditions that Matter* (Jossey-Bass, 2005).

Janet G. Lenz is associate director for career advising, counseling, and programming in the career center at Florida State University (FSU) and a senior research associate in the FSU Center for the Study of Technology in Counseling and Career Development. She has a courtesy faculty appointment in the College of Education's Department of Educational Psychology and Learning Systems. She received her bachelor's degree in sociology from Virginia Commonwealth University; she earned both a master's degree (1977) in student personnel administration and a Ph.D. (1990) in counseling and human systems from FSU. She has authored or coauthored numerous publications, including the *Career Thoughts Inventory* (Psychological Assessment Resources, 1996), *Career Thoughts Inventory Workbook* (Psychological Assessment Resources, 1996), and *Career Development and Planning: A Comprehensive Approach* (Wadsworth, 1999). She has made more than 100 presentations at regional, national, and international meetings. She is a master career counselor and national certified counselor. She is a past president of the National Career Development Association (NCDA) and an NCDA fellow. Janet's other memberships include the American Counseling Association, Florida Counseling Association, American College Personnel Association, National Academic Advising Association, and Southeastern Association of Colleges and Employers.

Louise M. Lonabocker is director of student services and university registrar at Boston College. She earned her Ph.D. (1981) in higher education administration at Boston College and has been employed there since 1970. She currently directs the college's one-stop organization. Louise is a past president of the American Association of Collegiate Registrars and Admissions Officers (AACRAO), has served on numerous AACRAO committees and task forces, and was a member of the AACRAO board of directors for six years. She has presented more than 40 conference sessions, written 20 articles and 5 book chapters, and was coeditor of *Breakthrough Systems: Student Access and Registration* (AACRAO, 1996). She is the current editor of *College and University*.

Michael McCauley is director of academic systems at Ball State University, a position he has held since 1988. Before this assignment, he was an academic advisor and advising administrator. He is one of the founders of the National Academic Advising Association (NACADA) and has served the organization as regional representative, treasurer, vice president, and president. He has authored or coauthored chapters and articles for several NACADA monographs and IBM-sponsored publications and contributed a chapter to *Academic Advising: A Comprehensive Handbook*. Mike has presented sessions and workshops at numerous NACADA national conferences, American Association of Collegiate Registrars and Admissions Officers conferences, and the Institute for the Study of Transfer Students. He served as a member of the NACADA Summer Institute faculty for nine years and has conducted numerous campus consultations. He currently sits on the national advisory board of AcademyOne, a software company that focuses on transfer solutions. In addition to his duties at Ball State University, Mike was recently named state director of the Transfer Indiana Central Office. This office oversees the development, implementation, and maintenance of the Transfer Indiana Initiative, sponsored by the Indiana Commission for Higher Education.

Thomas E. Miller is an associate professor in the College of Education at the Tampa campus of the University of South Florida, a position to which he was appointed in 2006. Before that time, he was a senior student affairs administrator at the University of South Florida. He previously held student affairs positions at Eckerd College, Canisius College, Indiana University, and Shippensburg University. Thomas holds a bachelor's degree from Muhlenberg College and master's and doctoral degrees from Indiana University. He is the author of many journal articles and book chapters, and he most recently coauthored the book *Promoting Reasonable Expectations*, with Barbara Bender and John Schuh. He received the Scott Goodnight Award for Outstanding Performance as a dean from the National Association of Student Personnel Administrators in 2001 and was chosen as a Pillar of the Profession in 2004. He has been on more than a dozen institutional accreditation teams and National Collegiate Athletic Association certification review teams. He received the Elizabeth Greenleaf Distinguished Alumnus Award from Indiana University's Higher Education and Student Affairs Program in 1989. Thomas currently serves as a member of the boards of directors for BACCHUS/GAMMA Peer Education Network and for the National Consortium for Academics and Sports.

Rebecca A. Mills has served as vice president for student life at the University of Nevada–Las Vegas (UNLV) since May 2000. She received her doctorate in secondary education from the University of Arkansas before joining UNLV in 1987. A professor of curriculum and instruction, she has published and presented nationally on such topics as organizational change, middle-level education, teacher beliefs, and teacher development. She has won several teaching awards, including the Carnegie Foundation's Nevada Professor of the Year Award. She is active in the National Association of Student Personnel Administrators, serving Region V as the public policy coordinator. She also belongs to and has presented at conferences for the American College Personnel Association. She coauthored a chapter in *Learning Partnerships: Theory and Models of Practice to Educate for Self-Authorship* and continues to work with staff to understand and implement the learning partnerships model and to enhance self-authorship among staff and students.

Diana G. Oblinger is vice president for EDUCAUSE, responsible for the association's teaching and learning activities, and is the director of the EDUCAUSE Learning Initiative. She has held positions in business and academia: vice president for information resources and chief information officer for the 16-campus University of North Carolina System, executive director of higher education for Microsoft, and IBM director of the Institute for Academic Technology. She was on the faculty at the University of Missouri–Columbia and at Michigan State University and was an associate dean at the University of Missouri. She is an adjunct professor at North Carolina State University. Known for her leadership in teaching and learning with technology, she has testified before the U.S. Senate and congressional subcommittees. She serves on a variety of boards, such as the National Science Foundation Advisory Committee on Cyberinfrastructure. Diana is a frequent keynote speaker as well as the coauthor of the award-winning book *What Business Wants from Higher Education* (Oryx Press, 1998). She is editor or coeditor of seven books and the author or coauthor of dozens of monographs and articles on higher education and technology. She has received several awards for teaching, research, and distinguished service. She holds three degrees from Iowa State University.

Terry D. Piper, vice president for student affairs and professor of educational psychology and counseling at California State University–Northridge, earned a bachelor's degree from Pennsylvania State University, an M.A. in college student development from the University of Iowa, and a Ph.D. in educational policy and leadership from the Ohio State University. He served the University of Nevada–Las Vegas as the director of residential life and then as associate vice president for student services. At Ohio State he was a residence hall director and area coordinator. He is recognized for his expertise in student development theory and practice. Terry's residence hall community standards model has been widely adopted. He has 13 publications, has made more than 30 presentations at national conventions, and has served as an invited or keynote speaker and as a faculty-in-residence at several conferences. He has held a variety of leadership positions in the American College Personnel Association (ACPA) and serves on the ACPA Educational Leadership Foundation. ACPA has recognized him with the Excellence in Practice Award and as a Diamond Honoree. He has received recognition from his graduate programs for his contribution to the profession.

Dave Porter retired after a 30-year career as a U.S. Air Force rescue helicopter pilot, aircraft maintenance officer, and permanent professor and head of the Air Force Academy's Department of Behavioral Sciences and Leadership to accept a position as Berea College's academic vice president and provost in 2001. He has a B.S. from the Air Force Academy in engineering mechanics, an M.S. in industrial relations from the University of California–Los Angeles, and a Ph.D. in experimental cognitive psychology from Oxford University. He has served as a consultant examiner for three regional accreditation organizations (the North Central Association, the Western Association of Schools and Colleges, and the Southern Association of Colleges and Schools) and the American Association for Higher Education's Urban University Portfolio Project. Over the past decade, he's played key roles in preparing institutional applications for accreditation and reaccreditation for the Air Force Academy, Western Governors University (where he serves as a member of the assessment and liberal arts councils), and Berea College.

Earl H. Potter III is president of St. Cloud State University. He earned his Ph.D. (1978) in organizational psychology from the University of Washington. He has been a Mellon Faculty Fellow at Yale University and an American Council on Education Fellow at the University of Colorado. As director of organizational development at Cornell University, Earl was responsible for change management in projects ranging from reengineering student services to the transformation of human resources management systems. He has been an evaluator for the Malcolm Baldrige National Quality Award and has consulted widely in higher education, including service as a member of the IBM Best Practices in Student Services project.

Robert C. Reardon has held full-time counseling and teaching positions at Florida State University (FSU) since 1966, when he was first employed as a counselor in the counseling center. In the 1980s he codirected the Office of Academic and Career Advising Services at FSU. He is a faculty member in the Division of Student Affairs, and his current position is director of instruction, research, and evaluation in the career center; professor in the Department of Educational Psychology and Learning Systems; and codirector of the Center for the Study of Technology in Counseling and Career Development. He received a bachelor's degree in social studies from Texas Lutheran College, and his graduate study at FSU earned him an M.S. in counseling and guidance and a Ph.D. in counselor education. He received the Eminent Career Award from the National Career Development Association in 2003 and was a corecipient of the Ralph Berdie Memorial Research Award and the Extended Research Award from the American Counseling Association in 1996 and 1999, respectively.

Saul Reyes is director of the career center at Florida Southern College. Previously he oversaw academic advising, career services, and academic support services for student athletes at Jacksonville University. He also served as a student affairs professional at Centre College, the University of Connecticut, and Bethany College. He is a doctoral candidate in the higher education program at the University of South Florida. He holds an undergraduate degree from Gordon College and a master's degree in counseling from West Virginia University. He is a member of the National Association of Student Personnel Administrators and the National Association of Colleges and Employers.

John H. Schuh is distinguished professor of educational leadership at Iowa State University. Previously he held administrative and faculty assignments at Wichita State University, Indiana University Bloomington, and Arizona State University. He earned his B.A. in history from the University of Wisconsin–Oshkosh, and he received an M.S. in counseling and a Ph.D. from Arizona State. He is the author, coauthor, or editor of more than 200 publications, including 24 books and monographs, more than 60 book chapters, and 100 articles. He most recently coauthored the books *One Size Does Not Fit All: Traditional and Innovative Models of Student Affairs Practice* (Routledge, 2006) and *Student Success in College: Creating Conditions that Matter* (Jossey-Bass, 2005). Currently he is editor in chief of the New Directions for Student Services series and is associate editor of the *Journal of College Student Development*. John has made more than 240 presentations and speeches to campus-based regional and national meetings. He is a member of the Evaluator Corps and the Accreditation Review Council of the North Central Association of Colleges and Schools. He received a Fulbright award to study higher education in Germany in 1994.

Deanna Sergel served as the associate director and then coordinator for the Center for Learning, Teaching, Communication, and Research at Berea College from 2002–2005. She worked with five faculty associates, a program assistant, and peer consultants to offer individual consultations, programs for groups, workshops for classes, publications, and other resources to the Berea College community. Before that, she taught for 10 years in the Department of English at Northwest Missouri State University, where she also coordinated the End-of-Core Writing Assessment. Deanna has presented workshops on course-embedded assessment, performance-based assessment of general education in Missouri, modular learning, and laying the groundwork for self-assessment. She has served on an accreditation team for the Western Association of Schools and Colleges and on the executive boards for the Missouri General Education Forum and the Missouri Association of Teachers of English. She is a charter member of the Consortium for Assessment and Planning Support. Deanna holds a B.A. in English from Florida State University and an M.A. in English from Northwest Missouri State University.

Tracy L. Skipper is editorial projects coordinator for the National Resource Center for The First-Year Experience and Students in Transition at the University of South Carolina (USC). Before her work at the center, she served as director of residence life and judicial affairs at Shorter College in Rome, Georgia, where her duties included teaching in the college's first-year seminar program and serving as an academic advisor for first-year students. She also served as director of student activities and residence life at Wesleyan College. Tracy teaches first-year English and University 101 at USC. She was coeditor of *Involvement in Campus Activities and the Retention of First-Year College Students* (USC, 2003) and author of *Student Development in the First College Year: A Primer for College Educators* (USC, 2005). She holds a bachelor's degree in psychology from USC, a master's degree in higher education from Florida State University, and a master's in American literature from USC.

Randy L. Swing is codirector and senior scholar at the Policy Center on the First Year of College. He developed, with colleagues John Gardner and Betsy Barefoot, the Foundations of Excellence self-study process used by colleges and universities to evaluate and improve their work with beginning college students. In addition, he is a fellow in the National Resource Center for The First-Year Experience and Students in Transition at the University of South Carolina, a visiting associate professor at Kansai University of International Studies in Japan, and the international advisor to the Quality Assurance Agency of Scotland. He has authored numerous articles, chapters, monographs, and books. His recent research is presented in the coauthored book *Achieving and Sustaining Institutional Excellence for the First Year of College* (Jossey-Bass, 2005). He is a frequent speaker at national and international conferences on institutional change, assessment, retention, and undergraduate student success. For two decades, he held various leadership positions at Appalachian State University in assessment, advising, Upward Bound, and the freshman seminar. He holds a Ph.D. in higher education from the University of Georgia, an M.A. and an Ed.S. in counseling from Appalachian State University, and a B.A. in psychology from the University of North Carolina–Charlotte. He also attended Davidson County Community College.

Vasti Torres is associate professor of higher education and student affairs administration in the W. W. Wright School of Education at Indiana University. She teaches courses in student affairs administration, student development theory, and research in higher education. Before joining the faculty, she had 15 years of experience in administrative positions, most recently serving as associate vice provost and dean for enrollment and student services at Portland State University. She has written numerous articles on Latino college students, survey development and use, and other diversity issues. She was the principal investigator for a multiyear grant investigating the choice to stay in college for Latino students. She is active in several student affairs and higher education associations. In 2007–2008 she will become the first Latina president of a national student affairs association—American College Personnel Association (ACPA). She has been named a Diamond Honoree and Emerging Scholar by ACPA, outstanding faculty by the National Association of Student Personnel Administrators' Latino/a Knowledge Community, and program associate for the National Center for Public Policy in Higher Education. She holds a Ph.D. in student affairs administration from the University of Georgia.

Lois Calian Trautvetter is associate director for Northwestern University's Higher Education Administration and Policy Program and assistant professor in the School of Education and Social Policy. She received her Ph.D. in higher education administration from the University of Michigan, an M.S. in chemical engineering from Carnegie Mellon University, and a B.A. in chemistry from the College of Wooster. She teaches college student development theory and research methodology courses. Her research interests include student development and faculty and professional development issues, such as productivity, enhancing research and teaching, motivation, and new and junior faculty. She is also interested in the role of church-affiliated colleges in American higher education as well as professional development for K–12 teachers to improve math and science teaching, gender issues, and the number of women in science. She recently coauthored the book *Putting Students First: How Colleges Develop Students Purposefully* (Anker, 2006). She has also written book chapters and articles on faculty experiences and teaching. Lois has patents as a chemist in the coatings and resins industry. She is currently a member of the Association of American Colleges and Universities, the American Educational Research Association, and the Association for the Study of Higher Education and continues to be a referee for a variety of professional journals and a speaker at conferences.

Faye Vowell is provost and vice president for academic affairs at Western New Mexico University. She has been a faculty advisor and directed a centralized advising center for freshmen and undeclared students that was staffed by faculty. Her experience also includes service as dean of graduate studies and research, dean of the School of Library and Information Management, and acting vice president for student affairs. She has been active in the National Academic Advising Association (NACADA) since the mid-1980s, presenting numerous papers at national and regional conferences. In addition, she has served as a faculty member at the NACADA Academic Advising Summer Institute. Her publications include many articles and book chapters on academic advising. She chaired the team that created the NACADA · advising training video.

J. James Wager is vice president for technology at SCRIP-SAFE Security Products and leads the development of new Internet-based products and services. He recently retired from the Pennsylvania State University as the assistant vice president for undergraduate education and the university registrar. While at Penn State, he provided direct oversight for all academic records and associated activities for the university's 80,000-plus students at 24 campuses across Pennsylvania. He was responsible for the development and implementation of numerous technology solutions that resulted in improved student services and reduced university expenditures. He played a leadership role in the enrollment planning initiatives of the university as well as strategic planning and total quality activities. He was a member of the university faculty senate and taught management courses. He served as the board chairman of the American Association of University Registrars and as the program coordinator of the Registrars' Summer Institute at Aspen. James has provided program consulting services to numerous universities across the country and in the United Kingdom. He has published more than three dozen monographs, professional papers, and contributions to professional books. He has also made numerous presentations to regional and national associations including the American Association of Collegiate Registrars and Admissions Officers and EDUCAUSE. He remains a strong advocate for the delivery of student services using secure web technology. He holds two degrees from Penn State—a B.S. in management and an MPA with an emphasis on managing information systems in higher education.

Lee Ward is director of career and academic planning and assistant professor of psychology at James Madison University. His experience in higher education also includes administrative appointments in athletics, first-year experience, recreation, student unions and activities, leadership development, and service-learning. In addition, he founded the Student Learning Institute and was its executive director for five years. Lee is a frequent consultant to other colleges and universities on issues of planned change, visioning, and leadership; he has also been an invited speaker and presenter at a variety of national and international conferences. He has written widely about change strategies and the elements of effective learning environments. He holds a doctorate in higher education administration from North Carolina State University and a master of education and B.S. in biology from Salisbury University. Lee is a member of several professional organizations and is active in service to the American College Personnel Association, from which he received the *Annuit Coeptis* honor in 1996. A native of Baltimore, Lee is a former college baseball coach and scout for the Milwaukee Brewers.

Eric R. White earned his undergraduate degree in history from Rutgers University and his master's and doctorate in counseling psychology from the University of Pennsylvania. He joined the Pennsylvania State University in 1970 as a psychological counselor at the Delaware County campus. Moving to University Park in 1975 as coordinator of the Freshman Testing, Counseling, and Advising Program, Eric was named director of the Division of Undergraduate Studies in 1986 and executive director in 1999. He was also named associate dean for advising in 2006. Active in the National Academic Advising Association (NACADA), he has served as the multiversity representative, as chair of the placement committee and the Commission on Standards and Ethics in Advising, as treasurer, and as a member of the board of directors from 2002–2005. He was president of NACADA in 2004–2005 and of the Association of Deans and Directors of University Colleges and Undergraduate Studies in 1993. He is an affiliate assistant professor of education at Penn State; author of monograph chapters and journal articles; and coeditor of *Teaching Through Advising: A Faculty Perspective* (1995), a monograph of the Jossey-Bass New Directions for Teaching and Learning series, and *Teaching From Mentoring* (2001), another Jossey-Bass New Directions monograph. He has also written a chapter for the NACADA/Jossey-Bass publication *Academic Advising: A Comprehensive Handbook* and coauthored a chapter on technology in *Faculty Advising Examined: Enhancing the Potential of College Faculty as Advisors*. Eric is the 2002 recipient of NACADA's Virginia N. Gordon Award for Excellence in the Field of Advising and the 2005 recipient of Penn State's Administrative Excellence Award.

FOREWORD

What? Another book about student services? Who needs it?

Two assumptions underlie these questions. First of all, these questions assume that we have already perfected the wheel on this topic. And second, they assume that this book is primarily about student services and, hence, for student services providers. I want to address these assumptions.

Clearly, we have not perfected the art, form, or substance of student services. We have been providing many of these services only since World War II—and many only since the Great Society legislation, especially the Higher Education Act of the mid-1960s. And, as we measure time in our 1,000-year-old enterprise, this is only a tick of the second hand. A substantial body of literature on this new field within higher education has been slow to emerge, just as traditional practices of assimilating and supporting students in higher education have been slow in changing and adapting. And from even a cursory glance at our performance in moving students through academic curricula to degree attainment, it would appear that we still have much to learn and perfect to maximize student achievement. Thus, for me, a work that stops and examines the current state of the art of student services is still very much needed.

But more than that, I believe this is not just a book about student services and for student services professional employees. This is a book about the requisite internal conditions, processes, and support mechanisms for collegiate student success. This is, in the words of my friends George Kuh and Jillian Kinzie, about how to create an infrastructure to support a "student-centered culture." Fundamentally, any campus culture is about values—what and whom a particular campus values, prizes, aspires to, and allocates resources to accordingly. Hence, I believe this book is as much as for faculty as for student services professionals. After all, we provide student services to support the work of the faculty. And it is the faculty who are most likely to ultimately become the administrative leaders of higher education institutions and then make critical decisions about student services: what services are needed, who should provide them, and how much they should be supported through resource allocation. Hence, I would argue that this book should also be read by faculty who have a big-picture interest in the overall effectiveness of their institutions and who are or may someday become campus leaders. In conclusion, this is not just a book for and about student services. If you are a student services reader, when you are finished with this work, pass it on to a faculty member who you believe is going to make still greater contributions to institutional leadership and student success.

I wish to commend my colleague, Gary Kramer, for his original vision for this project, one that led him to take this idea to my friends Jim and Susan Anker of Anker Publishing in the first place. That vision led Gary to recruit this stellar cast of contributors. I personally know and have worked with 16 of the book's 37 contributors. What an impressive and diverse array of intellectual investors he has attracted to this project.

I first came to know Gary through a similar process almost 20 years ago, when he came to me with another inspired vision, this one to create a monograph about which nothing had been published—the vital intersection between improving academic advising and improving the whole first-year experience. At that time Gary was the president of the National Academic Advising Association, and I was the executive director of the National Resource Center for The First-Year Experience and Students in Transition at the University of South Carolina. I find it very heartening to see that Gary is at it again, identifying a void, a need, in the literature base and being both willing and able to undertake the intellectual leadership effort to address it. Gary has exceptional skills in creating academic and administrative partnerships for the improvement of student support across the spectrum of institutional types. In this role he draws on both his own institutional and professional association experiences and his vast network of other practicing administrators, scholars, and intellectuals with expertise in this important field.

I have learned in my career that to become more successful with all our students, we have to change the value system of the academy. College was not originally designed to serve many of these students, students who don't represent the cohort that I epitomized when I began college—New England, white, property-owning, Protestant males. We have to persuade our colleagues to understand and value our new students and to serve them in new ways. And we need intellectually substantive literature, based in research and best practices, to perform this kind of persuasion. And that is a further reason why this work is needed. Our values ultimately lead to sets of institutionalized policies, practices, pedagogies, and systems of student support.

I saw how important it is to change basic societal values when I first arrived in South Carolina in early 1967, just three years after the Civil Rights Act. I was on active duty in the United States Air Force, which soon ordered me to become an adjunct instructor for my future and lifelong employer, the University of South Carolina. Some skeptical whites said to me in that era, "You can pass a law ordering this and that, but you can't change the way I think" and, by implication, the way they behaved. What I have seen over my now four decades in the Deep South proves just the opposite. When any group changes its basic rules and policies, it creates the framework in which people behave, interact, learn, and socialize. This then affects values formation. And so I believe that to improve student performance, we have to change many of our policies and procedures, which in turn shape the contexts in which we interact with our students and in which they learn or don't learn. This book helps show the way. Once again, Gary Kramer and his associates offer a better way to go about an important component of the total higher education enterprise. In that spirit I salute all of the contributors—and all of you who take this book seriously.

John N. Gardner
Brevard, North Carolina
November 2006

PREFACE

This book stands on the shoulders of a multitude of theorists and practitioners. Namely, the scholar-researcher-authors in this book, most of whom are currently or have been institutional or national professional organization leaders, bring to the forefront key issues on student success on the campus. From the first chapter to the last, this book's focus is on the campus community as facilitator and leader of the successful college student experience. This volume offers a unique blend of theoretical foundations with ample and relevant effective educational practices as well as suggested qualitative next steps for colleges to consider in fostering student success in the campus community. Using "students first" as the primary theme, the chapters present an examination of the concept of student success as it relates to the services and advice that help students succeed. Moreover, chapter contributors provide insights into the strategies and tools that institutions can use to create a successful campus environment. The key issues that make up the essence of this volume include addressing changing student demographics and needs, aligning institutional and student expectations, connecting student-oriented services systemically, organizing and fostering student services for learning, and creating and delivering services for students to achieve success in the campus community.

The following questions are addressed throughout the book and summarized in the final chapter: What do good institutions do beyond the routine or expected to actually create and achieve a student-centered environment or culture of student success? What are the essential or common ingredients found in successful programs? What does the research suggest as next steps that institutions should consider to promote student success? Finally, what do institutions and student services providers need to do better to align expectations, connect services, actively foster student development, and consistently achieve results through student-oriented services and programs? The response to these questions and others presented throughout this volume compose this work's 20 chapters and 4 parts on communicating expectations, connecting services, fostering student development, and achieving institutional success.

STUDENTS FIRST IN THE CAMPUS COMMUNITY

The foundation for this book stems from two individuals, both of whom have not only inspired me to assemble this volume but who have also over the decades invigorated all of us in higher education to do the real business of putting students first in the campus community. Harold Hodgkinson (1985), the educational demographer, often said that what determines institutional and student success is to know the students who are entering higher education and how they are progressing in it. And John Gardner, the first-year-experience and students-in-transition guru, aptly emphasized the importance of making a positive and profound difference in the lives of students. Like Hodgkinson, Gardner motivated us faculty and administrators to remember who in our own educational journey made a difference or served as a positive role model. Likewise, he asked who our students will remember long after they have left their college experience. Who will they remember as having made a difference in their lives, put them first, and enabled and ennobled them to achieve success?

These injunctions are still relevant today as higher education enrollments continue to rise to new levels (Hussar, 2005). For example, Hodgkinson's concern about knowing students is especially important as student demographics change. Increasing student diversity requires campuses to account for, know, and align the needs and expectations of students with those of the institution. Of equal value is knowing how students are progressing or, in today's language, showing evidence of student learning outcomes. Student success processes vary across groups. Not all students face the same barriers, nor do they need the same assistance to be successful in college. Institutions ought to strategically take into account the particular family, community, and policy context of specific students when forming policies and programs.

The United States has slipped in the rankings of worldwide higher education, particularly on measures of college participation, access to college, fostering student success, and degree completion. That fact suggests that the need has never been greater for institutions to provide improved student support services (see Hebel, 2006). However, the definition of student success transcends mere retention, degree completion, and related employment. Fostering a student-centered environment suggests a much broader definition of student success.

Today's institutions also face increased pressure to provide evidence of student learning outcomes and other measures of student success. This task is made more difficult by the characteristics and changing roles of the millennial generation. The millennial college student is older, more ethnically diverse, likely to almost exclusively use online student services, and may attend more than one campus concurrently (Coomes & DeBard, 2004; Lovett, 2006; Oblinger & Oblinger, 2005). Millennials struggle to meet institutional expectations of the traditional classroom and campus environment. Lovett notes that they often must hold more than one job to support families and thus are not always involved or engaged on campus. They must at times resist institutional pressures to participate in social, recreational, or cocurricular activities. So it is often difficult for the campus to build a sense of community, and institutions are left to find alternative ways to enrich student learning and success (Lovett, 2006). Vasti Torres, author of Chapter 1, adds that "today's higher education institutions are under constant pressure from external forces to reflect the changing landscape of U.S. society."

STUDENT SUCCESS AND THE RESEARCH LITERATURE

Researchers, scholars, administrators, and practitioners have long sought to understand and address these concerns. They've asked, "What constitutes student success given the changing roles of students, faculty, and even higher education itself?" Consider, for example, such lengthy volumes on the effect of colleges on students by Pascarella and Terenzini (1991, 2005). By bringing together several commissioned papers written by higher education scholars, in November 2006 the National Postsecondary Education Cooperative extended the discussion and research about the meaning of student success and what institutions need to do to create a culture of student success. In addition, the principles, standards, and frameworks required to achieve institutional and student success are well developed in the literature (Bailey, 2006; Barefoot et al., 2005; Baxter Magolda & King, 2004; Blimling, Whitt, & Associates, 1999; Braskamp, Trautvetter, & Ward, 2006; Braxton, 2006; Council for the Advancement of Standards in Higher Education [CAS], 2006; Hearn, 2006; Kuh, Kinzie, Buckley, Bridges, & Hayek, 2006; Kuh, Kinzie, Schuh, & Whitt, 2005; Miller, 2005; Perna & Thomas, 2006; Sandeen & Barr, 2006; Tinto & Pusser, 2006). Such scholarly attention has provided a connection between effective educational practice and research.

The research literature continues to provide significant insight and evidence on the factors that contribute to student success. However, what works for one institution may not necessarily work for another. No magic bullet or one-size-fits-all solution has emerged to drive policymakers, campus leaders, faculty, and service providers. Instead, researchers have provided more generalized guidelines for success that institutions can adapt. For example, Perna and Thomas (2006) suggest 10 approaches to address student success on the campus. These cut across the spectrum from pre-college readiness to post-college attainment. Similarly, Tinto and Pusser (2006) developed a framework to help guide college faculty, staff, and policymakers in achieving institutional effectiveness. Jillian Kinzie and George Kuh in their chapter in this book, and more specifically in their book (Kuh et al., 2005), provide specific conditions and institutional activities for creating a culture of student success. Braxton (2006) focuses on teaching and the development of recommendations about what institutions can do to enhance, align, and promote teaching performance as a contributor to student success. However, as Bailey (2006) points out, institutions must consider the influence of several factors as they apply these approaches: the impact of a student's family; general conditions in society; variations in the K–12 system; a student's personal characteristics, tastes, and attributes; the characteristics and policies of individual colleges and their pedagogic practices; state and federal policies on college regulation and financial aid; and the behavior of peers, advisors, faculty, and staff at any individual college.

The research suggests that an important factor in attaining student success is the willingness of institutions and policymakers to align policies and related assessment with student success indicators. The growth in size and diversity of student populations in these times of scarce resources and increasing demands for accountability challenge college administrators to more assertively measure and demonstrate student learning outcomes. At the same time, Tinto and Pusser (2006) caution that, despite the immense volume of research on college student outcomes, there are few well-supported insights and recommendations for colleges to apply to foster persistence and completion—even "a lamentable paucity of empirically sound research on effective education practice." Yet colleges must move forward, even when research does not definitively tell them what the best course would be (Bailey, 2006). Braxton (2006), Tinto and Pusser (2006), Kuh et al. (2006), and others have set forth specific recommendations to improve college teaching, build effective partnerships between institutions and policymakers, and develop our collective will to make use of what we know about improving student success. There is good evidence that when organizational structure and institutional commitment are both in place, they together influence student success (Berger & Milem, 1999; Braxton, Hirschy, & McClendon, 2004; Kezar &

Kinzie, 2006). Although there may be some things outside of an institution's control, there are many things that institutions can do to focus on students to ensure they reach their full potential, which is what this volume is all about. Each chapter emphasizes themes found on campuses that focus on helping students achieve success.

THE PURPOSE OF THE BOOK

The premise of this book is that student learning, growth, and success are the business of everyone on the campus. Involving the campus community in this strategic and systemic endeavor is essential. As institutions develop partnerships between policymakers, administration, faculty, service providers, students, and the educational community at large, a culture of student success will grow.

However, this book makes no attempt to define what student success is or should be for all institutions. Not all conditions and indicators of success given in this volume are readily applicable or transferable from one institution to another. Bailey (2006) suggests that institutions must consider the success indicators presented here in light of costs, resources, and time. They must also consider the impact of change on traditional faculty or administrator roles and organizational structures. Do institutional or individual incentives discourage reform? Does the institution have the will to make difficult changes to improve the institutional environment for students? Certainly, effective practices that cannot be implemented and sustained are not much more useful to student success than practices that do not work (Bailey, 2006).

This volume takes on this challenge by examining differences among institutions in higher education and offers considerations for action to improve and foster a student success culture. Although the book may not always perfectly connect research (what we know) to practice (what we should do), it does offer a host of suggestions for ways to better know the students who enter and leave an institution, to put students first by aligning expectations, and to regularly monitor those students' progress on goal achievement. Thus, the premise of this book is that any institution that does these things can make a collective positive difference in the lives of students by offering services that matter.

AUDIENCE

This book is specifically targeted at institutional leaders and practitioners who are responsible for the support, direction, and coordination of student services. That is, this volume is intended for anyone in the campus community charged with knowing what kinds of students are entering the system and how they are progressing in it. Specifically, this book is for those who are concerned with 1) supporting student development, learning, and achievement; 2) assessing student progress and achievement of learning outcomes; 3) working collaboratively, or through shared partnerships, to promote success for all students on the campus; and 4) determining and establishing the conditions for a student-centric culture on campus. Service providers, faculty, and other readers will learn how to encourage a variety of desired outcomes, including student persistence, satisfaction, learning, and personal development. Practitioners can also use this book to help examine their daily work—particularly the methods, models, standards, and success factors they use to achieve student success on their campus.

The target audience also includes administrators who are responsible for the support, direction, and coordination of student advising and related services. This includes vice presidents, deans, and directors as well as frontline administrators responsible for day-to-day student services. In addition, faculty and students in graduate programs may find this volume useful in their program of study, particularly as it relates to strategic approaches to student development, profiles of services that matter to students, and new directions for practice.

ORGANIZATION OF THE BOOK

This book is organized into 4 parts and 20 chapters. Part I, Communicating Expectations, examines and defines what responsibility policymakers, campus leaders, and faculty have in creating an environment that helps students succeed. The five chapters in this section set the conditions for student success on the campus through models, effective educational practices, and trends.

- *Chapter 1, "Knowing Today's and Tomorrow's Students":* Vasti Torres establishes the book's foundation and overall focal point by asking whether higher education is truly keeping up with its changing demographic landscape. Moreover, once a snapshot is provided for today's student, the chapter investigates how demographic changes influence students' access to higher education and their persistence, focusing on those students who are at risk. Sections of the chapter address creating a supportive environment for multiple types of students and related effective educational practices.

- *Chapter 2, "Creating a Student-Centered Culture":* Jillian Kinzie and George Kuh take the changing student demographics discussed in Chapter 1 and focus on establishing a student-centered culture. To help readers create and sustain a student-centered culture, which is documented as a major factor in the success of all well-performing institutions of higher education, this chapter draws on research on student learning and educational effectiveness to distill key features of student-centered cultures.

- *Chapter 3, "Aligning Expectations: A Shared Responsibility":* Thomas Miller and Saul Reyes explore the challenge of effectively aligning both institutional and student expectations to enhance the student experience on campus. The authors claim that a belief in the campus community that student expectations matter is an important ingredient in the student-institution relationship. To be effective, institutions must adjust to changing student demographics (and, therefore, needs) and establish a culture of student success by aligning student and institutional expectations.

- *Chapter 4, "Changing Student Services Through Assessment":* John Schuh argues that the most effective way to make decisions, especially those that bring about changes in the campus environment, is to base them on data. Assessment is central to knowing how students are progressing in the system and whether certain programs have an impact on and lead to achieving learning and development expectations. Specifically, the chapter describes assessing services, programs, and activities as a mechanism of change.

- *Chapter 5, "Promoting and Sustaining Change":* Earl Potter focuses on the commitment to put students first in the community. Specifically, he addresses the need to achieve near-term successes that will lead to long-term success. External pressures will force colleges and universities to become more student centered. Success will come as campus leaders concentrate on managing change within the organization to sustain student success.

Part II, Connecting Services, describes campus services that are central to putting students first. Each chapter in this section cultivates a systems perspective that encourages readers to evaluate and align their work with the needs and expectations of students and the institution. This section emphasizes admitting students to succeed, giving advice that makes a difference, providing learning technologies that serve students, connecting academic and career decisions, and providing one-stop student services both virtually and in a physical location.

- *Chapter 6, "Putting Students First in College Admissions and Enrollment Management":* Don Hossler focuses on those areas of student engagement that are commonly responsibilities of enrollment management professionals. Acknowledging the challenge such professionals face to bring in and retain students amid institutional enrollment pressures, this chapter advocates the importance of helping students make sound college choices to give them the best chance for success.

- *Chapter 7, "Connecting One-Stop Student Services":* Louise Lonabocker and James Wager describe model one-stop organizations and the planning required to create them. The phenomenon of one-stop student services—offering advising and counseling services from admission to graduation in one place—is a fast-spreading trend across the nation's campuses. To meet the expectations of today's students and families, this chapter promotes web-based and in-person services, which remove the runaround that students abhor. The emphasis on exchange (of forms, documents, signatures) in physical student centers is significantly altered by taking a virtual approach. Virtual one-stop services focus on campus web sites, electronic signatures, email, and other technologies. This chapter discusses the advantages of integrating and creating a virtual one-stop service center (with physical service centers as an additional service), especially for commuter students and long-distance learners.

- *Chapter 8, "Learning Technologies that Serve Students":* Peter DeBlois and Diana Oblinger make the case for a new understanding of technology as an enabler for student learning. This chapter is a call not only for understanding new learning technologies but for the active involvement of student services providers in helping students of the Net generation use those technologies. The authors further the discussion on what role technology should play in supporting on- and off-campus learners in such areas as one-stop (or no-stop) advising centers and business processes.

- *Chapter 9, "Giving Advice that Makes a Difference":* Wesley Habley and Jennifer Bloom discusses the need for collaborative partnerships in the campus community to help students identify and realize their academic goals and objectives. Academic advising is a service in which faculty members, academic departments, and professional advisors come together to ensure quality student experiences, progress, and the achievement of academic goals. This chapter emphasizes a systemic and strategic view of academic advising that includes a broad and strong institutional commitment to an interconnected academic advising program.

- *Chapter 10, "Planning Good Academic and Career Decisions":* Emily Bullock, Robert Reardon, and Janet Lenz conclude this section with a discussion of how to connect academic and career advising with planning. This chapter also emphasizes the importance of other related services—including career placement, academic internships, and career interventions counseling—in making good decisions. The chapter uses a theory-based model to provide hands-on advising tools, which are illustrated in a comprehensive case study.

In Part III, Fostering Student Development, core principles and practices of holistic student development and growth are presented. This section emphasizes student readiness, learning partnerships within the institutional environment, the organization of services for learning, preparing service providers, and engaging faculty in fostering student success. Several chapters in this section view student success through the lens of Baxter Magolda and King (2004) and consider how students can achieve self-authorship, or a personal awareness of their core beliefs, values, and moral directions through life. Institutions with such a focus strive to help students become the best people they can be and help them develop into fully realized, autonomous adults.

- *Chapter 11, "Learning Partnerships":* Terry Piper and Rebecca Mills begin this section by encouraging faculty and staff to be more intentional about helping students form partnerships that result in self-authorship. The authors describe student experiences and the changes that take place through epistemological, intrapersonal, and interpersonal dialogue. They argue that the learning partnerships model helps students express greater awareness of and comfort with the skills and abilities defined in learning outcomes. In addition, this model is an effective means to promote self-authorship. Fostering accountability for student learning outcomes is a result of shifting our focus from what we do to what students do. This approach assists students in their transition from depending on external authority to depending on internal self-reliance.

- *Chapter 12, "Developing Students' Search for Meaning and Purpose":* Lois Calian Trautvetter emphasizes that all colleges and universities, religious or secular, have the responsibility to contribute to the spiritual, moral, and character development of students. This chapter challenges administrators, service providers, and faculty to consider ways in which their institutions can improve holistic student development. Furthermore, Trautvetter discusses the importance of creating a supportive campus environment for students as they explore meaning, purpose, and the greater good. This chapter provides a framework that will not only enrich the personal lives of students but also deepen their learning.

- *Chapter 13, "Organizing Student Services for Learning":* Dave Porter, Joe Bagnoli, Janice Burdette Blythe, Donald Hudson, and Deanna Sergel state that the organizational structure and climate of an institution, built on various institutional paradigms and perspectives, have a strong bearing on what students learn. This chapter identifies the consequences of various institutional paradigms and perspectives and considers ways in which progressive approaches to educational administration can enhance student learning and success. The authors then apply theoretical underpinnings of student learning to effective educational practices.

- *Chapter 14, "Preparing Service Providers to Foster Student Success":* Tom Brown and Lee Ward focus on motivating and coordinating the work of student services providers in delivering high-quality, timely, comprehensive, and accurate services to students. It emphasizes developing staff and empowering them to foster student success. Overall, this chapter focuses on enabling students to take charge of their educational planning. The authors thoroughly discuss the role of those responsible for creating campus environments to make student success and development the highest priorities.

- *Chapter 15, "Engaging Faculty to Foster Student Development":* Faye Vowell addresses the role of faculty advising in fostering student success. The chapter emphasizes a thoughtful consideration of advising expectations and role definition. Divergent expectations of advising are often held by faculty advisors, their institutions, and student advisees. Thus, a great challenge faced by institutions is to create a common vision of what to expect from both advisors and advisees. To be successful, institutions must clearly express expectations and provide a culture of support for faculty advising on the campus. This chapter presents model faculty advising through case studies. It addresses such faculty advising issues as accountability, development, delivery, evaluation, and recognition and reward.

Finally, Part IV, Achieving Success, reasserts the central theme of this book, which is to identify conditions needed for achieving student success on the campus. This section illustrates success factors that are commonly found in effective institutions. It emphasizes the importance of partnerships between policymakers, campus leaders, faculty, service providers, and students in aligning expectations, connecting services, fostering development, and achieving success.

- *Chapter 16, "Intervening to Retain Students":* Wesley Habley and John Schuh synthesize the research literature on retention and degree completion over the past 50 years. The authors provide an insightful and thoroughly researched blueprint for broadening the definition of student success by outlining interventions that institutions and policymakers should consider. Critical issues regarding the retention/degree completion paradigm are reviewed. In particular, the authors note that the path to a college degree is neither linear nor constrained by time and that today college completion often comes via alternative means of earning college credit and multiple institutions of attendance.

- *Chapter 17, "Achieving Student Success in the First Year of College":* Randy Swing and Tracy Skipper review first-year students' unique struggles, especially their high attrition rates and developmental challenges. Using educational research, the authors present four significant ways to increase the success of first-year students who are at risk. Mirroring the major themes of this book, this chapter focuses on 1) entering students' characteristics, 2) the effect of external influences, 3) what students do, and 4) what institutions do.

- *Chapter 18, "Achieving Student Success in Two-Year Colleges":* Margaret King and Rusty Fox emphasize the unique challenges and opportunities two-year colleges face in fostering student success. The authors bring the reader up to date on what's changed in two-year colleges and on how campus leaders are fostering student success through various initiatives. The chapter demonstrates what needs to be done to create effective, interconnected educational practices.

- *Chapter 19, "Putting Students First in the Campus Community":* Gary L. Kramer (with Thomas J. Grites, Eric R. White, Michael A. Haynes,

Virginia N. Gordon, Michael McCauley, Wesley R. Habley, and Margaret C. King), all former leaders of the National Academic Advising Association, use the *CAS Professional Standards for Higher Education* as a framework to present six pathways to achieving student success. In this chapter academic advising is specified as the hub of student services and the key facilitator in helping students identify and realize academic goals and objectives. The authors note that academic advising depends on collaboration and shared partnerships with other campus departments. It is one of the very few institutional functions that connects all students to the institution. More important, academic advising has the potential to reach across the institution and coordinate the services that will assist students in their academic goals from point of entry to the time they leave the institution. The CAS standards are highlighted in this chapter to illustrate the importance of a framework to guide campus services.

- *Chapter 20, "Fostering Student Success: What Really Matters?"* Gary Kramer concludes this section and summarizes the book. This chapter addresses three questions raised here in the preface: 1) What do we know about student success on the campus? 2) What services matter to students? 3) What should institutions consider as next steps to fostering student success on the campus? In response to these questions, the chapter lists common educational practices found at institutions that have established a culture of student success. It also summarizes the recommendations presented in this volume that readers should consider as they seek to develop and implement programs that foster student success.

REFERENCES

Bailey, T. R. (2006, November). *Research on institution level practice for post-secondary student success.* Paper presented at the National Symposium on Postsecondary Student Success, Washington, DC.

Barefoot, B. O., Gardner, J. N., Cutright, M., Morris, L. V., Schroeder, C. C., Schwartz, S. W., et al. (2005). *Achieving and sustaining institutional excellence for the first year of college.* San Francisco, CA: Jossey-Bass.

Baxter Magolda, M. B., & King, P. M. (Eds.). (2004). *Learning partnerships: Theory and models of practice to educate for self-authorship.* Sterling, VA: Stylus.

Berger, J. B., & Milem, J. F. (1999, December). The role of student involvement and perceptions of integration in a causal model of student persistence. *Research in Higher Education, 40*(6), 641–664.

Blimling, G. S., Whitt, E. J., & Associates. (1999). *Good practice in student affairs: Principles to foster student learning.* San Francisco, CA: Jossey-Bass.

Braskamp, L. A., Trautvetter, L. C., & Ward, K. (2006). *Putting students first: How colleges develop students purposefully.* Bolton, MA: Anker.

Braxton, J. M. (2006, November). *Faculty professional choices in teaching that foster student success.* Paper presented at the National Symposium on Postsecondary Student Success, Washington, DC.

Braxton, J. M., Hirschy, A. S., & McClendon, S. A. (2004). *Understanding and reducing college student departure* (ASHE Higher Education Report, 30[3]). San Francisco, CA: Jossey-Bass.

Coomes, M. D., & DeBard, R. (Eds.). (2004). *New directions for student services: No. 106. Serving the millennial generation.* San Francisco, CA: Jossey-Bass.

Council for the Advancement of Standards in Higher Education. (2006). *CAS professional standards for higher education* (6th ed.). Washington, DC: Author.

Hearn, J. C. (2006, November). *Student success: What research suggests for policy and practice.* Paper presented at the National Symposium on Postsecondary Student Success, Washington, DC.

Hebel, S. (2006, September 15). Report card on colleges finds U.S. is slipping. *The Chronicle of Higher Education,* p. A1.

Hodgkinson, H. L. (1985). *All one system: Demographics of education—kindergarten through graduate school.* Washington, DC: Institute for Educational Leadership.

Hussar, W. J. (2005). *Projections of education statistics to 2014* (NCES 2005–074). U.S. Department of Education, National Center for Education Statistics. Washington, DC: U.S. Government Printing Office.

Kezar, A., & Kinzie, J. (2006, March/April). Examining the ways institutions create student engagement: The role of mission. *Journal of College Student Development, 47*(2), 149–172.

Kuh, G. D., Kinzie, J., Buckley, J. A., Bridges, B. K., & Hayek, J. C. (2006). *What matters to student success: A review of the literature.* Paper presented at the National Symposium on Postsecondary Student Success, Washington, DC.

Kuh, G. D., Kinzie, J., Schuh, J. H., & Whitt, E. J. (2005). *Assessing conditions to enhance educational effectiveness: The inventory for student engagement and success.* San Francisco, CA: Jossey-Bass.

Lovett, C. M. (2006, March 16). Alternatives to the smorgasbord: Linking student affairs with learning. *The Chronicle of Higher Education,* pp. B9–B11.

Miller, T. E. (2005). Student persistence and degree attainment. In T. E. Miller, B. E. Bender, J. H. Schuh, & Associates, *Promoting reasonable expectations: Aligning student and institutional views of the college experience* (pp. 122–139). San Francisco, CA: Jossey-Bass.

Oblinger, D. G., & Oblinger, J. L. (Eds.). (2005). *Educating the net generation.* Boulder, CO: EDUCAUSE.

Pascarella, E. T., & Terenzini, P. T. (1991). *How college affects students: Findings and insights from twenty years of research.* San Francisco, CA: Jossey-Bass.

Pascarella, E. T., & Terenzini, P. T. (2005). *How college affects students: A third decade of research.* San Francisco, CA: Jossey-Bass.

Perna, L. W., & Thomas, S. L. (2006, November). *A framework for reducing the college success gap and promoting success for all.* Paper presented at the National Symposium on Postsecondary Student Success, Washington, DC.

Sandeen, A., & Barr, M. J. (2006). *Critical issues for student affairs: Challenges and opportunities.* San Francisco, CA: Jossey-Bass.

Tinto, V., & Pusser, B. (2006, November). *Moving from theory to action: Building a model of institutional action for student success.* Paper presented at the National Symposium on Postsecondary Student Success, Washington, DC.

ACKNOWLEDGMENTS

I would like to thank my author-colleagues who have shared their experiences and scholarship on what it means and what it takes to foster student success in the campus community. Clearly, without them and their demonstrated good works over the years, there would be no book! We hope that this collection of insights will help faculty, student services providers, and campus leadership rethink, revitalize, and recommit to a student-centered environment, one that fosters student success in college. My colleagues have challenged us with ideas and strategies to make a difference in the lives of students.

Special thanks go to Peter Gardner and Shannon Openshaw of Brigham Young University (BYU) for their marvelous and professional assistance in editing the manuscript and organizing all the details associated with this project. Thank you for your feedback and for the long hours spent in final manuscript preparation.

And finally, I want to express appreciation to my colleagues at the McKay School of Education at BYU and to my family for their support and patience. My wife, Lauri, deserves special recognition. I am grateful for their willingness to adjust their needs and expectations to allow me the time and energy to complete this work. Thank you for understanding. I especially want to acknowledge Erlend "Pete" Petersen and Ford Stevenson, BYU student services administrators. They have taught me more than they will ever know—through their courage, will, and example—that it is possible to foster the success of others both on and off the campus.

PART I

COMMUNICATING EXPECTATIONS

The importance of knowing today's and tomorrow's students, creating a student-centered culture, aligning expectations, and sharing responsibility are discussed in Part I of this book. Central to the concepts of student learning, development, and success are assessing outcomes and promoting and sustaining change. Developed in these chapters is the important notion of aligning student and institutional expectations to develop measures of student outcomes and using the results to improve educational practices.

1 | KNOWING TODAY'S AND TOMORROW'S STUDENTS

VASTI TORRES

Today's higher education institutions are under constant pressure from external forces to reflect the changing landscape of U.S. society. Perhaps the most nebulous and critical of the forces is pressure to be responsive to the societal and demographic changes presently occurring and strengthening in society (Yankelovich, 2005). For example, one of the changes influencing higher education and garnering much attention is the effect that longer life expectancy is having on the order in which Americans accomplish life tasks. This longer life span influences higher education in two noticeable ways: First, students are creating new patterns of attendance by delaying college or taking longer to graduate (Yankelovich, 2005). This delay, in turn, affects other aspects of higher education, such as how access is measured. Second, more faculty and administrators are delaying retirement and working longer (Fogg, 2005). This trend creates an environment in which faculty and administrator expectations of what a college student should be may not match who today's, and tomorrow's, college students are.

Another factor influencing higher education is the advancement of technology (Yankelovich, 2005). Perhaps Marc Prensky (2001) best described this significant change in the landscape by calling today's students "digital natives," or native speakers of the digital language of computers, video games, and online socializing. The rest of us, especially those in senior administrative or faculty positions, tend to be "digital immigrants." Like most immigrants, we do our best to adapt to the current technological environment and hope we can keep up with the changes. But the expectations for mastering technology are getting higher and higher, and it's becoming more and more difficult to keep up with technology's rapid changes.

Even among the digital natives, there are differences that complicate this changing landscape. A phenomenon that is talked about in the media but not discussed much in higher education is the *digital divide,* which was originally defined in the early years of the Internet as the difference between the haves and have-nots. Eastin and LaRose (2000) say that today the "digital divide has been conceptualized primarily in terms of patterns of race and class discrimination that are reflected in unequal access to computers and the Internet." The existence of computer labs has led administrators and faculty to think that the digital divide in higher education is not wide. Yet there is much we don't know about our students' prior Internet activity and what influence income and education can have on their access to the Internet. The two examples of societal influences provided here, technology and changing life patterns, illustrate the changing landscape of higher education and how we must adapt our practice to encompass these changes.

To determine what we know about today's and tomorrow's students, this chapter will begin with an understanding of how student demographics have changed and then consider how these changes influence students' access and persistence, focusing on those who are at risk of not succeeding in college. And to help administrators know what to do, the chapter will end with a summary of best practices. Although there is no magic recipe that will help every institution understand the changing faces of higher education, it is important to understand administrator and faculty responsibilities in creating an environment that helps students succeed.

CHANGING STUDENT DEMOGRAPHICS

Many faculty and administrators began working with college students during the great expansion of higher education in the late 1960s, the 1970s, and the early 1980s. When faculty and administrators began their academic careers is significant because their impression of what a college student looks like may be tied to when they first entered the academy.

Coomes and DeBard (2004) posit that there are four distinct generations on most college campuses: silents (born between 1925 and 1942), boomers (born between 1943 and 1960), Generation Xers (born between 1961 and 1981), and millennials (born between 1982 and 2002). Each of these generations has differing values and seeks to correct something from the previous generation (Coomes & DeBard, 2004).

Understanding the diversity among our college students is critical to understanding how we can serve today's students. Comparing the college enrollment patterns from 1970 to 2000 reveals major growth and changes in the composition of the student body. Major shifts include the following:

Figure 1.1 **Undergraduate Attendance in U.S. Colleges and Universities, by Gender, 1970–2010**

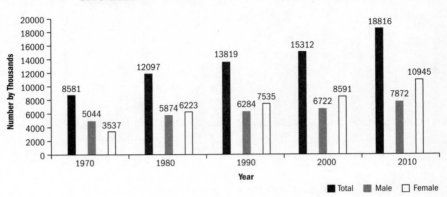

Source: Snyder, Tan, and Hoffman (2006). Note that the statistics for 2010 are projections.

- *Gender:* Figure 1.1 reveals that the number of women undergraduates has been increasing since 1980; today women make up 58% of the undergraduate student population (American Council on Education [ACE], 2005; Snyder, Tan, & Hoffman, 2006). Although much has been made of this increase in female attendance, research shows that this trend is not happening at the expense of men; rather, Latino and African American women are enrolling at higher rates than their male counterparts (King, 2006).

- *Attendance:* As indicated in Figure 1.2, the number of part-time students is increasing. It is estimated that in 2003, 59% of undergraduates attended college on less than a full-time, full-year basis and that 40% attend community colleges (ACE, 2005).

- *Race/ethnicity:* In 1980 the percentage of minority students (African American, Latino, Asian, and American Indian) was 16.5%. By 1997 there was a 10% increase to 26.8% (Hoffman, 2001); by 2003 the number had increased to 36% (ACE, 2005).

- *Immigration:* By 1999–2000, 20% of undergraduates either were born outside the United States or had at least one parent who was born outside the United States (Choy, 2002).

- *Age:* In 2003, 39% of undergraduates were at least 25 years old (ACE, 2005).

Figure 1.2   **Undergraduate Attendance in U.S. Colleges and Universities, by Attendance Pattern, 1970–2010**

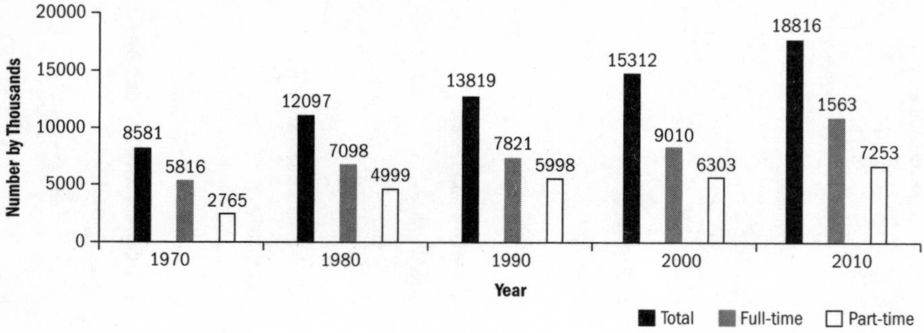

Source: Snyder, Tan, and Hoffman (2006). Note that the statistics for 2010 are projections.

- *Financial status:* In 1999–2000, 37% of undergraduates at four-year colleges were considered financially independent (Choy, 2002).

These changes in student characteristics influence the college environment and require faculty and administrators to adjust their thinking about college students. Research on higher education has identified the barriers to success for today's students, but this literature is less clear about how these changes influence retention. The remainder of this chapter will attempt to summarize what we know about how changing demographics influence access, persistence, and effective practices.

Influences Changing Demographics Have on Access

The growth of student enrollments and changing demographics have created different challenges for institutions of higher education. As a result, access has become a priority for many policymakers and it is one of the challenges for this century. There is evidence, however, that access alone is not sufficient and that more needs to be done to help at-risk students succeed. This section will consider how changing demographics have influenced access.

Some of the increases in the student body can be associated with an increase in first-generation college students. Students who are first-generation college goers experience a "disadvantage for access" (Choy, 2002, p. 22). Even after enrolling, they are twice as likely to drop out after their first year. Those who persist for three years still tend to lag behind and are less likely to be on track for a bachelor's degree (Choy, 2002; Ishitani, 2006). In a study of indicators of college success, first-generation students were less engaged and "less likely to successfully integrate diverse college experiences" (Pike & Kuh, 2005, p. 289); overall, they perceive "the college environment as less support-ive" (p. 289) than their peers do. These disadvantages were related to educa-tional aspirations and where the students lived while attending college. Many first-generation students have lower educational aspirations and commute to college, rather than live on campus. Even at institutions where on-campus housing is available, the cost can make living at home a more viable option.

First-generation college students, however, also vary greatly in certain respects. For example, Ishitani (2006) found that students who had a strong high school academic record and parents who had completed some college coursework were more likely to graduate in a reasonable time period. As a result, administrators today must know about students' high school academic attributes and obtain more detailed information about familial educational experiences.

Longitudinal research has also found that first-generation Latino stu-dents tend to seek information from trusted and familiar sources rather than from university officials (Torres, Reiser, LePeau, Davis, & Ruder, 2006). The Latino students at the four urban universities examined in Torres et al. did not change their information-seeking behavior until they experienced dissonance, which many times resulted in a negative situation (such as not meeting requirements or being denied admission to a program due to inaccurate course registrations). This style of information-seeking behavior could help explain why, even in the third year of college, first-generation students are often not on track for a bachelor's degree.

Providing information about college admissions, advising, and financing is essential for preparing low-income students and students of color for suc-cessful college experiences (McDonough, 2004b). A 1999 study found that only 18% of high school students and 30% of their parents had information about the actual cost of attending college (McDonough, 2004b). Accurate and timely information can make a difference in access for students (McDonough, 2004a), and institutions can no longer assume that this infor-mation is getting to everyone who is interested in attending college.

The lack of information also influences the academic preparation of at-risk students. A study conducted in six states found "that less than 12 percent of students knew the courses required for [college] admission" (McDonough, 2004b, p. 11). This statistic is worrisome because one of the best predictors of college attendance is a rigorous high school curriculum and advanced math-ematics (Adelman, 1999). Whether their source for information is family or schools, many low-income and underrepresented students lack knowledge about course requirements or advising. This lack of knowledge becomes an invisible barrier to access and then to persistence (McDonough, 2004b).

Academic preparation also influences the need to take remedial courses in college. Although previous research could not distinguish between the effects of poor high school preparation and the remedial education in college, more recent statistical techniques have found that the lower graduation rates among students in remedial courses are attributable more to poor academic skills carried over from high school preparation (Attewell, Lavin, Domina, & Levey, 2006). Attewell et al. also found that, although low-income students were more likely to take remedial courses (52%), there was a significant number of students from high-income families who also took remedial courses (24%).

A common approach to helping students achieve focuses on acquiring skills and knowledge (Anderson, 2006). Though this approach has been in effect for more than 30 years, the gap in achievement has only widened. Anderson (2006) referred to this approach as the "deficit remedial education model" (p. 4), noting that it focuses on removing the deficit without drawing on the students' strength. The starting point for assisting students is turning the deficit model around and, using an approach based on concepts of positive psychology, creating an ethos focused on the discovery of strengths rather than deficits (Shushok & Hulme, 2006). This focus on student strengths requires that campus policies and programs be evaluated to challenge existing assumptions about students' learning (Shushok & Hulme, 2006). Once students recognize their strengths, the role of the institution shifts to connecting them to communities where their strengths can be expressed and nourished.

Another barrier is the financial resources necessary to attend college today. The rising cost of tuition, the shift toward more merit-based aid, and unmet financial need all influence access (McDonough, 2004b). Research shows that low-income and underrepresented students tend to lack information and overestimate the cost of college. A longitudinal study of Historically Black Colleges and Universities found that "Black students are more sensitive to changes in need-based financial aid than White students" (Sissoko & Shiau, 2005, p. 203). The cost of college education influences low-income students more than middle- or high-income students. As a result, the gap between the haves and have-nots continues to widen.

An increasing issue in higher education today is unmet financial need. As increases in college tuition outpace those in financial aid packages, more and more students experience a gap between their need and the financial package offered to them. This gap can range from about $1,200 a year for students attending public institutions to more than $5,000 a year for those attending private colleges and universities (Pascarella & Terenzini, 2005). The research connecting unmet need to access and persistence suggests that students with unmet need are less likely to persist and complete their degree (Pascarella & Terenzini, 2005).

Influences Changing Demographics Have on Persistence

Although in the past most students began and completed their degree at one institution, today 54% of college undergraduates attend or have attended more than one institution (Choy, 2002). It is likely that this percentage will swell to 60% in the future (Adelman, 1999). Ironically, it is the students at each end of the academic spectrum who are most likely to transfer. Students beginning at "highly selective 4-year colleges and those starting out in open door institutions have the highest rate of multi-institutional attendance, though for very different reasons" (Adelman, 1999, p. vii). Although these statistics are disturbing, the number of institutions attended did not have an effect on degree completion. However, the fewer schools a student attended, the more likely the student maintained continuous enrollment. The completion rate for continuously enrolled students was twice as high as that for non-continuously enrolled students (Adelman, 1999).

One of the reasons that understanding transfer students is important is that 40% of undergraduates attend community colleges (ACE, 2005). There is contradictory evidence about community college attendance and bachelor's degree completion. If one looks at degree attainment within four to five years, the results are not positive (Choy, 2002). If no time frame is given, the completion rate tends to be the same for those attending community colleges and those at four-year institutions (Adelman, 1999). The main concern for community colleges is that more nontraditional and underrepresented students tend to enroll at these less expensive colleges. For example, 51% of undergraduates over the age of 25 and 43% of low-income students attend a community college. Among underrepresented students, 44% of African Americans, 46% of Latinos, 45% of American Indians, and 40% of Asian Americans attend community colleges. The low cost and geographic proximity to family attracts these potentially at-risk students to community colleges. To make a difference in the success of these students, much more attention and research focused on this sector of higher education and the process of transferring are needed.

The need for interventions to assist transfer students in their transition to a new institution is well documented (Hurtado & Carter, 1997). Yet only one-third of surveyed campuses have formal programs to assist in such transitions (Lester, 2006). Peer tutoring, instructional courses, and workshops tend to have the greatest effect on helping students transfer and succeed (Pascarella & Terenzini, 2005). To be most successful, these components need to be connected in a comprehensive manner. One-shot programs tend to have limited success with transfer students and do not address their ongoing needs.

The final influence on persistence among low-income and underrepresented students is the number of hours worked for pay. Attending part-time and working more than 15 hours a week are factors that reduce the likelihood of persistence (Choy, 2002; King, 2002). It is important to understand the connection between the cost of an education and working for pay. In a report from the Advisory Committee on Student Financial Assistance, it was estimated that "in the 1990s, between 800,000 and 1.6 million low and moderate income high school students who were both academically qualified for and intent on attending a four-year college did not go on to earn a bachelor's degree" (Lederman, 2006). The estimate is even higher for this decade: 1.4 million to 2.4 million. This report states that although there are other factors that can influence noncompletion, economic factors such as work, loans, rising tuition, and low need-based grants "continue to undermine advances in other areas."

EFFECTIVE PRACTICES

Looking toward tomorrow's students, faculty and administrators must consider the environment within their institution. The academic and social environment of an institution has an important influence on what students learn (Feldman, Smart, & Ethington, 2004). Although there is evidence that the academy tends to have low expectations of minority students, there is evidence that the opposite—high expectations—benefits students the most. Providing academic challenge with sufficient support is the combination that has the best effect (Kuh, Kinzie, Schuh, Whitt, & Associates, 2005). Supportive academic environments create positive student-faculty interactions as well as a collaborative learning environment (Kuh et al., 2005). The positive influence of faculty-student interactions is supported by a large body of evidence (Pascarella & Terenzini, 2005) and is common sense. These practices are more crucial today and will be even more crucial in the future.

An example of an institution that changed its culture to help students succeed is Fayetteville State University (McLeod & Young, 2005). The change in culture came after a review of existing data revealed that the institution was serving as a "revolving door" (p. 73) for many students. One of the major efforts to change this culture was to institute a comprehensive program called the Freshman Year Initiative. This initiative included a freshmen seminar that aided students in transitioning to college and developing skills to succeed there. Seminar instructors were also assigned as the freshmen's advisors to build the relationships between student and faculty. This relationship is important for many first-generation college students (Torres et al., 2006). The final element was a pledge card that was given to each student and discussed in the course. This pledge included issues of time commitments, asking for help, and taking responsibility. The immediate effect of this intervention was increased retention rate, greater student satisfaction, and higher benchmark scores on the National Survey of Student Engagement (McLeod & Young, 2005). This example illustrates how an institution can be deliberate in creating a positive environment for students and change a revolving-door culture to one of success.

One of the important components of a positive academic environment is socializing new faculty to the campus culture (Kuh et al., 2005). In a study of institutions that created environments that engage students in learning, such socialization took several forms. It began with the recruitment process and continued through a variety of campus activities that helped faculty understand their role in creating a positive learning environment (Kuh et al., 2005).

Another component is valuing diversity within the community. Efforts to understand other cultures will be one of the most salient influences on higher education in the future (Yankelovich, 2005). Engaged institutions infuse diversity activities into their campus culture to help their students understand today's global environment (Kuh et al., 2005). Even colleges with low structural diversity (the number of people of color) can use other techniques to help members of their community understand and experience the value of diversity (Umbach & Kuh, 2006).

There are several approaches that make a difference for adult students. Validation of prior experiences, customized educational plans, and support for distance learning are three of the components found in exceptional programs for these students (Compton, Cox, & Laanan, 2006). Programs that were successful in serving adult students tended to redesign their structure to be accessible to people who had less time to be a student. These institutions also evaluated instructional delivery to make sure it served adult students. Finally, these institutions considered the practical needs of adult students to better serve them inside and outside the classroom (Compton et al., 2006).

These components illustrate that the traditional college environment has to do more to prepare students to succeed in college and in today's global environment. Although there is no one way to create an engaging college environment, it is important for colleges to be intentional about creating a supportive environment for multiple types of students.

CONCLUSION

Is higher education keeping up with the changing landscape of today's society? The answer to that question is mixed. Some institutions are moving forward, evaluating their institutional data to determine and address their students' gaps and problems; other institutions are continuing with the same programs, as if students had not changed for the past 40 years. This chapter provided examples of ways institutions can better serve today's students. As a summary, the following are some of the ideas that have made a difference:

- *Colleges and universities ought to review institutional data about their students.* This simple activity can prompt institutional change. The Lumina Foundation grant Achieving the Dream is based on a culture of evidence: Community colleges look at their student data and research to determine the best solutions for local student issues. Fayetteville State University is a prime example of an institution that took to heart the results of its institutional data and created interventions that addressed the gaps (Kuh et al., 2005). By disaggregating their student data by race/ethnicity, gender, and class year, administrators and faculty can better see the gaps in their educational system.

- *With these findings, institutions can create local initiatives to respond to the types of students they serve.* As previously acknowledged, one size does not fit all; locally owned solutions are necessary to address the needs of a given campus's students (Tierney, 2000).

- *Institutions ought to reevaluate instructional techniques to make sure students' needs are being met.* The evidence indicating the importance of faculty-student interaction combined with the evidence on effective intervention components is a call for action: We need to reevaluate what we do to serve students. More recent research makes a compelling case for the use of active learning, collaborative teaching, and high expectations (Kuh et al., 2005; Wilson, 2004). No institution is immune from the changing demographics and social issues discussed in this chapter.

- *Institutions should review system-wide policy to make sure current policies serve all students.* Examples of K–16 initiatives illustrate the need to articulate a system-wide commitment to advancing all students toward higher education. In Indiana, for example, all students will automatically receive the college curriculum; they will not be required to opt into it or request it. Although this initiative will not be ready for full implementation for several years, this type of policy emphasis creates an ethos that students can meet expectations instead of a deficiency model that implies low expectations of certain student groups.

- *Institutions need to remember that students are individuals and make that fact the basic tenet of working with them.* Evidence about the diversity and differences among first-generation college students illustrates that remembering the individual student is central to success. This principle should be at the center of all that administrators and faculty do for students.

- *Institutions must be willing to challenge the expectations and assumptions of their faculty and administrators.* The negative influence of stereotypes is confirmed by research literature, yet institutions continue to react to some students from a deficiency model that reinforces stereotypes. Administrators and faculty must confront each other to establish an ethos that works with students' strengths instead of focusing on the deficits.

The use of traditional theories that do not consider the changing diversity of undergraduate populations will likely do harm rather than help students succeed. Successful colleges and universities are creating approaches that are informed by the literature but also grounded in the context of their students' needs. The research illustrates that, although there are many challenges, there are many ways to create environments that help students succeed. The challenge is to match the intervention to the actual needs of students. This requires administrators and faculty to understand the changing faces of today's and tomorrow's students.

REFERENCES

Adelman, C. (1999). *Answers in the toolbox: Academic intensity, attendance patterns, and bachelor's degree attainment.* Jessup, MD: Education Publications Center.

American Council on Education. (2005). *College students today: A national portrait.* Washington, DC: Author.

Anderson, E. (2006). If we want to boost retention and achievement, we need to work from student strengths, not weaknesses. *About Campus, 2*(4), 4–5.

Attewell, P., Lavin, D., Domina, T., & Levey, T. (2006, September/October). New evidence on college remediation. *Journal of Higher Education, 77*(5), 886–924.

Choy, S. P. (2002). *Access and persistence: Findings from 10 years of longitudinal research on students.* Washington, DC: American Council on Education.

Compton, J. I., Cox, E., & Laanan, F. S. (2006). Adult learners in transition. In F. S. Laanan (Ed.), *New directions for student services: No. 114. Understanding students in transition: Trends and issues* (pp. 73–80). San Francisco, CA: Jossey-Bass.

Coomes, M. D., & DeBard, R. (2004). A generational approach to understanding students. In M. D. Coomes & R. DeBard (Eds.), *New directions for student services: No. 106. Serving the millennial generation* (pp. 5–16). San Francisco, CA: Jossey-Bass.

Eastin, M. S., & LaRose, R. (2000, September). Internet self-efficacy and the psychology of the digital divide. *Journal of Computer-Mediated Communications, 6*(1). Retrieved June 21, 2007, from http://jcmc.indiana.edu/vol6/issue1/eastin.html

Feldman, K. A., Smart, J. C., & Ethington, C. A. (2004, September/October). What do college students have to lose? Exploring the outcomes of differences in person-environment fits. *Journal of Higher Education, 75*(5), 528–555.

Fogg, P. (2005, June 3). Advancing in age. *The Chronicle of Higher Education,* p. A6.

Hoffman, C. (2001). *Mini-digest of education statistics, 2000* (NCES 2001–046). U.S. Department of Education, National Center for Education Statistics. Washington, DC: U.S. Government Printing Office.

Hurtado, S., & Carter, D. F. (1997, October). Effects of college transition and perceptions of the campus racial climate on Latino college students' sense of belonging. *Sociology of Education, 70*(4), 324–345.

Ishitani, T. T. (2006, September/October). Studying attrition and degree completion behavior among first-generation college students in the United States. *Journal of Higher Education, 77*(5), 861–885.

King, J. (2002). *Crucial choices: How students' financial decisions affect their academic success.* Washington, DC: American Council on Education.

King, J. (2006). *Gender equity in higher education: 2006.* Washington, DC: American Council on Education.

Kuh, G. D., Kinzie, J., Schuh, J. H., Whitt, E. J., & Associates (2005). *Student success in college: Creating conditions that matter.* San Francisco, CA: Jossey-Bass.

Lederman, D. (2006, September 14). The children left behind. *Inside Higher Ed.* Retrieved June 21, 2007, from http://insidehighered.com/news/2006/09/14/lost

Lester, J. (2006). Who will we serve in the future? The new student in transition. In F. S. Laanan (Ed.), *New directions for student services: No. 114. Understanding students in transition: Trends and issues* (pp. 47–91). San Francisco, CA: Jossey-Bass.

McDonough, P. M. (2004a). Counseling matters: Knowledge, assistance, and organizational commitment in college preparation. In W. G. Tierney, Z. B. Corwin, & J. E. Colyar (Eds.), *Preparing for college: Nine elements of effective outreach* (pp. 69–88). Albany, NY: State University of New York Press.

McDonough, P. M. (2004b). *The school-to-college transition: Challenges and prospects.* Washington, DC: American Council on Education.

McLeod, W. B., & Young, J. M. (2005). A chancellor's vision: Establishing an institutional culture of student success. In G. H. Gaither (Ed.), *New directions for institutional research: No. 125. Minority retention: What works?* (pp. 73–85). San Francisco, CA: Jossey-Bass.

Pascarella, E. T., & Terenzini, P. T. (2005). *How college affects students: A third decade of research.* San Francisco, CA: Jossey-Bass.

Pike, G. R., & Kuh, G. D. (2005, May/June). First- and second-generation college students: A comparison of their engagement and intellectual development. *Journal of Higher Education, 76*(3), 276–300.

Prensky, M. (2001, October). Digital natives, digital immigrants. *On the Horizon, 9*(5), 1–2.

Shushok, F., Jr., & Hulme, E. (2006, September). What's right with you: Helping students find and use their personal strengths. *About Campus, 11*(4), 2–8.

Sissoko, M., & Shiau, L.-R. (2005, March/April). Minority enrollment demand for higher education at historically Black colleges and universities from 1976 to 1998: An empirical analysis. *Journal of Higher Education, 76*(2), 181–208.

Snyder, T. D., Tan, A. G., & Hoffman, C. M. (2006). *Digest of education statistics 2005* (NCES 2006–030). U.S. Department of Education, National Center for Education Statistics. Washington, DC: U.S. Government Printing Office.

Tierney, W. G. (2000). Power, identity, and the dilemma of college student departure. In J. M. Braxton (Ed.), *Reworking the student departure puzzle* (pp. 213–234). Nashville, TN: Vanderbilt University Press.

Torres, V., Reiser, A., LePeau, L., Davis, L., & Ruder, J. (2006, Fall). A model of first-generation Latino/a college students' approach to seeking academic information. *NACADA Journal, 26*(2), 65–70.

Umbach, P. D., & Kuh, G. D. (2006, January). Student experiences with diversity at liberal arts colleges: Another claim for distinctiveness. *Journal of Higher Education, 77*(1), 169–192.

Wilson, M. E. (2004). Teaching, learning, and millennial students. In M. D. Coomes & R. DeBard (Eds.), *New directions for student services: No. 106. Serving the millennial generation* (pp. 59–71). San Francisco, CA: Jossey-Bass.

Yankelovich, D. (2005, November 25). Ferment and change: Higher education in 2015. *The Chronicle of Higher Education,* p. B6.

2 | CREATING A STUDENT-CENTERED CULTURE

JILLIAN KINZIE AND GEORGE D. KUH

Many colleges claim to be student centered. Those that really do focus on students and their learning present students with rich and varied opportunities for learning inside and outside the classroom, challenge students to reach high levels of performance, and provide support to help meet students' academic and social needs.

Being student centered is not a new idea. Under different labels, the concept has been linked to student success for decades (Keeton, 1971; Kuh, Schuh, Whitt, & Associates, 1991). But focusing on students and their success has become even more important as greater scrutiny is given to institutional performance in the form of persistence and graduation rates, particularly gaps in these rates for different student populations, and as clarion calls have been made for more transparency and accountability for the quality of the student experience (Bauman, Bustillos, Bensimon, Brown, & Bartee, 2005; National Commission on the Future of Higher Education, 2006; Wingspread Group on Higher Education, 1993).

In *Greater Expectations: A New Vision for Learning as a Nation Goes to College,* the Association of American Colleges and Universities (2002) made a compelling case for reorganizing "undergraduate education to ensure that all college aspirants receive not just access to college, but *an education of lasting value*" (p. vi; emphasis added). Doing so requires that institutions place student learning and success at the heart of the enterprise. This is easier said than done because student-centered colleges and universities are products of many complementary, inextricably intertwined factors and conditions—educational mission, operating philosophies, resources, programs, and practices, to name just a few. Woven together, these threads of institutional life make up the fabric of the campus culture.

Culture is a major factor in the success of all high-performing organizations (Collins, 2001; Kuh, Kinzie, Schuh, Whitt, & Associates, 2005; Tagg, 2003; Tierney, 1999). To create and sustain a student-centered culture, colleges and universities must first understand the properties of campus cultures that foster student success.

To be clear, institutions with student-centered cultures do not attempt to address students' every want and desire. Rather, they set high expectations consistent with the differing characteristics, talents, and goals of their students and intentionally organize their resources to expose and encourage students to take advantage of a range of learning experiences.

This chapter draws on research on student learning and educational effectiveness to distill key features of student-centered campus cultures. Many of these ideas were described in *Student Success in College: Creating Conditions that Matter* (Kuh, Kinzie, Schuh, Whitt, & Associates, 2005), which reported the findings from the Documenting Effective Educational Practice (DEEP) project, an 18-month study of 20 four-year colleges and universities that had higher-than-predicted scores on the National Survey of Student Engagement (NSSE) and higher-than-predicted graduation rates. The DEEP project research team used the case study method to explore the practices, programs, and policies that accounted for each institution's performance. (For more on the study, see www.nsse.iub.edu.)

First, we briefly review the philosophical underpinnings of the student-centered concept and how this view evolved over time. Then we describe several key features of student-centered campus cultures. We conclude with some suggestions for creating and sustaining such learning-friendly environments.

OVERVIEW OF THE STUDENT-CENTERED PHILOSOPHY

Virtually all colleges and universities espouse an abiding interest in the welfare of their students, especially undergraduates. But students are not necessarily uppermost in the minds of campus policy and decision-makers, who try to balance the competing interests of such stakeholders as faculty members, trustees, community leaders, alumni, funding agencies, and legislators in the course of pursuing the institution's teaching, research, and service missions (Winston, 2003).

Over the past century various groups periodically issued reports about the need to focus on students and their success in the context of the other purposes of postsecondary education. Among the earliest such documents was the 1937 *Student Personnel Point of View* issued by the American Council on

Education, which underscored the need for nonfaculty specialists to work directly with students. Within two decades, the student affairs profession was established (Nuss, 1996).

Subsequent major reports appeared with increasing frequency, striking similar chords (American Association for Higher Education, American College Personnel Association [ACPA], & National Association of Student Personnel Administrators, 1998; ACPA, 1996; Education Commission of the States, 1995; National Institute of Education, 1984; Wingspread Group on Higher Education, 1993). The pioneering research on student development by the contributors to Nevitt Sanford's classic volume *The American College* (1962) precipitated a veritable explosion of studies into the characteristics of students and learning environments (e.g., Astin, 1977; Feldman & Newcomb, 1969; Pace, 1979). Thanks to periodic syntheses (Bowen, 1977; Feldman & Newcomb, 1969; Pascarella & Terenzini, 1991, 2005), almost everything known about college student development was made accessible to scholars and practitioners alike.

By the mid-1990s the body of research on effective teaching and learning had matured to the point where Barr and Tagg (1995) declared that a paradigm shift was under way from *teaching* to *learning*, wherein a student-centered institution could be intentionally fashioned by creating conditions that emphasized learning, not simply delivering instruction (Tagg, 2003). In the traditional teacher-centered approach, instructors are the authority, directing the learning process and regulating students' access to information. In student-centered pedagogy, learning is an active, dynamic process in which students have direct access to information and resources and work individually and in small groups to construct their own meaning (Baxter Magolda, 1999; Cross, 1991; Meyers & Jones, 1993). Student-centered approaches to teaching and learning also emphasize the importance of students' prior experiences and preferred learning styles while using activities that stimulate higher order thinking, thus setting the stage for lifelong learning (Brown, Collins, & Duguid, 1989; Driscoll, 1994).

Changing student demographics further fueled efforts to create student-centered cultures as greater numbers of historically underserved students began to matriculate. Research shows that racial tensions and group competition are diminished when students feel they are valued and faculty and administrators are clearly devoted to their development (Hurtado, Milem, Clayton-Pedersen, & Allen, 1998). Hurtado (1992) concluded that increased structural diversity in colleges and universities will likely fail in achieving the desired student development outcomes unless institutions become more student centered in their approaches to undergraduate education. On most campuses, student affairs personnel are at the vanguard of efforts to promote diversity.

In the 1990s calls for collaboration between academic and student affairs became more frequent and were based on research showing that students benefited more when they were actively engaged in learning activities inside and outside the classroom (Astin, 1993; Pascarella & Terenzini, 1991, 2005). To no small degree, what students do during college is associated with the quality of the learning environment—the campus ethos, policies, and programs—and whether they participate in educationally purposeful activities (Kuh, 2003). To emphasize this point, Pascarella and Terenzini (2005) concluded, "It is important to focus on the ways in which an institution can shape its academic, interpersonal, and extracurricular offerings to encourage student engagement" (p. 602).

Another external force also compelled institutions to take students and their learning seriously. By the end of the 1990s regional accrediting agencies and their counterparts in the disciplines required that institutions show evidence that they are measuring student outcomes and aspects of the campus environment associated with these outcomes *and* are using this information to improve student learning and success.

This abbreviated review of the recent past suggests three things. First, various groups on and off the campus have long been interested in what happens to students during college. Second, there is general agreement that student success is and must remain a high priority for postsecondary institutions. Finally, a substantial body of research indicates that colleges and universities can arrange their human and other resources to induce students to take part in educationally effective activities inside and outside the classroom. When these practices and the beliefs, values, and assumptions that support them are institutionalized, conditions are ripe for establishing a student-centered culture.

PERSPECTIVES ON CAMPUS AND INSTITUTIONAL CULTURE

Institutional culture is a multifaceted construct represented in part by deeply embedded, intertwined patterns of behavior, values, and beliefs that are more or less shared by members of the community (Kuh & Whitt, 1988; Schein, 1992). As an "invisible tapestry" (Kuh & Whitt, 1988), culture gives meaning to campus activities and events; provides a common language, purpose, and direction; and brings a measure of coherence to campus life (Kuh et al., 1991; Kuh & Whitt, 1988; Magolda, 2000; Manning, 2000).

Although the depth, complexity, and occasionally ambiguous nature of institutional life sometimes make cultural properties nearly impossible to thoroughly discover and describe (Martin, 2002), some of the more visible manifestations of culture can be identified. For example, often told stories, annual rituals, and institutional mantras can reveal much about institutional values and where students and their success fall among institutional priorities. Cherished campus rituals that reinforce the norms of student-faculty interaction outside class or rites of passage that introduce new students to the rigors of college work can signal the extent to which the institutional culture welcomes students. Campus signage can make plain or obfuscate how newcomers and physically limited persons navigate the campus. In this section we provide some illustrations of what these and other cultural properties look like in the context of institutions with student-centered cultures. In particular, we will discuss seven threads woven throughout the fabric of student-centered cultures. They are:

- A clear, coherent mission and philosophy

- An unshakeable focus on student learning

- High performance expectations for all students

- The widespread use of effective educational practices

- Human-scale settings

- A collaborative, improvement-oriented ethic

- Language and traditions supporting student success

We draw substantially from studies of high-performing campuses (Kuh et al., 1991; Kuh, Kinzie, Schuh, Whitt, & Associates, 2005) along with national reports, such as the "Seven Principles for Good Practice in Undergraduate Education" (Chickering & Gamson, 1987), *Making Quality Count in Undergraduate Education* (Education Commission of the States, 1995), and other related writings (Bailey & Alfonso, 2005; Bauman et al., 2005; Carey, 2004; Peter & Cataldi, 2005; Tagg, 2003). The examples provide glimpses of what a student-centered culture looks like, at least to outsiders. These institutions are places to get some good ideas for what to do and to— in Tom Peters's (1987) words—"creatively swipe" what seems to be working at institutions with student-centered cultures.

Clear, Coherent Institutional Mission and Philosophy

Colleges and universities that clearly explicate their educational objectives and align their educational policies and programs with these objectives generally are more effective and efficient (Bolman & Deal, 1991; Ewell, 1989). As Chickering and Reisser (1993) put it:

> Clear and consistent objectives, stated in terms of desired outcomes for learning and personal development, are critically important in creating an educationally powerful institution. These should not have to be deduced from course descriptions. They should be explicit and compelling. They should be defined by the members of the college community, taken to heart by campus leaders, and invoked as guides to decision-making. (p. 287)

Some institutions—mostly small colleges—have pithy, succinct mission statements. One men's college mission illustrates the point: "Wabash College educates men to think critically, act responsibly, lead effectively, and live humanely" (Kuh, Kinzie, Schuh, Whitt, & Associates, 2005, p. 52). Other institutions adopt a tagline that speaks volumes about what the institution is and values. Here is one such example: "Luther College has a higher calling—to help students connect faith with learning, freedom with responsibility, and life's work with service" (Luther College, 2005, p. 21).

Indeed, the enacted mission of a campus—what people actually do—appears to be more important to creating and sustaining a student-centered culture than the written mission (Kezar & Kinzie, 2006; Kuh, Kinzie, Schuh, Whitt, & Associates, 2005). In part, this may explain why some researchers (Astin, 1993; Hedlund & Jones, 1970) find correlations between student persistence and resources allocated to student services and personnel: The enacted mission and ethos of institutions that have a deep commitment to student success impel them to use their resources in this way (Kuh, 1995). That is, these institutions invest more in student support services because they believe students will perform better when those students' academic and social needs are recognized and addressed (Kuh, Kinzie, Schuh, Whitt, & Associates, 2005).

These cultural moorings may also partially explain why students at many special-mission institutions—such as single-sex colleges, Historically Black Colleges and Universities (HBCUs), and Hispanic-Serving Institutions (HSIs)—appear to benefit more educationally and socially compared with their counterparts attending other institutions (Dayton, Gonzalez-Vasquez, Martinez, & Plum, 2004; Harwarth, 1999; Holland & Eisenhart, 1990;

Outcalt & Skewes-Cox, 2002). Perhaps students succeed at higher rates at such colleges because "faculty who show regard for their students' unique interests and talents are likely to facilitate student growth and development in every sphere—academic, social, personal, and vocational" (Sorcinelli, 1991, p. 21). The University of Texas at El Paso, an HSI, expresses this ideal in its mantra: "Talent is everywhere, opportunity is not" (Kuh, Kinzie, Schuh, Whitt, & Associates, 2005, p. 50). Alverno College's mission is elegant in its focus: "Alverno exists to promote the personal and professional development of women" (Kuh, Kinzie, Schuh, Whitt, & Associates, 2005, p. 29).

Unshakeable Focus on Student Learning

Maintaining an unshakeable focus on students and their success is the second distinctive thread in a student-centered culture. This focus is anchored by a talent development philosophy that bleeds throughout the institution, a view that recognizes the importance of valuing and addressing students' diverse talents and needs (Chickering, 2006; Chickering & Gamson, 1987). Adhering to a talent development philosophy benefits all students, especially when pedagogical practices acknowledge and honor students' backgrounds and experiences and view their talents and skills as assets. Because all students have a unique perspective on the world and the topic under study, through sharing their knowledge and experience, they enrich their own learning as well as that of others (Alexander & Murphy, 1994). At California State University–Monterey Bay, for example, faculty members teaching first-year students assess their skills and allow students to select their preferred way of completing early assignments (multiple choice test, essay, oral presentation) to bolster their confidence, as contrasted with forcing all students to do the same thing, which may disadvantage those who do not typically perform well in a particular format. In subsequent assignments, after establishing themselves academically, students will have to demonstrate their ability to use other approaches to completing assignments.

Some faculty members view learning style differences as academic deficiencies in need of remediation (Pounds, 1987). Uri Treisman (1992) observed that many students from historically underserved groups at the University of California–Berkeley were failing calculus even though they had achieved the academic prerequisites and demonstrated ability to perform successfully. Discovering that environmental disorientation was the issue, not lack of motivation as some instructors assumed, Treisman developed strategies for these black and Hispanic students to further hone their mathematical and problem-solving skills. According to Treisman, "We did not question that minority students could excel. We just wanted to know what kind of setting we would need to provide so that they could" (p. 368). By adopting a talent development perspective and taking into account the backgrounds and characteristics of the students, Treisman and his colleagues were able to develop a model program that responded to the needs of a variety of students (Kuh, Douglas, Lund, & Ramin-Gyurnek, 1994).

Faculty and staff using a talent development approach believe all students can learn anything the college teaches (Kuh, 1997). A key step in enacting this philosophy is validating students, which helps them believe that they can succeed and that they are full members of the institution (Rendon, 1994, 1999; Suarez, 2003). For example, one explanation for why many African American students struggle academically at primarily white institutions is that they must contend with feelings of alienation and frustration, along with little encouragement for their efforts, relative to their peers at HBCUs (Watson & Kuh, 1996). But when faculty and staff validate students—address and praise them by name, work one on one with them, provide encouragement and support (Rendon, 1994, 1999)—students begin to see themselves as being capable of learning, which in turn contributes to an increased interest and confidence in their capacity to learn (Volkwein & Cabrera, 1998).

High Performance Expectations for All Students

Setting high expectations and then holding students accountable for reaching them is another earmark of a student-centered culture (Education Commission of the States, 1995; Kuh et al., 1991; Kuh, Kinzie, Schuh, Whitt, & Associates, 2005). Students tend to adjust their behavior to meet the demands placed on them, regardless of their prior academic history. This is what Blose (1999) found for students at selective institutions who exceeded their predicted performance when challenged with high expectations. Institutions with student-centered cultures set expectations appropriate to their particular students.

Students at George Mason University must take freshman composition, advanced composition, and at least one writing-intensive course in their major. Some writing-intensive courses require writing portfolios, such as in nursing, or design projects, such as in engineering. Every public and international affairs course at or above the 300-level is writing intensive.

At the University of the South (or Sewanee), the lynchpin for the first-year program is a small, academically rigorous seminar designed to foster communities of learning and introduce new students to college-level work. The Evergreen State College (2001) established six "expectations of an Evergreen graduate" (p. 10) to set forth what students are to attain as part of their individualized academic plan. These expectations flow from the college's five foci for teaching and learning: interdisciplinary learning, learning across significant differences, personal engagement with learning, linking theory to practice, and collaborative learning (Kuh, Kinzie, Schuh, Whitt, & Associates, 2005). Wofford College's Novel Experience first-year reading program assigns a common reading to all incoming first-year students, who then write an essay about the reading. The eight best are published, thus establishing academic excellence as what defines celebrity status in the entering class.

To achieve the desired effects, high expectations must be accompanied by reasonable amounts of support to help students respond to these academic challenges and do what is necessary to succeed. All new Macalester College first-year students take a discipline-based first-year seminar (FYS) in their first semester; the instructor is their advisor for the first two years or until the students declare a major. Because of the FYS instructors' dual role—seminar leader and advisor—they see their advisees several times a week, which provides frequent opportunities for informal conversation and monitoring students' academic and social adjustment. As a result, Macalester students have at least one faculty member who knows them very well and can make appropriate referrals, if necessary. Fayetteville State University's extension grade policy permits students in certain introductory courses to request a temporary "extension grade" in lieu of a D or an F if they sign an extension grade contract no later than the end of the fifth week of the semester, complete all course requirements, agree to use academic support services such as supplemental instruction, and reenroll in the course the next term.

Widespread Use of Effective Educational Practices

Colleges and universities with a student-centered culture organize their resources and create conditions for teaching and learning using research-based, educationally effective practices inside and outside the classroom (Kuh, 2001, 2003; National Survey of Student Engagement, 2005; Pascarella & Terenzini, 2005). This thread in the cultural fabric of student-centered institutions has two discernable features: 1) engaging pedagogies, and 2) programs and practices that guide students toward pathways to success.

Engaging pedagogies. Engaging pedagogies matter to student success in three ways. They involve students more intensely in learning. They increase students' time on task. And they harness peer influence in educationally purposeful ways. Engaging pedagogies include discussion-oriented classes, classroom-based problem solving, peer teaching and tutoring, study groups, supplemental instruction, one-minute papers, service-learning, and effective employment of various forms of electronic technologies (Twigg, 2003, 2005). These teaching approaches are especially powerful when aligned with student ability, preferred learning styles, and learning aims.

For example, if the goal is to provide students with current knowledge in a field, then lectures, guest lecturers, and use of the Internet may be effective methods. If the aim is to develop students' ability to test ideas and evidence, then seminars, feedback on written work, peer assessment, and self-assessment are likely to be effective. These latter approaches often require students to collaborate with others on academic work. Problem-solving activities prepare students to deal with the messy, unscripted situations they will encounter daily after college (National Survey of Student Engagement, 2005); increase the amount of time and effort they spend on learning tasks (Guskin, 1997); and more tightly connect them to others on campus. Participation in active and collaborative learning is linked to increased student contact with faculty members (probably because the nature of class activities and out-of-class assignments requires more contact) and more positive views of the campus environment (probably mediated by getting to know classmates better through the collaborative exercises).

The University of Kansas created a few supersize undergraduate classes to enable certain departments to continue to offer a reasonable number of smaller classes. But instead of adhering to the typical lecture format, active learning approaches are used in these large classes. For example, students are sometimes divided into small groups and given a problem to work through, occasionally leaving the large class venue to do so. Faculty members in Fayetteville State University's School of Business and Economics require students to evaluate one another's group projects. Following the evaluations, students must reflect on and summarize what they have learned from the process. At Longwood University students manage the Lancer Student Investment Fund, which is $250,000 of the university's portfolio. In addition to real-time hands-on responsibility, students must make a presentation on their work to the university foundation's board of directors.

Complementary programs and practices. Institutions committed to student success provide a host of integrated, high-quality academic and social support programs that complement their mission and student characteristics. Such efforts help students adjust to college and encourage them to more frequently use the institution's resources for learning (Kramer & Associates, 2003; Kuh, Kinzie, Schuh, Whitt, & Associates, 2005). They include effective orientation experiences, transition courses and first-year seminars, early-warning systems and safety nets, learning communities, intrusive advising, tutoring, supplemental instruction, summer bridge programs, study skills workshops, mentoring and student support groups, student-faculty research, and senior culminating experiences such as capstone projects.

Simply offering such programs and practices does not guarantee that they will have the intended effects on student success. Instead, they must be of high quality, carefully designed to meet the needs of the students they are intended to reach and philosophically and operationally consistent with the values undergirding a student-success-oriented campus culture (Kuh, Kinzie, Schuh, Whitt, & Associates, 2005). When these efforts touch large numbers of students in meaningful ways, they comprise clearly marked pathways to student success (Kuh, Kinzie, Schuh, Whitt, & Associates, 2005). In addition, although exposure to educationally effective practices is associated with desired outcomes for all students, historically underserved students benefit more from engaging in these activities than white students in terms of earning higher grades and returning for a second year at the same college (Kuh, Kinzie, Cruce, Shoup, & Gonyea, 2006).

One especially powerful form of experiential learning is the internship. Most majors at the University of Maine at Farmington (UMF) strongly encourage or even require an internship or practicum, which helps students integrate their liberal arts courses with professional preparation. To make cultural immersion experiences available to students, especially to older or part-time students who cannot be away from work or family for extended periods, such colleges and universities as George Mason, Alverno, Kansas, Wabash, Fayetteville, UMF, and Sewanee provide abbreviated opportunities, usually no more than three weeks in duration. Many of these short-term trips occur during spring break and include service-learning opportunities. Kansas offers the London Review, a two-week trip planned and coordinated by students. UMF sponsors a two-week Spanish immersion program in Mexico, replete with a home-stay program, daily language instruction, and visits to cultural sites. Upon their return, some students share their experiences with the community during UMF's Symposium Day. To promote community service, Winston-Salem State University requires such an experience, which is emphasized in its motto—"Enter to learn, depart to serve." For some students, community service is a life-changing experience.

Human-Scale Settings

Students are more likely to flourish in small settings where they are known and valued as individuals than in settings in which they feel anonymous.

Learning environments with these characteristics do not happen by accident; they are intentionally designed (Kuh, Kinzie, Schuh, Whitt, & Associates, 2005; Schroeder & Hurst, 1996). The natural and built physical environments of the campus shape behavior by permitting certain kinds of activities while limiting or making impossible other kinds. Moreover, students' commitment in terms of persistence and loyalty to the institution can be strengthened by intentionally creating a strong "sense of place" through connecting campus architecture and design to meaningful experiences and memories of activities (Kuh, Kinzie, Schuh, Whitt, & Associates, 2005). The Wofford campus is essentially an arboretum through which students move on the way to class, experiencing the rich sense of place in the midst of the collection of ordinary and extraordinary trees. At the University of Michigan the "diag" is a central gathering place where students can express their interest in a wide range of social issues, among other things.

The proximity of academic buildings to student residences can promote or inhibit interactions between students from different majors (Kuh, 2000). Institutions can encourage student-faculty interaction and peer interaction before and after class by placing benches and comfortable seating areas near classrooms. Student-faculty interaction can also be supported by creating well-equipped group study space proximal to faculty offices, thereby increasing the likelihood of spontaneous interactions between students and faculty (Kuh et al., 1991; Kuh, Kinzie, Schuh, Whitt, & Associates, 2005). Ursinus College redesigned space and added large tables, chairs, and laminated whiteboards to create "interaction areas" near faculty offices and classrooms in its science building. These areas became what one faculty member described as a "visual image of achievement and aspiration" by inspiring an intense focus on learning. Alverno classroom tables and chairs are typically arranged into small groups—"pods," in the institutional lexicon—that allow students to work closely with their peers and instructors and facilitate group work and peer evaluation, which are emphasized during the students' first two years. Coker College and Sweet Briar College are two other institutions that arrange classrooms in a similar fashion to promote discussion-oriented learning.

Human scale can be created programmatically through well-designed learning communities or programs that enroll groups of students in a common set of courses, usually organized around a theme and frequently linked with residence life experiences (Knight, 2003; Shapiro & Levine, 1999; Tinto, 1997). The National Learning Communities Project monograph *Learning Community Research and Assessment: What We Know Now* (Taylor, 2003) synthesizes the empirical evidence, concluding that participation in a learning community is linked to student persistence, academic performance (i.e., GPA), credit hours earned, and satisfaction. These findings hold for a variety of learning community settings and structures and types of students (Knight, 2003; Pike, 1999; Price, 2005; Zhao & Kuh, 2004).

For example, the University of Texas at El Paso (UTEP) found that students in science, technology, engineering, and mathematics learning communities were more likely to return for a second year. UTEP expanded these offerings so that most first-year students participate in some variant of a learning community. Wofford's first-year students spend most of Tuesdays and Thursdays in their seven-credit-hour learning community class, which allows field trips and overnight experiences such as the cosmology learning community (which links physics and humanities courses) that went to the Pisgah Astronomical Research Institute to learn about the satellite-tracking station and make astronomical observations. Michigan's Comprehensive Studies Program is a learning community that provides support services to more than 2,000 undergraduates and offers "enriched classes," which meet an additional hour each week for group study, and the Science Learning Center, where study groups and tutors are coordinated for students.

Collaborative, Improvement-Oriented Ethic

Institutions focused on student success forge collaborative working relations and partnerships between those people who have the most contact with students—faculty and student affairs professionals (Kuh, Kinzie, Schuh, Whitt, & Associates, 2005). Sharing responsibility for student success is not possible without respect, trust, and competence, which are products of confidence about goals, agreement between espoused values and the means used to achieve desired ends, and a willingness to continuously assess performance. Systematically collecting data helps pinpoint where improvement is necessary, inform change strategies, and monitor the effectiveness of new efforts. But too often data-based reports simply gather dust on a shelf. Not so at "positively restless" colleges and universities. They collect and *use* information for a purpose—they want to get better at everything they do. And they realize improving requires that people work together from different disciplinary silos and across the not-so-invisible academic and student affairs boundaries.

For decades Alverno College has set the standard for assessing student abilities and using the results to improve teaching and learning. A spirit of self-assessment permeates the campus and is now deeply rooted in the institution's culture, practiced by both faculty and student affairs professionals.

The faculty learning communities at Miami University bring faculty members together to discuss ways to improve teaching. Some groups focus on such issues as cooperative learning, ethics across the curriculum, team teaching, using technology in the humanities, small-group learning, and approaches to assessing student learning; others explore the utility of problem-based learning and teaching portfolios. California State University–Monterey Bay values continuous improvement as evidenced by the innovative and evolving interdisciplinary academic programs and service-learning that are integrated throughout the curriculum. George Mason reformed its general education curriculum in little more than a year—a rare feat for most institutions, but one that is consistent with Mason's innovative ethos. The University of Kansas (KU) uses results from its own assessments of general education and student surveys as well as the National Survey of Student Engagement to monitor and improve advising practices, curriculum requirements, and administrative structures. KU faculty conducting the annual general education assessment interviews "sit across" from 120 graduating seniors to better understand the experiences of students in their major fields.

Language and Traditions Supporting Student Success

The words people use and the rituals and traditions in which they participate send powerful messages about who belongs at the institution and what it values. Alverno students talk about their college as a "sisterhood." During our campus visit there as part of the DEEP study, one student told us, "All the cultural messages are about women, about cultural expectations of women." Another said, "Here I don't have anyone undermining my learning. You remove that factor, and it builds self-esteem." A common phrase at Fayetteville State University is "We teach the students we have, not those we wish we had." This emphasizes that all students can learn under the right circumstances. At Evergreen students quickly learn the language of "seminaring," the preferred approach to class discussion. At California State University–Monterey Bay, historically underserved students are commonly called "vision students." This reminds everyone in the campus community about the institution's educational mission and who it was founded to serve.

Two phrases capture UTEP's evolution from a predominantly white to a Minority-Serving Institution. In the 1960s some stakeholders envisioned UTEP as a "Harvard on the border," with a mission to serve the children of affluent West Texans. But by the mid-1980s the changing demographics of the region and the growing proportion of Hispanic student enrollments led to a public affirmation of UTEP as being a "Hispanic-majority" institution. Although the identification was at first unsettling to some faculty, the new label emphasized a distinct shift in the campus culture and allowed institutional leaders to press forward and accelerate plans to welcome and educate the increased number of Hispanic students.

At Traditions Night at KU, more than 3,000 students gather in the football stadium to rehearse the Rock Chalk Chant, hear the legend of the mythical Jayhawk (which is the campus mascot), and learn the "I'm a Jayhawk" school song. Stories and rituals are featured that deepen new students' loyalty and commitment to graduating from KU. For example, at one point in the evening second- and third-generation Jayhawks stand and are recognized for their families' achievements; this ritual culminates with a senior (often a fourth- or fifth-generation KU grad) passing a torch to a representative of the first-year class.

At Wofford "there is a right way, there is a wrong way, and there is the Wofford way." Wofford orientation leaders present skits that depict these and other Wofford dos and don'ts to incoming students. Often featured in the performance are rituals such as rubbing the misspelled word *benificence* on the plaque commissioned by the founder for good luck on tests, faculty-signed Bibles distributed at graduation, and a local neighbor's opening reception and welcome into the neighborhood. Learning communities are so much a part of the campus lexicon that first-year students are apt to identify themselves by the one they are in as often as they claim affiliation with a Greek organization. And the identity sticks. For example, when a junior or senior says, "I'm one of the 'water people,'" most people on campus know he or she is a member of the nature and culture of water learning community.

The mascot of Winston-Salem State University (WSSU) is the ram, and new students are challenged to do what is necessary for academic success during the Lamb to Ram pinning ceremony, a formal induction event held during orientation week. This program inspires confidence, builds a sense of membership in the community, and helps new students picture themselves as successful WSSU students. The ram ambassadors and the student government of the Lamb to Ram program initiate students into the "ram family" and communicate what it means to be a member.

Sewanee uses its first-year program to introduce new students to various terms of endearment and campus rituals. One such ritual is "getting a Sewanee angel"; that is, as students pass through the gates at the edge of the campus, they touch the roof of their vehicle—an invitation to a guardian angel to ride along and protect them while away from the campus. The angels are released by touching the roof again when students return. To outsiders, such practices may seem quaint and out of fashion, but at Sewanee they reinforce the academic ethos, communicate the core values of the institution, and integrate newcomers into the college's culture.

At Sweet Briar College scores of terms of endearment, traditions, and other cultural properties are interwoven in ways that bond Sweet Briar women to the college and to one another. For example, faculty and staff welcome new students with glow sticks during an induction ceremony on the last evening of orientation. The fall's Founders' Day features an organized march to the top of the hill where Daisy Williams—whose mother provided the funds to establish Sweet Briar—and the rest of her family are buried. The procession is led by a bagpiper, faculty in academic regalia, and seniors wearing their academic robes for the first time. In the spring, graduating seniors pass on their academic robes to juniors, thus keeping the chain unbroken from one class to another. Such rituals and traditions ensure continuity across generations of students as well as give students something to look forward to—a sense that they too can achieve something of significance, as did their predecessors. Much of the campus culture at Sweet Briar is transmitted from the intentional pairing of first-year students with juniors, a common practice at women's colleges.

These examples illustrate how high-performing campuses use their culture to instill and support success in their students. In subtle and sometimes not-so-subtle ways, a student-centered campus culture fosters a sense of student agency—expecting, encouraging, supporting, and rewarding students to take a full measure of responsibility for their learning and community affairs. Equally important, student-centered cultures intentionally make room for everyone and allow people with different points of view to be heard and affirmed.

CREATING AND SUSTAINING
STUDENT-CENTERED CULTURES

Campus cultures do not change easily or willingly. Long-held beliefs and standard operating practices are tightly woven into an institution's ethos and embedded in the psyche of faculty leaders and senior administrators, which makes cultural transformation difficult (Kuh, Kinzie, Schuh, Whitt, & Associates, 2005). That said, most institutions can do far more to use cultural perspectives to identify ways to enhance student success. We close this chapter with five first-order steps on the path toward creating and sustaining student-centered cultures.

Use a Cultural Lens to Systematically Discover and Examine Aspects of Institutional Life that Encourage or Discourage Student Success

To determine whether a campus is student and learning friendly, one must "make the familiar strange" (Whitt, 1993)—that is, look anew at the obvious, everyday patterns and activities and try to understand their meaning and influence on different groups, including students, faculty from different departments, staff, and so on. Consider, for example, what institutional values and widely held beliefs communicate about who can learn what here and who cannot, who deserves an education and who does not, and the importance of specific goals and activities (Kuh & Whitt, 1988).

To assist with this process, we developed the inventory for student engagement and success framework (Kuh, Kinzie, Schuh, & Whitt, 2005). This self-study framework can help a campus discover norms, values, and other conditions that are common or antithetical to student-centered cultures. Attempts to audit a campus culture must be sensitive to different interpretations that people may have of similar words or events. For example, some campus traditions may be viewed as alienating or offensive by some students, even though no one intends for them to be so. In addition, students' experiences are shaped profoundly by what they do at college as well as their perceptions of their interactions with the institution. It is essential that efforts to assess the properties of institutional culture invite students to provide their interpretations of what these properties mean and how they might be modified to achieve the desired effects and promote meaningful engagement in campus life.

Lessons learned from an examination of campus culture should be highlighted so that everyone understands their value and purpose. By transmitting these lessons in admissions material, at orientation, and regularly in courses and through campus activities, students gain a clear image of what being a successful student on campus looks like. For example, DEEP schools demonstrated that students are better prepared to manage successfully the many challenges that college presents if they have clear ideas of what to expect and when to expect it, how to deal with these issues, and what it will take to learn at high levels and graduate (Kuh, Kinzie, Schuh, & Whitt, 2005; Kuh, Kinzie, Schuh, Whitt, & Associates, 2005). Drawing attention to cultural practices that support student success reminds stakeholders about the institutions' commitment to student learning and instills and deepens students' commitment to graduating.

Periodically Review and Evaluate Institutional Policies and Practices with an Eye on Student Success

To what extent do practices, policies, and programs foster and perhaps even require students to take advantage of resources designed to support learning and success? For example, are advisors simply assigned to new students? Or is there a coordinated tag team model for first-year student advising that enlists faculty, administrators, librarians, and upper-class student mentors all working together in a first-year seminar, thus forming a responsive support network? Practices and policies that make certain students take advantage of academic support services, writing centers, tutoring, leadership opportunities, and other educational programs are central to creating and sustaining a culture that promotes student success. What are the policies that encourage students to engage in educationally purposeful activities? Equally important, what policies and practices discourage students from doing so? Data such as findings from the National Survey of Student Engagement and other instruments can point to areas of campus life that may have their origins in some aspect of campus culture. This information may be especially revealing when disaggregated by student background characteristics and by persistence and graduation rates. When analyzed by major field or course-taking patterns, curricular trouble spots—such as courses with high dropout rates or low success rates—may emerge. Other campus information—such as poor attendance at campus events, limited use of tutoring centers, or residence hall environments that are antithetical to the educational mission—may identify areas that are underperforming in general or for particular groups of students.

Perhaps the most difficult question to answer in any cultural change strategy is not what the university should do next, but what it should stop doing so that it can invest in promising new initiatives (Collins, 2001; Kuh, Kinzie, Schuh, & Whitt, 2005). Too often, campuses struggle to terminate programs and activities that are no longer effective. Creating student-centered cultures requires the prioritization of activities that support student success, as well as the difficult task of rededicating resources from ineffective programs.

Student-Centered Cultures Are More Likely to Be Created and Sustained When Support Is Widespread and Everyone Is Pulling in the Same Direction

No single office or unit is responsible for creating and maintaining a student-centered culture. Leadership is important, but it does not reside exclusively in the executive ranks. Rather, faculty, staff, and students must act collectively as caretakers of the culture. Students must be encouraged to take responsibility for establishing a collaborative, high-quality learning environment by supporting peers through formal activities—such as learning communities, tutoring, study groups, and mentoring and support networks—and also by helping peers become involved in productive educational activities. The dedication and efforts of everyone on campus are needed to make students feel valued and important.

Blending the contributions and talents of student and academic affairs and involving all units on campus are necessary to enact the seven threads of a student-centered culture. The notable programmatic initiatives at DEEP schools work as well as they do because people at these campuses work together toward mutually determined desired ends. Most important, student-centered cultures are created and maintained by many individuals who do remarkable things with and for small numbers of students every day. In particular, it is important to acknowledge the work of staff members who are regularly in the company of students. Their interest in students and concern for those students' success is essential to a supportive campus culture.

Seize Opportunities to Spark Cultural Change

The seeds of cultural transformation can take different forms. For example, both a campus crisis and sustained focus on students and their learning may be used as levers for culture change. A cataclysmic event affecting institutional performance, such as a sudden drop in student enrollments or persistence rates—events that effectively threaten the institution's existence—can be used to refocus administrators, faculty, and staff on what must be improved. Cultural change can also be stimulated more deliberately by citing patterns of information that point to places where student and institutional performance are falling short. Data showing low levels of student engagement in educationally purposeful activities, student dissatisfaction with support services, and faculty and student concerns about the quality of the academic climate on campus may provide opportunities to set a course for institutional change. In fact, viewing different kinds of situations as potential opportunities for cultural change is a marker of high-performing institutions.

For example, changing student demographics in the region prompted UTEP to focus on inclusive student success. At WSSU an external challenge—state mandates to graduate more students—was the stimulus. And at Ursinus College preparing for an accreditation visit was the mobilizing event. All these schools converted their challenges into initiatives to leverage their strengths into advantages for students. Indeed, as Kezar (2002) emphasized, organizational change requires openness to surprises, a focus on creativity, and an appreciation for chance occurrences.

Stay the Course

Meaningful change rarely occurs quickly or in dramatic fashion. Cultivating a student-centered culture is seldom a function of grand strategic initiatives. Rather, it is the product of many people regularly doing ordinary things well on a regular basis and with an eye to promoting student success. Sustaining a student-centered culture requires unwavering institutional leadership and a commitment by faculty and staff to use research-based, effective educational practices, to systematically assess the learning environment, and to use what they are learning about their performance to improve.

DEEP schools use a variety of approaches to firmly pursue their goals of institutional improvement. For example, UMF pursued its ongoing improvement agenda in an incremental, evolutionary way. The president and administrative leaders believed that good ideas are generally the result of collaboration, so they solicited and acted on suggestions from all corners of the campus. They also knew that these good ideas would need to be seeded and nurtured to take root. Though resources are in short supply at UMF, the university's leaders were able to provide small grants to support the faculty and administrators in making positive change. Ursinus College adopted a campaign approach to enhance the intellectual vitality on campus. The campaign metaphor for change values resolve, innovation, and flexibility; empowers faculty and staff; and celebrates achievements.

Other institutions benefited by having people work on one or more initiatives for an extended period of time to establish them and demonstrate their efficacy. The visionary leadership of President Natalicio and the hard work of countless faculty and staff at UTEP maintained a long-term course of action focused on transforming UTEP into a high-performing university committed to serving a diverse student body.

CONCLUSION

Student-centered institutions create and sustain campus cultures that challenge and support all students to high levels of achievement. Such colleges and universities send messages about becoming involved in different dimensions of institutional life and encourage students to share responsibility for their performance and that of their peers, inside and outside the classroom.

More often than not, this enviable level of performance is a product of intentionally designed approaches based on research on effective educational practices that are embedded in a web of cultural properties that value and support student success. Common to student-centered campus cultures are seven interdependent, complementary threads made up of assumptions and beliefs about teaching and learning and student success; normative behaviors that encourage high levels of performance by students, faculty, and staff; and language and myriad rituals and traditions that reinforce what students need to do to succeed. Examples from different DEEP colleges and universities show that creating such cultures is possible for any institution if people have the will to do so. Our students deserve nothing less.

REFERENCES

Alexander, P. A., & Murphy, P. K. (1994, April). *The research base for APA's learner-centered psychological principles.* Paper presented at the annual meeting of the American Educational Research Association, New Orleans, LA.

American Association for Higher Education, American College Personnel Association, & National Association of Student Personnel Administrators. (1998). *Powerful partnerships: A shared responsibility for learning.* Washington, DC: American College Personnel Association.

American College Personnel Association. (1996). *The student learning imperative: Implications for student affairs.* Washington, DC: Author.

American Council on Education. (1937). *The student personnel point of view.* Washington, DC: Author.

Association of American Colleges and Universities. (2002). *Greater expectations: A new vision for learning as a nation goes to college.* Washington, DC: Author.

Astin, A. W. (1977). *Four critical years: Effects of college on beliefs, attitudes, and knowledge.* San Francisco, CA: Jossey-Bass.

Astin, A. W. (1993). *What matters in college? Four critical years revisited.* San Francisco, CA: Jossey-Bass.

Bailey, T. R., & Alfonso, M. (2005). *Paths to persistence: An analysis of research on program effectiveness at community colleges* (New Agenda Series, 6[1]). Indianapolis, IN: Lumina Foundation.

Barr, R. B., & Tagg, J. (1995, November/December). From teaching to learning—A new paradigm for undergraduate education. *Change, 27*(6), 12–25.

Bauman, G. L., Bustillos, L. T., Bensimon, E. M., Brown, M. C., II, & Bartee, R. D. (2005). *Achieving equitable educational outcomes with all students: The institution's roles and responsibilities.* Washington, DC: Association of American Colleges and Universities.

Baxter Magolda, M. B. (1999). *Creating contexts for learning and self-authorship: Constructive-developmental pedagogy.* Nashville, TN: Vanderbilt University Press.

Blose, G. (1999). Modeled retention and graduation rates: Calculating expected retention and graduation rates for multicampus university systems. In G. H. Gaither (Ed.), *New directions for higher education: No. 108: Promising practices in recruitment, remediation, and retention* (pp. 69–86). San Francisco, CA: Jossey-Bass.

Bolman, L. G., & Deal, T. E. (1991). *Reframing organizations: Artistry, choice, and leadership.* San Francisco, CA: Jossey-Bass.

Bowen, H. R. (1977). *Investment in learning: The individual and social value of American higher education.* San Francisco, CA: Jossey-Bass.

Brown, J. S., Collins, A., & Duguid, P. (1989, January/February). Situated cognition and the culture of learning. *Educational Researcher, 18*(1), 32–42.

Carey, K. (2004). *A matter of degrees: Improving graduation rates in four-year colleges and universities.* Washington, DC: The Education Trust.

Chickering, A. W. (2006, May). Every student can learn–if. *About Campus, 11*(2), 9–15.

Chickering, A. W., & Gamson, Z. F. (1987, June). Seven principles for good practice in undergraduate education. *AAHE Bulletin, 39*(7), 3–7.

Chickering, A. W., & Reisser, L. (1993). *Education and identity* (2nd ed.). San Francisco, CA: Jossey-Bass.

Collins, J. (2001). *Good to great: Why some companies make the leap . . . and others don't.* New York, NY: HarperCollins.

Cross, K. P. (1991, Spring). Every teacher a researcher, every classroom a laboratory. *Tribal College, 2*(4), 7–12.

Dayton, B., Gonzalez-Vasquez, N., Martinez, C. R., & Plum, C. (2004). Hispanic-serving institutions through the eyes of students and administrators. In A. M. Ortiz (Ed.), *New directions for student services: No. 105. Addressing the unique needs of Latino American students* (pp. 29–40). San Francisco, CA: Jossey-Bass.

Driscoll, M. P. (1994). *Psychology of learning for instruction.* Needham Heights, MA: Allyn & Bacon.

Education Commission of the States. (1995). *Making quality count in undergraduate education.* Denver, CO: Author.

The Evergreen State College. (2001). *Evergreen advising handbook, 2001–2002*. Olympia, WA: Author.

Ewell, P. T. (1989, April). Institutional characteristics and faculty/administrator perceptions of outcomes: An exploratory analysis. *Research in Higher Education, 30*(2), 113–136.

Feldman, K. A., & Newcomb, T. M. (1969). *The impact of college on students.* San Francisco, CA: Jossey-Bass.

Guskin, A. E. (1997, July/August). Learning more, spending less. *About Campus, 2*(3), 4–9.

Harwarth, I. B. (Ed.). (1999). *A closer look at women's colleges.* Washington, DC: U.S. Department of Education, Office of Educational Research and Improvement.

Hedlund, D. E., & Jones, J. T. (1970, May). Effect of student personnel services on completion rates in two-year colleges. *Journal of College Student Personnel, 11*(3), 196–199.

Holland, D. C., & Eisenhart, M. A. (1990). *Educated in romance: Women, achievement, and college culture.* Chicago, IL: University of Chicago Press.

Hurtado, S. (1992, September/October). The campus racial climate: Contexts of conflict. *Journal of Higher Education, 63*(5), 539–569.

Hurtado, S., Milem, J. F., Clayton-Pedersen, A. R., & Allen, W. R. (1998, Spring). Enhancing campus climates for racial/ethnic diversity: Educational policy and practice. *Review of Higher Education, 21*(3), 279–302.

Keeton, M. T. (1971). *Models and mavericks: A profile of private liberal arts colleges.* New York, NY: McGraw-Hill.

Kezar, A. (2002, May). Overcoming the obstacles to change within urban institutions: The mobile framework and engaging institutional culture. *Metropolitan Universities: An International Forum, 13*(2), 95–103.

Kezar, A., & Kinzie, J. (2006, March/April). Examining the ways institutions create student engagement: The role of mission. *Journal of College Student Development, 47*(2), 149–172.

Knight, W. E. (2003, June–August). Learning communities and first-year programs: Lessons for planners. *Planning for Higher Education, 31*(4), 5–12.

Kramer, G. L., & Associates. (2003). *Student academic services: An integrated approach.* San Francisco, CA: Jossey-Bass.

Kuh, G. D. (1995, March/April). The other curriculum: Out-of-class experiences associated with student learning and personal development. *Journal of Higher Education, 66*(2), 123–155.

Kuh, G. D. (1997, September/October). You gotta believe. *About Campus, 2*(4), 2–3.

Kuh, G. D. (2000). Do environments matter? A comparative analysis of the impression of different types of colleges and universities on character. *Journal of College and Character, 2*. Retrieved June 22, 2007, from www.collegevalues.org/articles.cfm?a=1&id=239

Kuh, G. D. (2001). College students today: Why we can't leave serendipity to chance. In P. G. Altbach, P. J. Gumport, & D. B. Johnstone (Eds.), *In defense of American higher education* (pp. 277–302). Baltimore, MD: Johns Hopkins University Press.

Kuh, G. D. (2003, March/April). What we're learning about student engagement from NSSE: Benchmarks for effective educational practices. *Change, 35*(2), 24–32.

Kuh, G. D., Douglas, K. B., Lund, J. P., & Ramin-Gyurnek, J. (1994). *Student learning outside the classroom: Transcending artificial boundaries* (ASHE-ERIC Higher Education Report No. 8). Washington, DC: The George Washington University, School of Education and Human Development.

Kuh, G. D., Kinzie, J., Cruce, T., Shoup, R., & Gonyea, R. M. (2006). *Connecting the dots: Multi-faceted analyses of the relationships between student engagement results from the NSSE, and the institutional practices and conditions that foster student success.* Bloomington, IN: Indiana University, Center for Postsecondary Research.

Kuh, G. D., Kinzie, J., Schuh, J. H., & Whitt, E. J. (2005). *Assessing conditions to enhance educational effectiveness: The inventory for student engagement and success.* San Francisco, CA: Jossey-Bass.

Kuh, G. D., Kinzie, J., Schuh, J. H., Whitt, E. J., & Associates (2005). *Student success in college: Creating conditions that matter.* San Francisco, CA: Jossey-Bass.

Kuh, G. D., Schuh, J. H., Whitt, E. J., & Associates. (1991). *Involving colleges: Successful approaches to fostering student learning and development outside the classroom.* San Francisco, CA: Jossey-Bass.

Kuh, G. D., & Whitt, E. J. (1988). *The invisible tapestry: Culture in American colleges and universities* (ASHE-ERIC Higher Education Report, 17[1]). San Francisco, CA: Jossey-Bass.

Luther College. (2005). *A higher calling: The campaign for Luther College.* Decorah, IA: Author.

Magolda, P. M. (2000). The campus tour ritual: Exploring community discourses in higher education. *Anthropology and Education Quarterly, 31*(1), 24–36.

Manning, K. (2000). *Rituals, ceremonies, and cultural meaning in higher education.* Westport, CT: Bergin & Garvey.

Martin, J. (2002). *Organizational culture: Mapping the terrain.* Thousand Oaks, CA: Sage.

Meyers, C., & Jones, T. B. (1993). *Promoting active learning: Strategies for the college classroom.* San Francisco, CA: Jossey-Bass.

National Commission on the Future of Higher Education. (2006). *Commission reports.* Retrieved June 22, 2007, from www.ed.gov/about/bdscomm/list/hiedfuture/reports.html

National Institute of Education. (1984). *The progress of an agenda: A first report from the Study Group on the Conditions of Excellence in American Higher Education.* Washington, DC: Author.

National Survey of Student Engagement. (2005). *Student engagement: Exploring different dimensions of student engagement.* Bloomington, IN: Indiana University, Center for Postsecondary Research.

Nuss, E. M. (2003). The development of student affairs. In S. R. Komives, D. B Woodard, Jr., & Associates, *Student services: A handbook for the profession* (4th ed., pp. 65–88). San Francisco, CA: Jossey-Bass.

Outcalt, C. L., & Skewes-Cox, T. E. (2002, Spring). Involvement, interaction, and satisfaction: The human environment at HBCUs. *Review of Higher Education, 25*(3), 331–347.

Pace, C. R. (1979). *Measuring outcomes of college: Fifty years of findings and recommendations for the future.* San Francisco, CA: Jossey-Bass.

Pascarella, E. T., & Terenzini, P. T. (1991). *How college affects students: Findings and insights from twenty years of research.* San Francisco, CA: Jossey-Bass.

Pascarella, E. T., & Terenzini, P. T. (2005). *How college affects students: A third decade of research.* San Francisco, CA: Jossey-Bass.

Peter, K., & Cataldi, E. F. (2005). *The road less traveled? Students who enroll in multiple institutions* (NCES 2005–157). U.S. Department of Education, National Center for Education Statistics. Washington, DC: U.S. Government Printing Office.

Peters, T. (1987). *Thriving on chaos: Handbook for a management revolution.* New York, NY: HarperPerennial.

Pike, G. R. (1999, May/June). The effects of residential learning communities and traditional residential living arrangements on educational gains during the first year of college. *Journal of College Student Development, 40*(3), 269–284.

Pounds, A. W. (1987). Black students' needs on predominantly white campuses. In D. J. Wright (Ed.), *Responding to the needs of today's minority students* (pp. 23–38). San Francisco, CA: Jossey-Bass.

Price, D. V. (with Lee, M.). (2005). *Learning communities and student success in postsecondary education: A background paper.* New York, NY: MDRC.

Rendon, L. I. (1994, August). *Beyond involvement: Creating validating academic and social communities in the community college.* Paper presented at the American River Community College, Sacramento, CA.

Rendon, L. I. (1999). Toward a new vision of the multicultural community college for the next century. In K. M. Shaw, J. R. Valadez, & R. A. Rhoads (Eds.), *Community colleges as cultural texts: Qualitative explorations of organizational and student culture* (pp. 195–204) Albany, NY: State University of New York Press.

Sanford, N. (Ed.). (1962). *The American college: A psychological and social interpretation of the higher learning.* New York, NY: Wiley.

Schein, E. H. (1992). *Organizational culture and leadership* (2nd ed.). San Francisco, CA: Jossey-Bass.

Schroeder, C. C., & Hurst, J. C. (1996, March). Designing learning environments that integrate curricular and co-curricular experiences. *Journal of College Student Development, 37*(2), 174–181.

Shapiro, N. S., & Levine, J. H. (1999). *Creating learning communities: A practical guide to winning support, organizing for change, and implementing programs.* San Francisco, CA: Jossey-Bass.

Sorcinelli, M. D. (1991). Research findings on the seven principles. In A. W. Chickering & Z. F. Gamson (Eds.), *New directions for teaching and learning: No. 47. Applying the seven principles for good practice in undergraduate education* (pp. 13–25). San Francisco, CA: Jossey-Bass.

Suarez, A. L. (2003, February). Forward transfer: Strengthening the educational pipeline for Latino community college students. *Community College Journal of Research and Practice, 27*(2), 95–118.

Tagg, J. (2003). *The learning paradigm college.* Bolton, MA: Anker.

Taylor, K. (with Moore, W., MacGregor, J., & Lindblad, J.). (2003). *Learning community research and assessment: What we know now* (National Learning Communities Project Monograph Series). Olympia, WA: The Evergreen State College, Washington Center for Improving the Quality of Undergraduate Education.

Tierney, W. G. (1999). *Building the responsive campus: Creating high performance colleges and universities.* Thousand Oaks, CA: Sage.

Tinto, V. (1997, November/December). Classrooms as communities: Exploring the education character of student persistence. *Journal of Higher Education, 68*(6), 599–623.

Treisman, U. (1992, November). Studying students studying calculus: A look at the lives of minority mathematics students in college. *College Mathematics Journal, 23*(5), 362–372.

Twigg, C. A. (2003, July/August). Improving quality and reducing cost: Designs for effective learning. *Change, 35*(4), 22–29.

Twigg, C. A. (2005). *Improving learning and reducing costs—New models for online learning.* Keynote presentation at the 12th International Conference of the Association for Learning Technology, Manchester, UK.

Volkwein, J. F., & Cabrera, A. F. (1998, May). *Student measures associated with favorable classroom experiences.* Paper presented at the annual meeting of the Association for Institutional Research, Minneapolis, MN.

Watson, L. W., & Kuh, G. D. (1996, July/August). The influence of dominant race environments on student involvement, perceptions, and educational gains: A look at historically black and predominantly white liberal arts institutions. *Journal of College Student Development, 37*(4), 415–424.

Whitt, E. J. (1993). "Making the familiar strange": Discovering culture. In G. D. Kuh (Ed.), *Cultural perspectives in student affairs work* (pp. 81–94). Lanham, MD: University Press of America.

Wingspread Group on Higher Education. (1993). *An American imperative: Higher expectations for higher education.* Racine, WI: Johnson Foundation.

Winston, R. B., Jr. (2003). Stimulating and supporting student learning. In G. L. Kramer & Associates, *Student academic services: An integrated approach* (pp. 3–26). San Francisco, CA: Jossey-Bass.

Zhao, C.-M., & Kuh, G. D. (2004, March). Adding value: Learning communities and student engagement. *Research in Higher Education, 45*(2), 115–138.

ALIGNING EXPECTATIONS: A SHARED RESPONSIBILITY

Thomas E. Miller and Saul Reyes

This chapter will explore how student expectations are derived and why they matter, or should matter, to decision-makers. The challenges presented by student expectations will be explored. Those challenges are particularly difficult when students' expectations and the reality of their experiences do not match. Such dissonance may exist because the expectations are unreasonable or because institutional performance falls short. In any event, efforts to understand student expectations and compare them with reality are of value in the process of understanding students' connections to institutions and, ultimately, those students' success. Solutions to address unreasonable expectations focus on communication that is accurate, timely, fair, and thorough.

Administrators and faculty in American higher education have not always acted as though the expectations of students were of high importance. Through most of the past three centuries, institutional behavior seems to have been more focused on conveying to students the expectations that colleges had of them, not the converse. In the earliest period of higher education's development in America, colleges were founded to preserve the aristocracy and to prepare teachers and ministers to maintain civilization as it was known then (Vine, 1976). Although not much is documented about how institutions informed their constituents about the college-going experience, it seems likely that little was invested in trying to determine what the incoming student expected or anticipated about it.

Through the 1960s the college experience was a seller's market, with institutions picking and choosing their entering classes; those not admitted had to make other plans. As long as that condition persisted, colleges controlled the market and dictated the terms and conditions of the college experience (Thielen, 2004). The expectations of students were apparently of little concern to colleges, and students were forced to adapt if conditions differed from what they had anticipated.

Another factor that affected student expectations was the rather homogeneous nature of the college experience. College life was for those of traditional age, largely for young men from white middle- or upper-class families. It was for elite young people. Further, there were not many differences between institutions because many of them had followed a traditional path in their evolution. This sameness in the higher education industry may have led few to wonder what the experience would be like because it may have been rather predictable (Thielen, 2004).

All that has changed. College life is now, compared to even the recent past, extremely complex. The enrollment management movement has unfolded because higher education has become more of a buyer's market than ever, making recruitment extremely important for many institutions. Prospective students are potential customers, and like any good sales force, college recruiters are well served to consider their customers' expectations and to shape those expectations as much as possible.

Today there are many types of institutions offering many different experiences to students. Those choosing a college may have an underdeveloped notion of how the particular college they will attend may offer a unique and different learning environment and college experience. Even within individual institutions, particularly the larger universities, the complexity of an institution may generate a wide range of different college-going experiences, and a student may find it very different from what he or she expected.

Life experience demonstrates that some aspects of dissonance between expectations and real life are happy ones. Sometimes the experience is better than expected, and the person is happier than he or she thought would be the case. These pleasant outcomes, although quite common in the experiences of college students, are not the focus of this chapter. Rather, we will address what happens when the difference has a negative, not positive, effect.

THE PSYCHOLOGY OF EXPECTATIONS

There are psychological dimensions to how expectations are formed and how deeply beliefs are rooted. Some college student expectations are derived from dreams and ambitions for the future and are not the product of careful research. Regardless of the source, expectations are powerful forces in college choice and frame students' views as they begin (or restart) their journeys in higher education.

The Student-Institutional Relationship: Why Student Expectations Matter

A reason to attend to student expectations relates to how unmet expectations can create emotional reactions that negatively impact the connection between the student and the institution. Seeing that connection as a relationship is useful because all relationships begin with expectations that, if not met, may threaten the relationship. This is the case in marriage, in new jobs (or with new supervisors), and even in making major purchases.

When a couple is first married, each partner has expectations of what marriage will be like and how the other partner will behave. Many times, neither the marriage nor the spouse is what each thought it would be. Often these unrealized expectations are not problematic; if they are, the partners often sort out their differences. However, there are times when those differences are not easily resolved and the dissonance between expectations and real experiences becomes confounding and serious. When a person starts a new job, it is often based on an assessment of the work experience, the environment, and the setting that led him or her to certain expectations. When those expectations turn out to be inaccurate, they can create a sense of employee disaffection or dissatisfaction with the job choice that may lead to the person's resignation. In buying a house, the new owner has a set of expectations that, if unmet, can produce disenchantment with the home, another unhappy outcome.

Student expectations for college matter because they form the foundation of the relationships students have with a college or university. As with most relationships, each party presumes the other will act and respond in ways that will make the relationship mutually beneficial. In instances when expectations are not met, one or both parties must adjust their expectations (or otherwise cope with the dissonance) or risk becoming dissatisfied and deciding to terminate the relationship. Unmet student expectations may be a core cause of student attrition (Miller, 2005).

Studies associated with employment have developed the principle of the psychological contract. This is based on the notion that beliefs and assumptions about the work setting into which one enters produce a contract between the individual and the employer. The contract may only exist in the abstract, but the effect of it being broken is similar to the effect that results when more tangible contracts are broken. The disaffection that ensues is real, and it matters little whether the beliefs and assumptions that produced it are reasonable and accurate.

Much of the unhappiness and disaffection experienced by college students regarding their educational experiences may relate to similarly unrealized expectations. The entering student may well have expectations for the experience that are not made clear to institutional officials; they may even be unclear to the student. Regardless, they become the basis for a psychological contract between the student and the institution, and when unmet, they lead to the perception that the contract has been breached. The student may see the institution as not having met its obligation or as having violated the contract (Howard, 2005).

The Effect of Unmet Student Expectations

The challenge of adjusting to the college experience can be great or small. When college life is not what a student expected, it creates stress and often an unpleasant emotional reaction that threatens the student-institutional relationship. Stressful circumstances tax students' coping abilities, although many students can deal with their stress when expectations are incongruous with reality. When real experiences in college are not at all what students expected, the resulting stress and emotional turmoil can present turbulent personal circumstances and a difficult challenge (Howard, 2005).

What do students do when a difficult situation is beyond their ability to cope? They may become frustrated, they may resign themselves to failure, or they may engage in self-destructive behaviors, such as drug or alcohol abuse. In the worst of circumstances, their responses may be self-threatening.

When widely held student expectations are not met, other consequences could be broader and more public, extending into communities in which institutions aspire to good relations. Student expectations that remain unmet may point to the fact that the institution inaccurately portrays itself to students.

SOURCES OF EXPECTATIONS

It is helpful for colleges to anticipate and understand some of the origins of students' expectations. People create their expectations of an upcoming experience by blending their memories of past experiences in anticipation of some desired future state of affairs (Arnold & Kuh, 1999; Howard, 2005). Students who are just entering college form expectations based on various sources, including the observations of family members regarding their own college experiences, the entertainment industry and news media, the students' own past experiences with college, the college recruitment process, and the students' impressions of how they will fit in with their future college-going peers.

Generational characteristics help shape students' expectations. In *Millennials Go to College,* Howe and Strauss (2003) identify some of the unique qualities that characterize the current generation of students. Shaped by social forces and events during their development, students are confident, civic minded, technologically sophisticated, and inclusive. These characteristics impact their expectations and experiences in higher education. Institutions may need to rethink how they recruit, assimilate, and engage this new generation of students.

Institutions play a role in shaping student expectations as well. The college search process, in particular, influences students' perceptions of what college life will be like. Students are bombarded with recruitment messages before their senior year of high school. In the competition for new students, colleges attract prospects by promoting the best their institutions have to offer.

Previous educational experiences also shape students' expectations. It is not just students coming directly from high school who will be challenged by the transition to postsecondary education. The majority of college students today will have experienced more than one institution by the time they graduate with a four-year degree. Peter and Cataldi (2005) reported that nearly 60% of the students earning a bachelor's degree in 2001 had attended at least one other postsecondary institution. Transfer students' expectations may or may not match the reality they encounter in their new institution.

Expectations may also be shaped by students' home experiences. Students come to campus at varying levels of independence. Some are entirely independent and have raised their own families. Others may be living away from home for the first time. Sharing a room with another person often brings new challenges for those enrolling in residential colleges. Expectations for privacy, values, lifestyle, and involvement in like-minded activities may not match the reality of living with a new roommate.

Parents shape students' expectations for college. They paint a picture for their children of what college life was like for them. Students may come to expect that their experience will mirror their parents' college experiences. These expectations may cover a broad number of areas, including instructors, friendships, athletics, residential experiences, student government, clubs and activities, and campus traditions. In reality, students' experience may bear little resemblance to their parents' college experience.

Students typically come to college with expectations for career preparation and advancement. The primary reason they go to college is tied to an anticipated or desired outcome, their chosen career. Students have varying expectations of the programs and services that will help them transition to that career.

CHALLENGES AND OPPORTUNITIES OF EXPECTATIONS

The expectations of students present some difficulties to student affairs administrators. Students may have notions about aspects of higher education, including services they will receive and how their interactions with others will develop, that are inconsistent with the realities of college life. Evidence exists that students learn, grow, and develop in unexpected ways, and such a better-than-expected outcome is a positive factor in the college-going experience.

Student Services Expectations

Marketplace competition and customer orientation have increased expectations of students and parents. This market sensitivity is not just evident in the admissions process. Enrolled students crave the amenities institutions are spending money to provide. In his article "Room with a View: Student Demands Are Impacting University Facility Development," Jeff Conroy (2006) writes about institutions' increased spending on student quality-of-life amenities. He speaks of the "amenities arms race," a phrase he attributes to David Kirp, professor of public policy at the University of California–Berkeley. The amenities arms race is alive and well in our residence halls, student centers, recreation facilities, and dining facilities. Wireless Internet, coffee bars, climbing walls, water parks, apartment suites—students have an insatiable appetite for the amenities of college life. Institutions are increasingly willing to spend the money to feed that appetite.

Colleges should be and have become more responsive to student needs and wants. Students want immediate and personalized services. Web-based services have extended student affairs' capabilities. But a customer service orientation in student services areas may lead to unrealistic expectations. Students' just-in-time, 24-7 expectations can create a strain, and institutions must ask themselves whether they can meet student demands all the time.

In the area of career services, students often have unrealistic expectations. They want the career center staff to get them a job. They are not always interested in taking the time to learn and go through the career development process when a job placement meets their immediate need. What about the educational mission of career centers? Shouldn't a career center help students learn how to make informed career choices and how to effectively transition into the world of work? There is educational value in having students arrange their own internships; in the process they learn how to conduct an effective job search. On the other hand, a model in which a faculty member or professional staff member assigns students internships leads to passive student behavior.

Consumerism impacts virtually every student services area. In residence life there may be a hotel-guest mentality. Students may insist on switching rooms rather than learn to get along with roommates. Numerous dining venues replace cafeterias. Recreation centers become upscale fitness and entertainment facilities.

How is a campus to respond to this customer service orientation? Ardaiolo, Bender, and Roberts (2005) identify four expectations that students and their families have for campus services:

> [Colleges should] (1) provide what they say they will provide in promotional materials, (2) offer services and programs to make the college experience valuable and useful, (3) create opportunities to ease the transition to the world of work and graduate school, and (4) create and implement a collegiate environment that meets their perceptions of what the college experience should entail. (pp. 85–86)

Relationship Expectations

Upon arrival on campus, students have some notions about what their peer relationships will be like. Some of those notions are reasonable and accurate, and some are not. Students may base such expectations on their previous experiences. But the way they made friends in high school and the quality of those friendships may be similar to their college experience, or they may not. The student who aspires to better, more successful peer relationships in college may or may not have reasonable expectations.

How students think they will relate to faculty may also be shaped by previous educational experiences, but the relationships between college instructors and their students may be different from that of high school teachers and their students. Some aspects of the relationship may be affected by the performance of the student and how it compares to his or her expectations. In any event, when relationships with faculty are different (better, worse, or just different) from what was anticipated, the student will either adjust or experience confusion and, possibly, a disaffection from the relationship.

Regarding their relationships with student affairs administrators, many students have no experience on which to base an expectation. The professional and student staff members in residence halls, student activities, or the career center have no high school counterparts. Many students will forge relationships with such people, but it will probably be new territory.

Academic Performance Expectations

Students' academic expectations do not always match their experiences. Students who complete the *College Student Expectations Questionnaire* (Kuh & Pace, 1999) during orientation and then complete the *College Student Experiences Questionnaire* (Pace & Kuh, 1998) at the end of their first year often cite gaps in their expectations. Typically, students expect to work harder academically than they do, and they expect to earn higher grades than they do. The application of these questionnaires will be described later in this chapter.

Learning Expectations

There are other ways institutions communicate expectations to students, such as in the college catalog. The student handbook outlines the expectations for student life. Instructors communicate their course expectations in their syllabi. Orientation programs, summer mailings, and new student web sites can also communicate an institution's expectations.

Students do not always approach their college experience with an intrinsic motivation to learn and grow. Faculty are often frustrated that most students focus more on grades than on learning. Faculty and student affairs professionals can be more explicit with students about learning outcomes and expectations. Chickering and Gamson (1987) identified principles that promote deeper student learning in the undergraduate experience. These principles can be adapted for use in student affairs arena. Keeling (2004, 2006) suggests ways in which campuses can create a learning culture in and out of the classroom.

Meeting student expectations should be a concern of higher education institutions, and understanding students will continue to be a critical part of what student affairs administrators do. But as educators, we should be concerned with more than just meeting student expectations. We can help shape students' expectations and give them a greater picture of what to expect from their college experience.

ASSESSMENT OPPORTUNITIES

When college faculty members and administrators have good information about what students expect from college, they will be better prepared to design learning environments that appropriately challenge and support students. A commitment to study student expectations in a way that allows results to be compared and contrasted with real student experiences is necessary before addressing ways to close any gaps between the two. Little can be accomplished by guessing about what students expect or about the realities of college life. Decisions that will produce change need to be supported by reliable information that is the product of careful research; strategies for such study are readily available.

As valuable and necessary as institutional research can be to gaining understanding, it is equally important for the institution to be committed to individual assessment. Institutions can use private and personal encounters with students to elicit their perspectives about college life. Institutions can then explore how those perspectives might differ from what students expected and the extent to which those differences are problematic.

Tools for Researching Expectations

In this section we describe existing research tools that can support institutions' efforts to understand student expectations and help them become aware of disconnects between those expectations and what is known about students' real experiences.

Instruments with a national scope have many advantages, but locally developed tools may also be useful. Research instruments designed by the sponsoring institution make comparing data with that from national research difficult, but they do provide focused and well-targeted research. Institutions can study specific institutional aspects of the student experience and consider particular cultural and organizational characteristics.

A broad base of institutional support is needed for a study of expectations to have real value. Little will be accomplished with data about student expectations if the purpose of the inquiry is not understood and the results are not welcomed and widely disseminated. The monograph *Taking Student Expectations Seriously: A Guide for Campus Applications* (Miller, Kuh, Paine, & Associates, 2006) provides a framework for campus-based assessment associated with student expectations, as well as strategies for using the assessment results.

Research indicates that student satisfaction and success have much to do with the initial experiences in the first few weeks of college (Upcraft, Gardner, Barefoot, & Associates, 2005). Those crucial first few weeks may be influenced by the expectations that students bring with them. This may be the most prudent time to assess their expectations.

College Student Expectations Questionnaire. The *College Student Expectations Questionnaire* (CSXQ; Kuh & Pace, 1999) was developed to gather information about student expectations before matriculation. In response to data about students' beliefs related to the college experience, administrators and faculty members can consider program and instructional adjustments. An application of CSXQ also allows college officials to consider strategies for uniformly negotiating the expectations of students when those expectations are determined to be unreasonable. The CSXQ program was designed for this exact purpose; it is intended to measure students' expectations regarding the quality of the interactions they will have with faculty, the nature of their future relationships with their peers, their plans regarding the use of learning resource support, and the general satisfaction they will have with college. Armed with data about these expectations, administrators and faculty members can respond with well-informed programs of advisement and student orientation to better serve students and to inform them about what they can reasonably expect of the college experience.

As an example, the CSXQ can inform institutional researchers about the outcomes that students expect from college. If students have lofty goals associated with their engagement in the learning process, the institution can design learning activities and out-of-classroom programs that are intended to meet those expectations and enhance the learning process as a result (Miller et al., 2006).

College Student Experiences Questionnaire. The *College Student Experiences Questionnaire* (CSEQ; Pace & Kuh, 1998) has considerable value as a stand-alone project, and it has been in use since 1979. CSEQ is also a very useful tool for following up an administration of the CSXQ. Of the research tools available to study expectations and experiences of students, the CSXQ and CSEQ tools, when used in tandem, are the most directly relevant.

CSEQ allows institutions to compare what students expected from college with their subsequent experiences on the same basic set of considerations regarding in-class and out-of-class behaviors. An application of CSXQ before student matriculation and a follow-up administration of CSEQ at the end of the first year can provide rich information about the ways in which students' experiences vary from what they expected.

Institutional researchers can compare CSXQ and CSEQ results and discover that students may not report having the sort of learning experiences they expected. Solutions might include a summer jump-start program or requiring new students to live on campus. Before any direction can be chosen, the assessment of the dissonance between expectations and reality is a necessary first step to addressing the problem (Miller et al., 2006).

Cooperative Institutional Research Program. The Cooperative Institutional Research Program (CIRP; Sax, Lindholm, Astin, Korn, & Mahoney, 2002) is another appropriate instrument for assessing student expectations. Although it has purposes and applications far broader than the measure of expectations, specific survey items on expected experiences during college and on outcomes of attending college are useful sources of information. The instrument is generally administered before matriculation or shortly thereafter. From CIRP results, institutional researchers can learn about student expectations regarding academic performance, engaging the institution outside class, and persistence to graduation. If institutional leaders discover, for example, that a large proportion of incoming students expect to earn Bs or higher but do not, there is work to be done in orientation or in a summer program to help students achieve that performance objective.

Institutional data. Most institutions have substantial access to information about the real experiences of students; they also often have information about what students expect. The admissions application and early class registration information can give a glimpse into students' expectations. After enrollment, institutional data can include information on academic performance, credit hours carried, and cocurricular transcript information—all of which can be compared with students' expectations at entry.

Interviewing Students

Speaking with students in various settings can be rewarding and informative and can be an excellent source of information about the student experience. The research applications may be modest, but the opportunity to personally understand students' expectations and help them develop reasonable ones is an effective way to improve the relationships between students and the institution.

For example, personal encounters with students during new student orientation programs offer rich opportunities for asking them about what they believe the college experience will hold for them. Professional staff can hold such conversations, but they could just as easily be held by student staff who support student orientation programs.

Another example is the academic advisement process, which is a good opportunity for professional staff to engage students about their expectations, particularly early in the student experience. It is an optimal time to ask students about their original beliefs about college, how those beliefs may have changed, and what they think about their near future.

Also, in individual counseling sessions, professional counselors working with college students are often informed about student expectations. Although counselors need to provide quality client services and protect confidentiality, they can share information concerning student expectations with institutional decision-makers.

College residence hall staff members have a unique opportunity to engage students. In the informal residence hall setting, students are relaxed, and alert staff members can learn a great deal about student opinions regarding college life. The first few weeks of the academic year offer a distinct perspective about college, and feelings of dissonance between students' original beliefs and their actual experiences may be quite fresh.

Those who advise student organizations have a similar opportunity to collect perspective about expectations. When students with similar interests gather in a club setting, open conversations about the college experience and how it is different from what was expected can be common. Those conversations are fertile ground for gaining insight.

Intercollegiate athletics provides another opportunity to assess the expectations of individual students. Coaches and student athletes form close bonds because they spend a considerable amount of time together. In the practice setting, during travel for competition, and in many other sports-related situations, coaches, athletic administrators, and other staff and concerned students have many opportunities to learn from new students about what they expected regarding the college experience.

INFORMING ACCURATE STUDENT EXPECTATIONS

When student affairs administrators learn of generally held misperceptions of the college experience, they should respond by better informing students and helping them develop reasonable expectations.

There are at least two reasons why student expectations fail to be realized. In some instances, the expectation may be unreasonable. In others, the expectation may be reasonable, but institutional performance in the area associated with the expectation is not adequate.

When student expectations are unreasonable, it is important to engage them in a negotiation of sorts to help them develop expectations that are more consistent with what is known about real student experiences. Those negotiations can take place in many settings and forms (such as those discussed later), and institutions should explore multiple strategies for assessing individual student expectations and then comparing those expectations with what is known about real student experiences. The comparison may generate information that paves the way for a dialogue with the student to help form more reasonable expectations. The student who expects to be able to hold down a time-consuming off-campus job and still perform at a high academic level may have a disappointment in store for him. The student who discovers that her career aspirations were unreasonable may require help adjusting to the new reality. Taking the opportunity to engage students about their aspirations can afford administrators and counselors the chance to help before the matter becomes a serious problem.

When student expectations are reasonable but the institution fails to deliver on them, the correction is a more difficult one. The difficult choice is either to admit the inability to meet the expectation or to make the necessary corrections to meet it.

If a serious initiative is undertaken to understand student expectations and the results are compared to students' real experiences, the institution is armed to address the points of dissonance in an aggregate fashion. There are many settings to do this. Classroom conversations, campus convocations, and other activities and functions provide opportunities to engage groups of students about their expectations and to challenge their thinking in an effort to reframe their perspectives.

The following sections address four specific opportunities for student affairs professionals and properly trained student staff members to facilitate discussions about expectations: new student orientation; publications, printed materials, and web sites; first-year seminars; and student group meetings.

New Student Orientation

In new student orientation programs, student affairs staff members lead discussions about campus services, climate, and experiences for an audience of incoming students. These programs also provide a natural setting to discuss commonly held misconceptions of the student experience and ways in which student expectations might be misplaced. Using these early opportunities to address expectation myths can help students reflect on their beliefs and begin the college experience with a more accurate understanding of what lies ahead.

Orientation programs are opportunities for institutional representatives to clarify the amount of work and time needed for students to succeed. Students who think that a college workload is the same as a high school workload need to be better informed. Another common misconception is that an off-campus job will not compromise students' success. When research about the real experiences of students is provided to counter widely held notions about off-campus jobs, students can be better prepared for school.

Publications, Printed Materials, and Web Sites

Published materials developed by institutions have a tendency to create unrealistic expectations. Clearly, such materials are intended to show the campus in the best possible light. However, when photography in a publication depicts student diversity in a misleading fashion, for example, it creates a problem for the institution and for students who made a decision to attend based on that characterization. Likewise, if a listing of student organizations or sports teams includes some that are no longer active, a student who discovers the discrepancy may consider it a lapse in institutional integrity.

Student affairs professionals need to critically examine written materials that describe the campus experience. Those aspects of publications that are misrepresentative of the truth or that produce a biased or an unbalanced image must be corrected. Students need to be able to read the material that institutions publish and form accurate assumptions about what they can reasonably expect of the institution.

First-Year Seminars

Courses targeted to first-year students are extended opportunities to negotiate reasonable student expectations. As students discover that their beliefs about college are not accurate, first-year seminars give them a chance to discuss the aspects of college life that surprise them and to reframe what they expect on the basis of their real experiences.

Many student affairs professionals are involved as instructional staff in first-year seminars for new students. Such classroom experiences are clear opportunities for correcting the misguided notions that students might have about college life. The informed professional should seek ways to stimulate thought and perspective in those settings.

Student Group Meetings

Student activities staff often have early opportunities to meet with student organizations, student government, or students in Greek organizations. Those meetings are good opportunities to stimulate conversation about original expectations regarding life on campus and students' early impressions about how those expectations are not being met.

That sort of reflection can be freeing for students and give them the opportunity to process their impressions with peers. Student staff members can be very helpful in those circumstances, supporting students' problem solving and helping individual students set more reasonable expectations.

CONCLUSION

Institutions of higher education could do a better job of understanding students' expectations before or shortly after their academic experiences begin. Institutions could also learn much from the comparison of those expectations to the real experiences students have in college. Although a comprehensive approach to expectations is best, even without any broadly based institutional commitment student affairs staff members can make important progress on this front both with individual students and with groups of students.

This chapter has established why accurate knowledge about student expectations is important to institutions and has demonstrated strategies for gathering that knowledge. Policymakers and the public may well have a growing interest in student expectations, and institutions would be wise to measure them rather than waiting for some external agency to do so.

The simple process of asking students to reflect on their college experience and how it compares to what they may have imagined probably has a good effect on the student. The introspection and analysis that can come from such a discussion can be enlightening for the individual student and lead to self-understanding and reflection that can make him or her more comfortable with the college experience.

Student affairs administrators would be wise to engage this conversation and to assume responsibility for stimulating such thoughts. As full partners in the learning enterprise, student affairs professionals can have a positive effect on the students they serve and on those students' fit and comfort with the college environment.

REFERENCES

Ardaiolo, F. P., Bender, B. E., & Roberts, G. (2005). Campus services: What do students expect? In T. E. Miller, B. E. Bender, J. H. Schuh, & Associates, *Promoting reasonable expectations: Aligning student and institutional views of the college experience* (pp. 84–101). San Francisco, CA: Jossey-Bass.

Arnold, K., & Kuh, G. D. (1999). What matters in undergraduate education? Mental models, student learning, and student affairs. In E. J. Whitt (Ed.), *Student learning as student affairs work: Responding to our imperative* (pp. 11–34). Washington, DC: National Association of Student Personnel Administrators.

Chickering, A. W., & Gamson, Z. F. (1987, June). Seven principles for good practice in undergraduate education. *AAHE Bulletin, 39*(7), 3–7.

Conroy, J. (2006, June). Room with a view: Student demands are impacting university facility development. *University Business.* Retrieved June 21, 2007, from www2.universitybusiness.com/viewarticle.aspx?articleid=59

Howard, J. A. (2005). Why should we care about student expectations? In T. E. Miller, B. E. Bender, J. H. Schuh, & Associates, *Promoting reasonable expectations: Aligning student and institutional views of the college experience* (pp. 10–33). San Francisco, CA: Jossey-Bass.

Howe, N., & Strauss, W. (2003). *Millennials go to college: Strategies for a new generation on campus.* Washington, DC: American Association of Collegiate Registrars and Admissions Officers.

Keeling, R. P. (Ed.). (2004). *Learning reconsidered 1: A campus-wide focus on the student experience.* Washington, DC: American College Personnel Association & National Association of Student Personnel Administrators.

Keeling, R. P. (Ed.). (2006). *Learning reconsidered 2: A practical guide to implementing a campus-wide focus on the student experience.* Washington, DC: American College Personnel Association & National Association of Student Personnel Administrators.

Kuh, G. D., & Pace, C. R. (1999). *College student expectations questionnaire* (2nd ed.). Bloomington, IN: Indiana University, Center for Postsecondary Research.

Miller, T. E. (2005). Student persistence and degree attainment. In T. E. Miller, B. E. Bender, J. H. Schuh, & Associates, *Promoting reasonable expectations: Aligning student and institutional views of the college experience* (pp. 122–139). San Francisco, CA: Jossey-Bass.

Miller, T. E., Kuh, G. D., Paine, D., & Associates. (2006). *Taking student expectations seriously: A guide for campus applications.* Washington, DC: National Association of Student Personnel Administrators.

Pace, C. R., & Kuh, G. D. (1998). *College student experiences questionnaire* (4th ed.). Bloomington, IN: Indiana University, Center for Postsecondary Research.

Peter, K., & Cataldi, E. F. (2005). *The road less traveled? Students who enroll in multiple institutions* (NCES 2005–157). U.S. Department of Education, National Center for Education Statistics. Washington, DC: U.S. Government Printing Office.

Sax, L. J., Lindholm, J. A., Astin, A. W., Korn, W. S., & Mahoney, K. M. (2002). *The American freshman: National norms for fall 2002.* Los Angeles, CA: Higher Education Research Institute.

Thielen, J. R. (2004). *A history of American higher education.* Baltimore, MD: Johns Hopkins University Press.

Upcraft, M. L., Gardner, J. N., Barefoot, B. O., & Associates (2005). *Challenging and supporting the first-year student: A handbook for improving the first year of college.* San Francisco, CA: Jossey-Bass.

Vine, P. (1976, Winter). The social function of eighteenth century higher education. *History of Higher Education Quarterly, 16*(4), 409–424.

4 | CHANGING STUDENT SERVICES THROUGH ASSESSMENT

JOHN H. SCHUH

My colleague Lee Upcraft and I have argued that assessment is an essential function in student affairs (Schuh, Upcraft, & Associates, 2001; Upcraft & Schuh, 1996). Our view has been that, for several reasons, student affairs administrators and leaders have reached a point where they have no choice but to conduct assessments as part of the accountability process or they will suffer unwelcome consequences, such as having various units outsourced (Phipps & Merisotis, 2005) or done away with altogether. In addition, we have posited that leaders of student affairs units, programs, and services need to assure their stakeholders that the activities for which they are responsible contribute to student learning, are administered effectively, and are consistent with the institution's mission. These assurances are being sought not only from student affairs units but from contemporary colleges and universities in general. Leaders must be accountable to their various stakeholders so that better results can be achieved from institutions of higher education (National Commission on Accountability in Higher Education, 2005). An example of how accountability is sought from institutions can be found in the following observation of the Southern Regional Education Board (2006): "The quality of colleges and universities is regularly assessed and funding is targeted to quality, efficiency and state needs" (p. 1).

This chapter has three purposes. First, it will describe assessment as an essential contemporary administrative practice in higher education. I will assert that assessment has moved from a peripheral activity to an essential function in higher education and student affairs. Second, I will describe assessment as a process that student affairs units can employ to respond to a variety of external forces. Third, I will discuss the routine assessment of services, programs, and activities in student affairs as a mechanism of change. In developing this chapter I have assumed that the reader has a rudimentary knowledge of how to conduct assessment projects, so the chapter will not focus on the methodology of assessment.

ASSESSMENT AS AN ESSENTIAL CONTEMPORARY PRACTICE IN STUDENT AFFAIRS

Assessment in student affairs has been discussed in the literature for at least 30 years (e.g., Aulepp & Delworth, 1976), but interest in assessment has accelerated in the past decade or so. In 1996, Upcraft and Schuh asked, "In an era of declining resources, are student services and programs really necessary?" (p. 8). This question cuts to the heart of the assessment issue. It says that if student affairs cannot be justified as an institutional function, then perhaps colleges and universities, in times of ever tightening resources, might be better off without these services and programs. Certainly, as an approach to heading off elimination, outsourcing, or some other undesirable outcome, student affairs units and programs need to be able to demonstrate their usefulness.

Student affairs units, however, are not alone in needing to demonstrate their value to students' lives. Really, all aspects of institutions of higher education are expected to be able to demonstrate their effectiveness. In short, accountability is an important element on today's postsecondary education landscape. The National Commission on Accountability in Higher Education (2005) observed the following: "Public interest in accountability is rooted in the growing importance of higher education and uncertainty concerning its adequacy and affordability. We need better results from higher education, and better approaches to accountability are essential" (p. 32). This observation suggests that accountability is not an obligation that higher education should fulfill just when time is available; rather, it suggests that accountability is essential if institutions of higher education are to sustain their central role in improving the lives of this country's citizens. Similarly, a report from the National Center for Public Policy and Higher Education (Hunt & Tierney, 2006) emphasized the importance of accountability in developing an agenda for higher education to position itself to meet the challenges of global competition.

Student affairs divisions cannot meet these broad challenges by themselves, although they do represent a substantial commitment of institutional resources (Snyder & Tan, 2005) and can make important contributions to the education of students (see Pascarella & Terenzini, 2005). Consequently, these units must demonstrate how they contribute to the advancement of their institution. Upcraft and Schuh (2000) described the situation this way: "We may not know what we mean by assessment, or why we should assess, or what to assess, or how to assess, or how to use assessment, but we all feel the pressure to assess" (p. 249). Three years later, Upcraft (2003) updated this thinking with the following observation:

> Assessment is, quite simply, one of today's hottest issues in higher education and the student affairs profession for many reasons. Assessment is becoming more important because it can be used to improve the quality of student services and programs, guide strategic planning, analyze cost effectiveness, justify student programs and services, assist in accreditation, and perhaps more importantly, guide decision making, policies, and practices. (p. 555)

Some institutions have crafted a culture in which data drive decisions and the institutions themselves are committed to continuous improvement. Twenty such institutions were studied as part of the Documenting Effective Educational Practices project, an inquiry into the factors and conditions that have led certain institutions of higher education to perform above expectations. These institutions "rely on systematic information to make good decisions" (Kuh, Kinzie, Schuh, Whitt, & Associates, 2005, p. 152), which leads to a trajectory of improvement. They are also committed to innovation: "They are not afraid to invest in promising ideas, even though human and fiscal resources are stretched thin" (p. 156). In institutions such as these, data are collected routinely, and decisions about beginning, ending, or modifying programs are based on evidence. This practice means that student affairs and other major divisions of these institutions study the efficacy of their programs, and if changes are needed, those changes are based on information, rather than on hunches or intuition.

Accrediting agencies insist that institutions use data to demonstrate that students are learning. For example, in its resource manual on principles of accreditation, the Southern Association of Colleges and Schools (2004) discusses the need for institutions to provide evidence that demonstrates the effectiveness and adequacy of student support programs, services, and activities. The Middle States Commission on Higher Education (2007), as an additional illustration, provides a web site that includes publications for institutional improvement, such as assessing student learning and institutional effectiveness.

Thus, it becomes clear that assessment and accountability are important elements of current administrative practice in institutions of higher education. Regional accrediting agencies are placing a strong emphasis on institutions' ability to demonstrate their effectiveness, and exemplars of such are emerging in the literature. From this conceptual approach to assessment, a further look at assessment as a means of responding to external change is warranted.

ASSESSMENT IN RESPONSE TO EXTERNAL CHANGE

Institutions of higher education respond to a variety of forces, external and internal. External changes that may affect student affairs can include changes in the institutional mission, in the senior institutional leadership, or in the educational environment (e.g., changes in the physical environment or political change). Because external change affects student affairs, assessment becomes an important tool in measuring the extent to which student affairs has responded appropriately to the change. For example, if an institution of higher education opens a branch campus in another part of the city where the main campus is located, administrators can use assessment to identify the student services that are necessary at the branch campus and, after certain services and programs are implemented, determine the extent to which they meet student needs. Another example might be an evaluation of the programs and services for students of an institution that has been temporarily closed, as was the case with several institutions following the Hurricane Katrina disaster. Student affairs would need to consider how best to meet the needs of displaced students: What services do the students need? How well are these services provided? What special resources will the institution need to make available? These questions and others would form the heart of an assessment project related to this external force on the institution. The following are two case studies that illustrate how assessment relates to external change. Both cases are loosely based on actual situations.

South Central College Becomes a Four-Year College

South Central College (SCC) is a four-year, baccalaureate degree-granting institution located in the middle of the state. It is a private college, denominational in nature, with loyal graduates and a wonderful relationship with the city of Middletown. Five years ago the board of trustees conducted an exhaustive study and determined that important constituencies of the college—its graduates, its religious denomination, and the community of Middletown—would be well served if the college were transformed from a two-year college to a baccalaureate college. The college worked with the regional accrediting agency, the state licensing authority, and others to make this transition.

No one expected that it would be easy, least of all Harriet Jones, who as dean of students was the senior student affairs officer. Dean Jones knew that an expansion of services would be necessary at SCC. Students had typically transferred to a baccalaureate institution after two years at SCC; now many would stay at SCC to complete their degrees. She was not exactly sure what services would have to be added or expanded, but of one thing she was certain: SCC would be different upon completing its metamorphosis from a two-year to a four-year institution.

Dean Jones knew that a variety of tools were available to her to determine how student affairs might be changed to serve the needs of the new institution. One option was to bring in consultants from institutions that had undergone a similar change and seek their expert advice. She rejected this option because of SCC's distinctive culture. She thought that outside consultants not intimately familiar with the college might fail to understand the subtleties of what makes SCC unique and, therefore, would not be able to recommend fruitful suggestions. The other option she considered was to conduct a series of assessments of current SCC students as well as of recent graduates who were pursuing bachelor's degrees at other institutions. Dean Jones knew this approach would be time consuming and challenging, but she was convinced that it would yield the best data for making decisions.

Virtually all aspects of student affairs at SCC would be affected by the change. So Dean Jones assembled a leadership team that consisted of assistant deans for residential life, student activities, career and placement services, and counseling and health services, as well as the associate dean in her office who also oversaw judicial affairs. This group met and discussed how to respond to this change in the institution's mission. Team members agreed that simply adding staff and programs without assessing student needs would be unwise. They agreed with Dean Jones that the change in mission would provide a golden opportunity to assess what their units were currently doing and to determine how they might adjust their services, programs, and activities to meet the needs of future third- and fourth-year students at SCC. They also agreed that surveying current students and recent graduates was the appropriate strategy in their data-collection plan.

The residential life and student activities units decided to work together on the needs-assessment project. As a residential institution, SCC's locus for student activities was the residence halls (the modest campus union simply did not have the space to support a robust student activities program). These units would have to figure out how to accommodate the expected increase in the number of student organizations and activities that would result from the addition of the baccalaureate program.

The assistant dean for career services knew his office would have to change dramatically. Heretofore his office had been concerned primarily with helping students find part-time jobs and internships; because the vast majority of SCC graduates transferred to four-year institutions, helping students with career planning was a low priority. The scope of his unit would have to be broadened. He needed to work with the academic dean and other academic administrators to craft a plan.

The assistant dean for counseling and health services and the associate dean of students decided to collaborate on their areas of responsibility. The associate dean was responsible for administering the college's student health insurance program, and it would be important to ensure that any new student needs in this area were met.

In this scenario, thoughtful planning was conducted to develop plans to meet the needs of students that arose from a decision outside of student affairs. The student affairs division had no choice but to think about its services, programs, and learning experiences differently, and using data from two important groups of stakeholders—current students and recent graduates—would provide a very good start. Other possible options would be to use commonly adopted standards (see Miller, 1996, for an overview of the use of standards in assessment) or to use benchmarking (Bender & Schuh, 2002). But Dean Jones appeared to be on track to start the process.

Metro College Establishes a Branch

Metro College (MC) has a long history of serving the city and county in which it is located. This history extends back more than 100 years, and the citizens of the area are justifiably proud of the college. But because the neighborhood in which the college is located has deteriorated, some people have become uncomfortable making the trip to the college, especially at night.

To combat a decline in enrollment, a blue-ribbon committee recommended to the president that the college open a campus branch on the other side of town at night, which would make courses available to residents in that area of the city. Space was available for rent from the local high school. It appeared that this strategy would result in the boost in enrollment that the college needed.

Planning was conducted in the spring and summer, and a public relations campaign was conducted to make sure that residents of the area knew of these new educational opportunities. When the branch opened, courses were offered at night and on the weekends. Enrollments were strong, so the program appeared to be a rousing success—until the college conducted a satisfaction assessment at the end of the satellite campus's first semester of operation.

The results were disappointing. Although students reported that they liked having the courses in such a convenient location, with plenty of parking and comfortable classrooms, they were particularly critical of the lack of student services available at the satellite campus. Students couldn't do any of the following at the satellite campus:

- Receive academic advising

- Register for classes

- Order books

- Receive financial aid

- Pay college bills

- Check books out of the library

- Obtain an identification card

All these functions were integral to the college experience. And frankly, no one had thought about them, nor did anyone realize that they were so integral to the student experience. Students did not indicate that they needed recreation facilities or meeting rooms for student organizations, and they did not request health or counseling services. But students with disabilities did request special services under Section 504 of the Rehabilitation Act, which no one anticipated.

Something had to be done to make sure that rudimentary services were available; otherwise, college leaders feared that students would not continue to take classes at the satellite campus. The college decided that it needed to develop a targeted student services support program at the satellite campus. The vice president for student affairs decided to conduct a needs assessment to determine what services students felt they needed. Several people in the division of student affairs were knowledgeable about conducting a needs assessment, and working in cooperation with the provost's office, they prepared a questionnaire, which was administered through a special polling unit in the department of mass communications. A random sample of students who had enrolled at the satellite campus was surveyed, and the resulting data were used to develop a program of services on the satellite campus. Some additional space was rented from the high school to accommodate the necessary services, and representatives were made available to address student needs during the time that classes were scheduled.

A follow-up survey indicated that students were satisfied with the new services and that they planned to take other courses they needed to fit into their academic program. The addition of the new services was successful in providing the kind of services and support that the students needed.

The examples of SCC and MC are loosely based on actual circumstances. In each case it was clear that the student affairs program had to be adjusted to meet the needs of students as result of a fundamental institutional change. In the case of SCC, as the institution added a baccalaureate degree program to its portfolio of learning opportunities, careful planning was conducted in preparation for the third- and fourth-year students. The result was that students were well satisfied with their experiences. In the case of MC, because the vice president of student affairs was not involved in the initial planning for the satellite campus, many student needs were not addressed. The college temporarily lost the goodwill of the students enrolled at the satellite campus and had to scramble to create a needs-assessment program. Ultimately, the college provided the necessary services, which were really quite modest in nature. But the scenario underscores how central needs assessment is to the planning process.

ASSESSMENT TO MEASURE ORGANIZATIONAL RESPONSIVENESS AND MANAGE CHANGE

Assessment can also be used to study the effectiveness of student affairs programs, services, and activities and thus bring about organizational change. Because student affairs divisions are typically organized to help an institution achieve its mission (see Manning, Kinzie, & Schuh, 2006), they have features that are idiosyncratic to their institution. These features may be programs that usually are assigned to student affairs but are assigned to an academic unit because of a unique feature of the institution. For example, an institution with a college of health and human performance might have recreational sports services assigned to it rather than to student affairs because of internships and other practical experiences that are tied to students' curriculum. Another illustration is a service that is emphasized at a particular institution because of that institution's mission. For instance, a commuter institution may have an expansive child care program.

Regardless of the uniqueness of a given institution's division of student affairs, assessment is an essential activity in determining organizational effectiveness and can be used to bring about organizational change when necessary. In this section several different types of assessment are identified with examples of how they can be used to bring about organizational change.

Needs Assessment

The needs of students on a given campus will change for various reasons—some due to the normal evolution of an institution of higher education, some brought about by external factors. For example, as the characteristics of the populations served by an institution change, so will the nature of the student body. If an area experiences growth in the number of students who are the children of immigrants, the institutions serving that area will need to adjust their programs. Other examples include an institution's adding new undergraduate or graduate academic programs, committing itself to building more residence halls to increase the percentage of students living on campus, or changing its emphasis on intercollegiate athletics after moving from one NCAA division to another.

In situations like these, needs assessment is an essential tool for the institution to determine what student experiences, programs, and services should be provided. Consider the following example.

Mid-Central College (MCC) is a baccalaureate degree-granting institution that has a long history of serving the students of the local community and region. Due to several factors—including a population decline, an eroding base of feeder high schools, and residence halls that had not been updated for 20 years—MCC committed itself to broadening its recruiting activities geographically and to completely renovating its residence halls. A tremendous gift from a graduate covered much of the cost of the residence hall renovation.

During these changes, the issue before the senior student affairs officer was how to develop a program of activities that would provide for a robust first-year experience. He consulted with experts in the field on this topic, read widely, and studied MCC's Cooperative Institutional Research Program (CIRP) data to look for changes in the student body over the previous few years (CIRP, 2006). He found some valuable information, but in his mind more was needed.

The new program was to come on line in two years, but the recruiting process had already begun with excellent success. Students from a much wider geographic area had been attracted to MCC. Although these students were still living in the older residence halls, the senior student affairs officer believed it was time to begin a needs assessment in anticipation of the new program. He considered several tools to learn more about the new students' needs, including a series of mixed-methods studies. First, in the fall the college would administer the ACT needs-assessment survey to all entering first-year students. This instrument helps identify the perceived personal and educational needs of students (ACT, 2007a) and would provide baseline data about the entering class. Second, a series of focus groups would be conducted 10 weeks into the semester to elicit students' perceptions about their experiences after the first couple of months at MCC. Finally, another set of focus groups would be conducted with first-year students after spring break to confirm what had been learned in the fall. What was learned over the course of this year would provide the basis for program development over the following summer and the next year (the new program would be implemented the year after).

This example of a mixed-methods approach to assessing student needs has several laudable features. First, it was to be conducted far in advance of the implementation of the program. Plenty of time would be available to collect the data. The data were being collected in such a way that if the assumptions of the dean and the staff were incorrect, there would be ample time for them to adjust their plan. Second, data were being collected at several points throughout the school year. Thus, this process would provide longitudinal information about how student needs change over time, not just a snapshot of student needs. That would be very useful as the college planned its program for the first-year experience. Third, by using mixed methods, the research team would be able to elicit data that would not be available if just a quantitative or qualitative study were conducted. The plan ensured that MCC would approach this potential change in student needs in a thoughtful, deliberate manner and be ready for the new program when it was implemented.

Satisfaction Assessment

Satisfaction assessments usually should be conducted after changes in programs, experiences, or services have been implemented (Upcraft & Schuh, 1996). These could include assessments of new food services, of new campus bookstore management, or of new features to the campus identification card, such as a debit function for on-campus purchases.

In satisfaction assessment it is important to note that satisfaction needs to be framed by the institution's mission (Upcraft & Schuh, 1996).

Satisfaction assessment is not just about what students want, because there is virtually no limit to what an institution could provide to make students happy. Rather, satisfaction assessment is designed to measure student perceptions within the context of what the institution is trying to provide. For example, this might mean determining whether students who participated in the judicial process report that the process gave them an opportunity to present their side of the case, that the hearing officer followed the published procedures for judicial hearings, and that the hearing officer approached the hearing in an unbiased, objective manner. This is very different than asking the student who was charged with an infraction of the rules whether he or she liked the final decision. If assessment of student satisfaction of judicial hearings indicated that those charged with offenses did not have an opportunity to present their case or that the hearing officer appeared to approach cases with a bias against those charged, then further inquiry would need to be conducted.

At MCC when the needs assessment described in the previous section had been completed, various initiatives were planned for the new experience. Three elements of the program provided the foundation for the experience: a first-year tutorial course that would meet in the residence halls, a community service experience for all first-year students, and a special food service program that would allow students who lived in the first-year complex to invite faculty members to lunch any time they wished, without cost to the student or the faculty member.

After the first semester the senior student affairs officer and other senior members of the institution's leadership team wondered just how well this program worked from the students' perspective. They decided to collect data during the second semester to provide insights into how well the program achieved its objectives.

The senior student affairs officer—after consulting with several faculty, students, and administrators—decided that a broad-ranging satisfaction assessment process would be valuable to determine whether the new first-year students were pleased with their experience at MCC. If elements of their experience were unsatisfactory and could be linked to the special first-year program, then those could be explored in the next phases of the assessment process. Besides, the campus was committed to learning as much as it could about the student experience, so these data would be very useful to the campus in general. To help members of MCC's community get a sense of student satisfaction with their overall experience, the Noel-Levitz Student Satisfaction Inventory (2006) was to be administered to students who lived in the new first-year student housing complex.

The tutorial program consisted of sections of no more than 15 students each. These sections met in the residence halls in specially configured seminar rooms. Students enrolled in their sections based on their interests in the subject matter of the tutorials, which were taught by senior faculty members. These experiences also provided students with an in-depth orientation to MCC. All together, 30 sections of the two-credit tutorials were offered on campus in the fall. In developing a strategy to measure satisfaction with the tutorials, the senior student affairs officer and the senior academic officer decided to hold a meeting with students from each of the tutorial sections in the spring to learn more about student satisfaction with the experience. The senior academic officer also decided to hold several focus groups with faculty members who taught the sections. The interview protocols would be framed by the objectives for the tutorials, which had been developed the previous year by a faculty committee. These focus groups would also be used to examine the special meal program. Since MCC had committed substantial resources to the meal program, the college needed to measure student and faculty satisfaction with it and to determine whether the goals of the program had been met.

Finally, MCC needed a strategy to determine the level of satisfaction with the community service program. The college prepared a questionnaire based on the objectives of the program to measure student satisfaction. It was short and was designed to be administered online to all students who lived in the first-year complex. If the questionnaire elicited unanticipated or puzzling results, the college planned to conduct focus groups for clarification. The college also conducted a satisfaction assessment with partners in the volunteer program, surveying service agency representatives and clients to determine their level of satisfaction with the program and asking them to make recommendations to improve it for the future.

The approach taken at MCC to measure satisfaction with the new program used multiple methods. Each aspect of the satisfaction assessment was framed by the goals of the program. Because MCC's leaders were committed to this new approach to providing educational experiences for its first-year students, they could not move forward with the program until they were certain that students and other significant stakeholders were satisfied with it.

Measuring Student Outcomes

Measuring student outcomes is another assessment approach that can trigger change. Outcomes should be identified as programs are conceptualized. Then the success of programs can be measured on the basis of what students actually learn. Outcomes assessments are difficult to conduct (Schuh et al., 2001), but they are absolutely necessary in today's environment, in which institutions need to provide evidence that they are achieving their learning objectives.

Another step in developing the new first-year program at MCC was to determine whether the program achieved the learning outcomes that had been established for the students who participated in it. Because all first-year students participated in the program, the senior student affairs officer and the senior academic officer determined that they would include all first-year students in their study of learning outcomes. Associated with each feature of the program (the tutorial, the meal program, and the service program) were learning outcomes, which would form the basis for the learning outcomes assessment.

In the tutorial program one of the desired outcomes was that students learn about the library and other information resources on campus, how to take advantage of various student support units (such as the math lab and the English writing lab), and about MCC's academic honesty policy. The college had determined that students were beginning their academic work without understanding the fundamentals of how to prepare papers and other academic assignments according to the institution's requirements for attributing sources. Hence, the faculty senate pushed to incorporate a unit on academic honesty in the tutorial program. The faculty members who taught the tutorial courses were given several options for measuring these learning outcomes or could develop their own measures.

The meal program was much less structured; therefore, outcomes had to be measured differently. At the end of the term, records showed that more than half the students and about a third of the faculty members at MCC who were eligible to participate in the program had actually done so. To determine what benefits had accrued to students who participated in the program, a series of focus groups was planned. The interviews focused on why the students had asked faculty members to a meal, what they had learned from their experience with the faculty members, whether they had invited faculty members to a meal more than once, and, if so, why had they done so. This helped the college ascertain the students' motivations for participating in the experience and what they learned. Two focus groups for faculty members also were organized, and the faculty members were asked why they had participated in the program, what they had gained from participating in it, and what they thought the benefits were to the student participants. This assessment was not designed to be sophisticated. It was conducted to determine whether the meal program had contributed to student and faculty learning. Another short web-based survey was sent to students who did not participate in the program that simply asked why they had decided not to participate.

The service-learning program was somewhat more difficult to assess because some students had been engaged in projects over the course of the entire semester and others had participated in programs that lasted just a day. Residence hall directors organized the programs, and a staff member from student affairs coordinated the overall leadership for the service-learning component. This person had instructed students to keep journals of their experiences, which would ultimately be used to measure the efficacy of the program. Some journals were lengthy; others were just a page or two. Students were asked to address one question each day of their experience: What did I learn today from my experience in the service program? After discussing how to evaluate this element of the program, the two residence-hall directors and the central office coordinator met and decided to read the student journals and look for recurring themes related to student learning. These would then be compared with the learning outcomes developed for the program to see whether the program's objectives were met.

Measuring Cost Effectiveness

The costs of higher education are of ongoing concern to many individuals, including students and their parents, policymakers, and others (e.g., Stringer & Cunningham, 1999). Within institutions of higher education, student affairs units contribute substantially to the cost of attendance. For example, the cost of room and board can be greater than tuition at many public institutions (Schuh & Shelley, 2001). Kennedy, Moran, and Upcraft (2001) were prophetic in this admonition: "Clearly we must be prepared to answer cost effectiveness questions better than we have in the past, and one way is to develop more systematic ways of assessing cost effectiveness" (p. 175).

Student affairs units may be supported by the institution's general fund (i.e., tuition and, if it's a public institution, the state appropriation), student fees, and fees for service (Schuh, 2003). Units like student health services, child care centers, and perhaps recreational services are often supported by student fees and fees for service. If such units are supported substantially by student fees, a campus board or committee may conduct annual hearings about fee requests from the various units and recommend what the fee should be.

In preparing for such hearings, student affairs leaders should conduct a study of similar services provided off campus to determine the extent to which the charges levied to students are competitive or less expensive than what students can find elsewhere. In the case of student health, the cost of a visit to the campus health service should be compared with a visit to the local immediate care clinic. Other costs can also be compared to ensure that the costs of the health service on campus will be substantially less than the costs for similar services off campus. A similar comparison can be done of the fee charged to students for the recreation program and of the cost of joining a local health club. Campuses typically charge much less for use of recreational facilities than the cost of a membership in an off-campus fitness club yet provide far more extensive facilities and services. If special fees are levied for lockers, specialized equipment, or participation in special programs, these should be included in the comparison. Again, the goal is for the campus to provide more and better services at a lower cost than what students could find off campus. The last example is obvious: The cost of providing child care on campus should be less than what can be found off campus, whether student fees provide a subsidy or not.

Gathering financial efficiency metrics should be a goal for the leadership of all student affairs units. In some cases, such as a leadership development program for students, it may not be easy or even desirable to develop comparisons with off-campus programs because they may either not exist in the form that is found on campus or not be found at all. But where comparisons can be made, such as in the examples just cited, the resulting data provide a level of assurance that the services and programs are efficient and being managed to provide the best quality at the lowest cost for students.

Benchmarking

Benchmarking is defined as "a comparison of similar processes across public and/or private organizations to identify best practices in an effort to improve organizational performance" (Detrick & Pica, 2001, p. 55). Assessment is the most typical goal of benchmarking (Doerfel & Ruben, 2002). In some circumstances, broad performance indicators have been developed to measure institutional effectiveness (Southern Regional Education Board, 2000). Mosier and Schwarzmueller (2002) report that, "as in other areas of higher education, benchmarking practices in student affairs accelerated during the 1990s" (p. 104). Benchmarks may be internal or external.

An internal standard or benchmark might be illustrated in the following way. At Mountain Top Community College, academic advising is decentralized—that is, each academic division has its own academic advisors, and the division head oversees the overall advising program for these units. The division heads in turn report to an academic dean. The dean wants to make sure that advising services are efficient as well as supportive of students. To determine whether advising services are efficient, the dean organizes a retreat for the unit heads and the academic advisors. During this daylong event the various members discuss ways of measuring efficiency in academic advising. They determine, after a great deal of discussion, that during enrollment periods each year—the busiest times for academic advisors—each advisor should see a minimum number of students. Advisors who do not meet with a minimum number of students would have to provide justification for not achieving the standard in a conference with the senior advisor. Meeting this number is an internal benchmark. Another might be a minimum score on section IV ("Impressions of Your Academic Advisor") on the Survey of Academic Advising questionnaire (ACT, 2007b), which would be administered each semester to a random sample of students after they complete their advising/registration experience. Staff realize that simply seeing a certain number of students during the registration period is an incomplete benchmark; they also need to know that they have met the needs of the students they have served. This dimension of the advising process is another internal benchmark.

In the case of external benchmarks, certain practices of one institution are compared with a peer group, and institutional leaders can determine whether their institution is comparable to peer institutions in certain dimensions. An example of a for-profit benchmarking service is Educational Benchmarking, Inc. According to its web site, "Educational Benchmarking provides the most comprehensive, comparative assessment instruments and analysis to support quality improvement efforts" (Educational Benchmarking, 2005).

One of the challenges of external benchmarking is to make sure that the peer institutions selected for comparison in fact have institutional characteristics that are similar to the institution conducting the comparison. It is crucial that a good "fit" be developed for the comparison; otherwise, institutions might be compared when they are not similar enough to make the comparison useful.

Institutional leaders may choose to develop internal benchmarks, engage in external benchmarking, or do both. This form of assessment is designed to determine whether certain standards have been met. If those standards have not been achieved, then additional analysis is necessary to determine what needs to be done to meet them.

Cultural Assessment

Cultural assessments are complex processes in which the authors of the assessment desire to learn about the values of the institution they are studying as well as the quality of student life, both inside and outside the classroom. Several notable studies of campus cultures have been conducted in the past, including those published by Clark (1970); Horowitz (1987); and Kuh, Schuh, Whitt, and Associates (1991). Whitt (1996) observed that "student culture assessment offers a means to foster student learning and development in ways that support the educational purposes of the institution, and to assess the impact of campus environments on student learning" (p. 195). In 2006 a study of the culture of Duke University (Lipka, 2006) was called for after an off-campus incident involving a student group became a cause célèbre.

Although cultural assessments are complex processes (see the Involving Colleges Audit Protocol, published in Kuh et al., 1991), they are very useful in evaluating an institution's culture and how changes in the institution's composition over time affect its values. For example, consider an institution that has consciously decided to recruit and admit more academically able students over a five-year period. At the end of this time period, a cultural assessment might be in order, particularly if the entering students were demonstrably stronger than those who had enrolled five years earlier.

Cultural assessments often are a combination of quantitative and qualitative methodologies. Quantitative data from such surveys as the CIRP (2006) freshman survey and the National Survey of Student Engagement (2006) can provide useful information about students at the end of the five years. Then a series of interviews and focus groups with key students and others might be in order, as well as observations from students as they participate in various events and programs. Whitt (1996) provides a useful discussion of cultural assessment. In the end, institutional leaders can determine whether the change in the academic backgrounds of the students has resulted in any change in the values that they desire in their student body.

CONCLUSION

This chapter has asserted that assessment is an essential, contemporary practice in higher education and that a student affairs division must have an ongoing assessment component in the various programs, services, and learning experiences that it makes available to students. Without assessment, student affairs leaders can only guess at the effectiveness of their work, and guesswork in the current educational environment is unacceptable. In this chapter assessment has been described as a process student affairs leaders can use in crafting their response to a variety of forces that affect their areas of responsibility. Finally, assessment was described as a mechanism of promoting ongoing change and improvement in student affairs through the normal, routine study of services, programs, and activities that various units and programs within student affairs provide.

REFERENCES

ACT. (2007a). *College student needs assessment survey.* Retrieved June 22, 2007, from www.act.org/ess/fouryear.html

ACT. (2007b). *Survey of academic advising.* Retrieved June 22, 2007, from www.act.org/ess/fouryear.html

Aulepp, L., & Delworth, U. (1976). *Training manual for an ecosystem model: Assessing and designing campus environments.* Boulder, CO: Western Interstate Commission for Higher Education.

Bender, B. E., & Schuh, J. H. (Eds.). (2002). *New directions for higher education: No. 118. Using benchmarking to inform practice in higher education.* San Francisco, CA: Jossey-Bass.

Clark, B. R. (1970). *The distinctive college: Antioch, Reed and Swarthmore.* Chicago, IL: Aldine.

Cooperative Institutional Research Program. (2006). *CIRP freshman survey: The survey instrument.* Retrieved June 22, 2007, from www.gseis.ucla.edu/heri/cirp_survey.html

Detrick, G., & Pica, J. A. (2001). The power of benchmarking. In R. L. Swing (Ed.), *Proving and improving: Strategies for assessing the first college year* (pp. 55–59). Columbia, SC: University of South Carolina, National Resource Center for The First-Year Experience and Students in Transition.

Doerfel, M. L., & Ruben, B. D. (2002). Developing more adaptive, innovative, and interactive organizations. In B. E. Bender & J. H. Schuh (Eds.), *New directions for higher education: No. 118. Using benchmarking to inform practice in higher education* (pp. 5–27). San Francisco, CA: Jossey-Bass.

Educational Benchmarking, Inc. (2005). *Mission statement.* Retrieved June 23, 2007, from www.webebi.com/AboutEBI/companyhistory.aspx

Horowitz, H. L. (1987). *Campus life: Undergraduate cultures from the end of the eighteenth century to the present.* New York, NY: Knopf.

Hunt, J. B., Jr., & Tierney, T. J. (2006). *American higher education: How does it measure up for the 21st century?* San Jose, CA: National Center for Public Policy and Higher Education.

Kennedy, K., Moran, L., & Upcraft, M. L. (2001). Assessing cost effectiveness. In J. H. Schuh, M. L. Upcraft, & Associates, *Assessment practice in student affairs: An applications manual* (pp. 175–195). San Francisco, CA: Jossey-Bass.

Kuh, G. D., Kinzie, J., Schuh, J. H., Whitt, E. J., & Associates (2005). *Student success in college: Creating conditions that matter.* San Francisco, CA: Jossey-Bass.

Kuh, G. D., Schuh, J. H., Whitt, E. J., & Associates. (1991). *Involving colleges: Successful approaches to fostering student learning and development outside the classroom.* San Francisco, CA: Jossey-Bass.

Lipka, S. (2006, April 21). Duke incident raises questions about culture of the campus. *The Chronicle of Higher Education,* p. A1.

Manning, K., Kinzie, J., & Schuh, J. (2006). *One size does not fit all: Traditional and innovative models of student affairs practice.* New York, NY: Routledge.

Middle States Commission on Higher Education. (2007). *Guidelines for institutional improvement.* Retrieved June 22, 2007, from www.msche.org/publications_view.asp?idPublicationType=5&txtPublicationType=Guidelines+for+Institutional+Improvement

Miller, T. K. (1996). Measuring effectiveness against professional standards. In M. L. Upcraft & J. H. Schuh (Eds.), *Assessment in student affairs: A guide for practitioners* (pp. 252–272). San Francisco, CA: Jossey-Bass.

Mosier, R. E., & Schwarzmueller, G. J. (2002). Benchmarking in student affairs. In B. E. Bender & J. H. Schuh (Eds.), *New directions for higher education: No. 118. Using benchmarking to inform practice in higher education* (pp. 103–112). San Francisco, CA: Jossey-Bass.

National Commission on Accountability in Higher Education. (2005). *Accountability for better results: A national imperative for higher education.* Denver, CO: State Higher Education Executive Officers.

National Survey of Student Engagement. (2006). *NSSE 2006 survey samples.* Retrieved June 22, 2007, from http://nsse.iub.edu/html/sample.cfm

Noel-Levitz. (2006). *Student success and retention services.* Retrieved June 22, 2007, from https://www.noellevitz.com/Our+Services/Retention/

Pascarella, E. T., & Terenzini, P. T. (2005). *How college affects students: A third decade of research.* San Francisco, CA: Jossey-Bass.

Phipps, R., & Merisotis, J. (2005). *Is outsourcing part of the solution to the higher education cost dilemma? A preliminary examination.* Washington, DC: Institute for Higher Education Policy.

Schuh, J. H. (2003). The financial environment of student affairs. In J. H. Schuh (Ed.), *New directions for student services: No. 103. Contemporary financial issues in student affairs* (pp. 3–16). San Francisco, CA: Jossey-Bass.

Schuh, J. H., & Shelley, M. C., II. (2001). External factors affecting room and board rates: How much influence does the housing director have? *Journal of College and University Student Housing, 30*(1), 41–47.

Schuh, J. H., Upcraft, M. L., & Associates. (2001). *Assessment practice in student affairs: An applications manual.* San Francisco, CA: Jossey-Bass.

Snyder, T. D., & Tan, A. G. (2005). *Digest of education statistics, 2004* (NCES Publication No. 2006–005). U.S. Department of Education, National Center for Education Statistics. Washington, DC: U.S. Government Printing Office.

Southern Association of Colleges and Schools, Commission on Colleges. (2004). *Handbook for reaffirmation of accreditation.* Decatur, GA: Author.

Southern Regional Education Board. (2000). *Linking higher education performance indicators to goals.* Atlanta, GA: Author.

Southern Regional Education Board. (2006). *Holding colleges and universities accountable for meeting state needs.* Atlanta, GA: Author.

Stringer, W. L., & Cunningham, A. F. (with Merisotis, J. P., Wellman, J. V., & O'Brien, C. T.). (1999). *Cost, price and public policy: Peering into the higher education black box.* Indianapolis, IN: USA Group Foundation.

Upcraft, M. L. (2003). Assessment and evaluation. In S. R. Komives, D. B. Woodard, Jr., & Associates, *Student services: A handbook for the profession* (4th ed., pp. 555–572). San Francisco, CA: Jossey-Bass.

Upcraft, M. L., & Schuh, J. H. (1996). *Assessment in student affairs: A guide for practitioners.* San Francisco, CA: Jossey-Bass.

Upcraft, M. L., & Schuh, J. H. (2000). Assessment in student affairs. In M. J. Barr, M. K. Desler, & Associates, *The handbook of student affairs administration* (pp. 249–264). San Francisco, CA: Jossey-Bass.

Whitt, E. J. (1996). Assessing student cultures. In M. L. Upcraft & J. H. Schuh (Eds.), *Assessment in student affairs: A guide for practitioners* (pp. 189–216). San Francisco, CA: Jossey-Bass.

5 | PROMOTING AND SUSTAINING CHANGE

Earl H. Potter III

There are few college or university web sites today without a stated commitment to putting students first. Potential students and their families expect to see this commitment, and vice presidents for marketing have shaped messages to match these expectations. Moreover, university administrators have learned that students expect to be treated as customers whose legitimate needs must be addressed. Foremost among these is the need to achieve near-term success that will lead to long-term success.

College and university leaders know that student success is the cornerstone of institutional strength. Yet a cursory review of the Education Trust's College Results Online web site (www.collegeresults.org) shows that institutions vary widely in the degree to which their students achieve success. How can it be that although all institutions claim a commitment to student success, few reach the levels of success achieved by the best-practice leaders? Given the composition of the comparison groups used in College Results Online, the answer cannot be funding, nor can it be student ability.

We can look to an unlikely area of research for some ideas. In the 1980s Nicholas Allen did his dissertation research on leadership using U.S. Coast Guard cutters as the venue for his studies (Allen & Potter, 1985). At that time the Coast Guard fleet included twelve 210-foot medium-endurance cutters (210s) that performed search and rescue as well as law enforcement duties. The 210 fleet was a perfect setting for leadership research. Each ship had a mission similar to the others, the same funding, identical staffing, and the same physical plant. The only thing that differed from ship to ship was the people.

Allen was interested in leadership behaviors that might set high-performing units apart from units that achieved lesser results with the same resources. He surveyed the commanding officers of each ship to determine their goals and values. He also surveyed the crew members of each ship to assess their morale and their perspective on the ship's operations. He next asked the admirals commanding the districts in which the ships operated to evaluate the overall performance of each ship. Finally, he divided the ships into upper and lower halves in terms of their performance rankings. His findings were striking and relevant to the question we have asked about higher education.

Every commanding officer expressed the same set of objectives. These included, foremost, the welfare of the crew and the primacy of the mission. This is what might be expected in a relatively small organization with a strong institutional culture and in an industry that studies itself to the point of excess. Leaders know what they're expected to say.

Allen then looked at the crew members' perceptions of the captain's goals and priorities. Among the top-performing ships, the crew's perceptions matched the captain's self-reported goals. However, among the lower performers, there was disagreement. Although the captains said that their people came first, their crews said that the captain's career was the most important priority. In other words, leaders of the least successful units knew what to say, but their practices did not support their public statements.

In higher education the significance of leaders "walking the talk" is no different. At least this is the primary finding of a study of graduation rate outcomes conducted by the American Association of State Colleges and Universities (AASCU; 2005). AASCU identified 12 colleges and universities whose graduation rates were better than expected given student preparation and institutional funding. Six of the institutions were included in the study because of their consistently high performance; six others were included because of recent significant improvements in retention and graduation rates.

Each of these institutions had in place programs that had been recognized for their best practices for decades. However, unlike many other institutions whose programs operate in isolation from each other, the programs in these institutions were intentional and integrated. Strong advising, a first-year experience program, organizational structures that support integrated student services, and a curriculum that encourages student engagement were all key elements of the culture. Yet the research team did not find that the inventory of programs was sufficient to explain the observed success of these institutions.

In every case presidential leadership set these institutions apart. These presidents articulated a collective vision for student success; consistently took stock to assess progress toward the vision; acted strategically to build a coherent, integrated approach to student success; invested in building a culture consistent with the vision; and used the symbolic power of the presidency to repeatedly reinforce the institution's commitment to student success. Most important, the president in each of these institutions "actively model[ed] the institution's espoused values" (AASCU, 2005, p. 21) in ways that faculty and staff could see.

What then are student affairs leaders to do if student success is not the cornerstone of their president's agenda? The answer is that they must lead change from within the organization. Thankfully, there is solid evidence that this is possible.

LEADING FROM WITHIN

The Malcolm Baldrige National Quality Award was created by an act of Congress in 1987. Named for Malcolm Baldrige, who served as U.S. secretary of commerce from 1981 until his death in 1987, the Baldrige National Quality Program is a public-private partnership established for the purpose of improving national competitiveness. The selection process is rigorous; many organizations apply for several years before winning the award. The program is founded on a set of 11 core values: visionary leadership; learning-centered education; organizational and personal learning; valuing faculty, staff, and partners; agility; a focus on the future; managing for innovation; managing by fact; public responsibility and citizenship; a focus on results and creating value; and a systems perspective. The criteria are divided into seven categories: leadership; strategic planning; student, stakeholder, and market focus; information and analysis; faculty and staff focus; process management; and organizational performance results (National Institute of Standards and Technology [NIST], 2006).

The Baldrige Education Criteria for Performance Excellence were first offered in 2000. Although the criteria were designed for institutions, subunits of institutions that have a certain amount of control over the factors that determine organizational outcomes can apply independently. In 2004 the education winner was the Kenneth W. Monfort College of Business at the University of Northern Colorado. The award profile (NIST, 2004) for the Monfort College of Business outlines the strategy that allowed this college to win the award even though the university as a whole had not applied.

The Monfort College of Business achieved this goal by clarifying its vision, aligning its strategy with its vision, identifying a set of measures of its performance, and creating a benchmarking strategy to drive its goal setting and action planning. Persistent focus on its objectives led to ongoing improvement and results that ranked among the top in peer comparisons.

These results would not have been possible if the college had not created a culture in which faculty members and staff were actively engaged with planning and implementing plans to achieve shared goals. Furthermore, the college established and maintained a set of external partnerships that supported its objectives. These partnerships strengthened community-based learning opportunities and job placement results while boosting private support for scholarships and building public awareness of the value added to the community by the Monfort College of Business.

A very different example is offered by the way institutions are responding to the Higher Learning Commission of the North Central Association of Colleges and Schools' (NCA) Academic Quality Improvement Project (AQIP). AQIP is a developmental program that requires improvement and change but does not specify a level of accomplishment that must be achieved. In this respect it differs from the Baldrige program. The AQIP process begins with extensive self-evaluation that supports application for admission to the program. There are nine evaluation criteria that are based on the Baldrige criteria: helping students learn, accomplishing other distinct objectives, understanding students' and other stakeholders' needs, valuing people, leading and communicating, supporting institutional operations, measuring effectiveness, planning continuous improvement, and building collaborative relationships.

What really sets AQIP apart from the approaches to accreditation offered by the other five regional associations is its focus on specific programs rather than on the institution as a whole. The Northwest Council of Colleges and Universities also uses a Baldrige-based model for continuous improvement, but this approach is built on the expectation that the institution as a whole will demonstrate a commitment to continuous improvement. The NCA allows colleges and universities to focus their efforts, partly in recognition of the difficulty of moving the whole institution at once and partly in recognition of the power of smaller successes to influence a whole culture. This model allows any division to take the lead in building a strong institution.

A college unit need not adopt these specific approaches to lead institutional change. At Purdue University Calumet (PUC) the business services office decided to use the Baldrige criteria as the framework for assessing its own performance. At the same time the student services organization undertook the redesign of student services without using the Baldrige criteria. PUC's accomplishments in student services led to its designation as an IBM Best Practice in Student Services Partner. Now that the university is engaged in a campus-wide commitment to quality improvement, the experiences of both business services and student services are important assets. Instead of rigidly adhering to only one system, PUC has taken a more discerning approach by using the different perspectives developed by the two offices.

When one looks closely, it has not been a tradition in American higher education to put students first. Making students the top priority requires change, and not every student services organization in America really wants to change. There are still many student services leaders who measure success by activity. They count the number of students served, the hours of service given, and the attendance at events. They implement new programs that are being discussed at conferences and tell stories about student successes.

If student services leaders choose to put students first, in fact and not just in rhetoric, they should define their objectives in measurable terms, benchmark their results against peers, search actively for best practices that change results, develop goal-directed plans, align resources with those plans, enable student affairs staff and essential partners to become engaged in implementing the plans, and demonstrate a sustained focus on their goals. If leaders follow this course, they will achieve results that can influence a whole institution's way of working.

BUILDING THE CASE FOR CHANGE

The process of change begins with the recognition of a gap between the current state of affairs and a desired state. A leader must then develop a compelling case for moving to the desired state and show organization members how they are going to get there. Luckily, today's leaders have new tools for building the case for change, including new benchmarking options.

Advances in Benchmarking

Among the most compelling arguments for change is the revelation that similar institutions are getting much better results than you are. A gap in performance results is even more compelling when the results are in areas in which the institution has made a public commitment to excellence. The process of finding comparison data for a given set of measures is called "benchmarking." Even within the past few years, it would have taken weeks for a college or university to identify performance measures, choose a group of comparable institutions, gather comparison data from those institutions, and create a framework to compare measures. Benchmarking information, however, is becoming increasingly available.

In 2004 The Education Trust, an independent nonprofit organization that works to improve the academic achievement of students at all levels, completed work on a web-based tool that allows easy access to graduation rate data collected by the National Center for Education Statistics. This tool, College Results Online, allows interested parties to see the retention and graduation rates for most four-year institutions of higher education in the United States. It also allows institutions to see how their retention and graduation rates stand in relation to results achieved by a comparable set of American institutions. The groups have been built to be comparable in terms of 11 institutional and student characteristics that are related to six-year graduation rates (The Education Trust, 2007):

- Estimated median SAT (or ACT equivalent) of freshman class

- Admissions selectivity, per *Barron's Guide to American Colleges*

- Carnegie classification

- Percentage of undergraduates receiving Pell Grants

- Sector (public vs. private)

- Number of full-time equivalent (FTE) undergraduates

- Student-related expenditures per FTE student

- Percentage of FTE undergraduate students age 25 and over

- Status as a historically Black college or university

- Percentage of undergraduates who are enrolled part-time

- Status as a commuter campus

For an institution that is committed to improving student success results but has limited research capacity, this tool is invaluable in identifying improvement opportunities and building the case for change.

Tools for community colleges are also proliferating. The National Community College Benchmark Project (NCCBP; www.nccbp.org) is run by another former IBM Best Practice in Student Services Partner: Johnson County Community College. The NCCBP gathers data annually from participants and makes comparison reports available as a benefit of the $1,000 annual subscription fee. In 2005, 113 colleges participated in this consortium. Data are gathered and made available in more than 20 performance areas.

Some of these are:

- Proportions of students who completed a degree or certificate or transferred within three years
- Student performance at transfer institutions
- Student satisfaction
- Retention of remedial students
- Success in first college-level courses
- Ratios of students to professional student services staffers

Different kinds of benchmarking services are also available via The Kansas Study (www.kansasstudy.org) and Achieving the Dream: Community Colleges Count (www.achievingthedream.org).

Benchmarking by itself, however, may not be sufficient to build the case for change. A compelling case may require that leaders create a sense of the danger that will result if an organization fails to change.

Public Pressure for Accountability

Public pressure for accountability in higher education has been steadily increasing for more than two decades. Much of the public's interest can be traced to a lack of understanding of the role and value of higher education. Efforts by the American Council on Education and the Association of American Colleges and Universities to educate the public about the economic and cultural value of higher education in general, and of a liberal arts education in particular, address this problem. A certain amount of the public's discontent is attributable to rising costs of the predominant delivery systems in use throughout American higher education. Although the cost of computing power has declined and the globalization of industry has kept consumer prices in check, the cost of education continues to rise at a pace that outstrips the Consumer Price Index. The primary reason for this picture is that the way education is delivered has not changed even though technology and global markets have vastly increased productivity in other areas of the economy.

The public's discontent is also due to the kind of variability in effectiveness that is seen on the College Results Online web site. Rather than reject public and legislative criticism of the results that institutions obtain, higher education leaders might embrace this concern and turn public demands into a force for change. Failing to deal with rising public concern for quality and cost in higher education is a real threat to one of America's most successful enterprises. To build a case for change, leaders must convey the idea that an organization cannot afford to stay where it is—that there is peril in failing to change.

Legislative Pressure

Higher education leaders in the United States are keeping their eyes on the secretary of education's Commission on the Future of Higher Education (U.S. Department of Education, 2006). The development of the report and its reception are one thing; the direction of actions taken in response to the report will be another. Possible options include national degree standards, national accreditation processes, and linking new measures to future funding for higher education. Conversations about the options are likely to go on for years, but real change is already happening in state legislatures.

Oregon's Senate Bill 342 is just one example of legislative intrusion into the management of public higher education. The bill began with public concern for the rising costs of higher education. Legislators and Oregon's higher education officials hurried to deliver results to the public by creating a prescription for controlling costs. Embedded in the bill are eight specific requirements for Oregon's institutions of higher education:

> Community colleges and state institutions of higher education . . .
> shall cooperate in operating a statewide articulation and transfer
> system. The system must include the means for articulating lower-
> division general education credits, general elective credits and cur-
> riculum requirements for approved majors in order to allow
> students to transfer between community colleges and state institu-
> tions of higher education without losing credits that otherwise
> would be applicable toward a baccalaureate degree. . . .
> Community colleges and state institutions of higher education
> shall:
> (a) Revise the Associate of Arts Oregon Transfer Degree offered by
> community colleges;
> (b) Develop specific degree pathways as deemed appropriate by the
> state institutions of higher education and community colleges;
> (c) Develop an outcome-based framework for articulation and
> transfer that is derived from a common understanding of the crite-
> ria for general education curricula;

(d) Develop a seamless transfer of credits for all level 100 and 200 general education courses;

(e) Implement a statewide course applicability system that permits students and advisers to query and view online credit transfer options and conduct online degree auditing;

(f) Develop uniform standards for awarding college credit for advanced placement test scores; and

(g) Expand early college programs for 11th and 12th graders who earn college credit and intend to pursue a certificate or associate or baccalaureate degree. (Oregon Legislative Assembly, 2005)

The bill contained no funding to support institutions' efforts on this front but required an initial report on their progress toward fulfilling the criteria within 18 months.

There are a number of ways to deal with such a bill. The expectations included in it, in fact, embrace many practices that have been defined as important factors in supporting student success. Outcomes-based curriculum models support the assessment of learning, and clear program articulations simplify the challenge of student advising. One could decry the creation of mandates without funding, but one could also acknowledge that there is much in this bill that is already the legitimate business of public higher education. Student services leaders in states on the brink of or in the middle of legislative initiatives such as Oregon's have a ready-made case for the necessity of change. Leaders in states whose legislatures have not reached the point of pressuring for change on their public universities can use the specter of intrusive management to motivate change. In either case it is clear that the public is demanding or will demand improved results in terms of student success (Field, 2006). Student services leaders would be wise to become familiar with these conversations and build appropriate responses into their strategic plans. A leader who can put legislative demands in a positive light may well help his or her institution increase its standing in the public eye. Divisional leaders who help solve institutional problems gain value and influence with their peers and increase their ability to lead from within.

BUILDING SUPPORT FOR CHANGE

No leader should expect the announcement of planned change to be greeted by the cheers of employees. Change costs energy, and in organizations challenged by increasing demands and decreasing resources, energy is a resource that is often just as tight as public funding for higher education. When a leader introduces plans for change, even employees who will support the change in the end will have concerns. They have established routines that allow them to meet expectations, earn an income, and satisfy their needs for accomplishment. If an institution changes the rules, expectations, or tools, even the best will wonder how they will fit into the new order. When leaders understand that resistance to change is normal and assume the responsibility for leading the team to the future, change is possible.

Transitioning to a New Way of Working

The leader's challenge is to show employees how they can succeed in the new way of working. If new skills need to be learned, employees will need to understand how they are going to learn these skills. If new relationships need to be developed, they will need to understand the processes that will lead to these new relationships. Most important, employees will need to come to believe that they will be able to meet expectations in the new order. To address these needs, leaders need to accurately describe the new order, define new roles, and develop plans for current employees to move to the new way of working. This is best accomplished when those who have to change are part of the process of developing the plans for change. Involving employees in this planning increases their energy for change.

Nonetheless, there will be employees who cannot see themselves in the future. These may be staff members who understand the new expectations but do not accept them as legitimate. An example is the faculty member in an institution with rising expectations for scholarship who believes that research performance and teaching performance are mutually exclusive objectives. Another example is staff members who are nearing retirement and just do not want to adapt. (As the baby boomers near the end of their careers, the size of this group is growing.) Finally, these employees may include people who have been caught up in the changing nature of work in America. The organization may be moving from simple jobs requiring mechanical operations to integrated services that require cross-functional knowledge and multitasking.

Resistance to change is normal, and most of those who resist change can be helped. Leaders need to be patient as they lay out the case for change and engage their team members in moving toward changes. However, they also need to be prepared to encounter those who will not make the transition successfully. Leaders need to be ready to respond to those who will choose not to move with the organization. Unplanned attrition is very often one of the results of systemic change.

There will be costs associated with such attrition. Research shows that workers' compensation claims increase when employees who have not been required to perform to standards are held accountable. The number of early retirements may rise, resulting in increased hiring costs.

The cost of accommodation, however, is much higher. If leaders have carefully evaluated the case for change and planned well for the transition, the organization's performance will improve substantially. If leaders make adjustments for those who resist change because they do not have the will to focus on the goal, they will handicap the post-change organization and limit effectiveness. The lack of will might even cause the change efforts to fail.

Hiring for the New Order

Change is not the only catalyst for turnover in organizations. The number of retirements in higher education will be increasing over the next decade. Although the loss of institutional history and the cost of replacement are legitimate concerns, there has been perhaps no greater opportunity for change than the one that will occur naturally in the next 10 years.

Universities and colleges, especially in the public arena, have long sought to hire people who could do the jobs they were assigned. Seldom is the goal of hiring to find a superior performer. More often the goal is to fill the position—which in and of itself can be a challenge when universities cannot pay market rates for professional employees. Human resources practices and legal requirements have encouraged this approach. Position announcements emphasize minimum qualifications. Search committees look for a record of experience that is similar to the responsibilities associated with the position they are trying to fill. Moreover, future colleagues of the newly hired person tend to look for persons like themselves. These conservative forces limit the strength of an organization to the level of talent required for past performance. Conservative approaches to hiring will not develop the workforce needed to perform future work roles and face future challenges.

The studies conducted by Lyle Spencer, managing director of the Hay McBer Center for Research and Technology, show that a superior performer—defined as one whose performance is one standard deviation above the mean level of performance in like positions—contributes 19%–120% more value to an organization (Spencer, 1995). The percentage of value added by stronger performance depends on the complexity of the job. As redesigns lead us to integrate student services models with more complex roles, more and more student services jobs will be complex, rather than simple, in nature. The importance of hiring people with the ability to achieve superior levels of performance will only grow in significance.

Even if an organization seeks to hire superior performers, if it does so without changing hiring practices, it will not develop a workforce for the future. Evaluating applicants based on experience in roles that are being reshaped by change will not ensure future success. To ensure future success, colleges and universities need to hire team members with the skills for working in a world of continual change and continuously rising expectations. This requires that organizations base hiring decisions on competence rather than experience.

Through his research in high-tech, financial, military, and government organizations, Spencer (1995) has defined a set of competencies that are necessary for success in organizations that continually refocus and reorganize to meet changing expectations and conditions:

- *Achievement orientation:* thinking about doing better against a measurable standard of excellence

- *Analytical thinking:* the ability to take apart complex processes and issues

- *Customer service orientation:* initiating customer contact for the purpose of improving service rather than responding to customer input

- *Influence and persuasion:* bringing partners together to improve processes and results when you do not have the authority to compel cooperation

- *Initiative:* taking goal-directed action

- *Team orientation:* giving attention to the development of the team, not the accomplishment of the tasks assigned to the team

- *Discontinuous thinking:* the ability to look at radical out-of-the-box alternatives to the status quo

- *Technology know-how:* up-to-date knowledge of best practices in your area of responsibilities

Few of these competencies can be observed in the usual résumés submitted for jobs in student services. It is also hard to identify these competencies in traditional interviews, where applicants are asked to detail their attitudes and experience. At the very least, search committees should look for examples in past behavior that give evidence of particular abilities. There are powerful techniques for identifying competence, but they are seldom used, in part because of the skill required to implement them.

One technique is the scenario interview. In advance of these interviews, subject-matter experts create scenarios typical of the workplace so that applicants can demonstrate their abilities. Scenario-based interview approaches could include having the applicant role-play a team or customer interaction, prepare a plan, analyze a problem in real time, and so on.

Although a scenario interview offers a window for observing an applicant's competence, it is most important that members of the search committee understand and agree on what kind of competence is required. A committee with members who disagree about what they are looking for is likely to select the wrong applicant. In one example from a private university, the scenario required that applicants frame an approach to solving a problem that contained many uncertainties. The first applicant prepared an approach and presented a concrete solution to the panel. Upon further questioning, she opined that it was her job to make decisions and sell them to her team. The second applicant said he did not know what the answer was but that he would share his approach to resolving the uncertainties embedded in the scenario and detail how he would make his decision once the uncertainties were resolved. The search committee liked the decisiveness of the first applicant and, despite debate about the merits of making a decision with so many uncertainties unresolved, recommended that that she be hired. Two years later the new hire's employment was terminated largely due to the rigidity she brought to solving complex problems. The search was reopened and, surprisingly, the second applicant was hired. He is in place at the same institution to this day as his operation negotiates the twists and turns of an increasingly competitive and uncertain environment.

Student services leaders need to actively partner with human resources professionals in their organizations to define the competencies necessary both to operate in new work environments and to adapt to new ways of working. As new models are envisioned, human resources professionals will need to develop salary structures that allow superior performers to be hired at salaries that anticipate their greater contributions to the organization. Finally, team leaders will need to work with their teams, partners, and customers to design roles and processes that unleash employees' ability to serve.

No employees, even those with superior talent, will perform well if they are given poor tools to do their jobs. So, although hiring the best talent is essential for organizations to meet the challenges of the day, it is not sufficient without clear goals, efficient processes and tools, effective partnerships, and an ongoing process for performance review and improvement against objective benchmarks.

COPING WITH CHALLENGES THAT THREATEN SUSTAINED CHANGE

Functional leaders within colleges and universities could once focus solely on their own operations. They could meet with colleagues from other institutions to discuss best practices, but they did not need to attend closely to factors outside the university, let alone consider taking action to influence those factors. Today external forces increase the challenge of sustaining change and introduce change drivers, which may redirect plans for change and result in increased human and financial costs. Student services leaders must be much more attentive to movements outside their institutions to anticipate forces that will affect their plans for change.

Changes in Student Demographics

Most universities are aware that student demographics are changing. We know that women now enroll at higher rates than men, ethnic diversity is a powerful force on campus, and the need for psychological services is increasing in our student bodies. Student services have adjusted to address these changes.

Other forces on student services, however, are just beginning to have an impact, even though we have seen many of them coming for years. For example, university leaders have long known that the aging of the baby-boom generation would have a significant impact on communities, but it is only now that leaders in higher education are turning their attention to how the boomers' retirement behavior will impact their institutions. What, for example, will happen when we have multigenerational residential communities on our campuses? What might it mean for student services?

Observers have noted that students who take online courses are often those who also take face-to-face courses on campus. As higher education continues to move toward achieving learning outcomes as the objective of a university degree, delivery systems will likely change even more. As student relationships with the university increase in type and complexity, how will student services leaders help students engage with the institution? Do we have models for student engagement in such a complex environment?

Complexities of P–20

Student services leaders have long been attentive to the relationship between community colleges and universities. Academic student services have responded to issues of student preparedness for higher education. Increasingly, state governments are bringing together leaders of K–12 education, community colleges, and universities to develop integrated learning expectations, integrated data systems, and desired learning outcomes. The complexities and challenges associated with these efforts, called the "P–20 system of education," are enormous and affect nearly every component of student services.

Student services leaders cannot afford to be passive observers of these interactions. They must be leaders within their own institutions in developing an institutional approach to engaging with other sectors of the education enterprise. They must act with external partners to develop designs and approaches that do not do more harm than good. They must educate government leaders who press for change without understanding the cost of change. They must anticipate the impact of P–20 initiatives on expectations for the services they provide, and they must recognize that these forces could transform the nature of their business.

Higher Education Funding

In 1999 Neil Rudenstine, then president of Harvard, addressed the annual meeting of the American Council on Education. He began his remarks by noting that money was tight at Harvard. The audience of some 2,000 higher education leaders broke out in laughter. Rudenstine, who had not intended to tell a joke, paused and then said, "Well, everything is relative." Funding for higher education has always been tight, but the disinvestment in public higher education combined with the rising costs of traditional delivery systems has elevated this perennial issue to crisis proportions.

It is not just that money is tight. The public in many states no longer believes that higher education is worth the price it's asked to pay. To connect with students and families, leaders in higher education are going to have to frame their value proposition differently. Student services leaders are going to have to represent the value of their work in terms more familiar to business leaders and legislators. Doing so will require new approaches to valuing student services, new tools for analysis, and new partnerships between campus leaders. This challenge is compounded by the changing demographics of the student population. Different constituencies value different things about their university experience. Campus leaders have to learn the language of these new constituencies and become truly multilingual in expressing the value of higher education. To fail in this task would force leaders to continue to do more and more with less and less until they are expected to do everything with nothing.

Technology

The advent of new technologies is usually greeted with excitement as we consider the new things they will enable us to do. Then we discover the hidden consequences associated with those technologies. Today the introduction of new technologies has far outpaced our ability to figure out how to use them. Student services leaders are being forced to lead change in a technological environment fraught with uncertainty and risk.

The cost of new technologies—whether it is the cost of replacement technologies or the huge cost of enterprise resource management systems—is leading to a universe of haves and have-nots. Large universities can afford enterprise systems that support the seamless integration of business and student services. Many smaller universities cannot. Although portal technology is a given on many campuses across the country, underfunded institutions struggle with costlier approaches because they cannot afford the transition to more effective ways of working.

Student services leaders will have to join with other campus leaders to match strategic objectives to the institution's approach for managing technology costs. Among the challenges they will face is what is becoming known as "vendor-driven" increases in the cost of technology. In these cases the institution could function well with its current versions of software, but the vendors plan to discontinue support for them, which forces institutions to accept costly updates with little improvement in functionality.

The role of technology in the delivery of learning and student services will continue to increase. Student services leaders cannot afford to respond to circumstances that overtake them. More important, campus leaders cannot meet this challenge alone. To begin to drive the development of technology that addresses their strategic needs, higher education leaders will need to act in concert with each other. The wild card in this game is how students will respond to various technologies. To steer a course through this rocky channel, student services leaders and student leaders will need to work together to design new approaches to service while continuing to offer affordable opportunities for higher education.

CONCLUSION

Change in student services will happen. External factors will force colleges and universities to become more student centered. Student services leaders will face all the traditional challenges that leaders of change have always faced. Today there are new tools and new complexities that affect the change management process. Student services leaders will need to develop effective partnerships with campus colleagues, attend to the environment outside their institutions, work in new ways with student leaders, and be proactive in shaping the environments in which they lead.

Success will come as leaders define new workforce expectations, hire to those expectations, and turn technology into an asset rather than a threat to service quality. University presidents will need to hire student services leaders as much for their courage and insight as for their experience in an array of student services roles. Courage, candor, analytical ability, and persuasive skills will all be required. Hiring the right leaders for the job will make all the difference.

REFERENCES

Allen, N. H., & Potter, E. H. (1985, August). *U.S. Coast Guard efforts to support unit cohesiveness: Studied neglect in sympathy with excellence.* Paper presented at the meeting of the American Psychological Association, Los Angeles, CA.

American Association of State Colleges and Universities. (2005). *Student success in state colleges and universities: A matter of culture and leadership.* Washington, DC: Author.

The Education Trust. (2007). *College results online.* Retrieved June 22, 2007, from www.collegeresults.org

Field, K. (2006, July 21). Colleges propose accountability system. *The Chronicle of Higher Education*, p. A25.

National Institute of Standards and Technology. (2004). *2004 award winner: Kenneth W. Monfort College of Business.* Retrieved June 22, 2007, from www.nist.gov/public_affairs/Monfort_PDF_final.pdf

National Institute of Standards and Technology. (2006). *Baldrige National Quality Program: 2006 education criteria for performance excellence.* Gaithersburg, MD: Author.

Oregon Legislative Assembly. (2005). *Senate Bill 342.* Retrieved June 22, 2007, from www.leg.state.or.us/05reg/measures/sb0300.dir/sb0342.en.html

Spencer, L. M., Jr. (1995). *Reengineering human resources.* New York, NY: Wiley.

U.S. Department of Education. (2006). *A test of leadership: Charting the future of U.S. higher education.* Washington, DC: Author.

PART II

CONNECTING SERVICES

Part II furthers the concept of creating and maintaining a student-centered culture by involving the campus community. Taking the baton from Part I and knowing today's students, these chapters discuss admitting students to succeed and helping them make good academic and career decisions. They explain how to involve the campus community in student learning through physical and virtual one-stop student services, through technology, and through individualized academic and career planning. These developments have revolutionized the way colleges and universities offer services to an ever growing and diverse student population.

6 | PUTTING STUDENTS FIRST IN COLLEGE ADMISSIONS AND ENROLLMENT MANAGEMENT

DON HOSSLER

The history of college admissions and enrollment management is replete with periods of intense competition for students and concerns about student persistence. Even after World War II, with large numbers of GIs pursuing college degrees, the expansion of community colleges and regional four-year institutions resulted in such a competition for students, which led to increasingly complex and ethically dubious admissions practices. In the past two decades, the failure of some institutions to retain and graduate a sufficient number of students has garnered attention and criticism. As a result, some state governments and the federal government have used, or have proposed using, graduation rates as measures of institutional effectiveness. With institutions struggling to achieve enrollment objectives in this competitive environment, tensions related to admissions and persistence complicate and compete with the widely valued goal of putting students first in educational institutions' policies and practices.

What does it mean to put students first in college admissions and enrollment management? Does it mean that admissions professionals should admit only students who "fit" into their institution's culture? Does it mean they should admit only students who seem certain to graduate? Does it mean that institutional policies should be geared to recruiting students and enabling them to make a successful transition to college and to persist until graduation? The answer to all these questions is yes.

This chapter focuses on areas of student engagement that are commonly found among the responsibilities of enrollment management professionals. Because enrolled students help generate tuition and state monetary support for public institutions, many enrollment managers face real institutional imperatives to enroll and retain a sufficient number of students to ensure adequate revenue to keep the institution healthy and vital. I have never met an enrollment professional who did not believe that he or she was helping students make sound college choices or who did not want to make sure every admitted student succeeds, but enrollment managers are under pressure to bring in and to retain students.

Three broad strands of research and guidelines for good practice inform this discussion of putting students first in areas related to enrollment management. These include theory and research in student-institution fit, theory and research in student retention, and good-practice guidelines derived from research and the principles of good practice outlined by the National Association for College Admission Counseling (NACAC).

For some institutions, the trouble is often not that admissions professionals aren't trying to put students first but rather that it is not entirely clear how to be certain whether they've succeeded. For other institutions, more can be done to be equitable and to put students first. The mix of uncertainties regarding what it means to put students first and institutional pressures exerted in the area of enrollment management presents a complex set of issues for enrollment professionals as well as other senior campus administrators. The next section examines the institutional pressures faced by admissions professionals at many colleges. This is followed by an examination of student-institution fit, a review of the research on student retention, and institutional practices associated with successful student engagement and how they relate to the concerns of enrollment managers. The chapter closes with my reflections on the complex tensions enrollment managers face in their efforts to put students first and possible approaches toward resolving these tensions.

THE INSTITUTIONAL LANDSCAPE AND INSTITUTIONAL IMPERATIVES

In enrollment management it should never be forgotten that the number of students enrolled is linked with the financial health and vitality of most institutions of higher education. Public institutions are concerned about enrollment because the number of students enrolled affects both their state appropriations and the amount of tuition revenue they garner. Most private institutions receive approximately 80% of all revenue from the tuition students pay (Ehrenberg, 2000). If a small private college that serves a regional student market misses its enrollment target by 50 students, it might have to cut more than $1,000,000 out of its budget because of the loss of tuition and room and board. A reduction like this might result in layoffs of administrative and support staff. On the other hand, at some elite universities a class that is 20 students larger than the desired number can be viewed as a significant failure on the part of an admissions office. At many colleges and universities the pressure to increase the quality or diversity of the student body can also create strong imperatives for admissions professionals. None of these tasks is easily surmounted. There is a great deal of competition, for example, for top academic students and students of color.

The pressure to hit an exact enrollment target, to increase enrollment for additional revenue, to raise the average SAT score for an entering class, or to increase the proportion of enrolling African American students can present difficult challenges, and in this context, discerning what is best for students is not always easy. In addition, on many campuses the admissions office may be charged with achieving two or three of these goals simultaneously, increasing the pressure and difficulty. It is easier, for example, to increase quality if a smaller class can be recruited. It is easier to be selective when fewer students need to be admitted.

Other factors—such as an institution's mission, location, wealth, and prestige—also influence the extent to which it has the interest and capacity to admit only students who will succeed. For example, the mission of community colleges, which have few admissions requirements, is to serve anyone in their region who desires to enroll. Students enroll for many reasons, including to earn a degree or a certificate in a desired area of expertise, to enhance workforce skills, and to grow personally. Thus, many students enroll not planning to earn a degree (Dougherty, 1992). For community colleges, putting students first could be interpreted as a mandate to serve as many community residents as possible, regardless of their interests, abilities, or goals. In most instances enrollment and student affairs professionals at community colleges do not know the educational goals of many of their students. Therefore, it is very difficult to determine whether an institution has enrolled students who fit and can be successful if there is no way of determining whether a student has achieved his or her goals.

At the other end of the continuum are highly selective, elite private institutions such as Yale, Stanford, Williams, and Amherst—institutions that expend extraordinary amounts of time and effort to select an entering class of students they believe will fit, be successful, make positive contributions to the campus community, and find their educational experience satisfying. These institutions have high freshman-to-sophomore persistence rates and high graduation rates. The admissions staffs at institutions like these spend most of their time in the spring poring over information on applicants who have a serious chance of being admitted. The staff looks for students who will bring academic, geographic, ethnic, socioeconomic, and artistic diversity to their campuses. The admissions screening process is intended to shape the class and to admit students who will be successful in these challenging academic environments. However, from an empirical perspective it is difficult to determine whether a well-balanced and successful class is the result of the careful admissions process or is simply a function of the type of students who are admitted. Elite institutions admit only those students who have earned good grades in high school, who have high standardized test scores, and who are highly motivated. In addition, most of these students come from affluent and well-educated families. All these characteristics are attributes of students who are more likely to persist and graduate.

Most four-year institutions lie between these two ends of the continuum. For these schools, the extent to which the admissions office can focus on enrolling students it believes will be a good match—as opposed to ensuring there are enough students to fill all the chairs in the classrooms—is a function of the desired size of the entering class, the selectivity of the institution, and the size of the applicant pool. Small private institutions and regional public institutions that primarily attract students who live within 100 miles of their location and do not use selective admissions criteria are likely to be enrollment and tuition driven. Many commuter institutions also fall into this category. Colleges and universities in these broad categories are more likely to focus their efforts on enrolling a requisite number of students than on student-institution fit. Public flagship institutions and private residential campuses that are more selective are more likely to have an applicant pool sufficiently large enough for admissions professionals to devote more effort to carefully reviewing all applications and admitting students who are more likely to be successful.

The mission of institutions and the enrollment challenges they face exert a strong influence on enrollment management, but within this context, colleges and universities can make many efforts to serve students. Community colleges make heavy use of instruments such as the ACT COMPASS exam or the College Board's ACCUPLACER to assess the skills and abilities of entering students and make sure they are placed in courses in which they can be successful. Community colleges have a long history of providing excellent remedial education services and a wide array of courses to meet the interests and needs of their diverse student body. Most two- and four-year institutions also provide a wide array of services to meet the needs of entering students. These include orientation programs designed to help students make a successful transition to college. Tutoring, academic support, career planning, academic advising, and counseling services are also intended to put students first and help them make academic, career, and individual choices that will enable them to be successful college students.

LOOKING FOR A STUDENT-INSTITUTION FIT THAT PUTS STUDENTS FIRST

In the college admissions literature it is common to find recommendations that admissions professionals recruit only students who will fit. Among the theories of student-institution fit developed over the years, several focus on the environment's role in shaping students' behaviors and, thus, in affecting the degree of their involvement at the institution. Barker (1968), for example, posits that smaller campuses and smaller classes force students to be more involved to maintain the setting. Astin (1968) suggests that there are somewhat distinct peer environments, classroom environments, administrative environments, and physical environments—each of which shapes student behaviors. The more students' activities are consistent with the norms embedded in these environments, the greater the degree of student-institution fit. Cope and Hannah (1975) take these concepts one step further, arguing that factors like a poor choice of college, low quality of instruction, excessive institutional bureaucracy, or conflict between personal and institutional values can lead to a lack of congruency and compel students to drop out.

Clark and Trow (1966) outline what has become a popular theory of student-institution fit. They posit that colleges and universities are composed of student subcultures: the collegiate, the academic, the vocational, and the nonconformist. Small campuses may be composed of just one or two of these subcultures; large campuses probably are made up of all four of them. The authors suggest that if students cannot find a subculture that matches their orientation, they are more likely to drop out.

Additional theories of student-institution fit include Moos's (1974) classification of behavior settings, Pervin's (1968) person-environment transactional model, and Holland's (1973) personality theory. All these theories provide interesting conceptual leads for how students interact with their collegiate environments. However, efforts to empirically test and apply these theories toward enhancing student persistence have not proved successful. To date, no empirical studies have established the efficacy of these theories. Therefore, despite their intuitive appeal, they do not provide concrete guidance for serving students better during the college admissions process or for improving students' educational experiences and thus enhancing their satisfaction and persistence.

In recent years an approach has emerged from the world of marketing to operationalize the concept of student-institution fit. Many colleges and universities have started to use software based on the principles of geographic information systems (GIS) and derived from census data, SAT or ACT records, and other sources to identify the lifestyle, family income, and post-secondary educational interests of high school students (Litten, 1984; Mora, 2004; Murray, 1991). Using these databases, institutions have been able to identify sets of student characteristics that predispose them to be interested in specific colleges or universities. These marketing tools help identify prospective students who might be attracted, for example, to a small college with an emphasis on the arts or to a large public university with a major sports program and an active Greek life.

Student affairs professionals often react negatively to the idea of using tools developed for the for-profit world of marketing when considering college admissions and student-institution fit. A common fear is that the GIS tools will be used to recruit students just like the students currently enrolled, thus reducing the campus's heterogeneity and diversity. However, these same tools can be used in a strategic fashion, for example, to try to increase the number of Hispanic students or the number of out-of-state students. Such uses raise interesting ethical questions for admissions professionals and senior campus policymakers. Is it fair, in an effort to make an institution more diverse and less homogeneous, to recruit a selected group of students because there are very few students like them at the campus and enrolling them as a group increases the odds that they may not feel comfortable or find the campus to be a good fit? Also, many colleges and universities located in rural areas or in ethnically homogenous regions struggle with developing a diverse student body. To increase the odds of enrolling students who will find more students like them, thus enhancing fit, should institutions decrease efforts to enroll a more diverse student body?

There are, however, other ways that colleges and universities attempt to help students find a successful fit. Many institutions use their institutional research offices to identify the characteristics of students who are likely to be successful and of those who are more likely to struggle or drop out. Often students from small high schools or rural areas, students who are undecided about their major, and students who are first-generation college students are more at risk at the time they are admitted and matriculate. Once institutions have identified some of the characteristics of at-risk students, they often design special programs to help those students succeed. These may come in the form of targeted orientation programs, academic advising and career counseling services with focused outreach activities, and other forms of support services for at-risk populations.

RETAINING STUDENTS

Several theories and models of student retention have been proposed (Bean, 1990; Braxton, Hirschy, & McClendon, 2004; Terenzini & Pascarella, 1980; Tinto, 1993). The theory developed and refined by Tinto is the most widely used. More recently Braxton has devoted considerable effort to advancing retention research (Braxton et al., 2004). Most of the widely used retention theories share important key constructs and ideas to enhance student persistence. They all suggest the importance of a smooth transition to college; early socialization experiences for students during recruitment and the first year of college; high levels of interaction with socializing agents of the campus such as faculty, academic advisors, and other institutional administrators and staff; many opportunities for students to form strong peer networks; academic support programs for students who need them; and a pervasive campus culture that communicates high levels of care and concern for students. These ideas provide conceptual starting points for enrollment and student affairs professionals to create an array of important student services. For example, orientation programs should focus on helping students understand what kinds of behaviors and insider knowledge are needed to be successful. Campus administrators should create incentives for faculty to use engaging teaching techniques, promote high standards in the classroom, and provide students with timely feedback about their academic performance. Student life units should constantly search for ways to involve students in formal and informal organizations, one-time events, student government, and so forth. Retention research provides a wealth of leads for the kinds of programs enrollment managers, working with colleagues in academic and student affairs, should create to enhance student persistence and graduation.

A major problem for enrollment managers, however, is that to date it has proved difficult to ascertain the effects of such initiatives on students. Research on the efficacy of campus retention interventions is limited. After reviewing the published research on the effects of such interventions, Patton, Morelon, Whitehead, and Hossler (2006) conclude that surprisingly little research has been conducted. They found moderate levels of support for the following types of retention interventions: learning communities, academic support programs, programmatic efforts to enhance student-faculty interaction, and orientation and University 101 classes that help acculturate students and smooth the transition from high school to college.

Although enrollment managers appear to have some solid leads on ways to provide better services for students, the lack of certainty about the efficacy of many types of retention initiatives can leave them in a quandary. Because it is difficult to measure student-institution fit, and it is not certain how many institutional interventions actually improve persistence rates, enrollment managers face potential tensions about what is best for students and what is best for the image and prestige of the institution. Day to day, enrollment managers often have only gross measures of retention to work with, such as first-to-second-year persistence rates or graduation rates. The benchmarks that most faculty members, senior administrators, trustees, and alumni use for first-to-second-year persistence rates and graduation rates are part of the formula used in *U.S. News & World Report*'s *America's Best Colleges* (www.usnews.com/usnews/edu/college/rankings/rankindex_brief.php). The dilemma arises because sources like *U.S. News* or the web site of The Education Trust (www.collegeresults.org) do not include measures of engagement or other institutional factors that shape student success after enrollment. Rather, these sources rely solely on student and institutional characteristics—such as measures of student ability, socioeconomic status, and institutional selectivity—to rate how well institutions retain and graduate students. Because simple persistence and graduation rates are highly correlated with measures of institutional selectivity and wealth, the ratio of full-time faculty to students, and being a primarily residential rather than a commuter campus, these measures always make highly selective institutions look good; less selective commuter two-year and four-year institutions do not fare as well. Table 6.1 provides a comparison of graduation rates across an array of private and public two- and four-year colleges.

In lieu of more detailed information about the extent to which a college or university has implemented a successful set of retention efforts, the most obvious step enrollment managers can take to improve their retention rates is to enroll fewer students with low academic indicators. This can lead to enrolling fewer low-income students, fewer students of color, and fewer students from rural backgrounds.

As admissions selectivity declines at commuter institutions, the time students take to graduate increases. Thus, using traditional formulas for determining retention rates for community colleges may be unfair. As already noted, many students who enroll in them never plan to graduate because they have other goals.

Table 6.1   **Comparison of Graduation Rates at Selected Private and Public Two- and Four-Year Colleges**

Institution	Average SAT Score for First-Year Students	Residential Institution?	Graduate Rates After Six Years
Princeton University	1480	Yes	96.7%
Kenyon College	1325	Yes	84.3%
University of Colorado–Boulder	1165	Yes	66.2%
Wayne State University	945	No	31.7%
Average community college	N/A	No	28.9%

Sources: ACT (2005–2006) and The Education Trust (2007).

The broad variety of institutional missions, levels of selectivity, and sizes of markets from which institutions draw students complicate the issue of putting students first. How do enrollment managers advocate for programs to help students succeed when they know that not all these students will graduate and that the president and the board of trustees will be reading the annual issue of *America's Best Colleges*? The situation would look very different to one of the commuter campuses of the City College of New York than it would to Vanderbilt University, in Nashville, Tennessee.

Despite these complexities, institutions of higher education devote a great deal of energy to help students be successful and persist until graduation. Most colleges and universities have retention committees, often a senior administrator whose primary responsibility is focusing on student retention, and an array of programs and policies devoted to enhancing student success and persistence. Many of the types of programmatic initiatives have already been mentioned, including academic advising, academic support and supplemental instruction programs, career planning, and orientation programs. In addition, student activities, efforts to enhance student-faculty interaction, early-warning systems, and even financial aid and work study programs are offered by most colleges and universities in an effort to retain students. The success of such programs is not always certain, but retention initiatives and policies have, arguably, become one of the most important areas in enrollment management and a good example of efforts to put students first.

EFFECTIVE, FAIR, AND ETHICAL CAMPUS POLICIES TO PROMOTE STUDENT SUCCESS

The richest vein of research on campus policies that promote student engagement and success comes from the work of Kuh and his colleagues over the past two decades (Kuh, Kinzie, Schuh, Whitt, & Associates, 2005; Kuh, Schuh, Whitt, & Associates, 1991). Their work offers insights into effective educational practices in all facets of the college experience. In addition, principles for good practice in college admissions and enrollment management are provided by the NACAC.

Kuh et al. (2005) offer several recommendations that can help institutions serve students and put them first as they move through the college decision-making process and into their educational experience, including the following:

- Provide acculturation experiences to enhance student success by preparing students for the institution's expectations during the recruitment process and include strong transition and orientation programs.

- Enact institutional policies that provide tangible academic and social support from multiple sources for students who need it.

- Have a strong sense of institutional mission and a sense of integrity about the institution's goals and purpose. (Although not stated explicitly, this is a recurring theme throughout the work on student success by Kuh et al., 2005.)

In addition to these recommendations, the NACAC *Statement of Principles of Good Practice* (2006) has several relevant recommendations that follow naturally from the need for institutions to have a sense of integrity about their goals and purposes and how these relate to good practices in areas related to enrollment management:

- State clearly and precisely the requirements for secondary school preparation, admissions tests, and transfer student admission.

- Furnish data describing the currently enrolled freshman class, and describe all members of the enrolling freshman class in a published profile. Subgroups within the profile may be presented separately because of their unique character or special circumstances.

- Permit first-year candidates for fall admission to choose, without penalty, among offers of admission and financial aid until May 1 (a postmark date). Colleges that solicit commitments to offers of admission or financial assistance before May 1 may do so provided those offers include a clear statement that written requests for extensions until May 1 will be granted and that such requests will not jeopardize a student's status for admission or financial aid. Candidates admitted under an early-decision program are a recognized exception to this provision.

It is hard to determine the extent to which individual colleges and universities are following these guidelines. Although there are case studies on this topic, there are no definitive surveys that assess the use of good practices in many of the areas discussed by Kuh and his colleagues. In their book on the first-year experience, Upcraft, Gardner, Barefoot, and Associates (2005) draw attention to the important role of orientation and University 101 courses in acculturating new students to the colleges and universities of their choice.

Practitioner-oriented journals, books, and publications also include exhortations to create programs that provide both academic and nonacademic support for enrolled students, especially first-year students. However, the extent to which campuses create and fund these kinds of programs at a level where they can be successful is simply unknown at this time. I have raised questions about the amount of effort, resources, and institutional focus going into campus-based efforts to enhance student persistence and graduation (Hossler, 2006). Patton et al. (2006) raise similar questions. A recurring question is whether most colleges and universities subscribe to the "laundry list" approach to student retention programming—with campus professionals perusing recommendations from the literature to increase persistence and graduation rates; determining that their campuses already have these orientation, advising, and student support programs; and thus concluding, "We do that." The reality is that these professionals often have very little idea of how well the programs are funded, planned, and executed and, thus, very little idea of how effective they are.

Even though there is insufficient evidence about the effects of academic and student life programs designed to benefit students, most two- and four-year colleges continue to offer an array of programs. Scholarship from Kuh, Kinzie, Buckley, Bridges, and Hayek (2006) provides ample evidence that colleges and universities are attempting to offer programs and services that will help students make a successful transition and subsequently be successful. The lack of success on this front may mean institutions are not effectively organizing and managing their efforts, or it may mean that the issues associated with student transitions and subsequent persistence are complicated and not as easily addressed through institutional interventions as we might hope.

Currently there are some important admissions practices and policies that have attracted a good deal of attention by examining enrollment managers and their efforts to find balance in the matter of what comes first—students or institutions. These practices deal with the accuracy of admissions information and with early-decision and early-action programs. I will now describe each of these practices and discuss their implications.

Accuracy of Information

The accuracy of the information colleges and universities use to describe themselves has raised concerns for more than 30 years. (Indeed, in the 1970s the federal government considered enacting legislation about the accuracy of such information.) These concerns range from the correctness of descriptions of the academic and social programs offered by institutions to the truthfulness of information submitted to ranking organizations like *U.S. News & World Report*'s *America's Best Colleges*. It is difficult to get objective data on the extent to which colleges and universities provide accurate information. Without empirical studies we are left with the concerns admissions officers discuss in hallways and meetings. Such concerns often include the following:

- Not reporting the entrance exam scores of students admitted conditionally or during the spring or summer semesters because of low scores or high school grades enables an institution to garner a higher ranking in college guidebooks.

- Using a two-part admissions application can help give the impression that an institution is more selective. In such situations, the first part of the application is shorter and costs students little or nothing to submit. If students fill this part out but don't complete the second part, the institution can still count them as full applicants before rejecting them.

- Reducing the amount of information a college provides about admissions requirements encourages more students to apply so that more can be rejected, which again increases the institution's ranking in college guidebooks.

It is difficult to determine how frequently these practices are used. Most colleges and universities do not use such deceptive practices, but there is no doubt that some institutions do.

The use of misleading data for rankings reports will probably continue. However, there are no studies available showing how pervasive this problem may be. The Association for Institutional Research and the National Center for Education Statistics make every effort to improve institutional reporting of data. In addition, the federal Sarbanes-Oxley Act of 2002 is now being brought to bear on nonprofits, which may increase pressure on campus administrators to accurately report data used in rankings publications. Abuses and the lack of transparency in institutional practices in these areas are troubling. It seems unlikely that senior campus administrators would openly support a practice of providing inaccurate, false, or misleading information about their admissions requirements, the types of students enrolled, or the application process. Yet incorrect reporting continues to happen, and it erodes the public trust in higher education.

Early-Decision and Early-Action Admissions Programs and the Candidate's Reply Date

In 1948 members of the College Board agreed to establish what has become known as the Candidate's Reply Date. Initially set for June 15, in 1961 it was moved to May 1. The Candidate's Reply Date was established for two reasons: first, to give all students ample time to decide what college or university they would attend without pressure and, second, to give colleges and universities a definite date by which they would be able to predict how many students would be enrolling the following fall. But different institutions follow different practices; as a result, the May 1 deadline has lost much of its utility.

The most visible challenges to the Candidate's Reply Date come from early-decision and early-action admissions programs. These programs allow students to apply early, usually sometime in the late fall. Most early-decision (ED) programs are binding, which means that students can apply to only one campus during the ED process, and if admitted, they must enroll at that campus. In early-action (EA) admissions, a student applies to a school in the fall of the senior year and requests an early application review and notification of admission. If accepted, the student is not obligated to attend that institution and can still apply to other colleges during the regular admissions cycle. ED and EA programs are offered primarily by highly selective private colleges and universities; thus, most of the students who apply through them are good students.

The advantage to students applying through ED and EA programs is that they can learn much earlier whether they are admitted—which is likely a positive outcome. However, these programs have many potentially negative outcomes. The purpose of the May 1 deadline was to reduce some of the stress on students so they would not rush or feel pressured to make a decision about their college choice. Because the competition to be admitted to elite colleges has become so intense, the timing of ED and EA programs defeats the purpose of the Candidate's Reply Date.

These EA programs, however, are not the only recruitment practices undermining the purpose of the Candidate's Reply Date. Many institutions offer inducements, such as early course registration or early choice of housing, for students who pay early-enrollment deposits. Some colleges and universities now offer scholarships to students and require them to accept the scholarship before May 1 or lose it. These admissions and recruitment programs create a labyrinth of enrollment dates that have made the May 1 deadline increasingly meaningless.

ED and EA programs have other negative effects. There is ample evidence (Avery, Fairbanks, & Zeckhauser, 2003) that these programs result in significant advantages to students from affluent backgrounds. Very few ED and EA students come from low-income or minority backgrounds. Because these admissions programs are more complex and start earlier, affluent and well-educated families are more likely to know about them and to be able to afford private college counselors to help their children successfully traverse them.

Colleges and universities use these programs because they help them secure early-enrollment commitments for large numbers of good students—thus raising their yield rates and, consequently, their rankings. Although the advantages of these programs to institutions are clear, their effects on students raise questions about whether they are positive examples of putting students first.

It would be misleading, however, to suggest that all colleges and universities engage in these practices or to overlook the many efforts that are under way to address excesses in these areas of enrollment management. The issue of early decision has garnered a great deal of attention. Because of many of the negative outcomes of these programs, the University of North Carolina recently ended its ED admissions program (Lucido, 2002). More recently the president of Yale University called for the end of ED and EA schemes (Levin, 2003). In the fall of 2006 both Harvard and Princeton announced that they were dropping ED programs. The decision of these two leading institutions seems certain to pressure institutions that continue to use preferential admissions programs (Jaschik, 2006). Nevertheless, there is still much debate about ED programs, and it is important to note that only 25% of all four-year colleges employ some variant of early admissions (Hawkins & Clinedinst, 2006).

TENSIONS ABOUND EVERYWHERE

It should be evident by now that there is no dearth of theoretical and research-based insights, as well as guidelines for good practice, concerning ways enrollment managers can put students first in their practices. However, like most areas of university administration, our work lives are complicated. It would be easy for academic affairs and student affairs administrators to consider the discussion in this chapter and argue that students should always come first—and they should. But there is another question: Which students should come first? If enrollments fall because of efforts to enhance student quality or to focus more attention on student diversity, academic and nonacademic program budgets may be cut and currently enrolled students will suffer. If an institution that enrolls a relatively small number of students of color uses market-oriented models of student-institution fit and comes to the conclusion that students of color are not naturally attracted to the environment it offers, should it stop recruiting them? Or if retention studies conducted on a student body find that students of color and women from rural parts of the state are less likely to persist, should the institution stop recruiting these students? Should community colleges, founded on the mission of access to all local residents, stop admitting underprepared students because they do not persist despite a robust array of academic support programs? Putting students first can corner institutions in seemingly intractable complexities.

In other respects, however, the solutions seem more straightforward. Even if an institution might lose some students, providing inaccurate information to raise an institution's ranking is indefensible. It is hard to argue that ED and EA admissions programs are best for the majority of students, and it is evident that the benefits to institutions are primarily self-serving and on the margins of their missions. It is also hard to make a case for the current chaos around the Candidate's Reply Date.

Consensus is growing that there is too strong an impetus for enrollment management practices to put institutions, as opposed to students, first—as exemplified in a stinging critique of enrollment management practices in a recent issue of *The Atlantic Monthly* (Quirk, 2005). In 2005 and 2006 several professional associations held special meetings focusing on ethics in college admissions and enrollment management. It is possible the pendulum swinging between putting institutions first and putting students first is beginning to swing back in the direction of students.

CONCLUSION

Several recommendations flow from this discussion. Perhaps the most important is that enrollment professionals, as well as student affairs and academic administrators, should be thoughtful and reflective. Organizational lives are often messy environments with competing and conflicting goals. As is evident in this chapter, it is possible that doing what seems right for one group of students can have a negative impact on another group of students. Simplistic recommendations for complex issues seldom achieve any desirable goals.

Enrollment professionals need to be good stewards of the institutions that they serve. The varied missions of two- and four-year colleges and universities mean that what is right for students (or for institutions) in one setting might not be optimal in another. Mission and purpose matter when determining the best course of action to take.

There are ample insights from theory and research to help enrollment managers develop campus-based programs to ensure that students are well informed about the characteristics of various colleges and universities and what it takes to be successful at them. Indeed, the simple part may be identifying campus interventions to serve students. More complicated is securing sufficient resources and the institutional focus to effectively implement programs once they are identified. Here more may be less. Enrollment professionals may be better off implementing a small number of programs well than trying to sustain several inadequately funded and poorly implemented programs.

Ultimately, enrollment management professionals, like other groups of campus administrators, serve at the pleasure of the president and the board of trustees. A decision to implement an ED program or to engage in deceptive practices in admissions information may begin with recommendations from the enrollment management unit. But more often such decisions are shaped by senior campus administrators, who are at least consulted before a final decision is made. It is the duty of enrollment professionals to address the ethical dilemmas embedded in their policies and practices. Raising questionable practices with senior campus administrators or the board of trustees is one of the major responsibilities of all senior enrollment professionals. In the context of many other decisions about enrollment practices, individual professionals must determine the appropriate steps to take.

Trustees should also become more involved in the admissions process. It is common for private institutions to have trustee committees that deal with enrollment issues; it is uncommon for public institutions to have such committees. Having a single trustee committee that focuses on the full array of issues makes it more likely that its members will have a complete understanding of institutional practices and their implications. For both public and private institutions, trustees need to be better informed about national concerns in these areas and be proactive in requesting reports that fully disclose recruitment practices on their campuses.

After many years of observing institutions during my research, consulting, and service as a senior enrollment manager, I believe that most institutions make the right decisions to put most of the students first most of the time. Occasionally, however, a college or university president or an enrollment manager is so anxious to prove how good she is that she is willing to take dubious shortcuts to gather the proof. In the process she makes it clear that she is putting herself and her institution—not students—first.

REFERENCES

ACT. (2005–2006). *Retention/attrition analysis report.* Retrieved June 22, 2207, from www.act.org/research/services/predict/retent.html

Astin, A. W. (1968). *The college environment.* Washington, DC: American Council on Education.

Avery, C., Fairbanks, A., & Zeckhauser, R. (2003). *The early admissions game: Joining the elite.* Cambridge, MA: Harvard University Press.

Barker, R. G. (1968). *Ecological psychology: Concepts and methods for studying the environment of human behavior.* Stanford, CA: Stanford University Press.

Bean, J. P. (1990). Using retention research in enrollment management. In D. Hossler, J. P. Bean, & Associates, *The strategic management of college enrollments* (pp. 170–185). San Francisco, CA: Jossey-Bass.

Braxton, J. M., Hirschy, A. S., & McClendon, S. A. (2004). *Understanding and reducing college student departure* (ASHE Higher Education Report, 30[3]). San Francisco, CA: Jossey-Bass.

Clark, B. R., & Trow, M. (1966). The organizational context. In T. Newcomb & E. Wilson (Eds.), *College peer groups: Problems and prospects for research* (pp. 12–70). Chicago, IL: Aldine.

Cope, R. G., & Hannah, W. (1975). *Revolving college doors: The causes and consequences of dropping out, stopping out, and transferring.* New York, NY: Wiley.

Dougherty, K. J. (1992, March/April). Community colleges and baccalaureate attainment. *Journal of Higher Education, 63*(2), 188–214.

The Education Trust. (2007). *College results online.* Retrieved June 22, 2007, from www.collegeresults.org

Ehrenberg, R. (2000, March). *Financial prospects for American higher education in the first decade of the twenty-first century.* Paper presented at the annual meeting of the American Council on Education, Chicago, IL.

Hawkins, D. A., & Clinedinst, M. (2006). *State of college admission, 2006.* Alexandria, VA: National Association for College Admission Counseling.

Holland, J. L. (1973). *Making vocational choices.* Englewood Cliffs, NJ: Prentice Hall.

Hossler, D. (2006, Fall). Managing student retention: Is the glass half full, half empty, or simply empty? *College and University, 81*(2), 11–14.

Jaschik, S. (2006, September 19). Princeton ends early decision. *Inside Higher Education.* Retrieved June 22, 2007, from http://insidehighered.com/news/2006/09/19/princeton

Kuh, G. D., Kinzie, J., Buckley, J. A., Bridges, B. K., & Hayek, J. C. (2006). *What matters to student success: A review of the literature.* Paper presented at the National Symposium on Postsecondary Student Success, Washington, DC.

Kuh, G. D., Kinzie, J., Schuh, J. H., Whitt, E. J., & Associates (2005). *Student success in college: Creating conditions that matter.* San Francisco, CA: Jossey-Bass.

Kuh, G. D., Schuh, J. H., Whitt, E. J., & Associates. (1991). *Involving colleges: Successful approaches to fostering student learning and development outside the classroom.* San Francisco, CA: Jossey-Bass.

Levin, R. (2003, February). *Rethinking college admissions.* Speech to the annual meeting of the National Association of Independent Schools, New York, NY.

Litten, L. H. (1984). Extending the applications of portfolio analysis in higher education: The student body portfolio and enrollment management. *Liberal Education, 70*(2), 167–181.

Lucido, J. (2002, Fall). Eliminating early decision: Forming the snowball and rolling it downhill. *The College Board Review, 197,* 4–29.

Moos, R. H. (1974). Systems for the assessment and classification of human environments: An overview. In R. H. Moos & P. M. Insel (Eds.), *Issues in social ecology: Human milieus* (pp. 5–29). Palo Alto, CA: National Press Books.

Mora, V. J. (2004). Applications of GIS in admissions and targeting recruiting efforts. In D. Teodorescu (Ed.), *New directions for institutional research: No. 120. Using geographic information systems in institutional research* (pp. 15–21). San Francisco, CA: Jossey-Bass.

Murray, D. (1991). Monitoring shifts in image and recruitment efforts in small colleges. In D. Hossler (Ed.), *New directions for institutional research: No. 70. Evaluating recruitment and retention programs* (pp. 83–94). San Francisco, CA: Jossey-Bass.

National Association for College Admission Counseling. (2006). *Statement of principles of good practice.* Retrieved June 22, 2007, from www.nacacnet.org/NR/rdonlyres/9A4F9961-8991-455D-89B4-AE3B9AF2EFE8/0/SPGP.pdf

Patton, L. D., Morelon, C., Whitehead, D. M., & Hossler, D. (2006). Campus-based retention initiatives: Does the emperor have clothes? In E. P. St. John & M. Wilkerson (Eds.), *New directions for institutional research: No. 130. Reframing persistence research to improve academic success* (pp. 9–24). San Francisco, CA: Jossey-Bass.

Pervin, L. A. (1968, January). Performance and satisfaction as a function of individual-environment fit. *Psychological Bulletin, 69,* 56–68.

Quirk, M. (2005, November). The best class money can buy [Electronic version]. *The Atlantic Monthly.* Retrieved June 22, 2007, from www.theatlantic.com/doc/200511/financial-aid-leveraging

Terenzini, P. T., & Pascarella, E. T. (1980, September). Toward the validation of Tinto's model of college student attrition: A review of recent studies. *Research in Higher Education, 12*(3), 271–282.

Tinto, V. (1993). *Leaving college: Rethinking the causes and cures of student attrition* (2nd ed.). Chicago, IL: University of Chicago Press.

Upcraft, M. L., Gardner, J. N., Barefoot, B. O., & Associates. (2005). *Challenging and supporting the first-year student: A handbook for improving the first year of college.* San Francisco, CA: Jossey-Bass.

7 CONNECTING ONE-STOP STUDENT SERVICES

Louise M. Lonabocker and J. James Wager

In his best seller *The Tipping Point*, author Malcolm Gladwell (2000) describes tipping points as the magic moments when an idea or trend crosses a threshold, tips, and then spreads like wildfire. In higher education there are some notable tipping points that have had a profound effect on the enrollment services profession, transforming the way business is conducted. These tipping points have made it possible to give students greater control of their academic and financial transactions, have allowed them to conduct business at convenient times from convenient locations, and have resulted in significant improvements to service levels as lines of waiting students begin to disappear across campuses. This chapter will highlight some of these tipping points; describe model one-stop, including virtual one-stop, organizations; and discuss the planning involved in the development of a one-stop service organization.

STUDENT SERVICES TIPPING POINTS

In the 1970s institutional enrollments began to climb, and students spent a significant amount of time attending to administrative details such as walking from one department to another to register for courses, lining up in an arena to pay a student account, or being routed from office to office to determine why a hold had been placed on their record. In the 1980s new technologies emerged, and the first tipping points were introduced.

Voice-Response Registration

It all began when Brigham Young University (BYU) described its voice-response registration system at the American Association of Collegiate Registrars and Admissions Officers (AACRAO) annual meeting in 1982.

Before that time it hadn't occurred to registrars that they could allow students to process their own registrations, but BYU had been inspired by the banking industry, which had begun to make use of the technology. Everyone went away from that session inspired to recreate what BYU had done on its campus. Voice-response registration was the tipping point that led to distributed systems that were convenient and simple, offered students immediate feedback, and provided up-to-the-minute information for academic departments. Registration was transformed from a tedious, confusing process to an intuitive and convenient process (Peterson, 1993).

Student Access Systems

In 1988 Boston College introduced another breakthrough when it installed U-VIEW, a student access kiosk system, on campus. U-VIEW made use of ATM machines (without the cash-dispensing unit) to serve as an interface to the institution's legacy system. This gave students more localized access to their own academic, demographic, and financial information (Lonabocker, 1989). The devices were convenient for a residential population, and students went to these user-friendly machines to print their course schedule, access their grades, and check their student account. But the ATM machines, with their small screens and tiny print dispensers, did not offer the functionality of host-connected desktop computers and terminals. Within a few years Boston College and several other institutions introduced terminal-based student access systems, and students began to process registrations, search the schedule of classes, and access demographic and financial information without the assistance of a staff member.

At the 1997 AACRAO annual meeting, the University of Minnesota introduced the next leap forward when its representatives demonstrated their web-based student access system, which allowed students to process transactions and view information using a graphical user interface to access data in an interactive fashion. This marked another tipping point because it removed the boundaries of a transactional display and allowed students to view a schedule of courses; click on a specific course; view the time, location, course description, and availability of the course; place the course in a shopping cart of desired courses; and click on a link to the bookstore to review and purchase textbooks required for the course. Students became less dependent on administrative offices and more reliant on self-service transactions to conduct business from the convenience of their dormitory room, from home during school breaks, or from a remote location while on study abroad.

Now customer relationship management systems and campus portals allow students to customize their views to provide ready access to the information they need, such as email, clubs and activities, learning management systems, degree audit, course planning tools, institutional announcements, and media sources. These systems are geared toward today's students, who have demonstrated their preference for demand "pull" rather than producer "push." In demand pull, users determine for themselves the information they want to read. Typically, they prefer a quick headline so they can read it easily and move on to the next item (Hilton, 2006)

ONE-STOP ORGANIZATIONS

Some of the benefits of the emerging tipping technologies just discussed include self-service for students and families, a reduction in the number of student visits and telephone calls to campus offices, and opportunities for consolidating services into what are now commonly known as "one-stop organizations." Presented here are some examples of one-stop organizations, starting with the pioneers.

University of Delaware

In 1992 the University of Delaware created its own tipping point in higher education when its student services building opened, launching a transformation in service delivery that continues to be cited and hailed by enrollment services professionals. This student services building was formed at a time when colleges and universities were experiencing shrinking budgets and growing demands for improved service. Students encountering a registration hold might be sent to financial aid to determine whether their financial aid had been awarded, then to student accounts to see whether their loan had been disbursed, and finally back to the registrar to complete their registration. Often these offices were scattered around campus, administrative systems were limited in their functionality, and offices were reluctant to share information with other offices that might not have a thorough understanding of the data and related regulatory issues.

The University of Delaware attempted to identify comprehensive service models in which a student could perform a variety of administrative tasks in one stop. Like BYU it ultimately found its business model in banking, where branch banks were set up to be quick and efficient, provide various types of interaction, and use the latest technology to provide services to customers.

Banking also served as a model for staffing the service organization, including both generalists (bank tellers) and specialists (loan officers). The University of Delaware developed its organization to maximize self-help through kiosks, web-based services, and touch-tone telephone technology. Generalists would provide routine services such as issuing ID cards, processing payments, explaining financial aid procedures, and producing transcripts. Specialists would be available for expert advice about progress toward graduation, analysis of financial aid needs, and student accounts.

Carnegie Mellon University

In 1996 Carnegie Mellon launched its new student services office, which it called "the hub." New technologies implemented to improve service and processing included email to communicate with students, online access to student information, online registration, online academic auditing, the automation of needs analysis and financial aid packaging, and electronic grade submission. The institution also developed measures to assess its progress, including student satisfaction surveys and cycle time for subprocesses, such as registration and financial aid awarding.

Boston College

The Boston College Office of Student Services grew out of an initiative known as Project Delta, sponsored by the institution's executive vice president. The initiative aimed to increase service levels, reduce costs, and operate more effectively by offering an array of self-service transactions, new technologies, and cross-functionally trained staff. The goal was to provide outstanding service to students and their families and consolidate the in-person services in a fashion that replicated the services available to students on Agora, the university's web portal.

The Office of Student Services was formed in 1998 and includes the following services: registrar, financial aid, student accounts, credit and collections, campus-based loans, student employment, One Card (allowing access to all the campus's facilities and services), parking permits, notary, and veterans services. The goal of the new organization is to deliver services in one cross-functional unit and thus minimize the number of students referred to other offices. Associates in the service area of the office respond to approximately 90% of the telephone and visitor inquiries for academic, financial, parking, and One Card services. When the situation requires expert intervention, they refer callers or visitors to specialists in academic records, financial aid, student accounts, student loans, and student employment—all of which are housed in the same office.

The University of Connecticut

When the University of Connecticut remodeled its signature Wilbur Cross Building to house student services offices that had previously been located throughout the campus, senior administrators agreed to include an information desk, where staff would be available to refer students and visitors to the appropriate office. As the discussions unfolded, the concept soon grew into the design for a student services center, which would be staffed by generalists who could process many routine transactions. After extensive remodeling and renovation, the historic building reopened in 2001 and today serves as a one-stop service center for most student business needs. The building houses the following offices: orientation services, bursar, registrar, financial aid, dean of students, students with disabilities center, dining services, residential life, and the One Card office.

The New York Institute of Technology

In 2002 the president of the New York Institute of Technology (NYIT) rolled out a five-point retention plan that included improving communications and customer service in enrollment management and services areas. The president also created an enrollment management task force and committee to improve cooperation, communications, and processes; make recommendations about systems and infrastructure; and coordinate implementation of additional services, including web-based services. He also directed staff to cross-train members of the offices for registrar, bursar, admissions, and financial aid to better serve students.

One advantage that NYIT had in the service delivery arena was the fact that the offices of the registrar, bursar, and financial aid were all located in the same building on each campus in an area called "enrollment services." The admissions office was a short walk away from the other enrollment services offices. Though the operational units still functioned independently of one another, students, when referred to one of the other areas, did not have to shuttle all over campus or navigate several different buildings to accomplish their task.

The pioneers just described are some of the many institutions that have formed one-stop organizations. Other institutions that offer one-stop services include Belmont University, Massachusetts Institute of Technology, Pepperdine University, Seton Hall University, Tufts University, the University of Minnesota, and the University of Pennsylvania, to name a few. Each institution has formed its own unique one-stop organization based on institutional priorities, space, budget, and infrastructure. Common factors among the institutions include their desire to improve service delivery and student satisfaction using new technologies and highly trained staff. Staff generalists handle a wide range of routine transactions, which allows experts to focus on students who arrive with more complex problems. These one-stop organizations are all located in convenient, inviting spaces that are often designed specifically with the needs of the student and the staff in mind.

DEVELOPING THE ONE-STOP ORGANIZATION

A one-stop organization does not develop without leadership, vision, time, and effort. There is a lot to consider in the design and planning phases of an integrated one-stop service organization, as this section describes.

Benchmarking

Developing a one-stop operation should be preceded with six months to a year of preparation. During this time, service providers can consult and visit with other institutions, review relevant literature, and attend conferences or workshops where model one-stop organizations are described. Including staff members from all levels in the research and design phase will help them become invested in and supportive of the new organization.

Space

The space selected for a one-stop organization should be convenient for students and designed with their comfort and well-being in mind. Furnishings should be up to date, the space clean, the seating comfortable, and waiting times minimized. This can be a challenge on many campuses where space is tight, budgets are fixed, and different interests compete for limited funds. Most campuses have impressive visitor centers and admissions reception areas. To convey the institution's commitment to providing excellent service, it is equally important to provide functional space for enrolled students. The importance of such factors as the amount of space, noise, light, privacy, and airflow should not be underestimated.

Division of Responsibilities

Dividing responsibilities is a challenge for any organization, and a one-stop service center is no exception. There is no one-size-fits-all solution. Each school must develop job descriptions that are appropriate for its own environment, staff skills, and technological capabilities. For example, at some institutions generalist staff may discuss financial aid awards with students; other schools may elevate these discussions to a financial aid expert who is not part of the generalist staff.

Divisional Boundaries

Establishing boundaries between the divisions of the office should be determined with staff who understand the work and the workflow. For example, how much time should the service generalist spend trying to resolve an issue that may involve a staff member in the processing unit? Should the service generalist take ownership to see the issue through from start to finish, or should the caller be referred to the person in the processing unit who handles such matters? If the service generalist takes the call, researches the matter, and responds to the question, time to research and resolve issues will have to be included in the total time allotted to complete a telephone call.

Organizational Culture

The consolidation of staff from academic and financial areas may result in a need to smooth out differences in institutional subcultures. Policies regarding time off, attire, events, punctuality, meetings, and customer service may require review and agreement. If staff members at all levels are included in the planning for the new organization and if they can understand their role in the new organization, the change will be less stressful. Involving everyone may be unrealistic, but good communication can keep employees informed.

Internal Communication

Creating a one-stop organization will increase the number of staff who work together within one unit. Keeping everyone informed will be a critical factor for success. There are numerous ways to foster communication, including office listservs, electronic bulletin boards, blogs, newsletters, meetings, events, parties, book clubs, charitable initiatives, and a shared lunchroom. Listservs are useful for quick announcements, and electronic bulletin boards or blogs can post information that can be archived for a longer period of time. Electronic calendars are a good way to share key dates, deadlines, and staff absences. Newsletters can be used for informal updates such as birthdays, events, travel, or exchanges.

Process Redesign and Role Descriptions

Most institutions that engage in organizational change and process redesign begin with an identification of all tasks and activities performed by staff of the respective offices. When a one-stop organization is in a planning stage, process developers should ask a series of questions about each task. Is there is a better way to do it? Should it be automated? Should it be combined with another task? Should it be done at all? Every task should undergo this scrutiny before new job roles are created.

Training and Development

One of the most significant challenges faced by one-stop organizations is the development of well-trained staff who can seamlessly move from a student's question about financial aid to a parent's question about a student account to a student's request to replace his or her ID card. Seton Hall University and the University of Minnesota have developed training and development programs.

Seton Hall University. Seton Hall University's one-stop organization includes admissions, registrar, bursar, financial aid services, student employment, and student loans. Seton Hall has developed a comprehensive training program for all unit personnel and an intensive training program for those personnel whose main role is to provide frontline service as part of the customer response team (CRT). The comprehensive program is divided into a new-employee curriculum and ongoing cross-training. The intensive training program includes those components as well as extensive training for the CRT managers.

University of Minnesota. The mission of the University of Minnesota's one-stop student services is "to provide quality and professional service in the areas of enrollment, financial aid, and billing and payments, in support of students' academic and financial objectives" (University of Minnesota, 2006). With this dedication to customer service in mind, one stop has a comprehensive and intensive 12-week training program for new counselors to prepare them to assist students, parents, staff, and faculty.

Training is provided primarily by experienced one-stop counselors who also update training materials and develop examples, scenarios, and role-playing opportunities for the new counselors. In addition to classroom training, new counselors observe experienced counselors and are assigned a mentor, who supports the new counselor in becoming familiar with the university and office staff, provides useful materials, and is available as a resource during and after the training period.

Customer Service

College students seek consistent, trustworthy relationships with the service representatives at their institution. The variable in the service relationship is how an individual student defines personal service. Some students simply want to perform their desired tasks with little intervention by staff. Others need more attentive assistance by knowledgeable professionals throughout the process. The goal of most one-stop organizations is to offer students what they need when they need it and in the manner that makes them most comfortable (Nealon, 2005).

When the University of Pennsylvania restructured its student financial services (SFS) operation to create a one-stop organization, it wanted to ensure that service would be provided to students on a first-come, first-serve basis. The solution was software called Gamma Q, which was developed for Penn and has many applications. Now students who arrive at the SFS reception center swipe their ID card at the reception desk, which enters them into a queue that can be seen on monitors located in a comfortable waiting area. When a counselor is available, the student's name changes from white to red on the monitor, the counselor is identified, and the monitor notes the counselor's office location. Simultaneously, the counselor receives several items to facilitate the interaction, including a message on his or her desktop computer identifying the student, a display of the student's record, and a summary of previous student visits. At the conclusion of the appointment, the system automatically generates a follow-up survey about the quality and effectiveness of the interaction that is emailed to the student. Because the system tracks counselors and students in the queue, students know their wait time. This information is displayed on a plasma LCD screen in the SFS lobby and will soon be available on the SFS web site. Other enhancements include online appointments and follow-up to-do lists for the student and the counselor. The system has proved to be a success because students are treated with dignity and fairness.

Measures and Metrics

Measuring success is important for any organization, and it is especially important in the development of a one-stop organization to ensure that the goal of providing outstanding service is achieved. The consistent use of measures and metrics to track progress can be used to support requests for additional resources or to show increases in customer satisfaction.

Establishing benchmarks before the implementation of a one-stop organization helps institutions determine whether the new organization contributes to observed changes. Of course, because most institutions are continually trying to improve programs, activities, and facilities, it may be difficult to pinpoint the reasons for changes. Some institutions, such as Anne Arundel Community College, think that the creation of a one-stop center was a contributing factor in enrollment growth and in retention rate improvements.

Commonly used measures and metrics to evaluate one-stop organizations include the following:

- Satisfaction surveys conducted with students, parents, or internal customers

- Enrollment, retention, and graduation rates

- Telephone volume, including answered and abandoned telephone calls, average wait time, and percentage of calls answered within one minute

- Measuring the success in meeting critical deadlines, such as registration, graduation, the reading of financial aid files, and student account billing

- Rate of response to email inquiries and telephone calls within a specified period of time (normally 24 hours)

- Staff retention

- Positive and negative feedback received by staff and senior administrators

Other measures include benchmarking practices at other institutions and the use of balanced scorecards, a strategic management approach that measures customer service, internal processes, learning and development, and financial performance.

Perhaps the most important measurement for a one-stop organization is the measurement of telephone usage. At Seton Hall University there are several areas of measurement, but telephone response is perhaps the most advanced. This measurement combines the use of data and reports from an automated call distribution system with the monitoring of employees who answer incoming phone calls.

Career Development

The integration of several offices sometimes results in some unconventional role descriptions for staff. For example, at Carnegie Mellon University the registrar and the director of financial aid share the responsibility of overseeing the one-stop organization called "the hub." At the University of Connecticut the registrar oversees the student services center in the student services building, where students can obtain general information. At the University of Minnesota the former registrar is now the director of enrolled services and registrar. At Boston College the staff of the Office of Student Services include a director of academic and general services, a director of student accounts and student services operations, and a director of student services and university registrar. These unconventional pairings are the result of the skills and interests of staff as well as the needs of the organization. Whenever staff turnover occurs, role descriptions are deconstructed and reconstructed, and responsibilities may be reassigned to other staff members. Due to emerging technologies, new systems, and new responsibilities, job requirements have been changing rapidly over the past 10 years. These changes and the ensuing changes to role descriptions occur with or without the introduction of one-stop services.

CREATING VIRTUAL ONE STOP

In the immortal words of Yogi Berra, "The future ain't what it used to be!" Berra's words apply well to institutions of higher education in the early 21st century. The past two decades have brought rapid technology change, have introduced new thoughts about the role of higher education in American society, and have raised fundamental questions about the cost and value of higher education. At the same time there's a new generation of students— young men and women who have lived their whole lives in a technology-connected environment. Today parents are in closer communication with their students than perhaps ever before in the history of higher education.

Colleges and universities are people-intensive organizations that have seen exorbitant cost increases stemming from salaries, health care, and retirement contributions. Aging campus infrastructures, deferred maintenance, information technology investments, and various cost increases have all caused tuition to rise at a rate that has far outpaced inflation. The high cost of tuition in both public and private schools has resulted in pressures to do more with less, to become more efficient, and to simply reduce internal costs. A common desire within the student services arena has been to improve effectiveness in the delivery of services while becoming more efficient through organizational restructuring. Many have achieved this by combining disparate student services offices into more global and unified offices—one-stop service centers.

CHANGING PERSPECTIVES

Traditional-age freshmen entering college in the fall of 2006 were most likely born in 1989, well after the dawn of the information age. These students, known as the "Net generation," have grown up in an environment significantly different from the one most higher education faculty, staff, and administrators experienced during their developmental years. Oblinger and Oblinger (2005) outline many differences in educating this generation of students.

One of the most striking generational differences is that access to and use of technology is simply assumed by today's learners. For them technology is invisible and intuitive; students don't "learn technology," nor do they think of it as separate from the activities it enables. For the Net generation, television sets have always been in color with a remote control and a cable or satellite connection, and services have been available through the web for most of their lives. Because of their background, the Net generation has adopted a set of expectations that call for new—and sometimes challenging—responses from the academy. One of these student expectations is that they will receive customizable, personalized services, not a one-size-fits-all approach.

Some have described changing colleges and universities as akin to turning an aircraft carrier. Unlike a small pleasure boat that can maneuver and change course rapidly, an aircraft carrier requires a carefully planned maneuver and a large berth to complete its turn. Although information technology has had a significant impact on the Net generation, practices and expectations within the academy remain relatively unchanged. Classes continue to be taught by instructors in classrooms. Students are expected to navigate complex administrative processes. In many ways the academy continues to be staff centric. Some colleges and universities have demonstrated measurable progress in moving toward a student-centered philosophy, but many have not. That latter group's administrative structure, information systems, and approach to the delivery of student services continue to represent the traditional hierarchy experienced by previous generations of students.

The academy is changing. In addition to the changed expectations of the Net generation, external forces are influencing higher education. These include the following:

- The growing belief that the cost of a college education should be paid for by students, not taxpayers, is shifting the balance and delivery of federal student aid programs.

- A Supreme Court decision in a case involving admissions at the University of Michigan prompted a national examination of both admissions and financial aid practices.

- The Y2K phenomenon resulted in great angst for system administrators, often driving the replacement of administrative information systems.

- The rise of for-profit educational institutions has begun to change the delivery of both online and on-campus courses as well as associated services.

- Campuses are increasingly outsourcing services ranging from campus eateries, janitorial service, and printing/copying, to targeted student services such as transcript order/delivery and student aid.

- The rise of identity theft has forced colleges and universities to rethink their use of the Social Security number as the primary record identifier.

Such environmental changes have caused the academy to examine its policies, practices, and, more important, the application of information systems to create more efficient operations and more effective student services.

Melander (2002) extends this challenge as he ties the goal of becoming a student-centered university to the core institutional purpose of learning. Melander argues that although most faculty, administrators, staff, and students are not certain what it means to be student centered, no one seems to be suggesting that the academy should become less research or service oriented. Many feel that focusing on the student is what we already do—and do well—so what needs to be different? Being student centered does not necessarily mean more effort or resources are to be targeted to students. Rather, it means that teaching and learning are placed at the institutional core. Not only must faculty be focused on learning outcomes, but so must all others who have responsibilities for delivering programs and services in the learning environment. In other words, the focus on the delivery of student services is also at the core of the institution's goal of student learning.

Technology and One-Stop Centers

As discussed in the first part of this chapter, colleges and universities have improved the integration of student services through the one-stop model. Common characteristics of this multidisciplinary approach are the construction of a physical student services center that houses all appropriate student services offices and staff, as well as a student services desk staffed by trained personnel. Such a response is an improvement over the approach used during the arena-registration era; however, in practice this approach has serious limitations that stand in the way of true integration. It is expensive to build new buildings or to renovate existing buildings to physically establish a student services center. Completely integrating all student services into a single job description is not realistic—there is simply too much to learn.

Instead of this brick-and-mortar approach to improving and integrating the delivery of student services, a more robust approach is to capitalize on the power of information technology (IT). Creating a seamless virtual organization specifically tailored to exceed the expectations of today's Net generation students is a reachable objective.

It's Not About Technology

The continued use of technology to improve student services will be critical to the academy. The Net generation cares about the activity technology enables, not the technology itself. Technology is a tool; it represents the means, not the desired outcome.

But before focusing on technology, student services professionals must articulate a clear and unambiguous vision that provides the framework for technology. Because IT staff are important contributors to the desired outcome, they must be part of the process; however, leaders who will champion the vision for improved student services should not be expected to come from technology's ranks. Rather, they must come from the group of practitioners who are charged with advising and registering students, administering student aid, admitting students, collecting tuition and fees, and so on.

Each college and university is unique, and its structure, titles, and functions for student services offices vary. During the past decade, offices or divisions of enrollment management have become commonplace. Offices such as registrar, admissions, student aid, student accounts, student affairs, and housing all identify units responsible for the delivery of student services. But the functions of these units vary widely from school to school. The availability and adoption of technology-driven applications need not change the focus or responsibility of student services units.

Although the mission may remain unchanged, an institution's student services units will be faced with new issues as its technology-based services grow. For example, Net generation students are more inclined to email requests or to participate in interactive online chat sessions than to visit an office and ask for advice in person. Properly developed web applications should enable users to contact a business specialist if they encounter problems or have questions. Such questions are often emailed to a student services unit drop box. It is imperative that the student services unit has a plan to receive, read, and reply to this steady stream of incoming email messages. The student services office will likely need to reorganize its staff and service priorities in response to these types of changes.

Even though senior administrators may anticipate staff reductions after implementing new technology, those reductions rarely come to pass. Although administrative positions may decrease in number, there is typically an increase in the number of information technology positions. In many cases the growth of IT positions occurs in both the central IT support office and the student services units. In essence, IT becomes part of almost everyone's position because even nontechnical staff need to master new skills and learn to use the technology to its fullest.

It can be tempting to completely rely on the IT staff when problems arise or when a student challenges the process or results. Similarly, technologists might want to assume responsibility for the business process because they "own" the hardware that stores the data and the business logic. Both of these approaches are inappropriate: the student services unit must retain primary ownership of the process and the delivery of its set of student services, and the IT department should focus on infrastructure support issues such as networking, security, database management, backup and recovery, and other global issues. As technology-driven services are developed, they must continue to be the responsibility of the appropriate student services unit.

Technology as a Transformational Tool

For the Net generation, the quality of service matters. This requires more than automation; it requires transformation. How technology should transform the delivery of student services is a continuing challenge for administrators.

An example of how technology has transformed a basic student service is the National Student Clearinghouse (www.studentclearinghouse.org). In the mid-1990s, there was a three-way exchange of paper documents between an enrolled student, the school, and the student's financial lender. The lender required proof of enrollment for the student to remain in a nonrepayment status on his or her loan. The student would receive a document from the lender for the institution to complete; the school would receive the document from the student, complete it, and return it to either the student or the lender. This process was inconvenient for the student, time consuming for the institution, and difficult to manage for the lender.

Technology enabled a transformation that is much better suited to Net geners—or any busy student, regardless of age. Through the establishment of a central repository, colleges and universities can transfer pertinent enrollment data to the clearinghouse; lending institutions now make their enrollment status inquiries against this repository. The clearinghouse increased effectiveness for students and improved efficiencies for both lenders and institutions. In this example, the goal—validation of student enrollment to ensure continuance of borrower status—did not change. What changed significantly were the processes employed. Shifting from a manual to an automated system also added value by establishing a national database used for a variety of other purposes.

The Interrelationship of Service and Technology

The Net generation expects convenient, safe, reliable, and flexible access. The development of student services is not about technology, yet the support of today's extended and accessible services would be impossible without the presence of a robust technology infrastructure. Conceptually, there is a clear distinction between application development and the system that allows services to be delivered. In reality, the two issues are tightly coupled.

The constant and rapidly changing nature of technology requires those developing support services for the Net generation to be aware of both the current technology boundaries and the emerging possibilities. The following examples illustrate the interconnectedness between the service and the technology used to deliver it:

- *Due to changing core technology, lateral steps may be required that do not improve the service.* The half-life of software and hardware continues to decline; the period of time from acquisition to obsolescence keeps getting shorter. The laptop, desktop, or server purchased today will likely be improved by the manufacturer within a year. The resulting machine will be less expensive (all other attributes held constant) with greater performance capabilities. Although this does not necessarily make the original purchase an inappropriate decision, it does provide a warning that within a few years hardware or software may need to be replaced. It is necessary to maintain a current hardware and software base, but such efforts can become a distraction from the development and enhancement of direct services to students.

- *Inappropriate uses of technology require that developers take a defensive posture to ensure the integrity and stability of their services.* As the adoption of web-based services continues to expand, we are also experiencing the dark side of innovation—the use of technology to disrupt legitimate services or promote fraudulent services. The number and severity of Internet-spread viruses are on the rise, as are instances of fraudulent services that result in identity theft or credit card fraud. Many colleges and universities are responding by expending extensive resources to migrate away from using Social Security numbers as the primary identifier for students, faculty, and staff.

- *A reliable, fast, and secure network—both wired and wireless—is necessary to deliver the developed support services.* Another critical infrastructure issue is networking. During the past decade colleges and universities spent enormous sums of money wiring their campuses. The goal was to connect every classroom, residence hall room, and faculty office to the Internet. With much of this accomplished, these same institutions are now investing heavily in wireless networks to support the rapidly growing use of wireless computing on laptop computers, PDAs, iPods, smart cell phones, and other such devices. Although such wireless capabilities are needed, these expenditures divert investment from new support services and represent an ongoing commitment to maintenance and necessary upgrades.

- *The preferred solution is integration.* As the number and extent of support services continue to grow, students want the university to provide an integrated, full-service approach. It may be as simple as creating a single sign-on solution that verifies who the person is (authentication) and defines what the person is allowed to do (authorization). Or it may be more complicated (due to the complexity of typical university accounting systems)—for instance, providing integrated e-commerce applications for all billing issues.

- *Support services must be reliable, consistent, and available.* Mistakes happen and hardware fails. Files or databases may accidentally be destroyed. A virus may penetrate the security perimeter and cause damage. A failed hard drive might result in the inability to access a file. Whatever the root cause, there must be a data backup service so that critical information is not permanently lost. Institutions also need to consider their ability to recover from a larger disaster—fire, hurricane, earthquake, terrorist attack, and so on. Disaster recovery represents yet another necessary diversion of resources from support services development.

Higher education cannot ignore technology support issues. These issues are critical as strategic services are developed for our constituents.

Integration, Opportunity, and Service

The Net generation wants integrated and convenient services. Technology has the power to integrate the delivery of support services, create new opportunities, and deliver world-class levels of service. Many colleges and universities now use the web to organize, present, and deliver support services. The University of Michigan provides services through Wolverine Access (http://fordschool.umich.edu/current/wolverine.html). At the University of Texas students access UT Direct (http://utdirect.utexas.edu/utdirect). At BYU students, faculty, staff, and administrators use the AIM (academic information management) system (http://it.byu.edu/index.cfm?child_id=241&catID=72). The University of Maryland uses Testudo (www.umd.edu/testudo.html). At Penn State students, faculty, and academic advisors use eLion (http://elion.psu.edu).

Leadership and Vision

The development of the Penn State eLion system did not follow a traditional pattern; the development efforts were intentionally decentralized across many offices, and the project leadership was highly integrated through the use of collaborative teams. This is both an attribute of and a requirement for a successful one-stop implementation. The system was a result of strategic planning and not simply incremental planning or lockstep change. The evolution of systems within colleges and universities is often driven by external forces. The articulated need at Penn State was to improve academic advising services. Through the creative and collaborative efforts of staff in leadership roles, the early model and design of eLion emerged.

The first models were virtual prototypes that described the intended function and result. The models were presented to senior university administrators, who allocated modest development funds to pursue the creation of a functional prototype. These funds were used to provide training for existing staff and to purchase specialized software. Following a successful proof-of-concept demonstration, several teams were organized. One was responsible for the design of application standards and presentation techniques. Two additional teams were tasked with the development of the first student services applications. A fourth team focused on technical architecture requirements.

For the first three years progress was slow. During that time the Penn State leadership remained committed to the original vision and provided the fiscal and emotional support needed to keep the project moving forward. Today's system would not have been possible without this strong, top-down support and without a clear vision from the project team itself.

An important part of the vision was to provide a set of services that would quickly scale to a very large (100,000+) population of users, which required that the system be uniform, self-documenting, and reliable. Further, users needed to be able to offer comments and suggestions and receive personalized help. A standards document was developed to provide guidance to all eLion developers. This document included information on how to create a new application or modify an existing one, web standards, and technical programming standards, as well as general information about the structure and governance of the eLion initiative. Each eLion application required internal help documentation for users. Because the system is secure, a public demonstration service was developed to deliver a nonauthenticated view of typical applications. A statement in the standard footer of each page indicates that the page is maintained by eLion; behind this link is a page-specific email address that routes questions or inquiries to the appropriate developer.

PRACTICAL ISSUES: FROM ENROLLMENT TO GRADUATION AND BEYOND

The set of issues facing academic administrators discussed in this chapter is difficult and complex. The following are some practical approaches to address these issues and make a difference to our students, alumni, faculty, and staff.

Lifetime Relationship

Prospective students begin their relationship with an institution of higher education well before the traditional freshman admissions cycle. Students may be on campus during middle school years to participate in sports camps and organized student groups. Potential students may accompany their parents for alumni weekends. Some high school students may enroll in college courses and establish an academic transcript. While enrolled, students will have access to multiple technology services that will require ID cards and multiple user-ID and password credentials.

After graduation, alumni are encouraged to provide gifts, to receive ongoing news about the school, to join the alumni association, and to fill the seats at various sporting and artistic events. As the concepts of virtual one-stop student services are fully applied, institutions need to establish a single lifelong identity for each person. At a minimum this should result in the creation of a unique and persistent identification number, network credentials, and the ability to manage those credentials.

This is less of a technical challenge and more of a vision challenge. Creating a lifelong digital identity requires the cooperation of multiple academic and administrative offices. People will, over time, hold multiple roles— prospective student, applicant, enrolled student, graduate, alum, faculty, employee, and retiree. The effective use of a single digital identity will be necessary for a holistic virtual one stop.

Access to Academic Records

Given the typical design architecture of secure web services, only the designated student may access and modify his or her personal record. Student services staff may have the organizational authority to access and modify the student's record, but the technology may prevent staff access to the actual web transaction. Another technology challenge is to enable the staff member to see what the student sees without compromising the integrity of the system's security or data.

As students are provided with extended access to their academic records through virtual one-stop applications, it is increasingly important to grant access to their parents or guardians. Some have described the Net generation of students as having "helicopter parents"; cell phones, email, text messaging, and instant messaging have created opportunities for students' parents to be closer than ever to the academic and administrative issues their children are experiencing. A classic complaint that most registrars have heard from parents is along the lines of "I pay the tuition, so why can't I see my student's grades?" (This complaint is more prevalent at schools that have adopted Family Educational Rights and Privacy Act guidelines declaring students to be independent.) Most schools have strict policies against students' sharing their network credentials with others. Such policies place an especially difficult strain on students when their parents demand to have access to their user ID and password.

The concept of virtual one-stop can be logically extended to give access to parents. Such applications typically have several attributes, including prior permission by the student; specified and limited applications available to parents; and the establishment of a parent account related to, but separate from, the student's account.

Integrating Technology, not Adopting Technology

Academic administrators have used various metrics to measure academic quality. Registrars measure classroom utilization, class size, and scheduled class time. Enrollment managers measure graduation rates and time to graduation. Budget officers measure the number of underenrolled courses and the budget implications. Department chairs measure faculty teaching loads and student credit hours. These traditional metrics are important indicators but need to be thought of in new terms as the virtual one-stop approach is integrated into the teaching and learning environment. For example, technology-supported instruction, virtual discussion, and collaboration will reduce the need for scheduled class meetings. Virtual learning opportunities better prepare graduates for virtual team environments, which are rapidly being adopted by business and industry.

Laptops Required?

As online teaching and learning continue to permeate course modules, full courses, and even complete degrees, the need for students to access technology obviously increases. A critical tipping point for enrollment managers is to identify when public computer labs for students are no longer sufficient and when having a laptop computer should be a requirement for admission. Various experiments have already been conducted that resulted in providing first-year students with laptops or iPods. For example, the Duke Digital Initiative has explored the use of new and emerging technologies to support university priorities (see www.duke.edu/ddi/). Using various forms of portable technologies, the purpose of this initiative has been to find opportunities to promote innovative and effective teaching and to support curricular enhancement.

Going Digital

Although most applications have transformed from analog to digital form, some have not. Across the country, there are tens of thousands of academic transcripts that are printed, stuffed in an envelope, and mailed. On the receiving end, they are filed or, ironically, sometimes scanned into a document-imaging system. In many respects this paper-driven process is a result of tradition. New models have emerged that provide for increased document security, decreased cost, and much improved service to the student or alum and the transcript's receiver (an admissions officer or employer). The overarching principles of the virtual one-stop model can be applied to most any issue across the academy.

CONCLUSION

When BYU introduced voice-response registration, it was many students' first encounter with the technology. Today that paradigm has changed: Students expect their institution to provide services for the technologies they bring to school. They expect the technologies that their institution uses to conduct business to be integrated with the technologies they use to maintain their social networks. If we consider the devices and software used by students today—such as PDAs, cell phones, electronic auctions, blogs, instant messaging, text messaging, and gaming—it is clear that colleges and universities have some catching up to do to reach students in ways that are most convenient to them.

Most students expect to use self-service portals to conduct business wherever they are and whenever they're inclined to do so. They expect the back-end systems to be flawless. If they need assistance with a transaction, they expect in-person or telephone assistance that mirrors the online services. Students and families—who have been dealing with online service providers and businesses that pride themselves on providing easy, pleasant, quick, and accurate customer service—expect to find the same seamless service at colleges and universities.

The integration of student services and the development of a cross-functionally trained staff is a challenge, and some might ask whether it is worth the investment of space, time, and effort. Institutions with integrated services say that centralized services are valued by students and families, as evidenced by customer satisfaction surveys, verbal feedback, and letters written to senior administrators. Many of these improvements are the result of the collaboration that takes place when staff from various offices are brought together, get to know each other, and work together to help students. In a climate that nurtures continuous improvement and promotes excellent services, staff begin to recommend ideas for improvement.

Institutions also begin to realize benefits from integrated services as the peaks and valleys are smoothed out and more resources are made available. Consolidating services can also lead to reductions in staff, budgets, and equipment, thus providing more space for group work and meetings. Budget savings can be used where they're most needed to benefit staff, upgrade furnishings and equipment, develop new publications, or offer new services. The development of new systems can be planned from a more holistic perspective, and projects can be identified based on the needs of the institution, the organization, and the current functionality of the systems. A larger pool of talented staff makes succession simpler, and staff can be trained for career opportunities within their current role or office. Finally, the larger organization may be able to create full-time positions for staff who bring greater depth of expertise in project management, data analysis, and communication.

To meet the expectations of today's students and families, institutions should move away from silos to web-based and personal services, which remove the runaround that students abhor. The virtual approach provides a richer opportunity to integrate services and allows greater access without the restraints of time or distance. However, this approach requires a strong IT infrastructure.

But who in the institution decides where support services reside, and what are the implications of implementation? One of the leading factors will be the institution's ability to attract and retain a qualified IT workforce. In recent years, the supply and demand for IT professionals has become more balanced, but in many areas it remains difficult to retain IT staff because of colleges and universities' typically compressed salary structures. Further, recent graduates are often unfamiliar with legacy programming languages. To close this gap of technical needs and available talent, some institutions have established internal development programs to ensure a steady supply of interested and trained IT professionals. Others have purchased packaged systems and rely on external consultants to lead implementation efforts.

Matching institutional practice with technical features is another decision point. Should institutional practice change to align with the capabilities of the IT system, or should custom IT solutions be developed to meet the service needs? With the former, changing the institutional culture is difficult at best and divisive at worst. With the latter, the institution loses the leverage of maximizing future system growth and enhancements unless corresponding modifications are made to customize software.

There are more than 3,600 colleges and universities in the United States. Even when grouped by similar size, mission, and objectives, perspectives on the delivery of student systems are diverse. Individual institutions differ on student expectations, learning environments, academic and administrative policies, academic advising, and the role of faculty governance. Well-designed vendor-supplied student services recognize these variables and make provisions for flexibility. Yet there are practical limitations to the flexibility of any software.

Another decision involves the current IT infrastructure, including databases, enterprise-wide servers, authentication and authorization services, e-commerce support, web development, data warehouse capabilities, and help desk availability. Are the multiple campus systems interfaced to greater or lesser degrees? Does the institution have common or varied business practices for admissions, financial aid disbursement, and grade reporting? These student services and IT components combine to provide a launching point for the future development of any one-stop approach.

The need to provide improved student support services has never been greater. In recent years the cost of higher education has continued to increase, often outpacing other economic indicators. As tuition increases external pressures from students, parents, legislators, and alumni to contain costs mount. At the same time Net generation students expect improved and comprehensive services from the academy. Fortunately, the availability of technological solutions for student services has never been greater. The plethora of enterprise-wide solutions, outsourcing opportunities, and on-campus development tools provide a wide range of options for the design and deployment of responsive student services. Although the delivery of student services is not about technology, it is about using technology wisely. The use of technology requires a strong partnership between service providers and technologists. The Net generation's expectations for student services are high and rising. The opportunities for the academy to respond to—and even exceed—these expectations are equally boundless.

AUTHORS' NOTE

This chapter includes material adapted from L. Lonabocker (2006). One-stop shop and virtual services. In B. Lauren (Ed.), *The registrar's guide: Evolving best practices in records and registration* (pp. 101–120). Washington,

DC: American Association of Collegiate Registrars and Admissions Officers. This material is reprinted with permission of the publisher to expand upon the original material. All rights reserved.)

ACKNOWLEDGMENTS

The authors wish to thank the following one-stop experts for their contributions to this chapter: Frank Claus, associate vice president for finance, University of Pennsylvania; Thomas Green, associate vice president for enrollment services, Seton Hall University; Mary Koskan, director of one-stop student services, University of Minnesota–Twin Cities; and Jeffrey von Munkwitz-Smith, university registrar, University of Connecticut.

REFERENCES

Gladwell, M. (2000). *The tipping point: How little things can make a big difference.* New York, NY: Little, Brown.

Hilton, J. (2006, March/April). The future for higher education: Sunrise or perfect storm? *EDUCAUSE Review, 41*(2), 58–71.

Lonabocker, L. (1989, Summer). U-VIEW: A student public access record keeping system. *College and University, 64*(4), 349–355.

Melander, E. R. (2002, November 27). The meaning of "student-centered" advising: Challenges to the advising learning community. *The Mentor: An Academic Advising Journal.* Retrieved July 2, 2007, from www.psu.edu/dus/mentor/021127em.htm

Nealon, J. L. (2005). *College and university responsiveness to students-as-customers: The reorganization of service delivery in the enrollment service arena.* Unpublished doctoral dissertation, University of Pennsylvania, Philadelphia.

Oblinger, D. G., & Oblinger, J. L. (Eds.). (2005). *Educating the net generation.* Boulder, CO: EDUCAUSE.

Peterson, E. D. (1993). Landmark developments. In M. M. Bell (Ed.), *Touchtone telephone/voice response registration: A guide for successful implementation* (pp. 25–31). Washington, DC: American Association of Collegiate Registrars and Admissions Officers.

University of Minnesota. (2006). *Contact one stop.* Retrieved May 9, 2007, from http://onestop.umn.edu/onestop/services.html

8 | LEARNING TECHNOLOGIES THAT SERVE STUDENTS

Peter B. DeBlois and
Diana G. Oblinger

Just as technology has streamlined and opened up new efficiencies for student administrative services, so has it significantly transformed teaching and learning. This chapter discusses the technology expectations of the so-called Net generation student. It then gives an overview of technologies that students and faculty today are using to advance learning. Finally, it addresses student privacy in the increasingly networked world of teaching and learning and the cultural shift toward self-expression and self-empowerment with technology that those who advise students need to understand. At the heart of this overview is a call not only for understanding the "what" of new learning technologies but for active involvement by student affairs professionals in the "how" and "why" of helping students use them.

SERVICE EXPECTATIONS OF THE NET GENERATION

A key first step in understanding particular learning technologies is understanding the service expectations of those at the center of it all—students—and how technology can help us provide services. When we see students using a computer, cell phone, or game console, we observe their use of technology. Students who use such devices and see others use those devices do not see technology; they see activity—people connecting to information, communicating with friends, or entertaining themselves. Technology is only a means to an end for the Net generation; it is not an end in itself.

The Net geners' exposure to technology has changed their expectations of services. Immediacy is one example. Today's students don't expect to wait two weeks for the postal service to deliver an answer to an admissions query; they expect a response in a few seconds or a few minutes. Convenience is another example. Why go up and down the stairs to the residence hall laundry room to see whether a washer or dryer is free when you could log on to eSuds.net and find out which units are available? The Net generation expects to be listened to. Perhaps more a byproduct of marketing campaigns than information technology (IT), Net geners use technology to make their voices heard. Whether it is completing a web-based survey, blogging, or making purchases, they do not always accept traditional hierarchies or one-size-fits-all approaches.

Those who work with students need to consider the implications of five Net generation traits that relate to service expectations: Net geners are connected, engaged, participating, mobile and flexible, and visual.

Connected

Today's students are constantly connected—to friends, family, information, and entertainment. The devices vary. Whether it is a desktop PC, laptop, PDA, or cell phone, students use technology to connect with others.

Cell phones can be thought of as mobile computers. They access wireless networks for communication and information. They contain memory, which can store information, such as games. They have full-color screens and audio. And, increasingly, they have keyboards. A cell phone can be used for a conversation, whether it's a voice-to-voice conversation or one via text messaging. A photograph from that same cell phone can provide visual information about whom a person is with and what that person is doing. Students with location-aware cell phones can be alerted when friends are in the area, helping them get together. And as cell phone service expands to include TV, students can watch their favorite soap opera or sporting event in real time.

Engaged

Recently many faculty say they have been surprised by students' mind-sets that if class isn't engaging, they can choose not to pay attention. Although this has always been true (daydreaming and doodling are age-old pastimes), previous generations of students have felt less empowered to make such a choice. This expectation of being engaged is not surprising considering the environment in which today's students have grown up.

Many Net geners learned their ABCs with the Muppets or Barney. Rather than reading about the Civil War, they saw movies reenacting battles and accessed web sites with archives of photos, personal letters, and military campaign descriptions. Games and simulations allowed them to make their own decisions and witness the outcomes. Understanding the orbits of the planets was more than viewing a black-and-white mathematical formula; it was flying through a 3-D, full-color animation that could be viewed from all sides. Color, sound, and movement—coupled with opportunities for participation—have defined the informal learning environment for many young people. A formal chalk-and-talk educational environment may not contain the engagement today's students expect.

Participating

Net geners have participated in decision-making from the time they were very young. Where to eat dinner, the destination of the family vacation, even the color of the family SUV are joint decision-making activities in many families. Companies have asked kids what color of candy they like best or what flavor they prefer for their breakfast cereal—and have then responded. Participation has been encouraged because these kids have taken part in playgroups, soccer teams, and study groups since they were very young. And their learning environments have often been hands-on. Most Net geners identify themselves as experiential learners—they learn from doing, not just from listening.

Digital technology has provided additional opportunities for participation. Rather than simply consume the news, students can comment on articles or blogs and even create their own news feeds. Blogging, for example, has made it possible for individuals to self-publish on any subject—and not just by using words. Through podcasting and videoblogging, students can share their voices and images. Perhaps the most obvious example of the emergence of a participatory culture is Wikipedia. Anyone who chooses to add to this editable online encyclopedia can; participation is open to experts and amateurs alike.

Mobile and Flexible

Whether it is going to class, to work, to a club activity, or heading home, students are constantly on the move. And considering that the majority of students work part-time and commute, they have multiple time constraints. As a result, students expect to be able to get the information they need anywhere and at any time. Wireless networks have allowed any space to become a learning space—and students are taking advantage of that.

Podcasts allow students to replay lectures on the bus. Cell phone alerts notify them if a class is cancelled. Time-stamped assignments emailed to a professor eliminate the need to drop a paper off at the office. Phone and online registration mean students can choose classes while on spring break.

Visual

To this generation a picture really is worth a thousand words. Many teens say that they find reading boring (Starrett, 2005). Perhaps the reason is that between TV, radio, the web, and other sources, today's youth are exposed to an average of eight hours of media messages a day (Rideout, Hamel, & Kaiser Family Foundation, 2006). Studies of laboratories reveal that students are unlikely to read complex lab protocols; however, they will watch a video or simulation (C. Grisham, personal communication, January 15, 2003). Today's students are adept at interpreting complex visual images—at least in comparison to faculty and administrators. And they expect material to be presented to them in a visually interesting way. Beyond those expectations, students may intuitively know that images often reveal patterns and insights that words or numbers obscure. Whatever the reason, the Net generation is highly visual.

LEARNING TECHNOLOGIES

As the cliché says, "It's not about the technology; it's about what you do with it." The following review of specific learning technologies is by no means comprehensive. The technologies selected for coverage here are currently being deployed at institutions of all types and sizes, for both on-campus classes and distance learning, for traditional 18- to 22-year-old students and older learners (who actually outnumber the traditionals). An excellent resource for monitoring the full range of new learning tools and strategies is the 7 *Things You Should Know About* ... series, published by the EDUCAUSE Learning Initiative (ELI). Each brief in the series "focuses on an emerging technology or practice and describes: what it is, how it works, where it is going, and why it matters to teaching and learning" (ELI, 2005a).

Learning/Course Management Systems

Many institutions have web-based campus information portals, often customized for special audiences, such as current students, prospective students, alumni, faculty, and staff. Think of a learning/course management system (L/CMS) as a content portal tailored to registered students and the faculty of a particular course. During the past five years L/CMSs have matured and been widely adopted. According to the Campus Computing Project, their use in college courses at all types and sizes of institutions rose from 14.7% in 2000 to 45.9% in 2005 (Green, 2005, p. 10). In their present form, whether created in house or vendor supplied, L/CMSs typically operate in password-protected course web sites, restricted to faculty and enrolled students, and include:

- Templates for organizing and presenting syllabi, assignments, bulletin boards, reading selections, and multimedia files

- Links to discipline- and course-specific web sites, the campus library, computer training support, tutoring services, the counseling/advising center, and other on- and off-campus resources

- Platforms for synchronous (real-time) and asynchronous (anytime) communication between faculty and students, including email, two-way and multiway chat rooms, and discussion listservs

- Individualized student activity scheduling

- Joint project work spaces

- Secure individual student storage space for coursework

- Assignment submission and return channels

- Testing assessment tools

- Electronic rosters and grade books

Purdue University offers an impressive example of an institution adapting a commercial L/CMS (WebCT Vista) into a well-designed IT support environment. The frequently asked questions for students, instructors, and designers on Purdue's IT web page (www.itap.purdue.edu/tlt/vista) illustrate how particular courses at the university can deploy presentation, communication, assessment, management, and student tools.

Whether locally created, vendor supplied, or open source, L/CMSs have emerged as one of the most prevalent learning technologies in higher education. What stake do student affairs professionals have in L/CMSs? If these professionals haven't already, they would do well to connect with faculty and instructional support staff at their institutions to learn where and how deeply this technology has penetrated and to work to ensure that there is a well-designed link to student support services on every course-specific web site. That is a fundamental technical tie-in of the two service worlds.

E-Portfolios

As a technology with great potential to support academic and nonacademic advising as well as learning, the e-portfolio has special interest for student affairs professionals as well as students and faculty. It has been defined as

> a digitized collection of artifacts, including demonstrations, resources, and accomplishments that represent an individual, group, or institution. This collection can be comprised of text-based, graphic, or multimedia elements archived on a Web site or on other electronic media such as a CD-ROM or DVD. . . . (Lorenzo & Ittelson, 2005, p. 1)
>
> The benefits of an e-portfolio typically derive from the exchange of ideas and feedback between the author and those who view and interact with the e-portfolio. In addition, the author's personal reflection on the work inside an e-portfolio helps create a meaningful learning experience. (Lorenzo & Ittelson, 2005, p. 2)

E-portfolios are taking many forms on college campuses, from course-based collections of student and group work to advising tools for students to reflect on academic and professional goals, including degree program selection, major and minor choice, community service exploration, cocurricular activity records, and career development profiles. Student use of e-portfolios can begin during the admissions process and may extend well beyond degree completion. The technology has evolved into an all-purpose tool for campus life (and beyond) that showcases an individual's educational, professional, and personal achievements. Indeed, in some robust statewide systems, all state citizens and students enrolled in public colleges and universities can create personal e-portfolios (a notable example is eFolio Minnesota; see www.efoliominnesota.com). The following are examples of an individual student e-portfolio and an institutional project that illustrate important features of this learning technology.

Student professional e-portfolio. The e-portfolio of Sean Smallman, a graduating senior in the BFA theater production program at the University of Arizona (http://eportfolio.cfa.arizona.edu/cover.php?portid=93) uses a program-provided template that includes a home page he has populated with an image of a stage production on which he worked, an overview statement of his professional aspiration to be a lighting designer, and a link to his personal web site for more detail. Another page in his e-portfolio includes a scrollable résumé and a downloadable PDF version. The final page consists of linked thumbnails for two photo galleries—one of a Shakespearean stage production that Sean designed and the other of a special exterior lighting project he did for several buildings on the University of Arizona campus. Such an e-portfolio could supplement applications for a job or for graduate study.

Personal development e-portfolio. In the United Kingdom a unique partnership has developed a lifelong learning information system. The entities involved are Personal Development Planning (a national educational support program), the City of Nottingham Passport (a metropolitan information tool for citizens), and Nottingham University ePARs (an institutional model for managing personal and academic records). Originally conceived in 1996 by Ronald Dearing, the United Kingdom's Higher Education Policy Institute chairman, it was first widely implemented in 2005–2006, with such interactive components as the following (Jones, 2004):

- Work planning

- Self-assessment

- Private reflection

- Review of work with an advisor

- Self-presentation to an audience

An important feature of any well-designed e-portfolio is user control of access to its content. In Nottingham's ePARs system the student can grant access to any or all of three user categories: school or department administrator/advisor, academic tutor/instructor, and student. Without this fundamental privacy feature for managing users' access to various sections of the e-portfolio, a student will be less likely to trust the tool as a space for self-expression, materials collection, and honest reflection and will more likely see it as an administrative requirement.

Just as with L/CMSs, student affairs professionals have a vested interest in the evolution of e-portfolios on their campus. Do their institution's e-portfolio instructions, FAQs, and templates explain how students can link to academic and nonacademic support and counseling services? What are the policy and technical protocols for advisors to access all or part of a student's e-portfolio? Are there established guidelines for advisor and faculty partnerships and for interaction on common elements of a student's e-portfolio? Even when there are well-developed policies and procedures, they will remain viable only through regular dialogue between all stakeholders who use the technology.

These issues are discussed further in the Learning Technologies and Privacy Risks section later in this chapter.

Self-Publishing and Community Publishing

Self-publishing and community publishing refers to a cluster of electronic media technologies that have evolved over the past few years to support individual self-expression and group knowledge creation. These are typically available on public web sites, but they are often available only on password-restricted community learning spaces or private local networks. Pioneers and proponents of these technologies tout them as being as culturally transforming as Gutenberg's invention of movable type and the printing press in the 15th century, whereas critics and concerned devotees claim they have added immeasurably to Internet clutter and the digital age's propensity to waste time. In higher education these technologies are stimulating not only innovation in classrooms, laboratories, libraries, and social commons but broad debate within disciplines and institutions about academic missions and traditional faculty and student behaviors.

Blogs. Although there may never be a perfect solution for writer's block when engaging a topic or an issue in a course or for generating discussion in a classroom setting, blogging has helped many a reticent student interact with others. Shorthand for *web log,* a blog is a series of electronic journal entries and commentaries on either a focused topic or whatever stimulates the blogger at a given time. Blogs often include links to other sites and commentaries on particular blog entries by other bloggers. Hosted blog sites typically have features that allow bloggers to enter text directly or cut and paste from other sources, as well as add formatting, hyperlinks, and multimedia. Visitors can read, search by keyword or date, comment, and even subscribe to the site or receive alerts when entries on certain topics are made. Through Real Simple Syndication technology, bloggers can share postings via newsreaders that others employ to scan the web for content in which they are interested. In academic settings students may use blogs (voluntarily or by assignment) to reflect on specific course themes and on other students' reflections. Blogging facilitates informal but focused thought, monologue, dialogue, and synthesis.

"I knew firsthand the transformative power of social software in the hands of students. I have watched my students find themselves as community-minded learners, students who heretofore had been self-absorbed performers" (Ganley, 2006). This comment by Barbara Ganley, a lecturer in the writing program and director of the Project for Integrated Expression at

Middlebury College, is one of many provocative reflections on the impact of blogging on student learning and communication styles.

Wikis. According to the ELI brief on wikis, "A wiki is a Web page that can be viewed and modified by anyone with a Web browser and access to the Internet. . . . Any visitor to the wiki can change its content if they desire . . . permit[ting] asynchronous communication and group collaboration" (ELI, 2005c, p. 1). Wikis are powerful tools for group projects and knowledge creation. They allow users to add, delete, and modify what others have already submitted. Although by their very nature wikis may be populated with low-quality or even incorrect information and analysis, they also create a constructive pressure to always improve. Through transparent web page generation, a friendly graphical user interface, and HTML functionality, wikis constitute a democratic platform for information management, with the potential for rising or descending slopes of value, depending on the nexus of group trust, individual integrity, and joint commitment to truth.

A wiki is typically built on the backbone of a theme-based or group-identified web site whose URL is known to a set of users who use simple edit and submit buttons to modify the existing content. The best known and most widely used wiki is Wikipedia (www.wikipedia.org), begun in 2001 as an international, multilingual, editable, and searchable online encyclopedia, now with more than 4.5 million articles, including 1.2 million in English.

For teaching and learning, a course- or project-based wiki can be set up by a group of students who might come together to complete an assignment or who, on their own, decide to work together, dividing their collective resources to gather material, analyze, debate, critique, and reflect through the wiki. An excellent example is the Dickinson College series of wiki newsletters created by students in the global education program (http://itech.dickinson .edu/wiki/index.php/First_Issue). Students in the fall 2005 semester in Málaga, Spain, used their wiki to summarize research projects, describe art and architecture, record travel impressions, and comment on the culture and politics of modern Spain. In effect, their wiki could be considered a collective, editable blog.

Podcasting. Like Coke, Kleenex, and Xerox, Apple has reaped an enviable marketing boon in which one of its core products has spawned a word in the popular vernacular, or at least the language of wired techies: *podcasting.* The Apple iPod, a portable digital audio player—and, in some models, digital video player—was introduced in 2001, using the already established MP3 format for recording, uploading, and downloading media files. Podcasts are the files of recorded content that can travel over the web for sharing, storing, indexing, and playback at the user's convenience. Many college students are familiar with and use this technology regularly as an entertainment medium. Indeed, the issue of illegal file sharing on college campuses has brought a series of lawsuits from the recording and motion picture industries that have challenged the management of campus computing networks, our understanding of copyright infringement, and the value of open information exchange that is central to higher education.

Closely tied to the culture of blogging, podcasting enables anyone with basic recording equipment to easily create content that can then be posted on web pages and shared with others, making it a simple and cost-efficient strategy for self-publishing on the Internet. Educational uses of podcasting include making lectures and other course content available in audio and video file formats, interviewing experts and other students for content to embed into research projects, recording notes, and reflecting on course topics. Just as blogs and wikis can be incorporated into e-portfolios, so can podcasts. In fact, these technologies are fluid enough that any one could be the entry point to the others.

Duke University made educational history of a sort when it spent a half million dollars to give iPods and voice recorders to every member of the freshman class for the 2004–2005 academic year—the idea was to put in students' hands a tool with significant potential for engaging coursework and the world digitally. The results were mostly positive, garnering Duke kudos as much for institutional faith as for tangible innovation. Although it no longer gives an iPod to every entering student, the Duke Digital Initiative has helped transform several courses that now use podcasting technology as a standard learning tool (Duke Center for Instructional Technology, 2006). Consider the following examples from the spring 2006 semester:

- *Indian Cinema:* Students integrate iPods with digital editing tools to simulate the range of technical and artistic film-editing skills.

- *The Arts and Human Rights:* Students create podcasts of such things as recorded performances, news clips, and speeches and then analyze and reflect on the items' similarities and differences.

- *Intervention with Adolescents:* Students use iPods to take field notes on middle school students' perceptions of antidrug multimedia presentations.

- *Rebuilding from Ruins:* Students use iPods to keep audio journals of their activities in recreating the life cycle of a natural disaster.

To supplement the growth of podcasting with students and faculty, the university has developed DukeCapture, a service for automatic lecture recording through which, depending on faculty approval, students are able to download audio and video classroom lecture files from a central server (ELI, 2006). The issue this raises for some in higher education is "Why bother going to class at all?" Proponents argue that the anytime-anywhere opportunity to access and review classroom lectures and interactions is more compelling and meets a need that faculty and students alike have requested.

Social bookmarking. Classifying and creating subject hierarchies is a fundamental human way of knowing and may, in fact, be analogous to the neural structures of the brain. Typically, those who use web browsers regularly exercise this strategy when they set up folders for bookmarks of favorite web sites on their personal computers. Unfortunately, the phenomenon of folders-within-folders-within-folders can lead to chaos and uncertainty about where a bookmark that logically fits in two or more folders can be found. Ultimately, it is a solitary activity that's subject to individual whims and degrees of order (and disorder) and that's unaffected by the possibly greater clarity and search successes of other Internet users. Social bookmarking is a technology that can significantly reduce this chaos and increase the chances of efficient information management. In social bookmarking, individuals can organize their bookmarks with keyword tags selected by the user in a public or restricted group web site. The user can also access and copy others' bookmarks (ELI, 2005b). Three of the more popular social-bookmarking sites are Furl (www.furl.net), Simpy (www.simpy.com), and del.icio.us (http://del.icio.us).

The basic intellectual act at the heart of social bookmarking is tagging—that is, assigning one or more words to a particular resource that allows the user to retrieve the bookmark from the keyword and categories associated with it. Not only can registered users retrieve each other's bookmarks, but they can connect with each other because their contact information is associated with particular tags. Social bookmarking web sites track statistics on numbers of people using a tag to both search for and tag other web sites.

In learning settings, social bookmarking allows entire classes or project teams to organize online information resources that they discover collectively and individually. As an example of this technology in action, students in a course on the politics of immigration at the College of William and Mary developed a taxonomy of terms for the subject area that they then used to structure the web sites they discovered for their own research (Bryant, 2006).

In general, then, the learning technologies that support self- and group publishing encourage the individual student to generate thought with informality and ease and to share that thought with selected others or broad publics. These technologies also provide groups with tools to collaborate and share the explorations and knowledge that they generate together. To work with students in academic settings, whether in person or mediated by communications technologies, student affairs professionals need to understand which technologies are in use on their campus, where those technologies are being used by faculty and students, and what policies and technical opportunities would allow for using such technologies to bridge to student support services. Indeed, nearly all these technologies can be powerful tools and are starting to be used in advising and counseling services operations.

Gaming and Simulation

Games are part of today's culture. Handheld games, game consoles, computer games, and massive multiplayer online games are only some of the forms. Adventure games, strategy games, sports games, and first-person shooter games are among the existing genres. Aside from pioneers and proselytizers, higher education has only recently caught on to the power of gaming and alternative-reality simulation that the toy and game industries have understood for decades. Ultimately, it's not about games; it's about how they engage and energize players that makes them a potentially powerful learning tool. Although games' most obvious quality is that they are fun, more important attributes may be that "they are immersive, require the player to make frequent, important decisions, have clear goals, adapt to each player individually, and involve a social network" (Oblinger, 2006a; Van Eck, 2006). In addition, they require research and new learning because part of a game is learning skills that can be applied to winning. Problem solving is required. Players must learn the rules (which are codified in game play rather than in instruction manuals) and apply them to unique situations. And games are experiential. Game players take actions and see immediate responses. "For each action, there is a reaction. Feedback is swift. Hypotheses are tested and users learn from the results" (Oblinger, 2006b, p. 3; Oblinger, 2003).

In spite of the educational aspects of games, the importance of interface is often overlooked. Games have presented us with two new, and potentially transformative, interfaces:

> Most educators are familiar with the world-to-the-desktop interface
> that computers provide, enabling users to access resources, distant
> experts, collaborations, and communities of practice. The user "sits out-

side" the virtual world, but can access resources through it. An increasingly common interface—a critical one for games and immersive environments—might be called an Alice-in-Wonderland, multiuser virtual environment. Whether the technology involved is a computer or a hand-held ubiquitous device, participants can interact with computer-based agents and artifacts, virtually. (Oblinger, 2006b, p. 3)

The world-to-the-desktop interface is not psychologically immersive; virtual environments make players feel as if they are inside an environment. According to Dede (2005), the contrast is like diving rather than riding in a glass-bottom boat.

Many games and simulations allow students to "learn to be" or to simulate the experience of a professional. By participating in a community of practice and in immersive experiences, students learn through an apprenticeship model. For example, Flight Simulator allows students to learn what it is like to fly an airplane. America's Army allows players to go through a virtual basic training and experience being a soldier. In medicine, simulations enabled by tactile devices allow professionals to learn techniques, seeing and feeling the results of their actions. Marc Prensky, a leading-edge thinker and practitioner of gaming and simulation in higher education, has created the web site Social Impact Games (www.socialimpactgames.com), which lists more than 500 serious games that can be and are being used in learning situations.

Information Search and Literacy Tools

More than 60 years ago, Vannevar Bush, a visionary engineer and early computing pioneer, predicted that scholars would someday navigate computer-mediated files of all recorded human knowledge via a tool he called "memex." We now call it the Internet. "There is a new profession of trail blazers, those who find delight in the task of establishing useful trails through the enormous mass of the common record" (Bush, 1945). The "useful trails" have become powerful search engines that use keyword searches of multiple information databases and subscription services linking the library collections of numerous institutions and periodical publishers. What was unthinkable 10 or more years ago is now a cliché: It is possible for a student to earn a baccalaureate degree without ever setting foot in the campus building known as the library. "For most people, including academicians, the library—in its most basic function as a source of information—has become overwhelmingly a virtual destination" (Campbell, 2006, p. 20).

Academic libraries and librarians have adapted admirably to the challenge and opportunity of students' turning to the Internet as their central resource for information. The greatest challenge is helping students understand the value of library-provided search tools when they are tempted by the apparent ease and illusory wealth of material unearthed by such popular search engines as Yahoo! and Google. Hence, in addition to such new tasks as creating online reference services with links to full-text periodical and e-book collections, maintaining digital repositories, and managing resource licenses, librarians are deeply involved in teaching information literacy, often in partnership with faculty. The essence of information literacy is discrimination, being able to make judgments about what resources are likely to be useful—in particular courses, research topics, professional disciplines, and personal inquiry. Given students' comfort with being online, one of the most valuable tools for building information literacy is the online tutorial. Learn Enjoy and Play: Information Literacy Tutorial (LEAP; http://library.auraria.edu/leap/leappreview.html) is a publicly accessible information search tutorial in operation at the Auraria Library, serving nearly 37,000 students at three institutions in Denver, Colorado: the Community College of Denver, the Metropolitan State College of Denver, and the University of Colorado–Denver. Using Flash animation and perky, informal language, this interactive tutorial walks students through both successful and dead-end strategies for finding useful resources in six thematic areas: censorship and freedom of speech, global communities, Internet business, laws and regulations in cyberspace, new trends, and security and privacy.

A recent white paper from the ELI identifies three critical aspects of information literacy that have gained currency in education circles (Lorenzo & Dziuban, 2006). The first is visual literacy, or being able to use editing tools to manipulate images effectively in different media and to discern the truth and rhetorical purposes of images in the environment. The second is new-media literacy, which is the ability to communicate with and intelligently critique the cultural and political uses of mass media and digital media such as games, social software, virtual reality simulation, web sites, CD-ROMs, DVDs, and streaming audio and video. The final aspect of information literacy is information fluency, or being able to cultivate a blend of technical skills with various media and critical thinking skills. After finding out who on campus is responsible for teaching information literacy and where such skills are being cultivated, student affairs professionals must ask themselves how they, their services, and their department play a partnering role with others who view information literacy as a strategic mission. This sort of bridging occurs all too infrequently.

Evolving Learning Technologies

The following overviews deal with refinements and extensions of learning technologies discussed earlier in this chapter. Such developments are extremely fluid, with various innovation, acquisition, and implementation curves. The key point institutions must keep in mind is not to deploy or enhance particular learning technologies because some constituents want them to but, rather, to make choices based on departmental, divisional, and institutional missions and only then adjust IT funding allocations, human resources for instructional technology support, faculty and student training, and academic policies accordingly.

Smart information-on-demand systems. Information is becoming more personalized and being better filtered. Commercial web sites such as Amazon.com can track book and music search and buy patterns to make interest-based purchasing recommendations. Proprietary financial systems can analyze multiple economic data streams to guide stock and bond purchases. Medical diagnostic systems can process complex vital signs and real-time laboratory analysis to suggest patients' treatment options. In similar ways college and university information retrieval systems of the future will be able to interact with users at all stages of academic research to recommend productive paths of investigation. Indeed, prototypes are already delivering functionality that comes close to the artificial intelligence and decision support predictions of 30 years ago. Keyword searches that now depend on the user's knowledge of a subject area taxonomy and terms being typed into a search box will evolve into voice-recognition tools that interact with the student-scholar and, depending on her knowledge level, will either mentor her or be mentored by her (yes, the system will be a learner) to advance to a joint person-system interface in the search enterprise. Full-text resources will be brought to the student-scholar's desktop for sampling and possible reference categorization and storage in her personal catalog database. Smart information-on-demand systems will also integrate with L/CMS files for particular course sections, providing the student with a seamless connection between resources provided by the instructor and the universe of online information in a customizable, virtual learning space.

Of course, there is considerable debate among faculty, students, librarians, instructional designers, and academic administrators about the impact of such integrated systems. Will they, as was thought of digital calculators, render students into lazy, passive recipients of information, now brought to them by database "bot" crawlers; or will such systems enable more active learning by direct engagement with the search process itself? And what about the inherent privacy risks of systems that can become so thoroughly familiar with and store an individual's query patterns? It's not that much different from First Amendment concerns about library checkout records. What should student services professionals roll with, and what should they fight? The instinct of most professional librarians is captured in this reflection from a university library information specialist:

> Libraries, I think, have a choice. We can refuse to have anything to do with this sort of privacy-invading technology—on the grounds that it is so very dangerous to our civil liberties and against all the tenets of librarianship. Which it is. Then our students will use similar systems provided by others, who have less interest in educating them as to civil liberties. (Landesman, 2006)

Those who create, manage, and teach students how to use such systems need to balance technical innovation with learning theory, state and federal privacy law, law enforcement obligations, and rock-solid security infrastructure.

Mobile learning and the convergence of network services and personal devices. For years students had to seek out many online services at on-campus computer labs, registration centers, libraries, and student advising offices. But for some time they have been able to access these services via the Internet from locations on and off campus. The gradual penetration of wireless Internet access to more locations on college campuses has been paralleled during the past couple of years by other developments in technology: the explosive growth in student use of game devices, PDAs, MP3 audio and video players, and Internet-capable smart cell phones—and the inevitable physical compression, power and memory expansion, and functional integration of such devices. This convergence of smart devices and the progress toward any-where-anytime access is a seedbed for extending the classroom and facilitating interactive learning experiences. Wagner (2005) says this new direction in education is inevitable:

> Whether we like it or not, whether we are ready for it or not, mobile learning represents the next step in a long tradition of technology-mediated learning. It will feature new strategies, practices, tools, applications, and resources to realize the promise of ubiquitous, pervasive, personal, and connected learning. It responds to the on-demand learning interests of connected citizens in an information-centric world. It also connects formal educational experience . . . with informal, situated learning experience. (p. 44)

A notable example of a pilot effort to connect technologies that students already use for social communication with learning is Wake Forest University's MobileU program. In fall 2005 the program provided 100 students with pocket PCs to enhance their academic life. Combining functions of a cell phone and a mobile computer, the wireless devices allow faculty and students to use instant messaging and text messaging, the library information network, and the campus calendar—all mediated by voice-activated software. One chemistry faculty member is using the technology to send students course materials, such as audio files, so that they can preview upcoming class topics and review key ideas from previous classes (Walker, 2005).

Learning space design. A great deal of discussion and innovation in recent years has focused on the impact of evolving technologies and student behaviors on learning space design. Indeed, in the sense that technology is a tool, the places where learning occurs certainly constitute a technology in themselves. Most campuses have responded to increased faculty demand for instructional technology in the classroom by adding technology-enhanced "smart classrooms" with Internet access, multimedia presentation capability, user-friendly control consoles, and even direct phone connections with IT support staff (Carlson, 2006). But learning space design goes well beyond simply bringing more technology to existing classrooms. Informal spaces on campus are also potent learning spaces where students congregate, recreate, and, if facilitated, integrate learning with socializing. Technology is increasingly being used in student unions (e.g., in eating and entertainment areas, lounges, and game rooms), and it is starting to mediate food services (e.g., ordering online). But the major purpose of informal spaces is to encourage people to connect with each other.

Institutions with strategic computing plans that cut across organizational silos have brought together faculty, students, instructional technology staff, librarians, academic advisors, facilities managers, and architects to design new classroom buildings, enhanced library spaces, information commons, and student activity centers that reflect the interactive, collaborative, always-connected learning style of today's students. Oblinger (2006c) effectively captures the current thinking about learning spaces:

How do we turn the entire campus—and many places off campus—into an integrated learning environment? As we have come to understand more about learners, how people learn, and technology, our notions of effective learning spaces have changed. Increasingly, those spaces are flexible and networked, bringing together formal

and informal activities in a seamless environment that acknowledges that learning can occur anyplace, at any time, in either physical or virtual spaces. (p. 1.3)

In one notable example of an integrated learning space, the design team
that created MIT's Learning Lab for Complex Systems considered not only
the engineering curriculum but also students' inclination to use technology
tools in and out of the physical facility and their desire to extend the interactive use of those tools with fellow class members. The result was a facility that
has a central meeting room, multimedia classrooms, team breakout rooms,
chair and table configurations to facilitate face-to-face and group interaction,
informal spaces with whiteboards for brainstorming, student studios, a library
operations area, case study presentation rooms, immersive settings, social
spaces, connections between the design rooms and the system-build rooms,
accessibility during "student hours," and the ability to access project software
from residences. The designers summarized their core process and, by extension, the first principle in higher education learning space design, like this:
"We identified a variety of learning modes and then facilitated them with varied, flexible spaces" (Crawley & Imrich, 2004).

Future learning technologies. Which emerging technologies are further out
on the horizon? *The Horizon Report: 2006 Edition,* a joint effort of the New
Media Consortium and the ELI (2006), projects three technologies to be
adopted in 2008 or later:

- *Educational gaming* (two- to three-year adoption horizon): Research
  into gaming and engagement theory has led to increased use of gaming
  practice in disciplinary settings. Educational gaming should increase as
  students, faculty, and learning designers develop instructional game-
  building skills.

- *Augmented reality and enhanced visualization* (four- to five-year adoption
  horizon): This technology, the multidimensional visual modeling of
  large sets of data to create the effect of a physical presence for working
  with information, is already in use in medicine, engineering, the sciences, and archaeology.

- *Context-aware environments and devices* (four- to five-year adoption
  horizon): By using cues from the user's physical orientation, the time of
  day, space conditions, and other environmental features, as well as the
  user's current knowledge base and learning preferences and interests,

such tools will transparently and automatically respond to the user's needs.

LEARNING TECHNOLOGIES AND PRIVACY RISKS

Does the Net generation care about privacy and the risks of exposing personal information via social networking technology and the interactive Internet? You wouldn't think so given the wildly popular use of sites such as Facebook and MySpace, where users can "publish" themselves globally to literally millions of subscribers in supposedly secure communities. The scope of this phenomenon along with reported instances of abuse with occasionally tragic consequences have led some colleges to make awareness training about such services part of their technology and information literacy services for students. Cornell University, for example, includes a well-conceived web page called "Thoughts on Facebook" in its IT policy space (www.cit.cornell.edu/policy/memos/facebook.html). It covers caveats about attitude (invincibility), technology (caching), personal and institutional responsibility, and the law.

Learning technologies also create a challenge for institutional compliance with state and federal privacy laws regarding students' rights to control their educational records. The metaphor of an open hand next to a closed fist applies here. Because learning technologies support the collection, storing, publishing, and sharing of a great deal of personal and academic information, the understandable impulse is to structure systems to make this information readily available to encourage collaborative learning in courses and to support student success in advising settings (the open hand). However, the traditional role of academic administrators, data custodians, and privacy officers has been to restrict access to such information along precisely conceived rules grounded in legislation—namely, state privacy laws and the federal Family Educational Rights and Privacy Act (the closed fist). The only way to achieve an academically appropriate and legally sound balance between the two impulses is to adapt technology deployment to up-to-date policies and to ensure that all users are trained in both the technology and their obligations under policy and the law.

The Family Educational Rights and Privacy Act (FERPA) is grounded on two basic principles. First, the student controls the release of both directory information (defined as publicly accessible unless blocked by the student) and any nondirectory information (the "education record") maintained by the institution and its employees that is viewable by more than one employee. Second, elements of the education record may be accessed without student permission by either school officials with "legitimate educational interest" as part of their professional responsibilities or certain third parties under precisely defined legal circumstances. The ambiguity that has beguiled campus administrators and U.S. Department of Education officials since FERPA was enacted in 1974 is the meaning of the phrase "legitimate educational interest"; this phrase is especially challenging in the evolving distributed information environment and requires each institution to stipulate what it means. Five key questions should be at the nexus of learning technology and institutional privacy policy:

- Do students completely control access to all elements or portions of their personal web spaces and e-portfolios, for whatever purpose those technologies are used, or does their control vary by the type of learning or developmental technology?

- If access control is only partially available or not available at all to the student, does the student understand which individuals or categories of individuals (e.g., faculty members of courses in which the student is enrolled, fellow students in a course, faculty advisors, academic and athletic advisors, tutors, administrators, and other staff) are authorized to access some or all of the information stored by a particular technology to do their jobs? Annual notification to students of their rights, as required under FERPA, is the appropriate way to communicate this information (Rainsberger et al., 2000).

- Are privacy explanations and instructions for students about how to exercise access control clear and visible on the technology start-up page and in a training tutorial?

- Has the institution carefully defined "legitimate educational interest" by specifying which student data elements and information sectors in learning technology repositories school officials (such as faculty and staff) may view?

- Do faculty and staff with access to student information through learning technologies (above and beyond administrative systems) understand their obligations under FERPA and relevant state privacy laws? Is there a well-designed privacy awareness training program for all employees, whether administered by the registrar's office, the computing organization, or human resources?

Two examples of well-designed systems that integrate learning technologies, privacy policy, student control and training, and faculty and staff obligation training are at the University of Southern California and the Pennsylvania State University. The Online Academic Student Information System at the University of Southern California (https://camel.usc.edu/oasis/LoginGuest.aspx) allows students to create accounts and PINs for guest access to elements of their web-based academic records. Penn State's e-portfolio resources for faculty, advisors, and teaching assistants (http://eportfolio.psu.edu/build/psuresources/index.html#faculty) provides helpful links to FERPA and university privacy policies.

CULTURE CHANGE

Technology has presented society with many new tools and opportunities. As they are adopted, they become part of our culture, or our set of accepted norms and behaviors. Just a few years ago someone walking down the sidewalk listening to music on an iPod would be unusual; today students say that wearing an iPod is simply part of how they dress (EDUCAUSE, 2005). BlackBerries, iPods, and other digital devices are an accepted—and expected—part of our existence. And although the devices will change, fundamental elements of this culture shift may not.

Amateur as Authority

Technology has enabled a massive flattening of hierarchies. Want to write and share your work with the world? Write a blog. Think the news media has got it wrong? Speak up; almost undoubtedly someone out there will listen. "Experts" are no longer just those with advanced degrees or in selected positions. Individuals are becoming self-appointed experts, creating and contributing to wikis, blogs, and web sites. Wikipedia illustrates an increasingly common belief that hundreds of thousands of people can't be wrong. The power of the network and of the community appears to be surpassing the power of the hierarchy.

Participation

People's desire for individualization, customization, and control makes them want to actively participate in and influence the games they play, whether it's

Battlefield 2142 or Finance 101. Students are not content with allowing others to make decisions for them—they believe they should be able to participate. Participation does not mean that students take over; it does, however, imply that they have a voice, that they are consulted, and that their perspective is valued.

Integration

Once text, images, sound, and video became digital, all manner of things could be integrated. Students expect the integration of multiple media formats—and the opportunity to choose which suit them best. Students effortlessly integrate the physical and virtual—talking to someone next to them while instant messaging that person is just another communication channel. Social and academic life are not necessarily separate; in fact, much of academic learning is social, and students have increasing expectations that services will be integrated to address their needs. Rather than going to the library, then to the writing center, then to the IT help desk, students expect to see all three functions at an integrated services desk in the information commons.

Choice

Technology allows us to control many aspects of our environment: what music we listen to and when we listen to it, the TV programming we watch when we relax, the courses we take face to face and those we take online, whom we associate with, and how we will communicate with them—face to face, online, or both. Students choose potential friends based on information from social networks, such as Facebook. And they choose the persona they want to present to the world by the pictures they post, the hobbies they list, and the experiences they recount online. Technology has created the expectation that we can control time, place, and medium.

What then does the conjunction of evolving learner attitudes, behaviors, and expectations with converging learning technologies mean for the student affairs professional focused on student success? It means transforming professional practice in ways that use technology to foster connections with and between the new digital natives. This has ramifications for the individual advisor as well as for the institutional structure of service organizations. Here are some questions student affairs professionals should ask themselves:

- Do you know what technologies your advisees use inside and outside their courses? How do the technologies they use complement or conflict with their personal learning styles and social inclinations? Are they addicted to any particular technologies in ways that jeopardize their academic success and put them at personal risk? Are they aware of the risks and how to avoid those risks?

- Are there organizational silos for the delivery of academic and student services at your institution that make it difficult or inefficient to bring good counsel to students or students to good counselors through inter- active online information? How can technology bridge or break down the silos? Are executives and senior administrators prepared to yield tra- ditional organizational chart territories for new configurations to match learners' expectations of collaborative participation and independent control?

- Do student affairs professionals regularly talk to faculty members, librarians, instructional designers, admissions staff, registrars, financial aid counselors, and bursars about how technology is penetrating and transforming the traditional academic and administrative sides of the house? Are there forums to discuss ways of blending and making more seamless the technologies that facilitate learning and student support?

- What role should technology play in supporting on- and off-campus learners in such areas as one-stop (or no-stop) advising centers and business processes? What skills and cross-training do student ombudspersons and advisors need to reflect the connectedness, collabo- ration, and ease of navigation that networked systems have?

- Are students regularly involved in suggesting services and commenting on existing services? Have student affairs professionals adopted a phi- losophy of cocreation of services to ensure that student needs and expectations are met?

CONCLUSION

Ultimately, student affairs professionals and their institutions must ask them- selves what they are doing to find the right blend of learning technologies and service integration to make the bumper-sticker slogan "Students First" actu- ally run under the hood.

REFERENCES

Bryant, T. (2006). Social software in academia. *EDUCAUSE Quarterly, 29*(2). Retrieved June 23, 2007, from www.educause.edu/apps/eq/eqm06/eqm0627.asp

Bush, V. (1945, July). As we may think. *The Atlantic Monthly,* pp. 101–108.

Campbell, J. (2006). Changing a cultural icon: The academic library as a virtual destination. *EDUCAUSE Review, 41*(1). Retrieved June 23, 2007, from www.educause.edu/ir/library/pdf/erm0610.pdf

Carlson, S. (2006, July 11). Campus planners have a tech-savvy generation's needs to consider. *The Chronicle of Higher Education.* Retrieved July 11, 2006, from http://chronicle.com/daily/2006/07/2006071102n.htm

Crawley, E., & Imrich, S. (2004, September). *Process for designing learning spaces: Case study: The MIT learning lab for complex systems.* PowerPoint presentation delivered at the annual meeting of the National Learning Infrastructure Initiative, Cambridge, MA.

Dede, C. (2005). Planning for neomillennial learning styles: Implications for investments in technology and faculty. In D. G. Oblinger & J. L. Oblinger (Eds.), *Educating the net generation.* Retrieved June 24, 2007, from www.educause.edu/ir/library/pdf/pub7101o.pdf

Duke Center for Instructional Technology. (2006). *Digital technologies in courses.* Retrieved June 7, 2006, from http://cit.duke.edu/about/ipod_faculty_projects_spring06.do#aall170

EDUCAUSE. (2005). *Invasion of the iPods.* Retrieved June 24, 2007, from http://connect.educause.edu/node/1386

EDUCAUSE Learning Initiative. (2005a). *7 things you should know about . . .* Retrieved June 24, 2007, from www.educause.edu/7ThingsYouShouldKnowAboutSeries/7495

EDUCAUSE Learning Initiative. (2005b). *7 things you should know about social bookmarking.* Retrieved May 9, 2007, from www.educause.edu/ir/library/pdf/ELI7001.pdf

EDUCAUSE Learning Initiative. (2005c). *7 things you should know about wikis.* Retrieved June 23, 2007, from www.educause.edu/ir/library/pdf/ELI7004.pdf

EDUCAUSE Learning Initiative. (2006). *DukeCapture: Automated classroom lecture recording.* Retrieved June 7, 2006, from www.educause.edu/ir/library/pdf/ELI5011.pdf

Ganley, B. (2006). *At the UK's first edublogging conference: My talk.* Retrieved June 24, 2007, from http://mt.middlebury.edu/middblogs/ganley/bgblogging/2006/06/at_the_uks_first_edublogging_c.html

Green, K. (2005). *Campus computing 2005.* Encino, CA: The Campus Computing Project.

Jones, P. (2004). *What's the use of an e-portfolio? Defining the demand* [PowerPoint presentation]. Retrieved June 26, 2007, from www.notting ham.ac.uk/eportfolio/specifyinganeportfolio/keydocuments/presentations/ PRJNottingham%2008%2006%2004.ppt

Landesman, M. (2006, April). SNARB—Coming soon to a library near you. *The Charleston ADVISOR, 7*(4). Retrieved July 8, 2006, from www.charlestonco.com/features.cfm?id=206&type=ed

Lorenzo, G., & Dziuban, C. (2006). *Ensuring the net generation is net savvy* (EDUCAUSE Learning Initiative Paper No. 2). Retrieved June 24, 2007, from www.educause.edu/ir/library/pdf/ELI3006.pdf

Lorenzo, G., & Ittelson, J. (2005). *An overview of e-portfolios* (EDUCAUSE Learning Initiative Paper No. 1). Retrieved June 23, 2007, from www.educause.edu/ir/library/pdf/ELI3001.pdf

New Media Consortium & EDUCAUSE Learning Initiative. (2006). *The horizon report: 2006 edition.* Retrieved June 23, 2007, from http://nmc.org/pdf/2006_Horizon_Report.pdf

Oblinger, D. G. (2003). *Unlocking the potential of gaming technology.* Unpublished manuscript.

Oblinger, D. G. (2006a). Games and learning: Digital games have the potential to bring play back to the learning experience. *EDUCAUSE Quarterly, 29*(3). Retrieved June 23, 2007, from www.educause.edu/apps/eq/eqm06/eqm0630.asp

Oblinger, D. G. (2006b). *Simulations, games, and learning.* Retrieved June 23, 2007, from www.educause.edu/ir/library/pdf/ELI3004.pdf

Oblinger, D. G. (2006c). Space as a change agent. In D. G. Oblinger (Ed.), *Learning spaces.* Retrieved June 23, 2007, from www.educause.edu/ir/library/pdf/PUB7102a.pdf

Rainsberger, R. A., Baker, E. G., Hicks, D., Myers, B., Noe, J., & Weese, F. A. (2000). *The AACRAO 2001 FERPA guide.* Washington, DC: American Association of Collegiate Registrars and Admissions Officers.

Rideout, V., Hamel, E., & Kaiser Family Foundation. (2006). *The media family: Electronic media in the lives of infants, toddlers, preschoolers, and their parents.* Retrieved June 24, 2007, from www.kff.org/entmedia/upload/7500.pdf

Starrett, D. (2005, April). *Who are your future students?* Paper presented at the Teaching the 21st Century Learners conference, Cape Girardeau, MO.

Van Eck, R. (2006, March/April). Digital game-based learning: It's not just the digital natives who are restless. *EDUCAUSE Review, 41*(2). Retrieved June 23, 2007, from www.educause.edu/ir/library/pdf/erm0620.pdf

Wagner, E. D. (2005, May/June). Enabling mobile learning. *EDUCAUSE Review, 40*(3). Retrieved June 24, 2007, from www.educause.edu/ir/library/pdf/erm0532.pdf

Walker, C. (2005, August 24). *WFU first with campus pilot of pocket PC phones.* Retrieved June 24, 2007, from www.wfu.edu/wfunews/2005/082405m.html

9 | GIVING ADVICE THAT MAKES A DIFFERENCE

WESLEY R. HABLEY AND JENNIFER L. BLOOM

Few topics have garnered more tongue-in-cheek and cynical commentary than the topic of giving advice. Aesop suggested that one should never trust advice from a man in difficulty, and Harry S. Truman intoned, "I have found the best way to give advice to your children is to find out what they want and then advise them to do it." Most everyone dispenses advice informally, on any and all topics, on an almost daily basis, to whomever will listen, whether it's requested or not.

The focus of this chapter is not on such advice or on informal advice givers. Rather, its goal is to define and discuss a set of considerations for those who are charged by a college or university with giving advice to students to help them identify and realize academic goals and objectives. People with this responsibility are identified by a myriad of titles, including academic advisors, faculty advisors, educational counselors, mentors, and preceptors. And there are often others on campus who serve as academic advisors—even though their titles may not suggest an advising responsibility. Throughout this chapter, the generic terms *academic advisor* and *advisor* refer to all such individuals, regardless of their formal title.

This chapter includes five sections: institutional imperatives for quality advising; the roles advisors should play; advisor understanding of student development, diversity, and the stages of engagement; the relationship-building process; and the institutional and personal leadership necessary for advising to make a difference.

INSTITUTIONAL IMPERATIVES FOR ADVISING

Academic advising has existed at least informally on college campuses since the earliest days of American higher education. And although there is evidence of academic advising as an emerging field in the late 19th and early

20th centuries, the growth of academic advising and the theoretical, definitional, and practical literature supporting it has mushroomed since about 1965. In the years since, definitions of advising have evolved from the simple and narrow to the multifaceted and complex. In the 1970 *Handbook of College and University Administration,* Asa Knowles suggested that "the primary roles of advisors were teaching the mechanics of course selection and explaining the program of study" (p. 22). Shortly thereafter, however, two seminal articles challenged that traditional view that limited advising to helping students select courses during registration. Crookston (1972) articulated the dimensions of developmental advising, and O'Banion (1972) offered a five-stage paradigm for academic advising. Since that time, nearly every major advising resource has included a more expansive definition of advising. It is not the purpose of this chapter to review and critique those definitions or to provide yet another new and more compelling definition of academic advising. (Readers who are interested in a review of advising definitions should access the National Academic Advising Association's listing at www.nacada.ksu. edu/Clearinghouse/AdvisingIssues/Definitions.htm.)

The intent of this section, then, is to present and discuss six institutional imperatives that must anchor the advising program if it is to make a difference in the lives of students.

First, academic advising must be viewed as more than information giving for the purpose of selection and scheduling courses. Although it is essential that academic advisors provide timely and accurate course and degree information, in this day and age students have multiple, and far more efficient, means to access the information they need. To suggest, then, that giving information is the primary role of an academic advisor is to reduce the role of advisor to that of a clerk who makes sure that a student efficiently processes through a predetermined sequence of classes in a specified period of time to earn an academic credential.

Second, advising must be viewed as a process, not as an event or a series of events. *Merriam-Webster's Online Dictionary* (2006) defines *process* as "a natural phenomenon marked by gradual changes that lead toward a particular result" as well as "a series of actions or operations conducing to an end." It is not possible for advising to make a difference in the lives of students if each interaction with an advisor is viewed as a discrete, stand-alone event, void of context and lacking direction. Advising is marked by gradual changes and a series of related actions that lead to the achievement of student educational goals.

Third, advising must be characterized as a student-centered relationship. If advising is a process that involves more than information giving, then its positive impact can be fully realized only in the context of the relationship between advisor and advisee. Although there are numerous ways to define the advising relationship, Crookston (1972) offered a set of 10 dimensions that he described as characteristic of a quality advising relationship. Loosely paraphrased, those dimensions are:

- A focus on student potential

- The belief that students are striving and active

- The belief that students are growing, maturing, responsible, and capable of self-direction

- An emphasis on achievement and mastery

- Shared initiative

- Negotiated control of the relationship

- Negotiated responsibilities

- Learning and growth by both the advisee and the advisor

- Collaborative assessment of progress

- High trust

Crookston's dimensions suggest that the advising relationship is a two-way interaction rather than one in which the advisor prescribes a course of action that the student compliantly pursues.

Fourth, advising must be viewed as a teaching/learning function. In his 1972 article "A Developmental View of Academic Advising as Teaching," Crookston built a strong case for this imperative by advocating for two basic assumptions. He suggested that higher education provided the vehicle through which students work toward a self-fulfilling life and that teaching includes all activities that contribute to that goal. And, in a pointed and succinct affirmation of advising as teaching, Robert Berdahl (1995) suggested that "advising, rather than an extension of the educator's role, is integral to it. It is that part of teaching which stretches beyond instruction" (p. 7). Finally, the Council for the Advancement of Standards in Higher Education (CAS; 2003) asserts that the academic advising program must incorporate student learning in its mission and deliver services that enhance the overall educational experiences of students.

The first four institutional imperatives establish the context for the fifth imperative: Advising must be embedded in and central to the institutional mission. There is an increasing emphasis in the regional accreditation process to demonstrate that student support programs such as academic advising are consistent with and supportive of the institution's mission. The Southern Association of Colleges and Schools' Commission on Colleges (2004) includes a core requirement that "the institution provides student support programs, services, and activities consistent with its mission that promote student learning and enhance the development of its students" (p. 17). As Berdahl (1995) noted, "Advising . . . should be anchored in the institution's educational mission rather than layered on as a service" (p. 7).

Sixth, advising must function as the hub of support services for students. This final imperative can be realized only if each of the previous imperatives is achieved. Advising is unlike any other service or program on campus in that it provides students with a multifaceted, structured, and ongoing relationship with a concerned representative of the institution. Because of the unique nature of the advising relationship, there is a centrality to the function of advising. Knowledgeable advisors are in a position to span boundaries and build networks with a full array of other support services on the campus.

ROLES OF ADVISORS

Now that we have established the institutional imperatives for a successful advising program, our focus shifts to the advisors themselves and the multiple roles they play in the lives of students.

Advisor as Consumer Advocate

Advisors assist students in making wise choices—making the best use of the appropriate institutional resources. Implicit in this statement is the notion that students are consumers rather than customers. And although many institutions tout the concept of customer service, that analogy is not one that captures the essence of the educational process and should not, therefore, be applied to academic advising. The relationship with a customer is essentially adversarial. It involves a transaction in which both parties try to get the maximum while giving the minimum. Customer service implies that the student is always right and that obvious and immediate student satisfaction should be the outcome of an advising transaction. Experienced advisors know that some advice may be provocative and seem, temporarily at least, wholly unsatisfactory to the student.

To be a consumer advocate, alternatively, is to challenge students to explore, stretch, and grow, which may not always result in their immediate satisfaction.

Advisor as Intervener

Advising is not a passive activity. There may be times when it becomes apparent that a student's educational journey is heading in the wrong direction, is stalled, or is otherwise in jeopardy. Timely and assertive intervention can often spell the difference between success and failure in a class or an academic program. And, in some cases at least, a timely intervention can mediate the student's decision to withdraw from (or not return to) school. An advisor can assist a student in locating the source of the problem and in making connections with institutional resources that may solve the problem or help the student modify dysfunctional behavior. Moreover, assertive advisor intervention provides an opportunity for the advisor to build trust by demonstrating concern for the student.

Advisor as Orchestrator

To orchestrate is to arrange or combine to achieve a desired or maximum effect. In a musical sense, an orchestrator is an individual whose knowledge of instrument ranges, tonal quality, sonorities, and timbre comes into play when arranging a piece of music. Advisors function in much the same way, blending student goals, abilities, interests, and values with the full array of institutional programs and support resources. Inherent in this analogy of advisor as orchestrator are two requisites: 1) the advisor must know the student and demonstrate an understanding of the student's needs, and 2) the advisor must be knowledgeable of institutional programs, policies, and resources.

Advisor as Dissonance Mediator

For some students, the transition to college is a smooth one, but many students experience a transitional shock. Their expectations for college life do not jibe with their experiences. It is usually in an advisor's office that the difference between expectations and the realities of college life first surfaces. Habley (1981) offers a definition of advising that focuses on this dissonance, suggesting that academic advising "provides assistance mediating the dissonance between student expectations and the realities of the educational experience" (p. 46). Although it is neither possible nor desirable to totally eliminate these dissonances, it is possible for an advisor to reduce the disparity between what students expect and what they experience by providing timely and accurate information and, more important, by offering support as they seek to adjust to the realities of campus life.

Advisor as Dissonance Creator

At first, it may seem that the advisor's role as dissonance creator contradicts his or her role as dissonance mediator. In reality, the true art of advising derives from recognizing when dissonance should be mediated and when it should be created. It is important for advisors to know when and how much to challenge students to probe more deeply or to reach for loftier goals. The role of the advisor, like that of classroom teacher, is to create a tolerable level of cognitive dissonance and provocative but benign disruption. Anything less is an abdication of the advisor's role as educator.

Advisor as Boundary Spanner

Every student is unique. And although there is a temptation for advisors to generalize about the needs of all students, it is incumbent on advisors to assist students in designing a unique set of educational experiences that include the curriculum and the cocurriculum and a full range of student support services. This requires knowledge of the variety of institutional and external resources that enable students to identify and reach their educational goals. Advisors must be able to span these institutional boundaries.

Advisor as Bellwether

Relationships with students put advisors in the unique position of knowing not only what curricula and institutional policies support students but also what curricula and policies may impede student learning and growth. A bellwether advisor is an individual who takes the lead in bringing issues to curriculum committees and policymaking bodies on campus. By providing insight into the effect that program and policy decisions have (or will have) on students, the advisor becomes an advocate for student growth and learning.

Advisor as Cultural Guide

Each institution of higher education has its own norms and ways of doing business. Advisors educate students about written policies and unwritten expectations that will help them efficiently navigate the system and access appropriate resources. In addition, advisors can help students learn appropriate behavior norms for their particular institution. For example, advisors can coach students on how best to approach faculty members about joining their research labs. Advisors also can help prepare students for their future careers by letting them know which of their behaviors will be appropriate in the workplace.

UNDERSTANDING STUDENT DEVELOPMENT, DIVERSITY, AND THE STAGES OF ENGAGEMENT

The institutional imperatives discussed earlier provide a set of critical building blocks for implementing a successful advising program. Yet it becomes the advisor's responsibility to deliver on these imperatives. This section focuses on the need for advisors to demonstrate a basic understanding of both the diversity of student needs and the stages of student engagement with the institution.

Understanding Student Development and the Diversity of Student Needs

A working knowledge of student development theory provides academic advisors with a foundation on which to understand the diverse needs of the students with whom they work. Theories on how students develop abound. A review of the literature reveals a whole host of theories related to identity, making meaning, cognitive development, learning and personality, psychosocial development, and career development. The literature also features theories about the manner in which attributes like gender, race, and sexual identity affect student development. Although it is tempting to recommend that advisors become thoroughly grounded in each of these theories, the sheer number of theories makes that impractical. Nevertheless, it is essential that advisors have a basic understanding of the theoretical underpinnings of student development. Excellent summaries of the various theoretical perspectives can be found in Creamer and Associates (1990); Evans, Forney, and Guido-DiBrito (1998); Komives, Woodard, and Associates (1996); and Upcraft (1995).

In addition to understanding the general concepts of student development, it is equally important that advisors meet the diverse needs of several subgroups of students. Frost (1991) suggests that there are at least three subgroups of students, each of which may require differing techniques or advisor skills. The first subgroup is students in transition—that is, students who are integrating into college life. This category includes, but is not limited to, first-year students, transfer students, and adult students, as well as students who are undecided about a college major or who have changed majors. Students in this subgroup must assimilate into new expectations and make personal meaning of their relationships with the institution, its academic programs, and its social environment.

The second subgroup is composed of those who require additional services or accommodations. Among these groups are student athletes; honors students; students with disabilities; and gay, lesbian, bisexual, or transgender students. Ender and Wilkie (2000) suggest that although advisors should be cautious about making generalizations about the needs of students in any of these groups, it is important that they understand that student-institution interactions may be significantly different for these students. The authors go on to urge that advisors of these students focus on the student development themes of academic competence, personal involvement on campus, and developing a validating life purpose. They also suggest that these themes "be addressed within the context of a developmental advising relationship that is ongoing and purposeful, based in an interpersonal relationship, goal-oriented, and both challenging and supportive" (pp. 120–121).

The final subgroup of students identified by Frost is multicultural and international students. It is clear that college enrollments have been and will continue to be characterized by increasing diversity in students' racial-ethnic and sociocultural backgrounds. Habley (2005) projects that by the year 2013 the growth in racial and ethnic population cohorts will result in a national undergraduate enrollment that will be 13% black (non-Hispanic), 16% Hispanic, 9% Asian/Pacific Islander, and 1% American Indian. In addition, the National Center for Education Statistics reports that there are nearly 600,000 international students enrolled in American colleges and universities (Knapp et al., 2005). Race, ethnicity, culture, and economics influence communication styles, attitudes toward education, learning styles, responses to authority, definitions of personal space, approaches to problem resolution, and overall adaptation to campus life. Although it is impossible for advisors to completely understand the effect of these factors and it is unwise to overgeneralize about the needs of students based on factors like race, ethnicity, and culture, Priest and McPhee (2000) suggest that it is critical to provide them with culturally sensitive advising.

Evolving Stages of Student Engagement with the Institution

In addition to understanding student development and the diversity of student needs, it is incumbent on advisors to demonstrate an understanding of student needs at various stages of engagement with the institution. This section provides an overview of the work of four advising theorists concerning how students' advising needs and engagement with the institution evolve throughout their undergraduate careers.

First, Habley (1993) has proposed a two-stage model of intake and mentoring for engaging students in the advising process. All students enter college with many questions and some trepidation. These are the students that Frost (1991) refers to as students in transition. Their questions tend to be laden with insecurity: Have I chosen (or will I choose) the right major? Is this the right college for me, or should I be in college at all? Can I make it academically? Are policies and procedures really that important? Will I make new friends? An advisor working with students at the intake stage provides information, clarification, and support. When intake advising is successful, students will have identified and committed to programs of study, proved that they can be successful in the classroom, come to understand policies and procedures, and made an overall adjustment to the campus environment.

Habley posits that students who have achieved these intake outcomes should be ready to move on to the second stage: mentoring. Although definitions of mentoring abound, the mentoring advisor is one who develops with the student a relationship of trust that focuses on the exploration of options and the free exchange of ideas. Mentors provide insights into the discipline and connections with the post-baccalaureate world and challenge students to explore, examine, and analyze critical issues both within the discipline and across disciplines.

Second, Chickering (1994) suggests that there are three stages in the advisor-student relationship: Moving In, Moving Through, and Moving On. He suggests that assisting students in transitioning to college and developing motivation for learning (Moving In) are the most critical responsibilities of advisors. In the Moving Through stage, the advising relationship focuses on defining a major, optimizing learning, and developing mature relationships. In the Moving On stage, the focus of the advising relationship shifts to helping clarify the student's new and external identity as well as to cultivating a lifelong perspective on learning.

Third, Creamer (2000) approaches the topic of student engagement with academic advising by offering a continuous process model in which the need for information and the need for consultation is negotiated between the student and the advisor (see Figure 9.1). Creamer's model focuses on the gradual and incremental transition over time from an advising relationship that is characterized primarily as information sharing to one that is characterized by consultation.

Figure 9.1 **Changing Needs and Contexts for Advising**

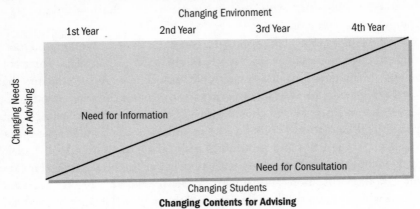

Source: Creamer (2000).

The fourth and most comprehensive model for understanding student needs at various stages of institutional engagement is provided by Kramer (2000). His model includes advising needs of students from before their entry to college through graduate school. For each of the academic levels, Kramer maps basic advising themes, a set of needs or educational tasks associated with each theme, and recommendations on the delivery of advising services.

This overview of student development, student diversity needs, and stages of student-institution engagement points to the conclusion that quality advising is far more complex than simply dispensing information and helping students pick and schedule classes. Advisors who make a difference view each student as a unique individual whose development, needs, attitudes, and values have been shaped by a variety of factors that fit no generalizations or stereotypes. Such complexity lends further credence to the assertions made earlier: Advising makes a difference when it is viewed as a student-centered relationship.

THE RELATIONSHIP-BUILDING PROCESS

As the preceding sections have illustrated, the advisor-student relationship is complex and multifaceted. Advising literature is replete with multiple theories yet does not contain many tangible steps for assisting advisors in building trust and developing their relationships with students. This section proposes one possible avenue for initially constructing viable and positive relationships with students.

Lipman (1995) shares the following insight:

> There are many ways to succeed. . . . It is no better to be Picasso
> than to be Rembrandt, to be Mozart rather than Beethoven. . . .
> We each have something unique to offer. To develop it, to offer it
> clearly, fully, and powerfully—is to succeed. Beethoven did not fail
> to become another Mozart; he succeeded at becoming Beethoven.
> Seen this way, success comes from developing your uniqueness. It is
> rare but not scarce. Everyone, potentially, can succeed. (pp. 29–30)

The challenge advisors face is determining the best method for helping students optimize their educational experiences and develop their uniqueness. Just as personal fitness trainers work individually with their clients to create and implement an individualized fitness-training plan, academic advisors collaborate with students to develop and execute a personalized academic plan. Arthur Chickering (1994) stated:

> The fundamental purpose of academic advising is to help students
> become effective agents for their own lifelong learning and personal
> development. Our relationships with students—the questions we
> raise, the perspectives we share, the resources we suggest, the short-
> term decisions and long-range plans we help them think through—
> all should aim to increase their capacity to take charge of their own
> existence. (p. 67)

Fulfilling this objective is no easy task given students' diverse backgrounds, goals, and aspirations. However, the organizational development theory of appreciative inquiry (AI) and its focus on developing powerful, positive questions and listening carefully to answers provides a framework that incorporates the institutional imperatives set forth earlier in this chapter. The AI framework is one that advisors can employ to help students recognize their potential and achieve their dreams.

AI was developed in 1979 by David Cooperrider, a doctoral student at Case Western Reserve University (Whitney & Trosten-Bloom, 2003). Enriched by the positive psychology movement, AI has been successfully implemented at large corporations (GTE, British Airways, Avon Mexico, McDonald's, Hunter Douglas's window fashions division); government agencies (NASA, the U.S. Navy, the U.S. Environmental Protection Agency); nonprofit agencies (United Religions Initiative, CARE, Imagine Chicago); and universities (Indiana University School of Medicine, Case Western Reserve University). Bloom and Martin (2002) were the first to make the link between AI and academic advising. Subsequently, Hutson (2006) reported that the University of North Carolina–Greensboro had incorporated AI into its advising system, resulting in higher academic recovery rates and an increase in students' self-perception of their own social behavior, academic preparedness, engagement with the institution, dedication, self-knowledge, and confidence.

The power of AI lies in the quality of the questions that advisors ask students and its focus on the enormous, often untapped, potential of each student. AI includes four stages: discovery, dream, design, and destiny (Cooperrider, Sorenson, Whitney, & Yaeger, 2000; Watkins & Mohr, 2001; Whitney & Trosten-Bloom, 2003). Bloom and Martin (2002) posit that for advisors to use AI successfully, they must first believe in the positive potential of each student who enters their offices. Future CEOs and astronauts do not walk in with a special tattoo that identifies them as such. Richard Herman (2005), chancellor of the University of Illinois at Urbana-Champaign, rightly states, "We do not as much lead people to our vision as we unleash them—their insight, ability, potential and ambition." The four stages of AI allow advisors to do just that—unleash the potential of students—through a series of positive, open-ended questions.

The Discovery Phase

The discovery phase is important because it gives advisors tools for building an initial rapport with students. A relationship of trust makes students more likely to be honest and forthcoming with the advisor. During the discovery phase, advisors attempt to ascertain the current strengths and abilities of students. Students have amazing stories of accomplishments, triumphs over insurmountable odds, and examples of how they have positively impacted other people's lives. In fact, the opportunity to be inspired by students speaks to Crookston's (1972) assertion that both advisors and students learn and benefit from their interactions. How can advisors draw out these stories from students? The answer is through positive, open-ended questions like these:

- When was a time you have positively impacted another person's life?

- What would your friends and family say are your top three strengths?

- What are your most cherished values? From whom do you think you learned these values?

- What are three skills that you would like to acquire or enhance?

The Dream Phase

The dream phase is focused on helping students explore their goals for life and career. This phase draws on the first two elements from O'Banion's (1972) work on the key components of academic advising: "exploration of life goals, exploration of vocational goals, program choice, course choice, and scheduling of courses" (p. 67). Today much of the information necessary for students to choose classes to fulfill degree requirements is available online. The value-added dimension of academic advisors is their ability to ask questions about long-term life and career goals and to listen carefully to students' answers before asking follow-up questions. Specific questions advisors can use to probe students about these long-term goals include:

- How is the world going to be a better place because of you?
- Twenty years from now, what does your ideal day look like?
- What are your top three life goals?
- What are your top three career goals?
- What are your top three goals for your undergraduate education?

The Design Phase

The design phase is when advisors delve into the details of fulfilling the long-term goals established in the dream phase. Students' answers to the dream phase questions serve as the context for discussion of more specific steps to attain these goals in the design phase. The advisor not only collaborates with the student to devise the concrete, incremental steps necessary to achieve goals but also directs the student to required resources. To paraphrase Hillary Clinton, it takes a village to ensure that students graduate and are positioned to attain their life and career goals. For example, a campus's career services office may have helpful information on creating a compelling résumé and cover letter, alumni working in the student's area of interest may be willing to answer questions, and a faculty member might have connections for a summer internship or research program.

This is also the phase when O'Banion's (1972) last three elements come into play: carefully selecting a program of study, choosing classes, and scheduling classes. The advisor works with students to compose a unique plan that will enable them to reach their potential.

An important element of this phase is working with students up front to devise an evaluation plan that will allow them to determine whether they have been successful. What outcomes is the student seeking? Questions for this phase include:

- What steps do you need to take during your college career to achieve your most important life, career, and college goals?

- What resources will you need to accomplish these goals and objectives?

- How will you know that you have accomplished them?

- How will you celebrate the accomplishment of them?

The Destiny Phase

Finally, the destiny phase allows advisors and students to celebrate the achievement of goals and to update and revise those goals regularly. This phase is a reminder that student interests often shift during college, so it is important to revisit life and career goals. Indeed, students will face roadblocks and make mistakes, but the advisor is there to encourage them to get back on track when they stumble, to take responsibility for missteps, and to understand the valuable lessons learned when dealing with failure. Equally important, the advisor congratulates students on their achievements along the way. Questions for this phase include:

- How and when will you update me on your progress?

- What will you do if you run into roadblocks?

- What will you do if you think your goals may be shifting?

To help facilitate advisor-student interaction, Appendix 9.1 provides an academic plan template with a series of questions that correlate with the four AI phases. Advisors should modify the questions as appropriate for their situation and advising style.

ADMINISTRATIVE AND PERSONAL LEADERSHIP

A vision without leadership is nothing more than a dream. Without both administrative and personal leadership it is not possible to deliver academic advising that makes a difference in the lives of students. This section relates both to individuals with administrative authority for advising and to those who deliver advising services.

Advising and institutional leaders are charged with establishing an environment in which students and employees can thrive. CAS (2003) has established clear standards for academic-advising programs. These standards are an excellent resource for institutional leaders who wish to establish and maintain effective advising programs or to improve the quality of current programs. CAS standards provide guidelines for advising programs on such topics as mission, student outcomes, leadership, organization and management, human resources, financial resources, facilities, technology and equipment, legal responsibilities, equity and access, campus and external relations, diversity, ethics, and assessment and evaluation. (Please refer to Chapter 19 in this volume for more details on the application of CAS standards.) The following are specific suggestions for leading an advising program that makes a difference.

It is imperative that leaders publicly and regularly acknowledge the importance of academic advising to both internal and external constituents. This can be accomplished in overt ways, such as mentioning academic advising as a key component to student success in speeches, featuring advisors in ad campaigns, or presenting faculty and professional advising awards at award ceremonies. In addition, advising staff also appreciate more subtle forms of support. Examples of this type of behind-the-scenes support include having institutional leaders attend advising events, seeking input from advisors on key issues, and inviting advisors to participate on committees related to curriculum, policy, and other departmental and campus-wide issues. This is a win-win for the campus leadership and the advisors. Because advisors are on the front line of the university and have their finger on the pulse of the students and the institution, they may quite possibly be better positioned than other members of the campus community to discuss certain issues. Leaders should also deliberately provide opportunities for advisors to interact with faculty, students, and academic affairs administrators. These relationships and the information sharing that will flow through them allow the institution to function more efficiently and effectively.

Leaders also need to ensure that the institution has advising mission and vision statements as well as a working definition of academic advising. If such statements do not already exist, institutional leaders can work with an established advising group on campus or can include members of the advising staff to create them. These statements should then go through the appropriate faculty governance committees to ensure that everyone on campus feels ownership of the advising process. Students must be notified in the campus catalog and in other key campus documents about the mission and vision statements as well as about what they can expect from their academic advisor and what their advisor will be expecting from them during interactions. Establishing succinct advising outcomes will ensure that all members of the campus community know what they can expect from their advising colleagues. Along these same lines, institutional leaders need to regularly evaluate whether the advising model employed on campus is meeting the needs of students and fulfilling the advising mission.

Campus leaders need to establish an advising career track that clearly delineates the credentials, skills, and abilities necessary for advancement. An essential component of this career track is a professional development plan that includes both institutional and external opportunities for advisors to stay up to date on the latest advancements in their field. Funding and time off for advisors to participate in conferences and other professional development opportunities are imperative. Adequate resources are also needed to provide financial, technological, and moral support of advising activities. As with all organizations, communication is the key, and both institutional leaders and academic advisors bear responsibility for keeping the lines of communication open.

Leadership for the quality of advising programs cannot be placed solely on the shoulders of campus administrators. Building on the advisor-as-bellwether role mentioned earlier, advisors must provide leadership in their area of influence, particularly when academic advising is not well supported on campus.

Jim Collins (2001), author of the book *Good to Great*, states that individuals do not have to be at the top of an organization to create "pockets of greatness" that focus on taking responsibility for what happens within their sphere of influence. So even when advisors are dissatisfied with how the rest of the institution is run, they can create a pocket of greatness by advising students to the best of their abilities, informed by CAS standards, student development theory, and a genuine commitment to student success. Advisors need to focus on how to reframe "problems into opportunities" (Jones, 1999).

Advisors are responsible for informing faculty and administrators not only of student problems and concerns but also of the positive things students are saying about their educational experiences. As boundary spanners, advisors need to be aware of cultural and language differences between academic and student affairs units. Advisors need to observe these cultural differences and get a good sense of when, how, and where it is appropriate to present student concerns and other matters. It is also important for advisors to do more than simply alert others to problems; instead, they need to present options for solving problems and demonstrate a willingness to brainstorm other possible solutions.

Advisors can also demonstrate leadership by proactively seeking out opportunities to interact with faculty, advisors, and colleagues on campus. Students appreciate when advisors can provide references to people they know personally throughout campus. Advisors should work together with advising colleagues to share best practices, frustrations, and shared concerns. In addition, advisors need to keep key administrators and faculty abreast of the advising group's activities and outcomes as well as recommend ways the advising group can contribute to student and campus success.

Advisors also need to take advantage of professional development opportunities. The National Academic Advising Association (NACADA) offers a host of resources—including national, regional, and state conferences and institutes; the *NACADA Journal;* and the NACADA Clearinghouse (www.nacada.ksu.edu/Resources).

In summary, student success requires strong leadership from institutional administrators as well as academic advisors. Two studies underscore the necessity of both micro and macro leadership. First, the National Survey of Student Engagement examined 20 institutions—from small liberal arts colleges like Alverno and Macalester to large research institutions like the University of Michigan and the University of Kansas—that had higher-than-predicted graduation rates and found that these institutions approached academic advising in comparable ways (De Sousa, 2005). These institutions incorporated many of the topics covered in this chapter: 1) There was a "talent development" approach to advising; 2) advising was a "tag team" activity; 3) advisors worked with students to develop a unique path to success; 4) advisors focused on connecting with students; 5) advisors connected students to learning opportunities outside the classroom; and 6) advisors encouraged students to learn from their diversity.

Similarly, the American Association of State Colleges and Universities (AASCU) released a report titled *Student Success in State Colleges and Universities* (2005) that described the characteristics of 12 colleges and universities that had higher six-year graduation rates than their peers. The AASCU found that these institutions had three things in common: 1) There was an intentional institutional commitment to student success, 2) student and academic services were integrated, and 3) there was a great deal of collaboration between student affairs, academic affairs, and faculty. One last source of information on exemplary advising programs is the listing of NACADA's Outstanding Advising Program Award recipients (www.nacada.ksu.edu/Awards/OP_Recipients.htm).

CONCLUSION

The field of academic advising is broad and encompasses a full range of topics, issues, and challenges. This chapter focused on a few select topics that present an overview of what academic advising is, the role academic advisors play, and what campus leaders can do to enhance the advising services offered on campus.

There is a significant body of evidence that undergirds the contention that advising, when properly supported and delivered, provides services valued by students. In his overview of more than 41,000 students included in the normative report of ACT's *Survey of Academic Advising,* Habley (2003) summarized student advising needs and impressions of advisors. Among the advising needs cited by students, he reported that discussions of academic progress, clarification of life and career goals, continuing education after graduation, and coping with academic difficulties as topics of high satisfaction among students. And included among the most favorable characteristics of advisors, students identified listening skills, respect for student opinions, approachability, and a sense of humor as being very important.

There is also mounting evidence that quality advising is seen by campus administrators as a major, if not predominant, strategy for improving first-to-second-year retention and persistence to degree completion. In *What Works in Student Retention,* Habley and McClanahan (2004) collected data on retention strategies employed at more than 1,100 campuses. They concluded that academic advising, first-year-transition programs, and learning support were the most common strategies employed by colleges with high retention and degree completion rates. Among the specific advising strategies cited were special advising services for selected student populations, integration of advising with first-year transition programs, integration of advising and career exploration, and the existence of an advising center or office.

Giving advice that makes a difference, however, will not happen without institutional and individual intentionality. It requires the commitment of both those in leadership positions and those who deliver advising. It requires a definition that focuses on putting students first.

APPENDIX 9.1

Academic Plan Template

Assessment of Current Status/Skills	
1. What are your top three strengths?	1. 2. 3.
2. What are your three most important values?	1. 2. 3.
3. Tell me about a time when you felt you had a positive impact on someone else's life.	1. 2. 3.
4. What are three skills that you would like to acquire or enhance?	1. 2. 3.
Goals	
1. What are your top three life goals?	1. 2. 3.
2. What are your top three career goals?	1. 2. 3.
3. What are your top three goals for your college experience?	1. 2. 3.
Plan for Achieving Goals	
1. What are concrete steps for fulfilling the top three goals listed above?	1. 2. 3.
2. What other resources should you use?	1. 2. 3.
3. How will you know that you have accomplished your goals?	1. 2. 3.
4. How will you celebrate the achievement of each goal?	1. 2. 3.
Assessment of Progress/Updating of Goals	
1. When will you visit your academic advisor next?	
2. What will you do if you run into roadblocks?	

REFERENCES

American Association of State Colleges and Universities. (2005). *Student success in state colleges and universities: A matter of leadership and culture.* Washington, DC: Author.

Berdahl, R. M. (1995). Educating the whole person. In A. G. Reinarz & E. R. White (Eds.), *New directions for teaching and learning: No. 62. Teaching through academic advising: A faculty perspective* (pp. 5–14). San Francisco, CA: Jossey-Bass.

Bloom, J. L., & Martin, N. A. (2002, August). Incorporating appreciative inquiry into academic advising. *The Mentor, 4*(3). Retrieved June 25, 2007, from www.psu.edu/dus/mentor/020829jb.htm

Chickering, A. W. (1994, Fall). Empowering lifelong self-development. *NACADA Journal, 14*(2), 50–53.

Collins, J. (2001). *Good to great: Why some companies make the leap . . . and others don't.* New York, NY: HarperCollins.

Cooperrider, D. L., Sorenson, P. F., Jr., Whitney, D., & Yaeger, T. F. (Eds.). (2000). *Appreciative inquiry: Rethinking human organization toward a positive theory of change.* Champaign, IL: Stipes.

Council for the Advancement of Standards in Higher Education. (2003). *Academic advising program standards and guidelines: Self-assessment guide.* Washington, DC: Author.

Creamer, D. G. (2000). Use of theory in academic advising. In V. N. Gordon, W. R. Habley, & Associates, *Academic advising: A comprehensive handbook* (pp. 18–34). San Francisco, CA: Jossey-Bass.

Creamer, D. G., & Associates. (1990). *College student development: Theory and practices for the 1990s.* Washington, DC: American College Personnel Association.

Crookston, B. B. (1972, January). A developmental view of academic advising as teaching. *Journal of College Student Personnel, 13*(1), 12–17.

De Sousa, D. J. (2005). *Promoting student success: What advisors can do* (Occasional Paper No. 11). Bloomington, IN: Indiana University, Center for Postsecondary Research.

Ender, S. C., & Wilkie, C. J. (2000). Advising students with special needs. In V. N. Gordon, W. R. Habley, & Associates, *Academic advising: A comprehensive handbook* (pp. 118–143). San Francisco, CA: Jossey-Bass.

Evans, N. J., Forney, D. S., & Guido-DiBrito, F. (1998). *Student development in college: Theory, research, and practice.* San Francisco, CA: Jossey-Bass.

Frost, S. H. (1991). *Academic advising for student success: A system of shared responsibility* (ASHE-ERIC Higher Education Report No. 3). Washington, DC: The George Washington University, School of Education and Human Development.

Habley, W. R. (1981, Spring). Academic advisement: The critical link in student retention. *NASPA Journal, 18*(4), 45–50.

Habley, W. R. (1993, July). *What do students need from academic advisors?* Paper presented at the 7th annual ACT-NACADA Academic Advising Summer Institute, Salt Lake City, UT.

Habley, W. R. (2003). Faculty advising: Practice and promise. In G. L. Kramer (Ed.), *Faculty advising examined: Enhancing the potential of college faculty as advisors* (pp. 23–39). Bolton, MA: Anker.

Habley, W. R. (2005, November). *The first year class of the future.* Paper presented at the regional conference of the Pacific American Association of College Registrars and Admission Officers, Tucson, AZ.

Habley, W. R., & McClanahan, R. (2004). *What works in student retention: Four-year colleges.* Iowa City, IA: ACT.

Herman, R. (2005). *The magic, mystery and mission of leadership.* Retrieved June 25, 2007, from www.oc.uiuc.edu/speeches/cicalp.html

Hutson, B. L. (2006). *Monitoring for success: Implementing a proactive probation program for diverse, at-risk college students.* Unpublished doctoral dissertation, University of North Carolina–Greensboro.

Jones, D. (Director). (1999). *Everyday creativity* [Video]. Zepher Cove, NV: Dewitt Jones Productions.

Knapp, L. G., Kelly-Reid, J. E., Whitmore, R. W., Huh, S., Levine, B., Berzofsky, M., et al. (2005). *Enrollment in postsecondary institutions, fall 2003; graduation rates 1997 & 2000 cohorts; and financial statistics, fiscal year 2003* (NCES 2005–177). U.S. Department of Education. Washington, DC: National Center for Education Statistics.

Knowles, A. S. (Ed.). (1970). *Handbook of college and university administration.* New York, NY: McGraw-Hill.

Komives, S. R., Woodard, D. B., Jr., & Associates. (1996). *Student services: A handbook for the profession* (3rd ed.). San Francisco, CA: Jossey-Bass.

Kramer, G. L. (2000). Advising students at different educational levels. In V. N. Gordon, W. R. Habley, & Associates, *Academic advising: A comprehensive handbook* (pp. 84–104). San Francisco, CA: Jossey-Bass.

Lipman, D. (1995). *The storytelling coach: How to listen, praise, and bring out people's best.* Little Rock, AR: August House.

Merriam-Webster's Online Dictionary. (2006). *Process*. Retrieved June 25, 2007, from http://m-w.com/dictionary/process

O'Banion, T. (1972). An academic advising model. *Junior College Journal, 42*(6), 62, 64, 66–69.

Priest, R., & McPhee, S. A. (2000). Advising multicultural students: The reality of diversity. In V. N. Gordon, W. R. Habley, & Associates, *Academic advising: A comprehensive handbook* (pp. 105–117). San Francisco, CA: Jossey-Bass.

Southern Association of Colleges and Schools, Commission on Colleges. (2004). *Principles of accreditation: Foundations for quality enhancement*. Decatur, GA: Author.

Upcraft, M. L. (1995). Insights from theory: Understanding first-year student development. In M. L. Upcraft & G. L. Kramer (Eds.), *First-year academic advising: Patterns in the present, pathways to the future* (pp. 15–24) Columbia, SC: University of South Carolina, National Resource Center for The Freshman Year Experience and Students in Transition.

Watkins, J. M., & Mohr, B. J. (2001). *Appreciative inquiry: Change at the speed of imagination*. San Francisco, CA: Jossey-Bass/Pfeiffer.

Whitney, D., & Trosten-Bloom, A. (2003). *The power of appreciative inquiry: A practical guide to positive change*. San Francisco, CA: Berrett-Koehler.

10 | PLANNING GOOD ACADEMIC AND CAREER DECISIONS

EMILY E. BULLOCK, ROBERT C. REARDON, AND JANET G. LENZ

Students faced with academic and career decisions may feel as though they are trying to solve a riddle. Are academic choices the same as career choices, are they related, or are they different? The answer depends on how students look at the issue. In some instances, academic and career choices could be the same; in others, they are different. It depends on how students think about their interests, values, goals, and abilities, as well as how they think about education and work. In this chapter we explore why these decisions can be so complex and confusing to students and a challenge to advisors and counselors. We also examine ideas, programs, and services that can help solve these dilemmas.

One factor contributing to the complexity of this issue is the increasing popularity of college majors in the so-called practical arts over the liberal arts in the United States. In an analysis of historical trends, Brint, Riddle, Turk-Bicakci, and Levy (2005) indicate that the number of students in academic programs in the practical arts has been increasing in recent years. More than 60% of bachelor's degrees are now in occupational or professional programs. This suggests that those academic advisors who help students plan their educational programs regularly deal with career-related questions and that career decision-making has become intertwined and fused with academic advising. Helping students clarify and establish career goals is an important task in the advising process. Institutions continue to explore new administrative schemes for improving academic and career advising.

UNDERSTANDING ACADEMIC AND CAREER COUNSELING SERVICES

Exploring the meanings of the terms *academic advising* and *career counseling*, determining where they overlap and where they are distinct, and how they inform professional roles and relationships are important in expanding our understanding of how to make good academic and career decisions. For persons working in these areas, Kuhn, Gordon, and Webber (2006) described a continuum of responsibilities that range from information giving to more in-depth counseling. Perhaps a new term is needed to identify those functions and skills that are shared by the two fields. Gordon (2006) has suggested that *career advising* captures the aspects of career work that academic advisors need to perform. We would add that it also captures those aspects of career counseling that professional and paraprofessional career counselors may perform. Let's begin with defining academic advising and career counseling.

According to Ender, Winston, and Miller (1984), academic advising is "a systematic process based on a close student-advisor relationship intended to aid students in achieving educational, career, and personal goals through the utilization of the full range of institutional and community resources" (p. 19). Creamer (2000) later defined it as "an educational activity that depends on valid explanations of complex student behaviors and institutional conditions to assist college students in making and executing educational and life plans" (p. 18). Thus, academic advising is focused on assisting college and university students in their life and career decision-making by helping them choose curricular and cocurricular activities that are necessary in the matriculation process and that lead toward graduation and possible graduate work. Professional career counselors typically do not do this work.

Academic advisors may have degrees from varied disciplines. Sometimes they are faculty members who serve as academic advisors within their respective departments. Academic advisors are usually trained informally through a variety of experiential one-on-one interactions with students that are focused on meeting course- or discipline-specific program requirements. Donnelly (cited in Gordon, 2006) reported that 74% of academic advisors do not have a counseling degree. Academic advisors affiliate primarily with the National Academic Advising Association (NACADA), which provides a variety of professional resources to promote quality academic advising in postsecondary education.

Sears (1982) defines career counseling as "a one-to-one or small group relationship between a client and a counselor with the goal of helping the client(s) integrate and apply an understanding of self and the environment to make the most appropriate career decisions and adjustments" (p. 139). Sears further defined a career as "the totality of work one does in his/her lifetime" (p. 139) and work as "conscious effort, other than that having as its primary purpose either coping or relaxation, aimed at producing benefits for oneself and/or for oneself and others" (p. 142). These definitions of career and job are very broad and include education, family life, leisure, and citizenship as well as work and job. Career counseling is not limited to educational settings and is typically performed by persons with a master's, specialist, or doctoral degree. For career counselors, a likely professional association is the National Career Development Association (NCDA), whose purpose is to promote people's career development over their lifetime. NCDA provides ethical guidelines for practice and specifies career-counseling competencies to guide the training of new career counselors.

We agree with Gordon (2006) that the term *career advising* can be useful in solving the long-standing dilemmas in this area because the distinctions between academic advising and career counseling are primarily a matter of scope and emphasis. Both functions involve a process of individual or small group interventions to help persons use information to make educational and occupational decisions that are consistent with their personal goals, values, interests, and skills. Both fields work with the same students throughout their time at the institution. Moreover, Gordon suggests that career advising may be thought of as academically related career planning or less psychologically intensive career counseling:

> The emphasis is on information and helping students understand the relationships between their educational choices and general career fields rather than how to cope with intense career-related personal concerns. Career advising helps students understand how their personal interests, abilities, and values might predict success in academic and career fields they are considering and how to form their academic and career goals accordingly. (pp. 11–12)

Career counseling includes many of the career-related elements of career advising. In addition, it focuses on testing and assessing personal traits, assisting in employment and work experience searches, resolving more difficult career problems, and providing longer term interventions and life-planning assistance. Academic advisors, career counselors, or even paraprofessional career services providers, often called "career development facilitators" (CDFs), may all provide career advising. Indeed, in some career services settings, CDFs may be called "career advisors." For these reasons, we will use the term *career advising* throughout this chapter to describe these shared functions.

THEORY IN ACADEMIC AND CAREER ADVISING SERVICES

Application of theory has long been a standard practice in the delivery of professional career counseling and career advising services. Theories can help advisors better understand clients and use techniques to help those clients function more effectively. Gordon (2006), in describing competencies for academic advisors who provide career advising, notes that "understanding theoretical frameworks can provide insights and give direction and meaning to advisors' daily contacts with students" (p. 23). Evidence- and theory-based practice and service delivery are marks of mature professional fields. In the next section we describe two that we believe can inform career advising.

Useful Theories in Career Advising

Theories in career services began with the work of Frank Parsons in Boston in the early 1900s. He developed a three-step model to guide people in making vocational choices (Parsons, 1909). Since that time, career development theories have become more varied and complex. *Career Choice and Development* (Brown & Associates, 2002), a popular text in the field of career development, describes nine theories commonly used in career counseling. We highlight two here that are directly applicable to the career advising process: cognitive information processing and Holland's theory.

Cognitive information processing. The cognitive information processing (CIP) approach is a counseling theory that provides a structure to explain how to factor in a person's interests and personality during life changes and decision-making (Peterson, Sampson, Lenz, & Reardon, 2002; Sampson, Reardon, Peterson, & Lenz, 2004). The CIP approach is rooted in information processing theory and Aaron Beck's (1976) cognitive theory. The main goals of the CIP approach are to help individuals make academic and career choices and improve their problem-solving and decision-making skills.

The CIP approach includes three information processing domains—knowledge, decision-making skills, and executive processing. These can be depicted as a pyramid. At the bottom of the pyramid is the knowledge domain, which is composed of self-knowledge and option knowledge. In our view, career advising is especially relevant to the knowledge domain because both academic advisors and career counselors are particularly equipped to help students in these two areas. To increase self-knowledge, for example, advisors can help students review their academic history, test scores, course preferences, interests, and goals. Counselors can use career assessments, computer-based guidance tools, and counseling techniques to do the same. Advisors have specialized information about an institution's curriculum that can help students improve their knowledge of different educational options, and career counselors, through career resource centers, have access to specialized information that relates to fields of study and employment options.

The middle section of the pyramid, the domain of decision-making skills, is conceptualized as a cycle. Called the "CASVE cycle," it is a recursive process through which students may have to proceed numerous times to arrive at optimal decisions (Sampson et al., 2004). The phases of the CASVE cycle include:

- *C (communication):* knowing that one needs to make a decision to remove a gap between where one is and where one would like to be

- *A (analysis):* understanding self and options in relation to the gap

- *S (synthesis):* expanding and then narrowing a list of options for removing the gap

- *V (valuing):* weighing the costs and benefits of options to make a decision

- *E (execution):* implementing a choice

Because it is a cycle, students return to the communication phase after the execution phase to understand whether the choice they made was a good one and the gap was removed.

The third tier of the pyramid, the executive processing domain, includes metacognitions. "Metacognitions control the selection and sequencing of cognitive strategies used to solve a career problem through self-talk, self-awareness, and monitoring and control" (Sampson et al., 2004, p. 24). Students experiencing difficulty at the metacognitive level may need the assistance of career counselors because problems with educational and career decision-making typically require more intensive, specialized, and long-term interventions.

The CIP approach is a practical theory with a manageable number of concepts that can be readily grasped not only by practitioners but also by students. Later in this chapter we will describe tools commonly used within the CIP approach and apply them to the practice of career advising. (To learn more about the CIP approach and its applications, visit www.career.fsu.edu/techcenter.)

Holland's theory. Gordon (2006) describes the theory of John Holland as "one of the most useful in helping students make connections between their personal characteristics and possible majors and occupations" (p. 25). A brief overview of Holland's theory will aid in the upcoming discussion of how the theory can be applied in the career advising process.

Holland's theory (1997) includes four key propositions:

- Most people can be categorized as one of six personality types: realistic, investigative, artistic, social, enterprising, or conventional (RIASEC).

- There are six environment types, which carry the same RIASEC labels. An environment may be a job, a leisure activity, a college major, or any other area of life. People with the same personality type dominate these environments. For example, a realistic environment is most likely to be populated with realistic personalities.

- People search for environments that will let them exercise their skills and abilities, express their attitudes and values, and take on agreeable problems and roles. In other words, people seek out life experiences that are similar to and complement their personality type.

- Behavior is determined by the interaction between personality and environment.

The six personality and environment types in this theory are defined by the vocational and avocational preferences, life goals and values, self-beliefs, and problem-solving styles. Many regard Holland's typological theory of persons and environments as the most influential in the field of career counseling (Brown & Associates, 2002). Reardon and Lenz (1998) discuss how considering client characteristics in terms of Holland types can be useful in determining appropriate career interventions. A summary of typical traits of the Holland types and examples of occupations is found in Table 10.1. Assessment tools have been created to operationalize Holland's theory and assess one's personal traits in relation to the RIASEC types. The Self-Directed Search inventory (Holland, Powell, & Fritzsche, 1994) is one such tool and is described later in this chapter.

Reardon and Bullock (2004) drew on research by Smart, Feldman, and Ethington (2000) to apply Holland's RIASEC theory to the academic advising field. Smart et al. showed that Holland's theory could provide an effective way to classify academic disciplines within higher education and serve as a guide to inform students about the intricacies and similarities of academic

Table 10.1   **Summary of Holland Types**

Type	Examples of Occupations	Typical Traits
Realistic	· Computer engineer · Forestry worker · Surveyor · Poultry scientist · Farmer	· Has mechanical and athletic abilities · Likes to work outdoors and with tools and machines · Might be described as conforming, frank, hardheaded, honest, humble, materialistic, natural, normal, persistent, practical, shy, and thrifty
Investigative	· Biologist · Chemist · Physicist · Geologist · Anthropologist · Laboratory assistant · Medical technician	· Has math and science abilities · Likes to work alone and to solve problems · Might be described as analytical, complex, critical, curious, independent, intellectual, introverted, pessimistic, precise, and rational
Artistic	· Composer · Musician · Stage director · Dancer · Interior decorator · Actor · Writer	· Has artistic skills · Enjoys creating original work and has a good imagination · May be described as complicated, disorderly, emotional, idealistic, imaginative, impulsive, independent, introspective, nonconforming, and original
Social	· Teacher · Speech therapist · Religious worker · Counselor · Clinical psychologist · Nurse	· Likes to help, teach, and counsel people · May be described as cooperative, friendly, generous, helpful, idealistic, kind, responsible, sympathetic, tactful, understanding, and warm
Enterprising	· Buyer · Sports promoter · Television producer · Business executive · Salesperson · Travel agent · Supervisor · Manager	· Has leadership and public speaking abilities · Is interested in money and politics and likes to influence people · May be described as acquisitive, agreeable, ambitious, attention getting, domineering, energetic, extroverted, impulsive, optimistic, self-confident, and sociable
Conventional	· Bookkeeper · Financial analyst · Banker · Tax expert · Medical laboratory assistant	· Has clerical and math abilities · Likes to work indoors and to organize things · May be described as conforming, careful, efficient, obedient, orderly, persistent, practical, thrifty, and unimaginative

disciplines. Their findings have a multitude of implications for career advising. Reardon and Bullock suggested the creation of institution-specific self-help resources for students. For instance, a college curricula planner could group majors in terms of RIASEC codes. Such tools could help students understand a college's academic culture, the expectations of each discipline, and the similarities and differences between various college majors.

The U-Maps project at the University of Maryland is a good example of such a tool (Jacoby, Rue, & Allen, 1984). U-Maps were designed to help students become aware of diverse campus opportunities, options, and resources related to RIASEC types. The project involved creating large posters for display and smaller brochures that were distributed by advisors. Each of the six RIASEC U-Maps had a standard layout that included academic areas of study (with office locations and phone numbers), sample career possibilities, internship and volunteer options, and student organizations and activities related to each type. Each map also had a short description of the RIASEC type and a brief self-assessment related to interests and skills. For example, all University of Maryland majors that fell under Holland's investigative type were included on a poster, along with information about those majors.

ASSESSING STUDENT NEEDS

Although theories can help guide practice, it is also important to consider students' decision-making readiness and how that might affect the impact of various career-advising interventions. Sampson et al. (2004) suggest that students may benefit from different levels of service when seeking career advising assistance. Some benefit from self-guided information gathering, and others require more intensive staff assistance due to the complicated nature of their academic or career-related issues and their level of readiness to engage in decision-making and learning (Peterson, Lenz, & Sampson, 2003). In this section, we first discuss readiness assessment and then three levels of service delivery related to readiness.

Readiness for Career Advising

Students' readiness for academic or career decision-making can have a great impact on their ability to benefit from and move through career advising interventions. Sampson et al. (2004) defined readiness as "the capability of an individual to make appropriate career choices while taking into account the complexity of family, social, economic, and organizational factors that influence an individual's career development" (p. 68). They proposed a two-dimensional model that helps academic and career advisors assess the readiness of students and their need for assistance.

The first dimension in the model is capability, which refers to the cognitive and affective capacity of an individual to engage in career problem solving and decision-making. The second dimension is complexity, which refers to contextual factors—originating in the family, society, economy, or employing organizations—that make it more or less difficult to process information necessary to solve career problems and make career decisions. Consider a student seeking to enter a highly competitive major. This student has many negative thoughts concerning his or her ability to be accepted and is feeling pressure from family members to enter that field. This student is dealing with a high level of complexity because of the choice of major and family influence and a low level of capability because of the negative thinking. He or she is at a low level of readiness and will likely require more staff-intensive assistance.

Levels of Service

Some students are capable of self-direction in academic and career decision-making. Colleges and universities can make resources accessible for such students to explore at their own pace. Delivering this self-help level of service involves providing a location where students can gather information on their own. In many universities this takes place in a career center's library or a similar resource center. Some academic advising offices have resource centers in the campus library and student union building. In such a setting students can browse at their leisure and ask staff for assistance as needed.

At Florida State University (FSU) the academic advising office and career center collaborated on a self-help tool, a pamphlet called the *Career Clock: A Four Year Academic and Career Planning Guide* (www.career.fsu.edu/advising/careerclock.html) This guide outlines activities students should be engaged in and decisions they should make during each year they are enrolled at FSU. George Mason University's School of Management (SOM) created a similar tool, SOM PACE (Plan for Academic and Career Excellence) Setter program (www.som.gmu.edu/pace/). This program recommends key steps to help students stay on track academically and in their career planning.

The second level of service delivery, brief staff-assisted services, may be required if students cannot find answers to their questions or if they are unable to complete activities and use resources on their own. This level of service may require the academic advisor or career counselor to create a written plan that outlines the materials and resources to be used by the student. Students can work through the written plan individually until they need additional guidance. More staff time is required with brief staff-assisted service than with self-help service, but this level of service delivery does not require multiple appointments with the same staff member. It also allows a staff member the freedom to work with more than one student at a time. Brief staff-assisted services may be enhanced through workshops or relevant courses with large group interaction.

As a supplement to the career center's brief staff-assisted service, FSU offers an undergraduate course in career development. This course is team taught by a group of three or four instructors, often with academic and career advisors teaching in the same section. This curriculum-based intervention permits students to focus on either academic or career decision-making, depending on their needs. The diversity of the instructors within a course section allows students to receive answers from a variety of perspectives. It also allows the academic and career advisors to learn more about how their respective offices contribute to educational and career decision-making. (More on the course can be found at www.career.fsu.edu/techcenter/instructor/undergraduate.)

The third level, services for individual cases, may be necessary for students who engage in negative thinking about academic and career planning. This level requires the most staff time and resources. It typically involves an individual appointment and requires guidance by a staff member as the student moves through various assessments, interventions, and information. Students in need of this level of service are typically at a low level of readiness for academic or career decision-making. This low level of readiness may have several causes and may require a referral for more in-depth counseling.

INSTITUTIONAL EXAMPLES

The issue of how academic and career advising can be structured in a particular institution to best provide services has been the topic of much discussion in related literature and on various web sites and listservs. We learned from our review of the literature and from interviews with selected program leaders that no one size fits all. What is reassuring to us is that the goal of improving academic and career advising can be achieved through a variety of approaches—completely separate offices for these functions, offices that share the same space but have different reporting lines, and offices that have successfully merged.

James Madison University

A school regularly cited for its best practice in this area is James Madison University. The academic advising and career services offices at James Madison University are completely integrated. According to its web site, the Office of Career and Academic Planning's mission is to "provide opportunities and support that engages students in the process of exploring, evaluating, and choosing academic programs and careers" (James Madison University, 2007). The web site also states that the office "will be innovative, adaptable, responsible, visible, and diverse so that we can enhance student learning and success."

The University of Illinois at Urbana-Champaign

An example of how theory has been combined with practice can be found at the career center at the University of Illinois at Urbana-Champaign (UIUC), where the staff have created a web-based program called EPICS (Exploring Pathways in Career Success; see www-s.epics.uiuc.edu/About.aspx). EPICS applies CIP theory to the process of making educational and career decisions. It provides a means for students to develop their self-knowledge and then connect that knowledge to academic and career choices.

The University of Northern Iowa

Another institution that presents a united front in these services is the University of Northern Iowa and its Academic Advising and Career Services. This unit's mission, according to the office's web site, is to "advise and empower individuals as they develop meaningful educational plans and skills to succeed in their life and career goals" (University of Northern Iowa, 2007). The office's staff "foster academic and career development, support self-exploration and effective decision-making, and provide resources to help individuals make successful academic and career transitions." Through WebCT, they offer a decision-making program for students called Major Decisions.

The University of Wyoming

The University of Wyoming's Center for Advising and Career Services web site describes the staff's commitment to "providing a comprehensive service that moves a student along a continuum of receiving academic advising as an undeclared student, exploring academic and career options, selecting a college major, and finally, implementing their degree in the world of work" (University of Wyoming, 2004).

Space does not permit us to highlight all the examples that might represent best practice for a variety of institutional and programmatic configurations. Readers are referred to the NACADA web site (www.nacada.ksu.edu) for additional resources. Information can be found in the clearinghouse section, as well as in the web site section on past NACADA awards for best practice.

CAREER ADVISING INTERVENTIONS

We have discussed two theories, CIP and RIASEC, that inform career advising services. These help determine what level of service will be most beneficial to students with various needs. They also provide tools that can be used within different organizational structures. In the following sections, we will explore examples of such tools.

Screening Tools

We have presented a model for determining the appropriate level of service based on student readiness. There are also formal screening tools that allow the academic or career professional to assess readiness. The career thoughts inventory (CTI) was designed to improve the quality of decisions made by individuals choosing an occupation or college major (Sampson, Peterson, Lenz, Reardon, & Saunders, 1998). The CTI is a 48-item, objectively scored, theory-based assessment. It allows trained academic and career advisors to assess the level of students' negative thinking associated with career decision-making in 7 to 15 minutes. It is accompanied by the CTI workbook, through which students can challenge and alter negative thinking to increase their readiness for decision-making.

The Self-Directed Search and Holland RIASEC Game

Holland's (1997) theory has provided a theoretical base behind many tools and activities used in career advising. For example, the Self-Directed Search (SDS) interest inventory (Holland et al., 1994) is based on RIASEC theory. To complete the 228 items, students rate their activities, competencies, preferences, occupations, and self-estimates in each of the RIASEC areas. Students also list their occupational aspirations or daydreams. The SDS is self-scoring and can be completed in 35–45 minutes. The results of the SDS generate a three-letter code from the six RIASEC options. Students can use the occupations finder or educational opportunities finder to explore occupations or college majors that best fit with their three-letter code. The SDS is available in paper-and-pencil, computer-based, and Internet-based versions.

The Holland RIASEC Game (Reardon & Lenz, 1998) can be used in academic advising or career-related workshops for students. This activity has students read descriptions of the RIASEC types, rank their top three preferences, and visit stations in the room that match those preferences. There students can be encouraged to discuss what led them to choose that interest area and what hobbies they share with other group members.

Individual Learning Plan

As mentioned in the section on levels of service, students may benefit from a written plan of action. Advisors and students can use an individual learning plan (ILP) to personalize a list of resources and activities that will aid in academic or career decision-making. This tool can be used with brief staff-assisted or individual case-managed services. The ILP shown later in Figure 10.1 includes the student's overall goals, appropriate activities, those activities' purposes, estimated times to complete the activities, goals the activities address, and the priority of each activity. An ILP makes choosing a major or occupation more manageable through the use of a flexible, step-by-step process, and it reinforces the student's ability to take responsibility for solving their academic and career concerns. The use of an ILP is also consistent with suggestions in the literature for making academic advising more of a student-learning-focused activity.

Computer-Assisted Career Guidance Systems

Computer-assisted career guidance systems (CACGS) are computer-based tools that provide students with self-assessment and information related to colleges, majors, occupations, job seeking, and various other academic and career-planning topics. This tool can be easily integrated into any level of service delivery, and students can access Internet-based CACGS from anywhere.

There are many comprehensive CACGS on the market. A few examples of commonly used ones are Choices Planner, Discover, Focus, and SIGI. In Florida one of these systems was integrated into a statewide tool for career advising: Florida Academic Counseling and Tracking for Students, or FACTS (www.facts.org).

E-Portfolios

As evidenced by the Portfolio Clearinghouse web site (http://ctl.du.edu/portfolio clearinghouse/search_portfolios.cfm), institutions are increasingly making use of online portfolios to help students connect their learning and skill development to their future career. These tools can be used in career advising to encourage student reflection about courses, campus activities, work experiences, and related activities in relation to academic and career choices. FSU has created an online portfolio for students (see www.career.fsu.edu/portfolio). Reardon and Lumsden (2003) noted that the portfolio provides a means for students to identify and communicate strengths and patterns within their educational and work experiences, which leads to more effective planning and goal attainment. If a student begins a portfolio and realizes that a desired skill has not been acquired, a career advisor can help him or her explore options for how to develop that skill through coursework, experiential opportunities, and related experiences.

Referrals

Referrals on a college or university campus may differ based on the institutional structure, service locations, and professional training of staff. As noted earlier, some institutions have completely integrated their career and advising services, making the referral process nearly seamless. Other academic advising and career services offices may employ staff from various fields, making it possible to address most student issues within one office. But this is not typical. More often the offices are separate. Although both academic advisors and career counselors can provide career advising, there are times when one office should refer students to another. Career services professionals may not have access to all of a student's academic information or knowledge of all university policies related to majors. When such information is necessary, it is important to refer the student to the academic advising office. Similarly, an academic advisor may encounter a student whose ineffective decision-making and negative thinking, coupled with other life complexities, makes a referral to a professional career counselor the most appropriate intervention. Referral to other offices may also become necessary. The most common one is likely to the student counseling center, such as when a student's deeper emotional issues are revealed in the process of career advising.

CASE STUDY: A STUDENT'S RESPONSE TO CAREER ADVISING

This chapter has discussed many ways of assessing students and helping address their academic and career concerns. Here we offer a case study to illustrate many of the topics that have been highlighted.

Abi was a 30-year-old female enrolled in a career-planning class at a community college. She had been referred to the class by her academic advisor. This class was team taught by both academic and career advisors. Abi was finishing her basic education courses and was planning on transferring to a university to complete her four-year degree. She was undecided about her major but was considering something in the social sciences that involved helping people. Her academic advisor helped her explore majors at the university, and Abi quickly realized that there were several that might be a good fit. She worked part-time on campus in the student disability resource center and, as a result of that experience, had thought about becoming a rehabilitation counselor. Abi also volunteered at a local senior care facility where her grandmother was living and had considered some type of work with the elderly. She said she planned to go on to graduate school, but she wanted to be sure about her career choice before she pursued additional education.

As part of her career class assignments, Abi measured her readiness for academic and career decision-making through the CTI. She also completed the paper version of the SDS Form R. Abi listed the following daydreams on her SDS:

Alcohol/drug abuse program administrator	ESR
Rehabilitation counselor	SEC
Aging program administrator	EAS
Equal opportunity representative	ESA
Social welfare administrator	ESA

Abi's SDS summary scale scores were as follows: R = 9, I = 12, A = 14, S = 41, E = 20, C = 22. (Scores on the SDS scale can range from 2 to 50.)

Her CTI results showed, among other things, that she had a high level of anxiety in relation to commitment:

CTI total score	61 (76th percentile)
Decision-making confusion	13 (62nd percentile)
Commitment anxiety	26 (99th percentile)
External conflict	1 (14th percentile)

The good news for Abi was that she was considering several options that fit well with the social and enterprising aspects of her Holland code. The bad news was that she was experiencing a great deal of anxiety about choosing the "right" field of study or occupation, as evidenced by her CTI commitment anxiety score. Although she had ideas about occupations and majors, she was unable to make a choice. She felt very frustrated. Her lack of detailed knowledge about the options she was considering made it difficult to prioritize her choices. Abi had office skills from her past jobs, but her low C score on the SDS occupations scale indicated she clearly was not considering options in that area. In contrast, Abi identified only two competencies on the E scale, yet this code appeared as the first letter in four of her five aspirations.

As part of her class assignments, Abi did three informational interviews with people in occupations she was considering. The class instructor referred her to a counselor at a local hospital who had graduated from a university with a degree in rehabilitation services. Abi also interviewed the administrator at her grandmother's retirement center about that job and spoke with a guidance counselor in her old high school. Abi reported that these interviews helped her think more about the kinds of settings where she might work and that she had felt most comfortable in the educational setting. It seemed to her to be a more positive place to work than the medical setting. While at a computer lab, Abi accessed the career center's web-based career guidance system to get printouts on several occupations. The instructor explained to Abi that she could use both of these activities as reference materials for the occupational analysis paper required in the class. As an extra-credit activity, Abi also attended the Major Discovery Fair, which was jointly sponsored by the advising center and career center. There she picked up information on the three majors she was considering and interacted with staff from those departments.

Abi then made an appointment with a career counselor in the career center and shared the results of her class assignments. In reviewing Abi's SDS results, the counselor observed the low score on the E competency scale and noted that Abi had listed four occupational daydreams that had E as their first letter. Together they reviewed the section on the SDS Interpretive Report that described E types. The counselor then asked Abi to say more about what she was thinking as she responded to the items on this scale. Abi said that although she had had a variety of jobs up to that point, none had given her a chance to take on a leadership role and she was looking to develop some skills in this area. Together they brainstormed ways that Abi might develop her E competencies—through involvement in campus organizations, class activities, and additional volunteer work.

Finally, after reviewing Abi's CTI results, the counselor provided her with a copy of the CTI workbook, and they discussed steps Abi could take to challenge her thinking about her ability to make career choices and to alter some of her negative career thoughts. Abi noted that she had been vaguely aware of having a problem taking charge of situations that affected her and of needing to be more proactive rather than reactive. She also became more aware of how her anxiety caused her to avoid acting on decisions that she needed to make. The workbook taught her how to take positive steps toward her goals. The ILP developed by Abi and her counselor (shown in Table 10.2) reassured her that she had a road map directing her where to go from here.

As a final class project, Abi wrote a strategic academic and career plan using the CASVE cycle of the CIP theory and incorporated the results of her other class assignments. In this paper Abi noted how much she had learned about herself from taking the SDS and the CTI. She said that she wanted to become a helping person and that becoming a professional counselor was now her career goal. Her first occupational preference was to be a school counselor, followed by career counselor and rehabilitation counselor. She also reported recognizing how being a helping person meant using enterprising competencies, such as making presentations to groups of people. Abi reported completing the CTI workbook and how she had taken some specific steps to become more assertive and clear in voicing her preferences. She had begun to lay out a specific plan for getting work experience in schools and community agencies and for applying to graduate school.

Throughout the class Abi had regular meetings with her academic advisor. The advisor verified that Abi's top three major choices—psychology, social sciences, and rehabilitation services—could all be good preparation for a career path in school counseling. Abi had enjoyed her general psychology course and thought that this major would give her some flexibility and be a good preparation for graduate studies. The advisor encouraged her to take the Careers in Psychology class to further expand her knowledge of options in this area. In another meeting Abi learned about the opportunity to complete a minor in leadership studies, which could be documented in her online portfolio. Abi's advisor, who had been involved with the campus first-year experience (FYE) class, also encouraged Abi to consider becoming a peer facilitator in one of the university FYE sections to further develop her leadership skills.

Table 10.2   **Abi's Individual Learning Plan**

Goals

1. To find a major I like and that will be good preparation for graduate school.

2. To improve my thinking and assertiveness when facing career decisions.

3. _____

Activity	Purpose/ Outcome	Estimated Time Commitment	Goal #	Priority
Review major descriptions in academic programs guide.	To compare and contrast options; to see which one might be the best fit.	30–45 min	1	1
Contact faculty member regarding leadership studies minor.	To see how I can use this minor to improve my leadership skills.	15–20 min	1	3
Use computer-based guidance systems to research occupations related to majors I'm interested in.	To learn more about requirements and how best to prepare.	30–45 min	1	2
Conduct information interviews with people in the field.	To get firsthand knowledge about occupations I'm considering.	1–2 hours	1	6
Complete selected activities in the CTI workbook.	To learn more about how my thinking impacts my career decisions.	Ongoing	2	5
Talk with advisors in majors I'm considering.	To get more detailed information about each major to further prioritize my choices.	30 min–1 hour	1	4
Follow up with career advisor.	To review above activities and determine next steps.	15–30 min	1 & 2	7
Complete the guide to good decision-making exercise.	To prioritize my options and take steps to implement my choice.	Ongoing	1	8

This plan can be modified by either party based upon new information learned in the activities of the learning plan. The purpose of the plan is to work toward a mutually agreed upon career advising goal. Activities may be added or subtracted as needed.

Abi	Corey	7/19/06
Student	Staff Member	Date

CONCLUSION

For many college students, making good academic and career decisions can be a daunting task—one that is full of riddles—and it can be challenging for those academic advisors and career counselors who seek to help them. With more students choosing the practical arts for their majors (Brint et al., 2005), it is important that all professionals who are responsible for academic and career advising have the training and tools necessary to accomplish that mission.

There are several steps practitioners can take to help students make effective career and academic decisions. First, all staff who provide these services must be thoroughly trained in the career advising theories. It is also important that staff are aware of their university's overall philosophy for addressing students' career and academic issues. As was noted in the descriptions of example institutions, the organization of the office and how services are provided vary greatly from one institution to another. Finally, the offices that serve students must acquire tools that reflect their philosophical and theoretical bases. Staff must be trained in the use of these selected tools and intervention strategies. As new staff are hired, the office can use training modules to provide them with the knowledge and skills they need to help students make good academic and career decisions. Critical to the success of these endeavors is a commitment by all stakeholders concerned with the academic and career advising process to forge collaborative efforts that ensure the highest and most effective level of service delivery to meet student and institutional needs. Through a series of learning activities, such as those discussed in this chapter, some of the decision-making dilemmas that perplex students can be worked out, using theory, practice, resources, tools, and skills that will empower students for a lifetime.

REFERENCES

Beck, A. T. (1976). *Cognitive therapy and the emotional disorders.* Madison, CT: International Universities Press.

Brint, S., Riddle, M., Turk-Bicakci, L., & Levy, C. S. (2005, March/April). From the liberal to the practical arts in American colleges and universities: Organizational analysis and curricular change. *Journal of Higher Education, 76*(2), 151–180.

Brown, D., & Associates. (2002). *Career choice and development* (4th ed.). San Francisco, CA: Jossey-Bass.

Creamer, D. G. (2000). Use of theory in academic advising. In V. N. Gordon, W. R. Habley, & Associates, *Academic advising: A comprehensive handbook* (pp. 18–34). San Francisco, CA: Jossey-Bass.

Ender, S. C., Winston, R. B., Jr., & Miller, T. K. (1984). Academic advising reconsidered. In R. B. Winston, Jr., T. K. Miller, S. C. Ender, & T. J. Grites (Eds.), *Developmental academic advising: Addressing students' educational, career, and personal needs* (pp. 3–34). San Francisco, CA: Jossey-Bass.

Gordon, V. N. (2006). *Career advising: An academic advisor's guide.* San Francisco, CA: Jossey-Bass.

Holland, J. L. (1997). *Making vocational choices: A theory of vocational personalities and work environments* (3rd ed.). Odessa, FL: Psychological Assessment Resources.

Holland, J. L., Powell, A. B., & Fritzsche, B. A. (1994). *The self-directed search professional user's guide* (4th ed.). Odessa, FL: Psychological Assessment Resources.

Jacoby, B., Rue, P., & Allen, K. (1984, March). U-maps: A person-environment approach to helping students make critical choices. *Personnel and Guidance Journal, 62*(7), 426–428.

James Madison University, Office of Career and Academic Planning. (2007). *Mission and philosophy.* Retrieved May 14, 2007, from www.jmu.edu/cap/about_cap/mission.htm

Kuhn, T., Gordon, V. N., & Webber, J. (2006, Spring). The advising and counseling continuum: Triggers for referral. *NACADA Journal, 26*(1), 24–31.

Parsons, F. (1909). *Choosing a vocation.* Broken Arrow, OK: National Career Development Association.

Peterson, G. W., Lenz, J. G., & Sampson, J. P., Jr. (2003). The assessment of readiness for student learning in college. In G. L. Kramer & Associates, *Student academic services: An integrated approach* (pp. 103–125). San Francisco, CA: Jossey-Bass.

Peterson, G. W., Sampson, J. P., Jr., Lenz, J. G., & Reardon, R. C. (2002). A cognitive information processing approach to career problem solving and decision making. In D. Brown & Associates, *Career choice and development* (4th ed., pp. 312–369). San Francisco, CA: Jossey-Bass.

Reardon, R. C., & Bullock, E. E. (2004). Holland's theory and implications for academic advising and career counseling. *NACADA Journal, 24*(1&2), 111–122.

Reardon, R. C., & Lenz, J. G. (1998). *The self-directed search and related Holland career materials: A practitioner's guide.* Odessa, FL: Psychological Assessment Resources.

Reardon, R. C., & Lumsden, J. A. (2003). Career interventions: Facilitating strategic academic and career planning. In G. L. Kramer & Associates, *Student academic services: An integrated approach* (pp. 167–186). San Francisco, CA: Jossey-Bass.

Sampson, J. P., Jr., Peterson, G. W., Lenz, J. G., Reardon, R. C., & Saunders, D. E. (1998). The design and use of a measure of dysfunctional career thoughts among adults, college students, and high school students: The career thoughts inventory. *Journal of Career Assessment, 6*(2), 115–134.

Sampson, J. P., Jr., Reardon, R. C., Peterson, G. W., & Lenz, J. G. (2004). *Career counseling and services: A cognitive information processing approach.* Belmont, CA: Brooks/Cole.

Sears, S. (1982, December). A definition of career guidance terms: A National Vocational Guidance Association perspective. *Vocational Guidance Quarterly, 31*(2), 137–143.

Smart, J. C., Feldman, K. A., & Ethington, C. A. (2000). *Academic disciplines: Holland's theory and the study of college students and faculty.* Nashville, TN: Vanderbilt University Press.

University of Northern Iowa, Academic Advising and Career Services. (2007). *Advising and career services.* Retrieved May 14, 2007, from www.uni.edu/acs/

University of Wyoming, Center for Advising and Career Services. (2004). *Who we are, what we do.* Retrieved May 14, 2007, from http://uwadmnweb.uwyo.edu/CACS/

PART III

FOSTERING STUDENT DEVELOPMENT

Although this volume emphasizes the campus as a learning organization, it also examines the important role of fostering student development. The chapters in Part III discuss learning partnerships, developing students in their search for meaning, organizing services for learning, and preparing service providers and engaging faculty as ways to put students first. These chapters focus on student and organizational learning in association with student and service provider development and assessment to help students achieve on the campus.

11 LEARNING PARTNERSHIPS

Terry D. Piper and Rebecca A. Mills

Imagine yourself on a journey to a destination that is not well defined and for which you do not have a map. A college student's journey into adulthood might be described that way. Students often have a fuzzy sense of what being an adult is about and are unlikely to have a clearly delineated pathway to get there.

Earning a college degree may be viewed by some as evidence that students have successfully navigated their way and are ready to assume their place as contributing adult members of society. Unfortunately, a college degree in itself does not certify that the student has achieved the maturity necessary to handle the challenges of modern society. In fact, concern that higher education is failing to meet society's expectation that graduates be able to meet the challenges of a changing workplace, of a diverse democracy, and of the global community led the Association of American Colleges and Universities (AAC&U; 2002) to call for a transformation of undergraduate education. Its report, *Greater Expectations: A New Vision for Learning as a Nation Goes to College*, expresses the societal need for individuals who are self-aware, purposeful, and self-directed; who are flexible and adaptable and able to integrate knowledge and pursue lifelong learning; who interpret, evaluate, and apply knowledge and experience to problem solving and decision-making; and who have an open mind, appreciate others, accept personal and civic responsibilities, and act ethically. AAC&U also called on faculty, staff, and students to become more intentional in their respective efforts to achieve these outcomes.

Just as it is difficult for students to navigate the journey to adulthood without a map, so it is challenging for faculty and staff to intentionally guide students without an understanding of the student journey. Baxter Magolda (2004b) suggests that the journey to adulthood and the achievement of the outcomes defined by AAC&U depend on whether a student becomes self-authored. To be self-authored is to be "guided by one's own vision" (Kegan, 1994, p. 172) or to develop an internal identity or sense of self from which to define and interact with the world. Self-authored individuals choose their own values and beliefs, form and sustain interdependent relationships, and are aware of and manage their thoughts and feelings.

Mark, Lydia, and Dawn—participants in Marcia Baxter Magolda's (1992, 2001) longitudinal study of young adult development—express this notion of self-authorship:

> Making yourself into something, not what other people say or not just kind of floating along in life, but you're in some sense a piece of clay. You've been formed into different things, but that doesn't mean you can't go back on the potter's wheel and instead of somebody else's hands building and molding you, you use your own, and in a fundamental sense change your values and beliefs. (Mark, in Baxter Magolda, 2001, p. 119)

> It [the college experience] was a fabulous experience. I did things I never would have thought I would do. It makes you feel small; there are so many other people out there! If you have experienced this much, how much more is out there? I have a thirst for more. If you stay in the same place, you get in a rut. It is so exciting! You don't know what you are capable of; you reinvent yourself as you gain new experience. (Lydia, in Baxter Magolda, 2001, p. 290)

> I have really started to open more and more and discover this intense passion I have for whatever it is I do. It's kind of a self-discovery of powers. I'm doing something that I've always dreamt about doing and never thought was possible. And that is so empowering. It just keeps unfolding and gets more intense and more passionate as I go along. (Dawn, in Baxter Magolda, 2001, p. 152)

Mark speaks of remolding himself; for Lydia college is a process of reinventing herself; Dawn says she gains empowerment through self-discovery. All are speaking about the transformation of self, the development that results in the outcomes identified by AAC&U. The purpose of this chapter is to map out the journey to self-authorship, suggest ways to partner with students on their journey, and provide two specific approaches that have been used in such partnerships.

THE DEVELOPMENTAL JOURNEY

Mark, Lydia, and Dawn's stories of college life and beyond reflect a developmental journey from dependency on external authority to reliance on themselves for leading their lives. They have taken ownership of and responsibility for constructing their world (cognitive maturity), defining for themselves who they are (integrated identity), and deciding how they will interact with others (mature relationships). Students' achievement of these outcomes depends on three dimensions of development: epistemological, intrapersonal, and interpersonal (Baxter Magolda, 2004b). The developmental trajectory of all three dimensions moves from reliance on external authority to reliance on one's own capacity. Epistemological development, or development of the student's way of knowing, transitions from the view that knowledge is certain and obtained from authorities to one that views knowledge as contextual and acknowledges that decisions regarding knowledge claims are based on evidence (Baxter Magolda, 1992). Intrapersonal development, or the development of the student's sense of self, evolves from a perspective defined primarily by the opinions of others to one that is based on self-awareness and choice (Chickering & Reisser, 1993). Interpersonal development, or the development of the relationships a student forms with others, shifts from relationships characterized by dependency to those reflecting interdependence (Kegan, 1994). Self-authorship emerges as maturity is achieved on all three developmental dimensions (Baxter Magolda, 2004b).

Although the stories of Mark, Lydia, and Dawn all differed in context and content, each has a common element: The journey was not made alone. Each of these young adults, as well as all others in the study who achieved self-authorship, had partners along the way. These partners helped create conditions that promoted the students' self-definition. Unfortunately, very few of the students completed this journey during college (Baxter Magolda, 2002). By the end of their college experience, they, like the majority of adults studied by Kegan (1994), had not yet achieved the self-authorship necessary to manage the complexity of modern life and to be effective citizens.

To strengthen the university's influence on students as they journey toward self-authorship, faculty, staff, and students must all be more intentional along the way. Student affairs professionals must take the lead in campus discussions about student development. The American College Personnel Association (ACPA) and the National Association of Student Personnel Administrators (NASPA) have articulated the role and responsibility of student affairs to promote learning (ACPA, 1996; ACPA & NASPA, 1997; American Association for Higher Education, ACPA, & NASPA, 1998). A more recent document from those two organizations, *Learning Reconsidered,* places at the center of student affairs work "identifying and achieving essential student learning outcomes and . . . making transformative education possible and accessible for all students" (Keeling, 2004, p. 3).

The emphasis on student learning and development also requires faculty and student affairs professionals to reorient their relationships with students. Just as faculty have been called on to shift their focus from teaching to learning through new pedagogies, student affairs professionals have been encouraged to shift their focus from providing programs and services to engaging students in partnerships (Piper, Baxter Magolda, & Trevan, 2004). Baxter Magolda (2002) characterizes such partnership as good company for the journey to adulthood and self-authorship. She offers the learning partnerships model (LPM) as a map to transform student affairs professionals' practice in higher education (Baxter Magolda, 2004b).

THE LEARNING PARTNERSHIPS MODEL

The LPM (Baxter Magolda, 2004a), depicted in Figure 11.1, is an approach to facilitate students' transformation from dependence on external authority to self-authorship. The process requires both the challenge of external authority and, simultaneously, support for the student's emerging developmental maturity. The LPM identifies sources of challenge and support and suggests a process for helping the learner achieve self-authorship.

Promoting Self-Authorship

The LPM is based on three core assumptions about learning. These assumptions challenge dependence on authority through exposure to epistemological, intrapersonal, and interpersonal complexity. Three corresponding principles for educational practice provide support to learners dealing with the challenges associated with this developmental process. Together the core assumptions and principles create conditions that promote self-authorship.

Core assumptions. The first assumption—that knowledge is complex and socially constructed—presents a challenge to the student's way of knowing. Students' beliefs about what they know—based on what they have been taught or have interpreted from experience—are challenged when they encounter alternative explanations and interpretations. The ambiguity or discomfort that students often experience when they realize that what they thought to be true may not actually be true can lead them to decide for them-

Figure 11.1   **The Learning Partnerships Model**

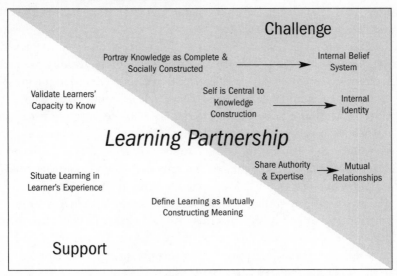

selves what to believe. Knowledge construction, or deciding what to believe, becomes a process of acquiring, analyzing, and judging knowledge claims based on evidence in collaboration with others rather than accepting others' knowledge claims without question. Transitioning from externally defined knowledge to an internal belief system is necessary for self-authorship.

The realization that people choose what to believe promotes the awareness that the self is intertwined with the perspectives an individual holds, which is the second assumption. The challenge to students to help define what they believe to be true calls for greater self-awareness and the use of that internal sense of self as they go about learning, working, and relating to others. To achieve self-authorship, students must transition from a sense of self that is defined by others to an internal identity.

The third assumption—that knowledge is mutually constructed via the sharing of expertise and authority—complements the second assumption. Mutual construction of knowledge implies that one considers multiple perspectives in dialogue and interaction with others, who are seen as equal partners in the process. To be self-authored, individuals must transition from being dependent on and defined by relationships to being able to define their relationships and function interdependently.

Principles. Learners need support as they begin establishing their beliefs, identities, and relationships. Baxter Magolda (1992) offered three principles of practice to provide this support.

The first principle—validating learners' capacity to know—is achieved by inviting learners into the knowledge construction process, seeking their ideas and opinions, demonstrating respect, and trusting their judgment. This strengthens their confidence in their ability to develop understanding and to make decisions. It also demonstrates to them the importance of hearing others' perspectives as they construct their own points of view. The second principle—situating learning in the learners' experience—is achieved by encouraging learners to use their existing knowledge and experience to guide them in new situations. This allows them to apply their identity to the context and to create a foundation to build on. The third principle—mutually constructing meaning—brings together the knowledge of the educator and the knowledge of the learner to create a more complex way of seeing the context or making decisions. This provides an opportunity to clarify perspectives and to negotiate those perspectives with others.

Autonomy and connection. Students are not passive recipients in the LPM. To achieve self-authorship, they must be actively engaged. What students do is best viewed through the interplay between autonomy and connections. Autonomy is found in the developmental challenges to define oneself and to use that definition to interact with the world. Connection is found in the need for support from others as one makes the developmental transition. Autonomy is represented in the three assumptions by the emphasis on the learner to take responsibility for engaging in the learning process. Connection is represented in those assumptions when the learner finds a relationship between his or her point of view and the perspectives of others. The three principles emphasize autonomy as learners bring themselves into the learning process and construct their own meaning; connection is demonstrated when learners use others' frames of reference to inform their own. Autonomy and connection are inherent in self-authorship and necessary for developing epistemological, intrapersonal, and interpersonal complexity.

The LPM provides staff and faculty with an approach to facilitating the student's journey to self-authorship. The applicability of the model is not limited to students. The following are examples from two universities that chose to use the LPM to guide their work with student affairs professionals and thereby their work with students.

PREPARING STUDENT AFFAIRS STAFF TO PROMOTE LEARNING PARTNERSHIPS

Becoming a partner with students on their journey to adulthood requires more than just the good intentions of student affairs staff. It requires that professionals have an understanding of that journey or, if you will, a road map. The road map used by professionals is often expressed in the assumptions, values, and philosophies that guide their work. At the Division of Student Life at the University of Nevada–Las Vegas (UNLV), we spent more than a year identifying, clarifying, and declaring our assumptions about students and our work with them. The division had focused for several years on creating learning outcomes, and the staff had grappled with that concept with varying degrees of success. The transition to a broad conversation about how to put students and their learning at the center of our planning, resource allocation, and divisional structure seemed to be the next logical step. Following a series of divisional conversations designed to create a shared vision of how we wanted to work and what we wanted to achieve on behalf of students, we reorganized the division to facilitate a focus on students, to support collaboration between departments, and to enhance efficiency. At that point we invited Marcia Baxter Magolda to campus to help us frame our efforts around student development and create a cohesive approach to our work. Although it seems self-evident now, we overlooked a step in our early planning: We failed to work intentionally or sufficiently with staff on their own process of self-authorship.

Promoting Staff Self-Authorship

After spending several days on campus, Marcia challenged the divisional leaders to consider the complexity of what we were asking of staff. This motivated us to acknowledge that our ability to partner with students to enhance their learning and development would be greatly facilitated or hampered by the degree to which those staff working directly with students were able themselves to move from a dependence on external authority to self-authorship. In short, before we could ask staff to provide experiences for students that were based on the principles of self-authorship—validating learners' capacity to know, situating learning in the learners' experience, and mutually constructing meaning—we needed to provide staff with developmental experiences and a divisional work context that were grounded in these principles.

Using the LPM in staff development. Opportunities for staff development were created to help us all better understand our assumptions about ourselves and our students, create a context that supported staff commitment to promoting learning partnerships, and focus on staff to enhance their focus on students. This development—planned by a staff committee—took a themed approach and focused on such topics as student development, student learning, socioeconomic barriers to learning, and how technology can support learning. The committee worked with speakers and facilitators to ensure that this development would be congruent with the core assumptions and grounded in the principles of self-authorship. Speakers and facilitators were asked to plan opportunities for staff to share their experiences, question their assumptions, and clarify their perspectives, thereby situating learning in the learners' experience, validating their capacity to know, and mutually constructing meaning.

The approach has made staff development interactive, engaging, and learner centered. As a result, participation has been high and evaluations have been strong. It is also evident that staff are using these principles as they work with students in program planning. In fact, in the intervening years staff have established student planning groups whose members enhance their learning and leadership skills by developing learning opportunities for their peers. Student groups such as the Rebel Pride Council, Rebel Service Council, and Student Health Advisory Council regularly demonstrate their learning and development as they share their expertise and authority as they plan with one another and with student affairs staff.

Using the LPM in the work context. Sometimes university administrators make decisions in a way that conflicts with the core assumption that knowledge is complex and socially constructed. We send memoranda that convey decisions, declare intent, or share learning without including others in those processes. Management processes provide opportunities to demonstrate the process of negotiating meaning. If we expect staff to engage students in the mutual construction of meaning to promote student achievement of self-authorship, then managers must engage staff in the same process. To do that, divisional leaders must be willing to share the ambiguities they face as they make decisions rather than masking the messiness of the decision-making process. This requires spending additional time with staff members, explaining the context and mitigating factors that influenced the decision and encouraging them when they face important decisions to look beyond the obvious answer and to consider the perspectives of the pesky parent, the irritating student, or the problematic colleague. This helps them mutually construct an understanding of the situation and solution.

As a result, at UNLV we spend considerable time in division leadership meetings and staff team meetings to reach agreement after considering supporting data and various perspectives. This management style is more time consuming and certainly messier than top-down models; however, we find that investing the time in the process means that staff move on to make more informed decisions and that staff team discussions, over time, become more substantive and thorough. We have watched staff grapple with the complexity of developing knowledge and making meaning.

To further ground the UNLV work context in the assumptions and principles of self-authorship, we created divisional work groups to address major goals such as staff learning about diversity, an integrated approach to student wellness, and the creation of a cocurricular agenda. These opportunities to grapple with the authentic challenges of leadership and decision-making have produced wonderful results for students and staff. Staff report more knowledge about and comfort in working with students of different races or backgrounds than theirs. We have designed space in our new recreation center to integrate staff's efforts in recreation, health services, counseling services, nutrition, housing, and other areas and work with individual students or groups of students to address a particular issue. In addition, through the process staff and student team members have enacted the principle of mutually constructing meaning. With colleagues and students, they have shared their expertise, considered multiple perspectives, created equal partnerships, and functioned interdependently.

We have worked to create an environment in which supervisors solicit staff members' opinions and demonstrate respect and trust for their staff, thereby validating staff members' capacity to learn and perform. Team meetings have become opportunities for individual staff members to use their past knowledge and experiences to guide their work with others. Staff are asked to mutually construct meaning by negotiating with one another and with student staff teams and to share authority with colleagues, subordinates, and students. It is in these settings that staff learning can be best encouraged and supported in a large division.

Inherent in our way of working—indeed, in our vision statement—is the concept of shared leadership. Through this value for shared leadership, we daily challenge traditional notions of authority and question internal perspectives about the chain of command. We ask everyone in the division to think of themselves as teachers and to recognize every opportunity to contribute to a colleague's or a student's learning. This requires that we challenge one another often to remember to place students first in decision-making and to create opportunities for staff and student learning from the vicissitudes of daily life in a large division of student affairs.

It has been remarkably rewarding to witness the results of staff learning. Although ours is a continuing saga, we have witnessed considerable change in the nature of the interactions between staff and students. In surveys of student affairs workers a large percentage of staff said that they believe their work makes a difference in the lives of students and that they are satisfied with the work they do. Staff involve students in planning and implementing programs and services much more consistently than they did five years ago. Major institutional events are no longer planned by a staff member who then manages a group of students; instead, they are planned and executed by student teams who are mentored and supported by staff.

PARTNERING WITH STUDENTS TO PROMOTE LEARNING

The Division of Student Affairs at California State University–Northridge (CSUN) responded to the call to put student learning at the core of our work during the 2001–2002 academic year. Declaring in a revised mission statement that the division "exists to advance student learning," the challenge became to identify and articulate exactly what we meant by "student learning." A review of our existing student affairs department goals revealed a primary focus on the administration and operation of the department (what the staff did) rather than on the impact of the department's efforts on students (student learning and development). Departmental goals that addressed student learning and development tended to also emphasize staff action (e.g., "to provide opportunities for students to understand diversity") or were so broad that they were neither practical nor feasible to accomplish (e.g., "students will develop awareness, insight, understanding, and appreciation of the races, ethnicities, cultures, and faiths as well as sexual orientations and gender identities of the campus community"). Little mention was made of assessing whether the various goals were accomplished. It became evident that advancing student learning required a shift in the way we thought about, expressed, enacted, and assessed our work; we needed a new map. We needed to be able to clearly and concisely state the learning outcomes we intended students to achieve through our programs and services, and we needed to be able to assess whether those outcomes were accomplished. The following section is based on the findings from this effort.

Learning Partnerships Model as a Framework for Developing and Implementing Learning Outcome Goals

Our first attempt to write learning outcome goals and assessment strategies began with creating a consistent format to guide our thinking and writing. We established common definitions:

- *Mission:* a global statement about the fundamental purpose of the department that represents the core functions and guides the development of goals

- *Goal:* a broad statement directly related to the mission that provides direction for the long term

- *Objective:* a focused statement concerning an action that contributes to the overall accomplishment of a goal

- *Strategy:* the specific action plan designed to accomplish the objective

- *Learning outcome:* a statement of what learners will know or be able to do as a result of the accomplished objective

We quickly discovered that writing learning outcomes was not simply about changing the language. It required transforming our thinking. The LPM became our guide in this process.

A series of workshops were planned during 2003–2004 to introduce and apply the LPM as a framework for developing and implementing learning outcome goals. Marcia Baxter Magolda served as the facilitator. The workshops were designed and delivered with five guiding assumptions:

- Promoting student growth on the developmental foundations of learning is essential to achieve student affairs' educational and service goals.

- Articulating these developmental foundations is essential to student affairs' being viewed as a core function in the current climate.

- Integrating developmental foundations with learning goals means thinking differently about and revising our current work rather than adding new work.

- Staff professionals maintain their unique expertise and specialties, yet they recognize how to realize this expertise more fully for students and help students put it all together into a holistic experience.

- Just as student learning is holistic, staff learning is holistic. Personal identity is part of professional identity. Personal growth and transformation support professional growth and transformation.

The overall approach was to model the framework for promoting self-authorship through the workshops.

First considerations. As noted previously, the LPM addresses three contemporary college learning outcomes: cognitive maturity, integrated identity, and mature relationships. These combine to enable effective citizenship. Each outcome is characterized by a set of skills, abilities, and attitudes; these can be the focus of a student affairs department's learning outcome goals. Cognitive maturity might be characterized by the ability to gather, interpret, and evaluate information; apply knowledge; recognize multiple perspectives; make decisions and solve problems based on evidence; and understand the rationale for policies. Integrated identity might be characterized by an understanding of self, engaging in self-assessment, displaying confidence for leadership roles, taking a position in dialogue with others, pursuing personal and academic growth opportunities, and advocating for one's self. Mature relationships might be characterized by engaging in collaboration, negotiating, managing conflict, understanding others and their cultures, and understanding and serving the community.

Before attempting to write learning outcome goals at CSUN to promote the achievement of these skills, abilities, and attitudes, it was necessary to consider the level of complexity of the desired outcome. The least complex level is represented by basic awareness of resources, policies, procedures, and information. A more complex level is demonstrated by the use of basic skills, such as how to do tasks, organize responsibilities, access information, and share information. Advanced skills—such as negotiation, collaboration, conflict management, and working in teams—reflect greater complexity. At the most complex level students demonstrate nebulous abilities such as interpreting and evaluating data, making wise judgments, acting responsibly, and integrating diverse perspectives.

Targeting the appropriate learning outcome complexity requires staff to consider the developmental capacity of the learner to achieve the desired outcome. Some learners may be able to achieve the basic skills but do not possess the developmental capacity to integrate and use them to manage their own affairs or work with others. Some learners can achieve advanced skills to manage their own affairs and work with others but do not possess the developmental capacity to do so without continued guidance. Other learners have the developmental capacity to fully achieve the outcomes and internalize these processes, make good judgments, and act on them. To promote the achievement of increasingly complex learning outcomes, the learner's developmental capacity must also be understood and promoted.

Developmental foundations. As noted previously, the journey to self-authorship is the process of increasing epistemological, intrapersonal, and interpersonal development—which serve as the foundations for cognitive maturity, integrated identity, and mature relationships, respectively, and are manifested through effective citizenship. This journey begins with a reliance on external formulas; moves through increasing awareness of context, self, and others; and ends with self-authorship. Table 11.1 displays Baxter Magolda's representation of the developmental journey toward learning outcomes (Baxter Magolda, 2004b). Understanding what students do along this journey—how they go about gaining and using knowledge, how they express who they are, and how they interact with others—provides insight into their developmental capacity and informs developmentally appropriate learning outcomes. We at CSUN focused on three questions to aid us in this process:

- *Cognitive maturity:* How would students have to "know" to achieve the learning outcome?

- *Integrated identity:* How would students have to see themselves to achieve the learning outcome?

- *Mature relationships:* How would students have to see relationships to achieve the learning outcome?

The answers to these questions identified the gap between students' capacity and the desired learning outcome.

Designing strategies to bridge this gap became the focus of our efforts as student affairs practitioners at CSUN. We found that the best learning outcome strategies for creating the conditions of connection and autonomy inherent in self-authorship were those that simultaneously provide guidance and empowerment. The three core assumptions and three principles of the LPM provide direction to craft these strategies.

As senior student affairs officers, our work with staff informs our work with students. Both UNLV and CSUN expect student affairs practitioners to focus their planning and decision-making on students; however, both also recognize that it is essential to address staff learning to create student affairs divisions that focus on student learning. By modeling a commitment to and a

Table 11.1   **Developmental Journey Toward Learning Outcomes**

Dimension	External Formulas	Crossroads	Self-Authorship
Epistemological	View knowledge as certain or partially certain, yielding reliance on authority as source of knowledge; lack of internal basis for evaluating knowledge claims results in externally defined beliefs	Evolving awareness and acceptance of uncertainty and multiple perspectives; shift from accepting authority's knowledge claims to personal processes for adopting knowledge claims; recognize need to take responsibility for choosing beliefs	View knowledge as contextual; develop an internal belief system via constructing, evaluating, and interpreting judgments in light of available evidence and frames of reference
Intrapersonal	Lack of awareness of own values and social identity, lack of coordination of components of identity, and need for others' approval combine to yield an externally defined identity that is susceptible to changing external pressure	Evolving awareness of own values and sense of identity distinct from others' perceptions; tension between emerging internal values and external pressures prompts self-exploration; recognize need to take responsibility for crafting own identity	Choose own values and identity in crafting an internally generated sense of self that regulates interpretation of experience and choices
Interpersonal	Dependent relations with similar others are source of identity and needed affirmation; frame participation in relationships as doing what will gain others' approval	Evolving awareness of limitations of dependent relationships; recognize need to bring own identity into constructing independent relationships; struggle to reconstruct or extract self from dependent relationships	Capacity to engage in authentic, interdependent relationships with diverse others in which self is not overshadowed by need for others' approval; mutually negotiating relational needs; genuinely taking others' perspectives into account without being consumed by them

plan for staff learning, senior student affairs officers and their departmental managers can create an environment in which discussions of staff learning can lead to enhanced focus on student learning.

LEARNING-CENTERED PRACTICE

As staff members at UNLV learned more about the LPM, their work with students began to change. In divisional planning for a new student recreation center, we chose to house the student health center and student counseling and psychological services within the facility. The concept of shared space has led to discussions of innovative ways to address students' health and well-being. As one example, staff designed a concept that will be known as the Rebel Wellness Zone. This space will be staffed and comanaged by individuals from Campus Life and from Student Wellness. The Zone will provide students with an integrated approach to wellness. For example, in this space a student who is struggling with an eating disorder can meet with a nutritionist, a fitness coordinator, and a case manager who will coordinate with a health care professional and a clinical psychologist to ensure that the student has a reliable support system. In the Zone the student will have access to online resources as well as books, videos, and manuals. The staff-led planning for this space demonstrates well the changes within the Division of Student Life since we first began discussions about shared leadership and learning partnerships. There has been virtually no sense of territoriality, and cross-cluster work groups continue to grapple with how to best serve students in that space.

Five years ago, the health center and student counseling were struggling with the idea that they could share information about a student; now a case manager works across the two areas to ensure that students keep appointments, fill prescriptions, consider options, and integrate their wellness regimen in their lives. With the student's permission, staff use electronic charts to share information with other wellness staff to best serve the student. In making the changes, staff members were required to reframe their perspectives, share their knowledge, and consider other experiences. They truly shared their authority and expertise to build mutual relationships, and students were the beneficiaries.

The CSUN student union provides a wide range of programs and services that are responsive to the needs of the university community. The student union staff began reframing their goals, objectives, strategies, and learning outcomes in 2001–2002. The comparison with the 2005–2006 statements, presented in Table 11.2, reveals a dramatic change.

Table 11.2   **Comparison of Learning Outcome Statements, 2001–2002 and 2005–2006**

2001–2002	2005–2006
Goal: Promote the university student union and its board of directors to improve the quality of life for students on campus	**Goal:** Support student engagement in campus life through volunteer service at the union and use the service opportunity to promote skill development
Objective: Reinstate the visibility committee and have it develop marketing strategies, funding request procedures, and communication methods	**Objective:** Provide student programmers, committee chairs, and volunteers with skill development in areas of responsibility specific to program planning, personnel management, and group leadership
Strategies: 1) Expand the union web site; 2) develop a new logo; 3) improve relationships with the campus newspaper; 4) use promotional giveaway items	**Strategies:** 1) Orient volunteers to program policies, practices, and procedures related to goal setting and achievement; 2) in collaboration with each student, establish learning outcomes and a process for monitoring progress; 3) provide support for committee work through ongoing training focused on transferable skills, such as team building, group dynamics, delegation, communication, parliamentary procedure, meeting, facilitation, and multiculturalism
Learning outcomes: 1) Committee members will develop, learn, and enhance marketing techniques and creative abilities; 2) committee members will understand the critical role of marketing in increasing rates of customer satisfaction	**Learning outcomes:** Students will develop or enhance and demonstrate skills in communication, customer service, analysis and decision-making, and project management

The focus in 2001–2002 was the organization, its processes, and the tasks to be accomplished. Learning was specific to those tasks that the organization needed to be successful. Note the shift of emphasis in 2005–2006 from the organization to the student. Emphasis on developing organizational structure and procedures had shifted to developing students who are engaged with the organization. A focus on tasks to accomplish became a focus on the development of understanding, skills, and abilities. Learning outcomes related to the development and use of transferable skills and abilities.

The change implemented by the student union staff is more than using new words to describe old practice. Old practice—that is, seeing students as vehicles for the accomplishment of organizational tasks—has given way to new practice: using organizational tasks as a context through which intentional student learning and development are promoted. Staff have structured their work with students to incorporate the three assumptions and three principles of the LPM. The first assumption—that knowledge is complex and socially constructed—is evidenced through orientation and training sessions as well as group discussion about ways to apply the concepts and ideas presented. Students negotiate what they will do and how they will do it. Students are encouraged to contribute their prior experience, to listen to and incorporate the experiences of others, and to decide collectively on a course of action. This invites the students into knowledge construction and validates their capacity to know—the first principle of the LPM. The second assumption—that self is central to knowledge construction—is evidenced through the use of self-assessment and the setting of learning outcomes. Each student is asked to reflect on his or her level of knowledge and ability and then to establish personal learning goals in negotiation with a staff member. The second principle—situating learning in the learner's experience—is facilitated by encouraging students to consider what they already know and to use it as a starting place for their involvement. The third assumption—that knowledge is mutually constructed via the sharing of expertise and authority—is evidenced through the use of group processing and the evaluation of programs and services. The third principle—mutually constructing meaning—is achieved through staff members' offering information, probing for clarification, raising questions, and contributing to the process as a participant in other ways.

CONCLUSION

Early evidence suggests that the LPM is a useful map for guiding students toward the desired destination: self-authorship. The CSUN student union assessment results find that students express greater awareness of and comfort with the skills and abilities defined in the learning outcomes. Observational data suggest improvement in students' ability to use their knowledge, work effectively in groups, and assume responsibility. At UNLV student satisfaction with and use of wellness services and programs continues to increase. Staff members work far more often across departmental lines to address students' needs and assess their progress. Additionally, the LPM has been effectively used to promote self-authorship through residence hall community development (Piper & Buckley, 2004), interdisciplinary writing (Haynes, 2004), diversity education (Hornak & Ortiz, 2004), and leadership development (Egart & Healy, 2004).

If student affairs practitioners are to contribute to the campus's ability to respond to increasing societal demand for accountability for student learning outcomes, then we must shift our focus from what we do to what students do—that is, we need to help students develop an internal belief system based on evidence and frames of reference, choose values that are manifested through an integrated sense of self, and establish relationships that are authentic and interdependent. To help students develop in these areas and eventually achieve self-authorship, we should join them in learning partnerships in which we become the metaphorical bridge (Kegan, 1994) that allows them to transition from dependency on external authority to internal self-reliance. Mark, Lydia, and Dawn—like the vast majority of students—did not find the bridge to self-authorship during their undergraduate education. We owe it to the future Marks, Lydias, and Dawns to do what we can to equip them with the epistemological, interpersonal, and intrapersonal capacities that modern society requires. The assumptions and principles of the LPM can aid us in achieving that goal.

REFERENCES

American Association for Higher Education, American College Personnel Association, & National Association of Student Personnel Administrators. (1998). *Powerful partnerships: A shared responsibility for learning.* Washington, DC: American College Personnel Association.

American College Personnel Association. (1996). *The student learning imperative: Implications for student affairs.* Washington, DC: Author.

American College Personnel Association & National Association of Student Personnel Administrators. (1997). *Principles of good practice for student affairs.* Washington, DC: Authors.

Association of American Colleges and Universities. (2002). *Greater expectations: A new vision for learning as a nation goes to college.* Washington, DC: Author.

Baxter Magolda, M. B. (1992). *Knowing and reasoning in college: Gender-related patterns in students' intellectual development.* San Francisco, CA: Jossey-Bass.

Baxter Magolda, M. B. (2001). *Making their own way: Narratives for transforming higher education to promote self-authorship.* Sterling, VA: Stylus.

Baxter Magolda, M. B. (2002, January/February). Helping students make their way to adulthood. *About Campus, 6*(6), 2–9.

Baxter Magolda, M. B. (2004a). Learning partnerships model: A framework for promoting self-authorship. In M. B. Baxter Magolda & P. M. King (Eds.), *Learning partnerships: Theory and models of practice to educate for self-authorship* (pp. 37–62). Sterling, VA: Stylus.

Baxter Magolda, M. B. (2004b). Self-authorship as the common goal of 21st-century education. In M. B. Baxter Magolda & P. M. King (Eds.), *Learning partnerships: Theory and models of practice to educate for self-authorship* (pp. 1–35). Sterling, VA: Stylus.

Baxter Magolda, M. B., & King, P. M. (Eds.). (2004). *Learning partnerships: Theory and models of practice to educate for self-authorship.* Sterling, VA: Stylus.

Chickering, A. W., & Reisser, L. (1993). *Education and identity* (2nd ed.). San Francisco, CA: Jossey-Bass.

Egart, K., & Healy, M. P. (2004). An urban leadership internship program. In M. B. Baxter Magolda & P. M. King (Eds.), *Learning partnerships: Theory and models of practice to educate for self-authorship* (pp. 125–149). Sterling, VA: Stylus.

Haynes, C. (2004). Promoting self-authorship through an interdisciplinary writing curriculum. In M. B. Baxter Magolda & P. M. King (Eds.), *Learning partnerships: Theory and models of practice to educate for self-authorship* (pp. 63–90). Sterling, VA: Stylus.

Hornak, A. M., & Ortiz, A. M. (2004). Creating a context to promote diversity education and self-authorship among community college students. In M. B. Baxter Magolda & P. M. King (Eds.), *Learning partnerships: Theory and models of practice to educate for self-authorship* (pp. 91–123). Sterling, VA: Stylus.

Keeling, R. P. (Ed.). (2004). *Learning reconsidered 1: A campus-wide focus on the student experience.* Washington, DC: American College Personnel Association & National Association of Student Personnel Administrators.

Kegan, R. (1994). *In over our heads: The mental demands of modern life.* Cambridge, MA: Harvard University Press.

Piper, T. D., Baxter Magolda, M. B., & Trevan, T. (2004, November). *From service to learning: One student affairs division's transition.* Paper presented at the meeting of the Association of American Colleges and Universities on Educating Intentional Learners: New Connections for Academic and Student Affairs, Philadelphia, PA.

Piper, T. D., & Buckley, J. A. (2004). Community standards model: Developing learning partnerships in campus housing. In M. B. Baxter Magolda & P. M. King (Eds.), *Learning partnerships: Theory and models of practice to educate for self-authorship* (pp. 185–212). Sterling, VA: Stylus.

12 | DEVELOPING STUDENTS' SEARCH FOR MEANING AND PURPOSE

Lois Calian Trautvetter

Spirituality and religion are part of the pluralistic nature of American culture. As such, higher education needs to address these dimensions of today's society, and colleges and universities should contribute to the faith and the spiritual, moral, and character development of students.

The objective of this chapter is to better understand holistic student development—or developing whole students, which includes spiritual and faith development—and to acknowledge the contributions and roles that student services practitioners, advisors, and other campus leaders can play in their campus communities in developing students' personal values, purpose and meaning, and faith, as well as cognitive and intellectual learning outcomes. After all, for any campus community, it takes a whole campus of whole persons to develop whole students.

This chapter is divided into four sections that discuss the role of faculty and student affairs professionals in developing students' search for meaning and purpose. First, we will look at how research from church-related institutions can be used to develop college students' search for meaning and purpose; then we will define terms such as *holistic student development, faith, spirituality,* and *religion* and their interrelationships; next we will examine the importance of today's college students' search for meaning and purpose. The final section will discuss the characteristics, practices, and challenges of those colleges that succeed in encouraging students' holistic development and will suggest how those qualities apply to all colleges and universities, faith based and secular.

Data gathered from in-depth institutional case studies of 10 church-related institutions from a three-year project called Fostering Student Development Through Faculty Development will be used to provide best practices. The goal of the project was to learn more about the role of faculty, student affairs professionals (including campus ministry members), and administrators in guiding student development. *Putting Students First: How Colleges Develop Students Purposefully* (Braskamp, Trautvetter, & Ward, 2006) presents a comprehensive overview of this project.

Why were church-related institutions used for this project? These institutions were chosen for their mission to revivify the life of the mind by incorporating faith, spirituality, and religion and to prepare students for lives of moral and intellectual complexity. These institutions have a history of addressing issues related to how faculty and student services professionals can reinforce learning and development through curricular and cocurricular practices. They have a history of intentionality about the integration of faith and learning. And because these institutions are dedicated to the development of the whole student, they provide settings from which we can learn how to help prepare students for both their careers and their lives as good citizens and persons of character (e.g., Dovre, 2002). As these findings are shared with more secular institutions, student affairs professionals will discover parallels with their own work environments.

The church-related institutions, ranging from enrollments of 1,800 to 6,500 undergraduates, were deliberately selected to reflect different geographic regions, church denominations, sizes, affinity levels with the sponsoring church, and levels of adherence to a dominant religious or faith perspective. The colleges included Bethune-Cookman College (Florida), the College of Wooster (Ohio), Creighton University (Nebraska), Hamline University (Minnesota), Hope College (Michigan), Pacific Lutheran University (Washington), Union University (Tennessee), the University of Dayton (Ohio), Villanova University (Pennsylvania), and Whitworth College (Washington).

DEFINING HOLISTIC STUDENT DEVELOPMENT

Recently some human development scholars have argued for a more holistic approach to educational research and practice to better help students develop the wide range of skills necessary for approaching the complex problems and "dissonance" of today's world (Baxter Magolda, 2004; Colby, Ehrlich, Beaumont, & Stephens, 2003). Some have acknowledged the more personal dimensions of student development (such as racial, ethnic, and sexual orientation; faith; spirituality; and purpose in life) and are calling for more expanded views of college students (Fowler, 1981; Parks, 2000). Colleges have a responsibility to help develop students as persons in cognitive learning by expanding their knowledge and intellectual powers; in their affective domain by enhancing their moral, religious, and emotional interests; and in their practical competence by improving their competence in work, family, and community (Bowen, 1991).

The members of a campus community—faculty, student affairs and campus ministry professionals, and administrators—contribute to the holistic development of students by who they are and what they do. Student affairs professionals, for example, tend to organize their campus activities, curricular and cocurricular, in ways they believe will develop students most effectively. Generally speaking, these activities are framed in terms of student learning and development goals. For some colleges and universities, such goals include a mastery of skills needed for a specific career; for others, moral and civic responsibility may be emphasized; still others may highlight character development and religious formation. Overall, in varying degrees of intentionality, colleges should pay attention to both the interior lives of students (values, spirituality, identity, purpose, and meaning) and the exterior lives of students (observable patterns of behavior).

Braskamp et al. (2006) examine and analyze how students grow and develop in a campus environment. They concur with Kuh, Kinzie, Schuh, Whitt, and Associates (2005):

> What students *do* counts more in terms of what they learn and whether they persist in college than who they are or even where they go to college. . . . The time and energy students devote to educationally purposeful activities is the single best predictor of their learning and personal development. (p. 8)

However, Braskamp et al. (2006) argue that institutions also need to consider who a student is (the student's sense of self, which includes sense of purpose, personal goals, strengths) and foster this element through the campus environment. In other words, just being busy is not enough for an authentic and purposeful life. Rather, an authentic and purposeful life involves connecting commitments and behaviors. Colleges can fulfill the goals of fostering holistic student development by helping students be introspective, reflective, and self-knowing.

Before delving deeper into this subject, several terms need to be defined. First, *holistic student development* is used to describe the connections between the intellectual, moral, social, faith, and spiritual aspects of student development and how students develop within campus and societal contexts.

Therefore, the term is used to include a full spectrum of holistic student learning and development goals that include vocational, professional, intellectual, cognitive, social, civic, political, moral, ethical, spiritual, and religious dimensions, as well as focus on values clarification and character development. Research on college students has explored different aspects of this spectrum, and more attention has been paid to some aspects than to others. This wide array of goals is not necessarily a new way of viewing student development; holistic student development was the core of the mission of the first colleges and universities in America, whose purpose was to assist men and women to be persons of character and integrity (Boyer, 1987).

In general, students searching for meaning and purpose seem to be asking for help in answering questions such as these: How do I know? Who am I? What relationships do I want with others? How can I best contribute to making this a better place to live? In past decades spiritual and religious development often was not included in student development efforts. More recently, the terms *faith, spirituality, religious commitment, character,* and *vocation* have become common in the literature on college student development (see, e.g., Astin, 2004; Chickering, Dalton, & Stamm, 2006; Jablonski, 2001). The use of such terms, however, differs from institution to institution.

Faith usually refers to an intentional effort to make meaning of one's life or to obtain a higher stage of moral reasoning. For example, Fowler (1981) describes faith as "the ways we go about making and maintaining meaning in life" (p. xii). Parks (2000) says that faith has

> both affective and cognitive dimensions. . . . [It] is the ground of ethics and the moral life. Faith is intimately linked with a sense of vocation—an awareness of living one's life aligned with a larger frame of purpose and significance. (p. 26)

Furthermore, faith is described as the "interior" of one's life (Astin, 2004). *Spirituality* is a different concept:

> [Spirituality often includes] all forms of reflection and introspection in which the primary goal is to explore one's relationship to the transcendent in order to deepen and enrich practice as well as non-religious or secular beliefs and practices in which the inward search for meaning and purpose, authenticity, and wholeness is the guiding purpose. (Dalton, Eberhardt, Bracken, & Echols, 2006, p. 5)

Dalton et al. argue that *spirituality* is a general term that includes religion. Spirituality is defined as turning inward to oneself but in such a way as to experience "an encounter with otherness" (Palmer, 1990, p. 5). It is also referred to as being full of affect, but it is not merely an emotional quest. It touches the core of our being and existence. It helps one know oneself (Astin, 2004); to claim an authentic identity, cohesiveness, integration, and wholeness (Tisdell, 2003); and to be socially and morally responsible (Dalton, Russell, & Kline, 2004). It is finding one's purpose in life through inner reflection and introspection and taking action that may lead to vocation. This inward journey or quest that college students take is an attempt to answer the big questions of life (Parks, 2000).

Usually, developing an authentic spiritual identity involves moving away from or deeply questioning one's childhood religious traditions and authorities and engaging in a critical reflective process. This kind of development typically occurs with college students (Fowler, 1981; Parks, 2000; Tisdell, 2003) and not just in the religious aspects of their lives. It is important to note that college students engage in a wide variety of spiritual practices and are receptive to new forms of spiritual searching. In fact, Dalton et al. (2006) have categorized college student spiritual seekers into two groups: religious and secular. The secular seekers are further identified as being mindfulness seekers, those who focus their inner search on ways to heighten self-awareness and understanding, and wellness seekers, those who engage in spiritual activities to achieve a more holistic, healthy, and integrated way of life.

Religious seekers' development takes place within the context of religious faith orientation or religious commitment because faith and the practice of faith are intractably connected. Miller (2005) says:

> Religion describes a social entity . . . [and] religions are defined by their boundaries. There are group members and nonmembers, prescribed and proscribed behaviors, and characteristic beliefs.
> Spirituality is a central concern of religions, but not the only concern. A religion can also involve important social, political, and economic goals. (p. 13)

The terms *religion* and *religious commitment* are associated with a given set of beliefs about the supernatural and one's relationship to a transcendent source or being. Religions often have a set of doctrinal standards and involve public expression, worship, and sacraments. They imply community with shared beliefs, commitments, and convictions—a community for celebrating and mourning the lives of others (Marty, 2000). According to Dalton et al. (2006), college students who are religious seekers can be multireligious in nature as they seek to deepen their spirituality and faith through interfaith and multireligious exploration, dialogue, and practice.

In view of student development, there are interrelationships between faith, religious commitment, spirituality, and intellectual dimensions. All are involved in a student's journey of finding purpose and meaning, but colleges vary in how interrelated those factors are and can be. Some may argue that finding meaning is independent of religious commitment. But a student comes to college, goes to class, and engages in campus life as a whole person, not as one dimension of a person. Defining these terms on a campus provides a good start and allows dialogue to continue in an open environment. In many ways students are often more receptive and willing to discuss issues of spirituality and religion than are many other members of the campus community.

This chapter argues that making connections between the intellectual, social, and faith dimensions of student development is valuable even if it is difficult. Asking the big questions in life that involve faith and meaning is not easy to do. But a more holistic view of student development will help students develop their convictions and articulate their views of the world and their place in it.

COLLEGE STUDENTS' SEARCH FOR MEANING AND PURPOSE

Howe and Strauss (2003) have cautioned campus administrators and faculty that they will "face increasing scrutiny of what values they impart or appear to impart" to today's college students and that they need to "find creative ways to inform [college students] that their ultimate contribution and worth will not be determined by their starting salary, the prestige of their first employer, or the rank of their professional school" upon graduation (p. 134). Furthermore, Astin (2004) has suggested that colleges should search for ways to incorporate spiritual and religious questions into the curriculum—helping students explore those questions with each other and in their coursework. If campus leaders are to encourage students' exploration of purpose and meaning in life, they may need to rethink their roles and consider new tools that can be used (Capeheart-Meningall, 2005; Tisdell, 2003).

In an academic environment in which students explore their individuality and student affairs professionals guide them in cognitive and social development, it may seem that the student's own personal quest of making meaning of life is missing. Even though many institutions, both private and public, have people working with students of a particular religious affiliation, many do not address their students' overall spiritual development. Buley-Meissner, Thompson, and Tan (2000) argue that "students with spiritual interests suppress their spiritual life or split their spiritual life apart from their formal education" (p. 15). As a result, such students may experience a period of displacement, confusion, and discomfort as they develop (Love & Talbot, 1999).

When we think of developing whole students, we are reminded that, increasingly, college students are compassionate and caring individuals, often immersed in service and community activities (Higher Education Research Institute [HERI], 2005; Howe & Strauss, 2003; Kuh et al., 2005). They are also becoming more interested in religion and spirituality for meaning, comfort, and certitude (Astin, 2004; HERI, 2005). In a survey of 100,000 first-year undergraduate students at 236 institutions, 80% responded that they were interested in spirituality, 76% said that they were searching for meaning in life, 69% reported using their beliefs for guidance, 74% said that they discuss their life philosophies with friends, 81% said that they attend religious services, 79% said that they believe in God, and 69% said that they pray (HERI, 2005). More than half said that they believe it is essential that colleges encourage students' personal expression of spirituality. In fact, many reported expecting their colleges to provide them with opportunities to develop and continue their search for meaning and purpose. Students are not always sure what they believe and are interested in grappling with big questions like the meaning of life and looking for ways to incorporate these questions into their college experiences. They also want to associate with faculty, student affairs professionals, and other adults who are willing to assist them in their search for meaning (e.g., Gallup & Lindsay, 1999; HERI, 2005).

CREATING A CAMPUS COMMUNITY FOR MEANING AND PURPOSE

This section discusses four institutional characteristics that can guide a campus community in developing meaning and purpose for college students: developing a supportive institutional culture, creating a meaningful curriculum and cocurriculum, collaborating with academic affairs, and helping students reflect on their own talents and development. Good practices from the institutions studied will be shared. Following the discussion of each of these characteristics is a set of suggestions or insights that can be employed in all types of colleges and universities, as well as a set of questions that can be used for reflection and discussion.

Developing a Supportive Institutional Culture

Culture is a word often used to represent the shared values, character, mission, and identity of an organization or group of people (Tisdell, 2003). Campus culture has a direct impact on an institution's commitment to nurturing holistic student development.

Institutions that foster holistic student development are very clear about their mission. The importance of having a mission has been written about profusely in the past decade (Braskamp et al., 2006; Kuh et al., 2005). It is not surprising that the institutions and departments in this research are interested in fostering holistic development and are committed to helping students examine their lives in terms of an Aristotelian "good life," which is independent of—and often in conflict with—material success. These institutions' mission is to assist students to know themselves—who they are and what their purpose in life is—and to develop their intellectual abilities.

Institutions such as Creighton University, Hamline University, Pacific Lutheran University, and Union University use special programs, conferences, and roundtables for staff, faculty, and students to engage in continuous, deliberate communication that keeps the institutional mission and identity on the front burner. Furthermore, in 2000 Villanova University established its Office for Mission Effectiveness to promote the institution's commitment to living out its mission and to support programs and research that perpetuate the university's Augustinian intellectual and moral legacy.

These colleges use a variety of strategies to form and communicate their mission and identity. It may be a quote from a significant person in the campus's history, a catchy phrase used by institutional leaders, or a slogan from recruitment materials. For example, a common phrase at Creighton University is "We exist for students and for learning." Whitworth College's motto is "An education of mind and heart." The University of Dayton's identity phrase is "Living and learning in community."

Because a large part of mission is vision, campus leadership is critical in creating purposeful campus cultures. Effective leaders inspire others in the community to become self-aware and use their talents. Because assisting students in their faith development and other personal issues can be controversial work, it is important that leaders repeat the institutional mission at convocations, graduations, programs, forums, and public events. Faculty and staff professionals may be reluctant to engage in such work unless the core administrative leadership supports holistic development (Braskamp et al., 2006).

Campuses that help students search for meaning and purpose also provide a career perspective on professional staff development. This includes considering prospective employees' institutional fit, providing thorough orientation, and offering professional and personal development at different career stages. As Creighton's president stated in an interview, "Who we bring in—students, staff, and faculty—creates the culture" (Braskamp et al., 2006, p. 65). As a way to begin conversations about the types of students enrolled and their needs, most of these institutions use student profiles in training new faculty and staff members. Such colleges also provide information about faculty and staff roles in student development.

Insights for institutions. The strategies to embody mission mentioned here can be employed by any type of institution. Although private faith-related colleges and universities are most active in supporting an institutional culture of faith and spiritual development with such activities as worship, study of religious texts, prayer groups, religious speakers, and retreats, private nonsectarian colleges can also support these activities within the context of interfaith activities, such as interreligious programs and interdenominational services. For example, Princeton University has created the Interfaith Dialogue Program, and Swarthmore College has a private meditation room. Colorado College has its Sacred Grounds Coffee Shop, which is a community center, concert hall, and movie theater in the basement of the institution's chapel. Williams College and Northwestern University have both created special spaces for the activities of religious groups on their campuses, such as a Muslim prayer room.

Public institutions usually support a culture of faith and spiritual development through a variety of indirect student support services, such as providing information about campus and community religious organizations, offering campus meeting facilities, and sponsoring programs that include secular forms of spirituality like meditation and yoga. For example, the Pennsylvania State University has created multifaith spaces on its campus— including the Pasquerilla Spiritual Center, Eisenhower All-Faith Chapel, and Meditation Chapel. The University of Wisconsin has a student residence for spirituality and religion; the University of California–San Diego has the Center for Ethics and Spirituality. Such campuses provide many opportunities for students to develop their faith, including campus speakers, student organizations, films, music, campus rituals and celebrations, living-learning situations, and service activities.

How do institutions and student services providers achieve a culture that helps develop whole students? And what can they do better to align expectations, connect services, and actively encourage this type of student development? First, they need to be intentional about using college students' experiences on campus (such as providing community service activities, stimulating intellectual discussions, encouraging travel abroad, and facilitating interactions with peers) to promote spiritual growth outcomes. These types of experiences can be structured to include the mission and goals of developing whole students at any institution.

Second, it is important that the campus mission, identity, and culture all reinforce the community. Campus leaders; the organizational structure; the collaborative arrangements between faculty, student affairs, and ministry professionals; and the campus setting and identity are all integral to building a strong campus community. Campuses that are most effective in fostering holistic development are clear about their mission, advocate for spirituality and religion as part of the mission, and publicize and communicate effectively about the activities that foster faith development so that everyone in the campus community feels free to believe in, participate in, and rally around the mission. Leadership and communication are critical to advancing the mission and empowering the entire campus community to take ownership in developing students (Braskamp et al., 2006).

Third, mentoring and development programs on campus can also create collegiality; help develop a sense of commitment to the college's mission and ideals; provide feedback to student services providers about their effectiveness; and provide opportunities and ways to help faculty and staff learn and appreciate the traditions, rituals, and ideals behind holistic student development. Here are some questions that you can ask about your institution's culture:

- How does your institution promote values, character formation, and social and moral responsibility for students in the campus community and beyond?

- Who do you consider to be champions or leaders of holistic student development on your campus? What strategies do they employ to enhance dialogue with others on your campus about supporting students' search for purpose and meaning?

- How are you expected to guide students intellectually, socially, civically, physically, religiously, spiritually, and morally?

- How does your institution's mission influence curricular and cocurricular priorities?

- How does your institution orient and develop staff and faculty to ensure the centrality of the campus's mission and vision in their work with colleagues and students?

Creating a Meaningful Curriculum and Cocurriculum

Campuses interested in holistic student development also contribute to students' learning by creating meaningful curricular and cocurricular activities. Because students are asking those big questions, it is important to understand the process of integrating learning and development (Pascarella & Terenzini, 2005). Institutions that are successful in developing students who search for meaning and purpose constantly ask themselves what is best for the students. They work on creating a meaningful curriculum and cocurriculum that includes engagement and reflection. Many of the institutions that were studied believe that student affairs professionals can be full partners in the daily processes of teaching students, just as faculty can be full partners in developing students. For example, student affairs experts can bring skills and knowledge to classrooms that some faculty members may lack, such as how learning occurs at different stages of a person's life and in different cultures.

In addition, the cocurricular environment plays an important role in developing students in their search for purpose and meaning. Astin (2004) argues that this is where campuses can strike the balance between the interior and exterior of students' lives. Students who are fully involved in the cocurriculum are more likely to persist in college and be academically successful (Kuh et al., 2005). Cocurricular involvement is not just about being involved in multiple activities; it is about becoming involved in activities and organizations that help connect in-class and out-of-class experiences. In such a cocurricular environment students can become more fully immersed in particular interests and can make connections between and meaning from classroom experiences (Braskamp et al., 2006; MacKinnon-Slaney, 1993). These experiences can take place in campus locations like the library, computer labs, residence halls, chapels, recreation centers, and dining halls as well as in off-campus locations. Such experiences help students express and deal with feelings and ideas (related to character, spiritual development, and religion, for instance) that might be viewed as too personal in other domains, like the classroom.

Campuses that take students' search for meaning and purpose seriously recognize the importance of the cocurricular environment and the campus community as a whole. The curricular and cocurricular ideas gathered from the research usually fall under one of these proposed strategies: 1) providing developmental experiences for students, 2) using pedagogy of engagement—field-based and community-based learning, 3) encouraging and supporting student interaction with faculty and staff, 4) being role models for students, 5) programming through residential life, and 6) student-initiated leadership. The following pages provide examples of each of these strategies.

Providing developmental experiences for students. Many institutions offer developmental experiences for students (such as first-year, sophomore-year, and senior-year experiences). The first-year focus is usually on smaller, highly interactive groupings that work on integrating into the college community through using common books and attending campus events. Faculty from any discipline and professionals from student affairs and ministry may teach sections, using their own perspectives and experiences. The goal is for students to get to know a faculty or staff member on a personal level during their first year of college. The senior year focuses on integrating knowledge and understanding, encouraging reflection, and applying knowledge to personal life.

For example, Bethune-Cookman College requires all first-year students to take a two-semester seminar that encourages them to give back to society while still in college. The broad goals, as indicated in the freshman seminar manual, are to learn how to function in this liberal arts educational community where enduring values should relate to lifelong goals and to further understanding and acceptance of core ethical standards that "good" people use to govern their daily civil interactions. Both faculty and staff professionals from the college teach the seminar. The course is structured to clarify and renew students' values. Students are asked to write about how they feel about social issues, such as election results, in the form of a journal. After the first semester, students are then engaged in a service-learning experience.

The colleges in the study also have a special type of academic offering for seniors, often referred to as "capstone experiences." Hope College, for example, requires all seniors to enroll in a senior seminar, taught by a variety of professors, which is intended to serve as the capstone to their educational experience. The seminar uses primary texts, short lectures, and small group discussions, but it also incorporates local and campus talks as a way for students to express and test their worldview in real-life discussions. For example, a recent campus speech may be discussed in class, incorporated in a paper, or serve as a springboard for discussion in the dining hall, residence hall, or chapel. Participants in this type of capstone course have their learning reinforced through both curricular and cocurricular activities. The seminar is described in the school catalog as "stressing personal assessment of one's education and life view." One professor of philosophy at Hope organized her senior seminar course (called Saints, Heroes, and Ordinary People) around this question: How good should the good life be? Students read a number of biographies, novels, and stories that illustrate the lives of various people, some Christian and some not. Students write a number of papers based on the readings either from a "believing" or a "distanced" stance. Each student also writes a "life view paper" that "articulates a philosophy for living a coherent, disciplined, yet personal way." Students are told to do their best to express themselves and grapple with the issues of the course and of their life.

Using pedagogy of engagement. Many of the institutions use several variations of pedagogy of engagement, such as study abroad, service learning, and student research. There are many examples of times when faculty, students, and student practitioners collectively participate in immersion experiences. Such experiences sometimes develop from the curriculum. For example, Bethune-Cookman College requires all first-year students to take a course that includes a service-learning component. Each student spends several hours in community service to fulfill the institution's mission to give back and serve society. At Whitworth College an Amtrak trip is part of the Prejudice Across America course. It allows students to participate with a faculty or staff member in a cultural experience. Students at Hamline University have developed a program called LEAD—Leadership, Education, and Development. Students who want out-of-classroom experiential learning can work in a local setting, attend classes abroad, and be in contact with a faculty member or a practitioner with the university's career development center about career opportunities. These experiences tend to be more authentic for students, faculty, and staff alike.

Undergraduate research can also offer experiences to develop whole students. The College of Wooster requires all seniors to complete an undergraduate research project in which they work closely with faculty members. At Whitworth College, Hope College, and Bethune-Cookman College, faculty often hire students for summer research projects that also help students learn about research.

Encouraging and supporting faculty-student interaction. Faculty members tend not to have the same relationships with students as do student services practitioners. Faculty are more likely to compartmentalize students. Therefore, it becomes the student affairs professional's role to bring faculty, staff, and students together as a community by supporting and encouraging faculty-student interaction. It is also extremely helpful if the chief academic officer is on board with such an initiative.

Participating in immersion experiences and social events provides ways of addressing more personal issues with students and faculty members. A Jewish student at the University of Dayton, a predominately Catholic institution, provides a good example of what interaction with students can accomplish. In an interview she explained that she had been pushed by her parents to attend a Jewish university but decided against it because she was struggling with doubts about her faith. Because the cultural environment of the University of Dayton in and out of the classroom integrated faith and learning, she felt free to begin her own faith exploration. Through this journey, she came into contact with a few Jewish professors on campus who offered her support and guidance. Likewise, Dayton's campus ministry also supported her, along with other students she led, in establishing a Jewish student group, which grew to include more than 30 students. These students attend religious ceremonies and share meals in professors' homes. They have found a community to explore their faith. The student confessed that she would not be at this point in her faith if it were not for these experiences with faculty and staff who were supported and encouraged by student services practitioners.

Being role models for students. Student interactions with faculty, coaches, professional staff, and ministry who demonstrate their convictions and values by what they do and how they do it can play an important role in challenging students to be their best in and out of the classroom.

Faculty involvement—especially serving as mentors and role models to students—is an important component of holistic student development (Pascarella & Terenzini, 2005). The interactions between faculty and students in the cocurricular arena develop trust and respect. The institutions that were studied encouraged a great deal of contact between faculty and students through faculty office hours, joint work on campus initiatives and programs, research, and student leadership. Students frequently mentioned that their most meaningful interactions took place during faculty office hours. One student from Pacific Lutheran University stated, "Faculty know the details of your life. . . . They are not just professors. They have a willingness to take an interest in my life and go out of the way to help me" (Braskamp et al., 2006, p. 149).

However, faculty on these campuses often expressed the need for more information on addressing common student concerns (such as career ideas and class help). They also desired more information about the boundaries for helping students with personal problems (such as mental or physical health concerns) and about available resources for students who need more personalized and professional help. These are areas in which student services practitioners can help, encouraging faculty members to think about the type of interaction they want to have with students.

The out-of-classroom experience usually is very important because it creates a natural setting for people to get to know each other in a nonthreatening way. Student services practitioners, including campus ministry professionals, play critical roles as counselors and mentors in such experiences and reinforce the importance of developing the whole student. It is essential that out-of-class activities be recognized by the entire community.

Coaches can also play important roles in students' lives and can provide role models for character formation. For example, along with promoting individual successes, coaches can teach good sportsmanship. A coach at the University of Dayton mentioned, "Emphasizing and role-modeling such behaviors as dressing for the occasion, respecting the opposing team, and teamwork are a large part of the student experience" (Braskamp et al., p. 145). In another example, a group of students on the swim team at the College of Wooster said their coach encouraged them in their athletic prowess and challenged them in their academic endeavors by sharing his own personal journey.

In addition, many of these campuses have opportunities for the whole campus community to model commitment and involvement in society. For example, "A Day of Remembrance" at Union University is used to give back to the local community, which provided assistance after a tornado hit the campus in November 2002. Most classes are suspended for the day to allow students, faculty, and staff professionals to work on service projects on and off campus and to attend a worship service together.

Programming through residential life. Residence-life programs play a prominent role in the cocurriculum. Residence halls are places where living and learning come together. Resident assistants and hall directors play key roles in student learning and development by capitalizing on educational opportunities (e.g., Pascarella & Terenzini, 2005). As the vice president of student affairs at Hope College said, "You cannot just compartmentalize. Residential life challenges us to integrate" (Braskamp et al., 2006, p. 137).

Most campuses in the study went to great lengths to capitalize on the learning and development opportunities in residence halls. First, the residence halls were seen as places of cocurricular learning. Students formed study groups and special interest meetings to augment in-class learning. For example, students and faculty at Union University read the same book and then discussed it in out-of-class settings, including residence halls. At Whitworth College students initiated and ran Bible studies, which provided opportunities for them to grapple with connections between faith and learning. Students said that it is often in Bible studies that questions related to classroom topics are discussed to figure out how a particular biblical concept might connect to a disciplinary one.

Organized living and learning communities were also very popular. For example, Creighton University provides a living and learning environment in which students can participate in service projects for the campus and the Omaha, Nebraska, community. At the College of Wooster students can arrange to live together based on their common interest in a mutual service project. At Hope and Whitworth students can live in houses that have a unified interest. In an effort to encourage learning related to student developmental stages, the University of Dayton offers unique living arrangements by school year. Certain housing configurations create different types of community.

Residence halls are prime locations for teachable moments. At these institutions subjects that surface in the halls are often discussed in the classroom or vice versa. Creighton University's provost had this to say: "What happens in class is then replayed a thousand times in the dorms and the impact of what happens in student residence life hits every classroom the next day" (Braskamp et al., 2006, p. 138). Students frequently mentioned residence life professionals as being essential to student life and development. Training is an important part of taking advantage of these residence hall educative moments; campuses were mindful to prepare their residence life staff for the types of issues that they might encounter.

Student-initiated leadership. It is important to keep in mind that students who are given leadership opportunities and have the responsibility to carry out programs experience the most growth. Students at the colleges studied were generally an empowered and highly involved group. Opportunities to lead helped develop self-responsibility. For example, at Whitworth College students were able to propose ideas and programs, ranging from themed housing to off-campus service projects. Students put proposals together that reinforced student learning and development that were then evaluated by a committee of student affairs practitioners and faculty.

Voluntary chapel and religious activities also provide opportunities for students to lead and perform. Chapel programs prove to be largely driven by student interests, and follow-up interviews confirmed that students initiated and led the chapel programs. For example, the chapel program at Hope was largely student focused and was mentioned as an important element of the cocurriculum on campus. Almost half the student body voluntarily attends chapel; the school attributes this interest to the high level of student leadership in creating the chapel experience.

A negative outcome for students taking on leadership roles in the cocurriculum can be overcommitment and overinvolvement. Some faculty members and student affairs professionals expressed their concern that this can sometimes work against the intellectual life of a campus, explaining that too many activities can compromise the quality of a student's curricular work.

Insights for institutions. Many of the strategies mentioned here are also widely used at secular institutions to create a meaningful curriculum and cocurriculum. In addition, due to the growing interest in spirituality on campuses, many institutions are seeing an increase in new student organizations with a spiritual focus, requests for speakers and programs on spiritual topics, and the need for more space and opportunities for these types of campus activities. Also, many institutions are creating new educational and administrative services aimed at developing students spiritually. For example, the University of South Carolina has a contact person in student affairs who works with chaplains of different faith communities. Bowling Green State University sponsors the "values initiative," which includes academic and cocurricular opportunities that encourage reflection on moral issues and integrates college students' search for meaning and purpose through campus experiences. It is worth noting the importance of hiring for fit and developing personnel for these types of roles.

It is also essential to provide a safe and open environment within these campus communities. Students need to feel safe and be able to express their ideas and to celebrate and defend pluralism on campuses both in and out of the classroom environment. In fact, the whole campus community must allow for diversity and pluralism in individuals' unique viewpoints and perspectives by encouraging hospitality and not stressing conformity (Bennett, 2003). A successful campus community uses events to provide similar experiences for all individuals and promotes dialogue in and out of the classroom. A safe and open environment is also a community that supports and challenges students (Braskamp et al., 2006). A campus community fosters support and challenge by creating a hospitable environment that honors academic freedom, inquiry, diversity, and pluralism and fosters both critical and constructive thinking and action. "This agenda cannot be pursued successfully simply by establishing special courses or programs" (Chickering, 2003, p. 42).

Successful campus communities develop a creative tension between challenge and support. In other words, colleges need to push and challenge students academically and personally. As Parks (2000) states:

At its best practice, higher education [plays] a primary role in the formation of critical thought and a viable faith. . . . It offers both challenge and support and thus offers good company for both the emerging strength and the distinctive vulnerability of the young adult. (p. 159)

This concept of supporting and challenging students is not new; it was first introduced by Sanford (1967) and has been recognized as a foundation of good student development and learning. Holcomb and Nonneman (2004) state that it is important to have a balance: "Too much of either challenge or support effectively stunts development" (p. 102). This dual role of support and challenge is especially relevant to those goals that extend beyond cognitive and skill development into students' values, civic responsibility, and faith development. There is a shift from the perception that faculty do the challenging and student affairs professionals do the supporting, but developing students requires that both of these groups support and challenge.

This can be accomplished at all institutions by providing a campus environment that is open to student reflection, courses that are tailored to development, more structured opportunities in and out of the classroom to explore meaning and purpose, more student leadership programs and peer advising, more staff members who have experience and knowledge in religious and spiritual development, and more interfaith opportunities as a part of campus diversity programming.

Here are some reflective questions about creating a meaningful curriculum and cocurriculum on your campus:

- How do you present new ideas in your programming?

- What do you think is on the minds of students regarding their interpersonal relationships?

- How are these students interacting with people of different cultures and ethnicities?

- What are you doing on your campus to expand students' experiences?

- To what extent do you address the big questions in life in your programming?

- How accepting is your campus community of pluralism and diversity based on race, ethnicity, religion, and lifestyle? What are the challenges in creating a community that honors diversity?

- How do you know that your campus has created a community of support and challenge?

Collaborating with Academic Affairs

Student services professionals are often concerned that faculty do not see students holistically. However, at most of the institutions studied both academic and student affairs professionals expressed a desire to learn more about each other's work experiences and goals. Student services professionals have an important role to play and an incredible amount of experience to help the campus community develop students as whole persons. They have had the inside track on student development for decades, so it is important that they educate faculty on student development issues. In *Our Underachieving Colleges*, Derek Bok (2006) admonishes:

> Don't equate what an undergraduate education should accomplish with what professors can achieve in their classrooms. . . . [This] overlooks all that admissions policies, residential living arrangements, and extracurricular life can contribute to an undergraduate's development. There is much evidence that these aspects of college do have significant effects on the attitudes, the values, and even the behavior of students. (p. 60)

It is important for student services providers and advisors to take the time to pass knowledge on to faculty members who do not know as much about the personal development of college students and to encourage and provide the means for them to interact more with their students. In fact, faculty members want student services providers to share the most current research in student development and their experiential knowledge so that faculty will understand students better.

On the other side, department chairs and faculty need to explain to student services practitioners what faculty do, their constraints and challenges, and some of the influences on their work (including discipline, career stage, employment conditions, etc.). Such collaboration is essential to make the campus a unified community.

Unfortunately, nearly all campuses struggle with collaboration between student affairs and academic affairs. The institutions in the study are aware that developing students holistically requires academic affairs and student affairs to work together. Pacific Lutheran University's motto is "Support and

Challenge." That institution tries to address the tension of balancing challenge and support by intentionally creating collaborative arrangements. Faculty and student practitioners talk in terms of how they both support and challenge students. Other institutions have some strategies that encourage this collaboration and at the same time foster holistic student development. New programs, centers, and positions are being created that provide support to student services providers and faculty to engage students more frequently.

Often special programs, especially externally funded initiatives, provide excellent opportunities for colleges to enhance a high-priority goal, create new administrative structures, and recommit to its mission. At successful campuses programs are offered in informal gatherings, such as book clubs and brown-bag events, where staff professionals can express their personal values and perspectives with colleagues and faculty members. For example, recognizing the importance of office hours with students, Villanova's Institute for Teaching and Learning established a brown-bag discussion about the importance of boundaries and how to make the best use of office hours for faculty and student affairs professionals. Other institutions have found it beneficial to include issues like office hours in new faculty orientation sessions.

It is also important for student services practitioners to encourage faculty-student interactions. At many of the institutions that fostered holistic student development, student affairs professionals deliberately encouraged faculty to invite students to their homes or provided campus venues for faculty to interact with students in homey environments (such as student lounges and special dining hall areas). Union University, in particular, had many different venues for student services practitioners to support faculty. Union's dean of students said:

> We make it easy for faculty with programs such as Be Our Guest,
> where we arrange the placement of first-year students at faculty
> homes with meals. . . . Also, we organize Leading You, where 130
> students were hosted by faculty members with a speaker and dessert
> served on campus. We want to be intentional, but it is not auto
> matic.

Insights for institutions. Regardless of the differing views about the need to collaborate, both academic and student affairs professionals in colleges overall agree that developing students takes time and requires places for students to gather, discuss, reflect, learn, and receive feedback from more experienced adults. Although discussing the big questions of life is not easy to do, it can be rewarding. For this collaboration to take place, the campus needs to buy into the essential idea that learning and development must be integrated. In other words, there must be a commitment to connect the intellectual and moral purposes of students and to help them discover their life's vocation. In doing so, there usually is a focus on self-understanding and service to others. These types of campuses create an engaging curriculum and cocurriculum that encourages self-reflection.

In addition to those ideas, other examples of collaboration and strategies for secular institutions can include 1) new administrative positions that cross organizational boundaries (such as coordinators of spiritual life or a center for sports and spirituality); 2) collaborative opportunities for the vice president for student affairs and the vice president for academic affairs; 3) placing student affairs representatives on what are typically thought of as faculty committees (such as ones dealing with academic dishonesty or leadership) and vice versa; 4) cosponsoring speakers and using campus events and experiences as learning opportunities; 5) sharing service-learning and study abroad opportunities; and 6) supporting faculty in such ways that encourage more interactions between students and faculty and helping faculty see the relationship between spirituality and learning.

Here are some questions to encourage reflection on the collaboration of student affairs and academic affairs on your campus:

- How do faculty and staff members collaborate at your institution to develop students holistically?

- How can you use your knowledge and skills in student development to help faculty?

- How can student services professionals and faculty be more involved in both curricular and cocurricular activities?

- Are there events and programs that are more successful than others? Why?

Reflecting on Your Own Talents and Development

Finally, successful campuses develop student services practitioners to lead holistic lives themselves. Successful campuses know that to have a whole campus developing whole students, the persons encouraging the development also have to be developing as whole individuals. It is important to these campuses to provide times and places for reflection and dialogue on these issues. They recognize the need for more education on college students' spirituality and faith development as a part of staff development and training.

How student services providers become involved and engaged with students is connected to their sense of self and personal goals and strengths. They have a vocation, or a calling, to put students first, but they must also remember to reflect on their purpose from time to time.

Here are some reflective questions to ask yourself:

- Do you see what you do as a job, a career, or a calling? In what way is your work meaningful? Does your work reflect who you are?

- What are challenges at your institution that need to be addressed to foster your own development? What opportunities have you found to foster your own holistic growth?

- To what extent is a community of support and challenge fostered on your campus?

CONCLUSION

A college education should prepare students to examine and develop purpose for their lives, form meaningful relationships, and learn the value of giving back to society. Because colleges have a responsibility to assist students with all aspects of their development, this chapter has presented a broad view of students' development—one that considers the spiritual, emotional, moral, and cognitive sides of developing whole students. Campus communities are intent on preparing students to be competitive in the marketplace, educating students to be productive workers in the labor force and to contribute to society as good citizens, but their involvement in helping students find purpose and meaning is what can make colleges and universities particularly distinctive.

However, there are challenges for student services providers and others in cultivating and developing whole students in all colleges and universities, faith based and secular. Not all desire or know how to engage students in activities in which students are expected to integrate their inner life of spirituality, personal values, and religious commitments with their intellectual and academic pursuits. Independent of the explicit nature of an institution's religious affiliation and mission, faculty and administrators need to view faith, spirituality, and religion as a rigorous, intellectual challenge. Colleges need to recognize that students, as well as faculty and staff, best develop their identity in community with others, within a safe environment to question, test boundaries, and refine identity.

Integrating a meaningful curriculum and cocurriculum is a driving force in student life in and out of the classroom. With the help of student services practitioners, faculty can also be involved in assisting students in their search for purpose and meaning. That is why fostering holistic student development requires a mixture of both support and challenge and a strong collaboration between student affairs staff and faculty.

It is also important to note that relationships, not programs, are more important in the long run. Students desire to have collegial relationships with faculty and other professionals on campus who demonstrate qualities of character such as integrity, perseverance, and courage. Student formation is not to be relegated to the offices of student affairs or campus ministry. However, this leads to the need to establish boundaries for staff professionals and faculty. The establishment of boundaries will vary depending on the college and institutional tradition. Acknowledging the vulnerability of all parties is an essential role that student services practitioners can take the lead in.

Providing a supportive campus environment for students to explore meaning and purpose will not only enrich their personal lives but deepen their learning. There is evidence that college students who actively search for purpose and meaning have a greater personal satisfaction, are more satisfied with their college experiences, study more, have higher grades, party less, and are more likely to perform community service (Astin, 2004; Kuh & Gonyea, 2006; Mooney, 2005). To be successful in developing whole students who are prepared for lives of meaning and purpose, colleges and universities of all types must be aware of students' spirituality and faith.

REFERENCES

Astin, A. W. (2004, April). Why spirituality deserves a central place in higher education. *Spirituality in Higher Education Newsletter, 1*(1). Retrieved June 27, 2007, from www.spirituality.ucla.edu/newsletter/past/volume%20I/1/4.html

Baxter Magolda, M. B. (2004). Self-authorship as the common goal of 21st-century education. In M. B. Baxter Magolda & P. M. King (Eds.), *Learning partnerships: Theory and models of practice to educate for self-authorship* (pp. 1–35). Sterling, VA: Stylus.

Bennett, J. B. (2003). *Academic life: Hospitality, ethics, and spirituality.* Bolton, MA: Anker.

Bok, D. (2006). *Our underachieving colleges: A candid look at how much students learn and why they should be learning more.* Princeton, NJ: Princeton University Press.

Bowen, H. R. (1991). Goals: The intended outcomes of higher education. In J. L. Bess & D. S. Webster (Eds.), *Foundations of American higher education* (pp. 23–37). Needham Heights, MA: Ginn Press.

Boyer, E. L. (1987). *College: The undergraduate experience in America.* New York, NY: HarperCollins.

Braskamp, L. A., Trautvetter, L. C., & Ward, K. (2006). *Putting students first: How colleges develop students purposefully.* Bolton, MA: Anker.

Buley-Meissner, M. L., Thompson, M. M., & Tan, E. B. (Eds.). (2000). *The academy and the possibility of belief: Essays in intellectual and spiritual life.* Cresskill, NJ: Hampton Press.

Capeheart-Meningall, J. (2005). Role of spirituality and spiritual development in student life outside the classroom. In S. L. Hoppe & B. W. Speck (Eds.), *New directions for teaching and learning: No. 104. Spirituality in higher education* (pp. 31–36). San Francisco, CA: Jossey-Bass.

Chickering, A. W. (2003, January/February). Reclaiming our soul: Democracy and higher education. *Change, 35*(1), 38–44.

Chickering, A. W., Dalton, J. C., & Stamm, L. (2006). *Encouraging authenticity and spirituality in higher education.* San Francisco, CA: Jossey-Bass.

Colby, A., Ehrlich, T., Beaumont, E., & Stephens, J. (2003). *Educating citizens: Preparing America's undergraduates for lives of moral and civic responsibility.* San Francisco, CA: Jossey-Bass.

Dalton, J. C., Eberhardt, D., Bracken, J., & Echols, K. (2006, October). Inward journeys: Forms and patterns of college student spirituality. *Journal of College & Character, 7*(8), 1–22.

Dalton, J. C., Russell, T. R., & Kline, S. (Eds.). (2004). *New directions for institutional research: No. 122. Assessing character outcomes in college.* San Francisco, CA: Jossey-Bass.

Dovre, P. J. (Ed.). (2002). *The future of religious colleges.* Grand Rapids, MI: Eerdmans.

Fowler, J. W. (1981). *Stages of faith: The psychology of human development and the quest for meaning.* New York, NY: Harper & Row.

Gallup, G., Jr., & Lindsay, D. M. (1999). *Surveying the religious landscape: Trends in U.S. beliefs.* Harrisburg, PA: Morehouse.

Higher Education Research Institute. (2005). *Spirituality in higher education: A national study of college students' search for meaning and purpose.* Los Angeles, CA: University of California–Los Angeles.

Holcomb, G. L., & Nonneman, A. J. (2004). Faithful change: Exploring and assessing faith development in Christian liberal arts undergraduates. In J. C. Dalton, T. R. Russell, & S. Kline (Eds.), *New directions for institutional research: No. 122. Assessing character outcomes in college* (pp. 93–103). San Francisco, CA: Jossey-Bass.

Howe, N., & Strauss, W. (2003). *Millennials go to college: Strategies for a new generation on campus.* Washington, DC: American Association of Collegiate Registrars and Admissions Officers.

Jablonski, M. A. (Ed.). (2001). *New directions for student services: No. 95. The implications of student spirituality for student affairs practice.* San Francisco, CA: Jossey-Bass.

Kuh, G. D., & Gonyea, R. M. (2006, Winter). Spirituality, liberal learning, and college student engagement. *Liberal Education, 92*(1), 40–47.

Kuh, G. D., Kinzie, J., Schuh, J. H., Whitt, E. J., & Associates (2005). *Student success in college: Creating conditions that matter.* San Francisco, CA: Jossey-Bass.

Love, P. G., & Talbot, D. M. (1999, Fall). Defining spiritual development: A missing consideration for student affairs. *NASPA Journal, 37*(1), 361–376.

MacKinnon-Slaney, F. (1993, Spring). Theory to practice in co-curricular activities: A new model for student involvement. *College Student Affairs Journal, 12*(2), 35–40.

Marty, M. M. (2000). *Education, religion, and the common good: Advancing a distinctly American conversation about religion's role in our shared life.* San Francisco, CA: Jossey-Bass.

Miller, W. R. (2005). What is human nature? Reflections from Judeo-Christian perspectives. In W. R. Miller & H. D. Delaney (Eds.), *Judeo-Christian perspectives on psychology: Human nature, motivation, and change* (pp. 11–29). Washington, DC: American Psychological Association.

Mooney, M. (2005, August). *Religion at America's most selective colleges: Some findings from the National Longitudinal Survey of Freshmen (NLSF).* Paper presented at the annual meeting of the Association for the Sociology of Religion, Philadelphia, PA.

Palmer, P. J. (1990). *The active life: A spirituality of work, creativity, and caring.* New York, NY: Harper & Row.

Parks, S. D. (2000). *Big questions, worthy dreams: Mentoring young adults in their search for meaning, purpose, and faith.* San Francisco, CA: Jossey-Bass.

Pascarella, E. T., & Terenzini, P. T. (2005). *How college affects students: A third decade of research.* San Francisco, CA: Jossey-Bass.

Sanford, N. (1967). *Where colleges fail: A study of the student as a person.* San Francisco, CA: Jossey-Bass.

Tisdell, E. J. (2003). *Exploring spirituality and culture in adult and higher education.* San Francisco, CA: Jossey-Bass.

13 | ORGANIZING STUDENT SERVICES FOR LEARNING

DAVE PORTER, JOE BAGNOLI, JANICE
BURDETTE BLYTHE, DONALD HUDSON,
AND DEANNA SERGEL

Student success, as measured by what students learn, is often determined by the context in which learning occurs. Organizational structures and climates, reflecting various institutional paradigms and perspectives, profoundly affect the learning process. Learning in college may be inevitable, but the paradigms and perspectives on which organizational structures and policies rest are likely to influence *what* is learned. Students can learn helplessness and cynicism just as readily as intellectual engagement and civic responsibility. This chapter identifies the educational consequences of different institutional paradigms and perspectives and considers ways in which progressive approaches to educational administration can enhance student learning and success.

Harvard educator Richard Light (2001) has asked what colleges might do to improve the chances that on graduation day more students would conclude that they really had learned what they came to college to learn. Graduation seems to be a necessary component of student success at four-year institutions. We can identify cases in which students achieved great personal or professional success despite not graduating; however, failure to complete a program is frequently accompanied by broken dreams, squandered opportunities, and bitter disappointment. On the other hand, graduation alone is not a sufficient measure of student success. As John Merrow (2006) suggests, in many cases teaching and learning have become far less important than earning a degree. He cites mounting evidence that many students complete programs or earn degrees having learned little of real value. A student's failure to attain required competency is not simply a personal disappointment; it is a failure of higher education to fulfill its promise to society. *Greater Expectations*, a report by the national panel of the Association of American Colleges and Universities (AAC&U, 2002), demands that higher education provide "the kind of learning students need to meet emerging challenges in the workplace, in a diverse democracy, and in an interconnected world" (p. vii).

Learning itself "is a complex, holistic, multi-centric activity that occurs throughout and across the college experience. . . . Knowledge is no longer a scarce—nor stable—commodity" (Keeling, 2004, p. 4). The more we discover the learning process, the more we appreciate the importance of context. Many of the prosocial dispositions we value most in our graduates are likely to be *caught* during students' experiences rather than *taught* through formal classroom instruction.

Human behavior (including administrative and faculty behavior) often reveals an individual's underlying perceptual frame, or paradigm. More than 30 years ago, Chris Argyris and Donald Schön (1974) argued that there is a critical distinction between *espoused theories* (things we claim to believe) and *theories in action* (beliefs implied by patterns in our behaviors). Unfortunately, higher education has a tradition of cloaking regressive bureaucratic practices with a thin but dazzlingly progressive rhetorical veneer. Consequently, public images seldom distinguish progressive from traditional educational organizations. For example, most college presidents publicly and proudly embrace expanded access, increased accountability, enhanced inclusion, more authentic engagement, deeper learning, and greater student achievement. Despite this similarity in rhetoric, the actual experiences of faculty, staff, and students in different schools varies greatly.

Causes of these differences can be found within the bureaucratic and hierarchical systems we create and work in. There may be great tension between what is taught in an institution's classrooms and what is done behind the scenes in its administrative offices and faculty meeting rooms. Enhancing student success, in the broadest sense, requires us to become aware of inconsistencies between our educational purposes and administrative and academic policies and practices; these inconsistencies must then be engaged and resolved with integrity and persistence. Student success requires that we narrow the gap between our rhetoric and our practice.

The term *leadership* is sometimes used to refer to particular people or positions; in this chapter, however, we will use the term a little differently. From our perspective, it is useful to recognize that leadership includes all the processes and activities that affect individuals' commitment to achieving common institutional goals. Thus, *leadership* will be used to refer to processes, not to a person or position. In healthy organizations (including many higher education institutions), leadership is widely distributed—everyone is encouraged to participate. Even in organizations that are less healthy, faculty and staff are likely to have many opportunities to influence student success by the ways in which they engage students and as they implement policies and procedures. But the recognition of such opportunities is greatly facilitated by a conceptual framework that helps illuminate the potential for improvement.

In the following pages we will contrast traditional hierarchical structures and processes with progressive alternatives we believe to be more consistent with the aims of higher education and what we understand about student learning and, thus, to be more likely to facilitate authentic student success. First, we will compare organizational structures and three characteristics that distinguish these archetypal organizations. Next, we will consider alternative models of education represented by two distinct conceptualizations of what college learning is and how it occurs. We will then explore the question of leadership and suggest ways in which change might occur within educational organizations.

In each case we will describe the theories in action as implied by observable policies and practices within traditional hierarchical organizations. We will provide an account of what it has meant to attempt to put progressive educational rhetoric into practice. Finally, we will provide brief accounts of these processes at the United States Air Force Academy and Western Governors University as well as a more detailed discussion of our efforts at Berea College, to "walk the talk" by aligning policies with our educational mission and practices with these policies.

Pure examples of the traditional and progressive archetypes do not exist. Because of this, the depiction of traditional hierarchical leaders and institutions that follows is likely to be more of a caricature than an exact likeness. However, this admittedly exaggerated comparison will be helpful in clarifying the distinctions between these two fundamentally different ways of approaching higher education administration.

Our objective in this chapter is not to vilify those who find comfort in the familiarity of traditional perspectives and approaches. Often the back-to-basics traditional approach to administration can help get the academic trains to run on time and create educational systems that appear to be as orderly and disciplined as any factory. Image is important, especially when institutions approach potential donors or politicians to solicit support, as they must increasingly do (Merrow, 2006). The confidence and clarity exuded by some traditional leaders can be quite persuasive to potential donors. Leaders whose style may alienate an entire campus may also prove themselves to be particularly adept at recruiting wealthy donors and influential board members. We believe that in most cases student success will depend on the integration of efforts by individuals with attitudes and perspectives representing a wide range of views and values.

Paradigms of leadership and organizations are somewhat like the flu—they are quite contagious. Knowledge of alternative theoretical frameworks provides an opportunity to observe and assess patterns within the myriad of mirrors and the billows of smoke that frequently attend higher education and its administration. Just as each individual must struggle with internal conflicts and uncertainty, each institution—with its unique mission, constituencies, and player personalities—must do the best it can in the circumstances in which it finds itself.

ORGANIZATIONAL STRUCTURES

Educational organizations are similar to other bureaucratic hierarchies. Once organizations are formed, they are molded by internal and external pressures that are similar across many different industries. Concerns with productivity, efficiency, accountability, competitiveness, control, debt, financing, alignment, and continuity are no less urgent in the education industry than in mining, manufacturing, sales, or agriculture.

Traditional Approach

In *Pedagogy of the Oppressed* (1997), Paulo Freire argues persuasively that preparing individuals to accept their roles within traditional corporate bureaucracies is one of the primary, though largely implicit, functions of many traditional educational systems. Although seldom proclaimed publicly, several organizational characteristics help distinguish institutional administrations that adhere to traditional hierarchical models (Porter, 1991, 1998):

- Centralized decision-making

- Continuing selection through competition

- Emphasis on conformity and compliance

By definition, hierarchies contain distinctive levels with subordinate units reporting to the organization's next-higher level. In education the classroom teacher or staff member interacting directly with students represents the lowest academic level; the disciplinary or administrative department represents an intermediate level; the division or college forms the next higher level; and finally, overall institutional or system administration constitutes the apex of the traditional organizational pyramid. In such hierarchies the most consequential decisions are the prerogative of those who occupy the administrative penthouse.

The management of information often establishes and sustains centralized decision-making. In traditional hierarchies information (particularly information related to both individual and collective performance) is treated as a confidential commodity reserved for only those with hierarchical privilege. Although administrators may provide limited information to subordinate offices or departments, such specific feedback is usually insufficient to allow for real participation in policy considerations or assessment. Because so much of information's meaning depends on its context as revealed by trends or cross-sectional comparisons, subordinates cannot integrate the specific information they are provided into meaningful wholes.

Traditional hierarchical administrators cite concerns about privacy, confidentiality, or institutional legal exposure to justify withholding information. As a result, many individuals at lower organizational levels know only what they have been told about how well the school is accomplishing its mission and supporting student success. Many traditional administrators believe that problems should be resolved before they are admitted. In such centralized systems, staff and faculty members in critical support functions are sometimes unaware of feedback that may show that students are struggling unnecessarily or failing. Ironically, subordinates' general lack of awareness is sometimes cited by senior administrators as a justification for not allowing wider participation in decisions about personnel, curricula, programs, or operating budgets.

Although extensive networks of faculty committees exist at traditional institutions, as long as adequate information is not publicly available, the most substantive decisions must be made behind the closed doors of senior administrators' offices. Some administrations collect the data and then hoard it for private use, but it is just as common not to collect such information at all. If there is low trust between the administration and the faculty and staff, ignorance about performance may be mutually desirable. Faculty and staff members are more comfortable not having their work measured, and administrators realize that the dearth of data makes their decisions more difficult to challenge. After all, the traditional hierarchical default when relevant information is lacking is to defer to executive intuition.

Thus, in traditional hierarchical organizations a conspiracy of ignorance may emerge between fearful faculty and staff members and administrators who are protecting their authority against data-based challenges. For example, faculty may resist student ratings of teaching because they do not trust administrators to use the information fairly and appropriately; administrators may resist such ratings just as strongly because the aggregate data may provide evidence of systemic failures in faculty development. In such organizations substantive initiatives designed to enhance student success are likely to be difficult to develop, awkward to implement, and nearly impossible to sustain. To enhance student success, traditional hierarchies need to decentralize decision-making and collect and share more and better information about the achievement of educational objectives.

The second common characteristic of traditional hierarchical organizations is their emphasis on competition as a means of selecting individuals for retention and promotion. In the corporate world the most notorious manifestation of this approach was Enron. As Malcolm Gladwell (2002) made clear, Enron's obsessive reliance on competition had devastating effects on the integrity of individuals within this twisted corporate culture. Alfie Kohn (1992) has documented extensively the costs and negative consequences of competition in both academic and occupational work groups. He provides strong evidence that competition erodes standards and undermines quality. Whichever particular aspects of the educational process are selected for measurement, emphasis on the unselected others is likely to decrease. Organizational processes may become increasingly warped and inefficient as a result.

The ill effects of selection through competition can be seen in the tenure and promotion systems of some institutions. Although faculty committees may carefully and conscientiously consider the qualifications of candidates against published criteria, presidents and trustees technically make the final decisions. Extensive definitions of criteria and the impossibly high explicit expectation that every candidate be excellent in every category of consideration create ambiguity and anxiety. The heightened perception of interpersonal competition can drive some junior faculty members into a dilettantish frenzy of superficial activity. As Kohn (1992) suggests, competition may increase activity but suppress actual productivity because so much of the extra activity is invested in things that create appearances rather than contribute to substance.

Current conceptualizations of the learning process provide many reasons to reduce reliance on interpersonal competition within educational systems. In general, competition is likely to cause faculty and staff to focus on the wrong things. Many academic and administrative tasks that are essential for student success may be neglected in favor of traditional activities—such as lecturing, testing, and committee work—that are likely to be more consistent with upper administration's expectations. Similarly, perceived competition between curricular and cocurricular programs is likely to lead to endless squabbles about who deserves credit for success or blame for failures—both of which are usually the result of the interaction of many factors. Under such conditions an institution is unlikely to achieve the integrated vision of learning and development called for by both student affairs professionals and national faculty groups (AAC&U, 2002; Keeling, 2004).

The third component characteristic of traditional hierarchical bureaucratic institutions is their emphasis on conformity. This characteristic is a natural consequence of traditional systems' reliance on competition. To appear fair and objective, criteria must be specified in great detail. Little value is assigned to those who have a penchant for coloring outside the lines; individualism (especially when demonstrated in novel ways) is perceived as a threat to established institutional values. For example, imagine the case of a faculty member who conducts research over several years to plan and develop technology for a new language laboratory at the institution but does not publish the results. Some might insist that, without publication, such activity is not truly scholarly. To consider the merits of the endeavor, they claim, would undermine the integrity of the tenure system. In traditional organizations critical decisions tend to be made on the basis of appearances rather than on a consideration of the actual contributions to the institution's mission or student success.

Thus, many traditional hierarchical institutions maintain policies and practices that reflect centralized decision-making, reliance on interpersonal competition, and an emphasis on conformity. Such an approach was widely accepted in the past; however, increasing emphasis on assessment and accountability by regional accreditation agencies, and others, appears to be highlighting the shortcomings of this approach. Unfortunately, the more strongly an institution is wedded to preserving its image, the more difficult it is for those interested in providing real support for student success and progressive reform to create opportunities for improvement.

Progressive Alternatives

In contrast to their actual practices, some educational institutions claim to adhere to more egalitarian and progressive models. Those in positions of power may use trendy phrases such as *total quality, servant leadership,* and *learning organizations* without actually understanding these approaches. The gap between rhetoric and practice becomes increasingly salient when the implications of servant leadership and learning organizations are compared to the hierarchical practices just described. No matter how lofty the ultimate goals, how venerable the mission, and how inspiring the rhetoric, if the prevailing means to accomplish these goals relies on hierarchical authority, the institution is likely to fall short of its potential for supporting student success. A brief review of progressive alternatives will clarify these distinctions.

Progressive organizational structures are built on the assumptions that people doing the job know a great deal about how to achieve desired outcomes and that they will respond positively to opportunities to improve organizational effectiveness. Somewhat surprisingly, this approach can be seen in military practices. General Colin Powell's *Leadership Primer* (2000) states:

> The commander in the field is always right and the rear echelon is wrong, unless proven otherwise. . . . Too often, the reverse defines corporate culture. . . . Shift the power and financial accountability to the folks who are bringing home the bacon, not the ones who are counting . . . the beans. (slide 17)

In progressive organizations the primary function of the upper administrative echelons is to inform and facilitate rather than to criticize and control. Service to subordinates is the essence of Robert Greenleaf's (1970, 1977) concept of servant leadership, an approach with profound implications for all types of organizations. All that is required to discover the prevailing orientation of the organization in which one works is to look around and listen. How well do current programs and practices reflect the understanding, perspectives, and wisdom of those who are directly engaged in supporting student learning? Do the individuals on the front lines believe they have the power to influence (or even eliminate) policies and administrative practices that waste resources or impede student success? Do faculty and staff feel that their service is appreciated and their insights valued? The more negative the responses to such questions, the more traditional, hierarchical, bureaucratic, and oppressive the administration is likely to be.

In progressive organizations there is much greater emphasis on cooperative and collegial development than on competition and selection. Not only are resources provided so that everyone has opportunities to learn and grow, but funds are directed at the individual and organizational needs that faculty and staff have helped identify as being of particular importance to supporting student learning. In progressive organizations individuals are likely to be assessed in terms of their potential to contribute to organizational goals rather than their allegiance to the most current administrative policy. Education is likely to be seen as a team sport rather than a series of individual contests. The advantage of this interdependent perspective is that people throughout the institution become more willing to do the small things essential to support student success, things that are sometimes not even noticed, let alone counted, by senior administrators (Porter & Sergel, 1998).

In progressive organizations it is easier to speak the truth. Individuals are more willing to take risks, learn from unexpected outcomes, and improve processes continuously. The accumulation of knowledge about what doesn't work balances information about past successes and creates a robust and reliable knowledge base for the institution. In progressive administrations, failures are not feared; they are recognized as an important source of learning. Traditional hierarchies' relentless emphasis on evaluation, competitive selection, and image tends to obscure failures in an effort to project an image of ubiquitous and continual success. This has a chilling effect on organizational learning: The need to improve simply would be inconsistent with the administration's pretense of perpetual perfection. Some traditional bureaucracies stagnate because innovative initiatives for enhancing student success are considered to be just too risky.

Decision-making in progressive organizations is widely distributed. Continuous improvement is achieved through individual and communal learning rather than through competitive selection. A rich diversity of talents and perspectives is likely to emerge. In contrast to traditional institutions' extensive use of performance metrics, individual faculty, staff, and students are engaged in ongoing conversations about their own learning, their performance, and contributions to important collective goals. Progressive organizations tend to become more stable as incumbents learn how to do their jobs better and find ways to adapt what they are doing to support institutional priorities with continuously increasing effectiveness.

In some traditional hierarchical organizations, senior administrators are shuffled around to create an appearance of progress and to compensate for able administrators who depart. Although the turnover turmoil in such organizations is often masked by euphemistic rhetoric, perpetual externally driven change is likely to create anxiety and uncertainty for those who remain within the organization. People hunker down and focus on accomplishing their particular prescribed tasks, doing whatever is necessary to avoid attracting negative attention. Authentic support for student success is likely to be neglected. Many incumbents in hierarchical organizations conclude that if the minimum weren't good enough, it wouldn't be the minimum. In progressive organizations the focus is on finding better ways to contribute to student success.

MODELS OF EDUCATION

Institutions of higher education distinguish themselves from organizations in other industries in one way: The work done by colleges and universities is education. It is more than the provision of simple services that can be measured by customer satisfaction or profitability alone. Education involves learning, a measurable increase in students' adaptive capacity. The way administrators understand the learning process determines how accurately they perceive the challenges students confront and how effectively they can provide the support necessary for students to learn.

The educational process has been illuminated by evolving theories of learning and human development. Over the past century our knowledge of human development has become increasingly refined and complex. Jean Piaget (1926) developed the notion of distinct stages of mental development. He was particularly interested in how infants and young children learn, noting the sequential transitions from the most basic sensorimotor stage to the stage of formal operations (i.e., abstract thought). His identification of the complementary processes of assimilation (using internal knowledge to engage the world) and accommodation (rearranging internal knowledge to better deal with the world's challenges) accounts for the hypothetical stair-step structure that underlies most modern developmental theories. Lawrence Kohlberg (1963) agreed that development occurs in sequential stages, but he focused on moral development in older children (primarily those who had already attained Piaget's formal operational stage). Later, William Perry (1970) interviewed male students during their years at college and proposed a comprehensive model of intellectual and ethical development for that life stage. He suggested that most students let go of notions of absolute right and wrong and learn to accept and integrate multiple perspectives through a series of distinct stages from dualism through multiplicity to contextual relativism.

However, Perry's scheme was seen by some as being too rational and too detached. Noting that Perry had relied entirely on male students' development, Belenky, Clinchy, Goldberger, and Tarule (1986) identified alternative developmental paths from their interviews with a diverse group of college women. Although confirming the general developmental trajectory that Perry proposed, Belenky et al. introduced a new path to sophisticated thinking and analysis that involved "a personal and intimate approach to knowledge acquisition: stepping into what one was trying to know" (Baxter Magolda, 2006, p. 52). Many others have provided further elaboration and nuance to our understanding of the diverse ways in which students develop through their college experiences (Baxter Magolda, 1992; Fischer & Bidell, 1998; Gardner, 1999;

King & Kitchner, 1994). Richard Light's *Making the Most of College* (2001), along with other recent research (Pascarella & Terenzini, 2005), has concluded that active student engagement, the use of multiple pedagogies, and interaction between students and faculty foster effective learning. Student engagement has been identified as a particularly significant ingredient for student success (Kuh, Kinzie, Schuh, Whitt, & Associates, 2005).

Although most presidents and provosts now espouse some version of the learning paradigm (Barr & Tagg, 1995), a review of their institutions' policies and administrative practices may reveal which ones are actually committed to this approach. Initially, Barr and Tagg's identification of higher education's need to shift from an *instructional paradigm* to a *learning paradigm* met with resistance on many campuses. The juxtaposition of two distinctively different paradigms made the gulf between some institutions' espoused theories (the learning paradigm) and their theories in action (some version of the instructional paradigm) uncomfortably obvious. Some traditional institutions committed extensive resources to denying the significance, accuracy, and, at times, even the existence of the instructional paradigm (Tagg, 2003). The contrast of these alternative paradigms rendered many traditional rhetorical strategies untenable.

In other instances, however, senior administrators became so mesmerized by measurement that they subjected their institutions to unending cycles of mostly meaningless data collection. In such cases it was as if the resultant piles of data themselves might create an impression of excellence worthy of recognition. Awards such as the Malcolm Baldrige Total Quality Award for education can place so much emphasis on the collection of data that relatively little attention is given to analysis and improvement. The transition from the traditional cultures of argument (in which assertions of authority or prestige prevail) that have characterized much of higher education's discourse over the past half century to more egalitarian cultures of evidence has been difficult and complex. Once again, characteristics of traditional hierarchical institutions and more progressive ones will be contrasted to highlight these distinctions.

Traditional Approach

Many traditional educational bureaucracies focus on inputs and pay less attention to measures of educational processes and even less to students' achievement of outcomes. For administrators of such traditional bureaucracies, measures of educational inputs were relatively easy and inexpensive to collect. For struggling institutions, input measures may have been attractive because they directed attention to the many external causes of students' academic difficulties (e.g., declining entry test scores). Yet another possible reason for this somewhat myopic focus on inputs was that rankings and ratings such as those published annually by *U.S. News & World Report* focus almost exclusively on inputs; thus, such measures are imbued with instant credibility. Entering students' SAT or ACT scores and class ranking; faculty members' research grants and professional publications; administrators' past accomplishments, awards, and salaries; and alumni giving have all been used to assert institutional prestige even in the absence of any evidence of student learning.

By selecting students who have already shown themselves to be the most intellectually absorbent and faculty who have generated scholarship most effusively, some traditional hierarchical institutions assume that all that is required for education to happen is bringing the right kind of students and the right kind of faculty together. This model implies that education occurs by mere exposure to information. This osmotic model suggests that if inputs are controlled, learning is only a matter of time. The accumulation of knowledge is periodically marked by the award of course credit, which in turn becomes a degree after a sufficient number and type of units have been acquired. One result of this superficial administrative understanding of the learning process is that "our educational practice has emphasized information transfer without a great deal of thought given to the meaning, pertinence, or application of information in the context of the student's life" (Keeling, 2004, p. 10).

An unfortunate (and unintended) consequence of outcomes assessment and accountability within traditional hierarchical institutions is that education has been reduced to a series of discrete measurements. Without holistic theoretical models of educational processes, traditional institutions are particularly susceptible to the dangers of reductionism. Rather than struggle to measure complex aspects of human learning, institutions eager to show compliance with external mandates are likely to select the metrics that are most available and to use jargon and rhetoric to inflate these data's significance.

Student learning increases a graduate's capacity to contribute to society. Such contributions depend on students' acquiring increased perceptual prowess as well as the mastery of a set of behavioral skills. After all, leadership (the process of influencing and supporting others in the attainment of common goals) requires that one be able to read situations accurately and respond effectively. These two types of outcomes distinguish two distinct but complementary processes: training (the acquisition and refinement of skilled behaviors) and education (the development of perceptual and reflective abilities). Skilled behaviors are most likely to be acquired by clear prescription and repetitive practice. With regard to skill development, practice may not make perfect, but it does tend to make the behaviors practiced more efficient and more likely to occur in the future.

Perceptual and reflective skills, referred to by some as "consciousness" and by others as "insight," are just as important. However, these skills are likely to follow complex and varied developmental pathways. Improvement of perceptual skills tends to be more difficult to measure and control than the acquisition of behavioral skills. The development of perceptual abilities is likely to require periods of independent as well as collective reflection; this allows students to integrate emotional and intellectual aspects of their own diverse encounters and experiences.

At many traditional hierarchical institutions, outcomes relating to curiosity, creativity, or consciousness are deemed too complex or elusive to be measured, so they are ignored. Enlightenment is relegated to small liberal arts colleges or particularly eccentric academic departments and other similarly peripheral educational entities. Evidence of these underlying beliefs can be found in the practices and policies of many traditional institutions of higher education. And yet such an instructional paradigm is likely to be vigorously denied by administrators. Although many institutions and administrators have eloquently espoused various aspects of the learning paradigm, very few have changed policies and practices to ones that are more consistent with this progressive approach (Tagg, 2003).

Progressive Alternatives

The learning paradigm recognizes that learning is a process occurring within a broader system. This realization forces the focus of inquiry to expand beyond the inputs. In a learning institution, inputs, despite their apparent ease of measurement, are not given priority over the other components of educational systems—processes and outcomes. The emphasis shifts from looking good to doing well.

The transformation toward becoming an institution aligned with the learning paradigm is likely to begin with consideration of outcomes. Learning paradigm colleges must articulate what they want their students to learn. It is not sufficient to simply collect extensive lists of desirable qualities of graduates. Outcomes must be organized, integrated, and prioritized into coherent wholes. This statement of outcomes becomes the focus of the institution's mission, a concise statement of what the institution values most. Institutions that create mission statements that sprawl over several pages miss the opportunity to prioritize and fail to realize the full value of having a mission. If the institution promises to be all things to all people, it is likely that the institution will regularly disappoint many of its constituencies and that subordinates will have to continue to rely on senior administrators to help them understand and prioritize alternatives.

There are several obvious advantages to clarifying and prioritizing outcomes first. Clarifying outcomes increases accountability. Rather than using input measures to support arguments for institutional excellence, administrators committed to an outcomes-first approach engage the difficult task of identifying what matters most and then seriously considering the question of how these outcomes might be measured. Administrators, faculty, and staff at such mission-driven institutions have a sense of identity and share beliefs about priorities consistent with that identity. If this process of organization, integration, and prioritization is undertaken at the highest level, it provides a model for other departments. However, the process itself can occur at any level within the organization even without support (or even permission) from above.

When there is greater clarity concerning what students are to learn, educators can turn their attention to the learning process itself. Process matters; it lies at the heart of the learning paradigm. Persisting in doing what has always been done is almost certain to ensure that student learning will not increase. Developing new processes to enhance student learning is critical work in which all educators must be encouraged to participate. They should ask such questions as these: What do the students need to know that they do not know already? What must they be able to do that they cannot do now? What attitudes or dispositions will contribute to our most valued outcomes?

In the classroom educational processes implemented by teachers to enhance learning are called "pedagogies," but the principles that underlie these practices apply more broadly. Collected under the rubric of powerful pedagogies, approaches such as cooperative and collaborative learning, problem-based learning, service-learning, and experiential learning have demonstrated the capacity to energize and engage many students who may not respond to traditional lectures. Because institutions and the students they serve differ, it is important that educators adapt rather than merely adopt (i.e., import) these processes. In a sense, all learning, like politics, is local. Certain principles may consistently lead to success, but the ways in which general learning principles need to be implemented to achieve the desired results vary dramatically. This is one of the reasons that classroom assessment techniques (Angelo & Cross, 1993) and course-embedded assessment (Walvoord & Anderson, 1998) continue to receive such strong support from progressive educators: They provide practical frameworks for adaptation and improvement.

MODELS OF LEADERSHIP AND CHANGE

It should not be a surprise that the distinctions between traditional and progressive organizational structures and educational paradigms also apply to models of leadership and organizational change. The practices of many traditional organizations show their adherence to an outdated and empirically discredited but perpetually popular concept of leadership referred to as the Great Man Theory (Hughes, Ginnett, & Curphy, 1999; Lipman-Blumen, 1996; Stogdill, 1974). Far more problematic than its lack of empirical support is the tendency of this leadership conceptualization to exacerbate problems inherent in traditional hierarchical organizations. Adherents of this theory often attempt to make changes through the assertion of their administrative power. Together this theory of leadership and authoritarian hierarchical structures exemplify an approach to leadership that Douglas McGregor (1966) labeled Theory X.

In contrast, leadership practices in progressive institutions are more likely to reflect approaches to leadership (both ancient and contemporary) that emphasize the interdependence of individuals and the catalytic potential of senior administrative positions. Induction through modeling and encouragement is observed more frequently in these organizations than power assertion. This approach to organizational change through induction and support reflects McGregor's (1966) Theory Y and, we believe, is far more consistent with the goal of enhancing student success. More recently Jean Lipman-Blumen (1996) elaborated on this approach in her development of the concept of connective leadership as being both a more appropriate and effective style than the traditional hierarchical and authoritarian styles.

Traditional Approach

Leadership has not always been understood to be a process. In fact, the notion that leaders are born rather than made has exceedingly deep historical roots. However, this myth may have reached its zenith in the early 20th century in America. The notion that some set of special qualities and characteristics reliably distinguishes leaders from followers has enjoyed great popularity, especially among those whose inheritance or wealth placed them at the pinnacle of various industries and organizations. However, the personal characteristics of effective leaders vary greatly across different kinds of tasks, different times, and different groups of followers. Relationships between leader characteristics and group performance tend to be complex. In 1985 Bennis and Nanus concluded that thousands of leadership studies over the previous 75 years had failed to identify *any* substantial distinctions between leaders and nonleaders as well as any personality characteristics that distinguished effective leaders from ineffective ones.

Because the Great Man Theory is a myth, it is difficult to gather evidence to justify its continuation. In some traditional hierarchical institutions, leaders may at times provoke apparent crises to persuade external audiences, such as boards of trustees or state legislatures, that leadership continuity is vital. Such leaders may also reinforce their authority by surrounding themselves with those who are eager to display loyalty by reassuring these leaders of the reality of their mythic prowess and power. Thus, the use of hierarchical power to reward loyalty and conformity serves to keep "great men" in their privileged place. These manufactured crises also provide convenient justifications for the leader's assertion of power as the primary mode of effecting organizational change. In a crisis there simply is no time for democracy; the current situation, such leaders claim, is just too dire. Unfortunately, leaders who engage in such practices divert attention (and resources) from real problems and from real opportunities to enhance support for student success.

For many traditional institutions, periodic accreditation reviews exacerbate already oppressive hierarchical control. Extensive external specification of academic and administrative standards, combined with implicit threats of institutional probation or loss of accreditation, heighten institutional anxiety; therefore, interest in innovation and improvement is likely to be suspended. Despite more than a decade of efforts at reform in regional accrediting associations, many institutions are still evaluated on the basis of the impressions they create in their self-studies and during the relatively brief campus visit rather than on a systematic and objective assessment of their true capacity to accomplish their educational mission and enhance student success.

Douglas McGregor's (1966) description of the ideas and beliefs that characterize Theory X leaders provides some insight into how individuals might justify such practices. McGregor suggests that those who hold this perspective have a rather pessimistic view of human nature. They consider most subordinates to be less intelligent, less skilled, and less committed than they are themselves. Data from employee satisfaction surveys tend to show that expressed commitment is likely to decline rapidly as responses from successively lower levels in bureaucracies are analyzed. In fact, a steeply declining satisfaction gradient across different levels of the organization is a nearly certain indicator of this pernicious leadership approach. In Berne's (1996) popular vernacular, Theory X leaders are likely to believe that they themselves are OK but that the vast majority of their subordinates are not OK—and, unfortunately, a hierarchical leader's perception often becomes a self-fulfilling prophecy.

Collectively, the consequences of this approach to leadership within a bureaucracy that already emphasizes centralized decision-making, competition, and conformity are likely to undermine or obstruct initiatives designed to enhance student success. Structures that emphasize the management of information and the assertion of power as the way to bring about change create an environment in which idealism can quickly turn to cynicism among faculty, staff, and, in turn, students. This is perhaps the greatest cost to the institution.

Progressive Alternatives

However, there are alternatives. In organizations where information and knowledge are shared widely and decision-making has been delegated to the lowest level, different administrative practices emerge. In organizations where there is less competition for scarce resources and squabbles over who will receive credit for successes or blame for perceived failures are rare, more resources are available to devote to institutional priorities. In organizations where individuals feel they are respected for their unique perspectives and capabilities, the appearance of conformity is not achieved through bullying and intimidation (Porter & Sergel, 1998). In such organizations careful listening and conscientious modeling of desired behaviors are the most common form of influence. Individuals within these institutions feel free to organize and align themselves with appropriate institutional priorities, such as enhancing student learning.

Robert Greenleaf's (1977) concept of servant leadership is well suited for such organizations. Unlike the elitist implications of the Great Man Theory, servant leadership is an approach that is available to everyone; it is a set of behaviors based on a system of beliefs and positive expectations rather than something mysterious and ill defined such as personal charisma.

It is critical that people in positions of authority within the organization help synchronize the efforts of others as the organization transforms itself to meet the needs of its students more effectively. Understanding and trust are both critical (Porter, 1991). Without trust, even complete clarity about priorities and how the institution's most important goals are to be achieved is not likely to result in much progress. On the other hand, an organization with high levels of trust but insufficient understanding of the task or external circumstances can also encounter problems. Irving Janis's *Groupthink* (1982) documents the disastrous results of powerful administrative groups that developed too much trust and confidence with far too little understanding of their tasks and contexts.

Two things necessary for the development of trust within an institution are for those occupying senior positions to become worthy of trust and for these same senior administrators to demonstrate a sincere and enduring willingness to trust others. Highly competitive systems almost always induce those within them to cut corners or play politics to gain an advantage over those they perceive to be adversaries (Kohn, 1992). People who have won the competition for senior administrative positions often bring with them undesirable personal characteristics. But this is often not the greatest challenge to developing organizational trust. Simply being trustworthy is not sufficient to engender trust in others; it is also necessary to convey trust in others. Because many traditional hierarchical leaders view themselves as being in competition with others (especially those who ask impertinent questions and insist on using evidence to support conclusions), they find it difficult to display the trust necessary to get others to trust them.

In the age of information, organizational systems and the process of education have become both increasingly complex and more dynamic. In such an environment, information from across the institution must be collected and integrated into knowledge that can inform institutional decisions at all levels. High trust and good intentions are not sufficient; individuals need to become aware of the consequences of their actions on others within the system as well as on the system as a whole. Knowledge of failures (or unexpected results) is especially valuable. It may be reassuring to collect extensive evidence that the system is working well, but information about the times when and places where the system fails is what is needed to improve support for outcomes such as student learning and success.

Organizational learning (just like individual learning) requires regularly reconciling experiences and observations with prior expectations. Expectations need to be more substantive than individual hunches or opinions; they should be based on theoretical models of key institutional processes. A model is simply a way to combine beliefs about what causes what within a system. Even a bad model is better than no model at all because a bad model can be improved every time additional information about processes and outcomes is garnered. Systemic models provide a way of storing and contextualizing evidence of institutional performance and organizing it in a way that will be accessible to all constituents. Articulating one's model is a matter of both integrity and accountability. It is also one of the best ways that people in positions of administrative responsibility can model appropriate behavior for subordinates.

This approach to ensuring continuous improvement in quality and effectiveness of organizations is simply not compatible with McGregor's (1966) Theory X leadership style. The perspectives and characteristics of McGregor's Theory Y approach, on the other hand, fit with the progressive approach well. As McGregor suggests, those who hold to Theory Y assume that most others (students, faculty, and staff) are intrinsically motivated to contribute to common goals of the organization. Theory Y leaders are likely to provide their subordinates with increasing autonomy and responsibility. Trust and knowledge increase together naturally. Another significant advantage of this progressive alternative is its effects on student success. By relying on democratic and egalitarian behaviors and relationships, faculty, staff, and administrators come to embody the changes they hope to achieve in their students.

OVERCOMING BARRIERS TO EDUCATIONAL SUCCESS

We must admit that some traditional hierarchical bureaucracies have demonstrated the capacity to support student success. Although some of these demonstrations were relatively short lived and others were more apparent than actual, there are some circumstances when centralized decision-making, competition, and conformity serve the interests of the institution and students. But when such practices and policies become a part of institutional identity or determine administrative structures and policies, colleges and universities are likely to fall short of their full potential to support student success. Clearly, students dedicated to their own learning can sometimes overcome long odds and many obstacles to achieve success. But the AAC&U's *Greater Expectations* (2002) identifies several common systemic barriers to the quest for educational quality: "professors trained and rewarded more for research than for teaching, a prestige hierarchy built on reputation and resources rather than educational success, and a lack of meaningful or comparable measurement to assess student-learning outcomes" (p. x). In our collective experience, traditional paradigms and perspectives have contributed significantly to the construction and maintenance of each of these barriers.

As we have observed repeatedly, every system is perfectly designed to yield the results observed. Low faculty morale, lack of student engagement (and excitement), and a tendency to elevate mediocre accomplishments into examples of educational excellence persist in many institutions of higher education. We must pause and consider our own paradigms and perspectives and their consequences on the choices we make and the educational systems we create.

It is much easier to create a caricature of the traditional great man, brimming with ego and arrogance, than it is to imagine an idealized alternative: the servant leader. Servant leaders come in both genders and all shapes, sizes, and colors; some may not even wear suits (or pants). They may occupy different roles within organizations and possess a variety of temperaments (Greenleaf, 2004). What they have in common, however, is the willingness to ask supportive questions of their colleagues and students (such as "What have you done that has made you proud?" or "How do you hope to contribute to our mission in the future?"); they provide sustained and authentic support for the efforts of others. They also have the temerity to ask themselves and the institution questions such as "What are we really trying to accomplish?" and "How do we know that what we are doing is working?" Adopting a progressive paradigm allows faculty, staff, and administrators to align themselves with one another and the unique mission of their particular institution in ways that can enhance student success substantially. But, admittedly, the details and particularities of such paradigmatic shifts conceal many devils. We now turn to some of these.

PROGRESSIVE INSTITUTIONS

Our challenge is to provide illustrations and examples showing how progressive paradigms and perspectives have been put into practice. Many caveats are relevant. As participant-observers in the events we describe, none of us can claim to have been unbiased (Tavris & Aronson, 2007). The activities we describe are ones about which we have cared (and continue to care) deeply. We have done several things to help reduce the distortion our biases might introduce. We have made bona fide efforts to disprove our own assumptions, and each of us played devil's advocate in reviewing the accounts provided by our coauthors. We have asked for evidence to support conclusions and tried to be fair as well as truthful. However, what we saw (and what we remember) was undoubtedly influenced by who we are and where we stood. We confess that we believe the progressive paradigms and perspectives described previously not only have broad academic and theoretical support but that they are extraordinarily practical. These perspectives contributed to a variety of initiatives in many institutions across higher education. As an introduction to a more extensive and detailed account of ways in which these ideas influenced developments at Berea College, brief descriptions of two somewhat different institutions—the United States Air Force Academy and Western Governors University—are provided.

The United States Air Force Academy

Established in 1959, the United States Air Force Academy in Colorado is both an undergraduate, degree-granting institution and an Air Force organization. This dual identity makes it a rather unlikely candidate as a model for a progressive educational transformation. The academy's student body of approximately 4,000 cadets receives instruction from an academic faculty of about 500 as well as an additional 100 military officers who develop and implement a variety of military training programs and activities. Each year cadets are selected from among the top high school graduates across the nation.

Most of the academy's faculty members are military officers, the majority of whom have earned only master's degrees and are assigned to the academy for a single three-year military tour of duty. A third of the academy's academic faculty are civilian professors; nearly all have earned doctorate degrees and many are retired military officers. Similar to other military organizations, the academy's culture was very receptive to the idea of articulating objectives and measuring results. This openness to assessment provided a comparative advantage over many other higher education institutions in the mid-1990s.

The academy's curriculum includes approximately 140 semester hours with about two-thirds of this requirement dedicated to a core of more than 30 required courses in math/sciences, humanities, social sciences, and engineering. However, many educators thought that despite its great curricular breadth, the academy's lack of depth limited its educational effectiveness. Some courses were considered to be superficial, and extensive reliance on curve/mean grading seemed to create a curriculum that involved far more activity than actual learning.

In the early 1990s, Lieutenant General Bradley Hosmer, a graduate of the academy's first class in 1959 and a Rhodes scholar, assumed institutional command as the new superintendent, a position with administrative responsibilities similar to those of a president at most colleges. His vision and integrity, as well as his engaging and progressive personal leadership style, engendered changes that ultimately transformed the academy and allowed both the institution and its students to achieve unprecedented educational success over the next decade. His emphasis on student learning and institutional responsibility to provide necessary support established a model and set the standard for the entire institution.

Image was just as important to the Air Force Academy as it was to the nation's other major military academies, West Point and Annapolis. Conversations about what the institution (the Air Force and the nation) really expected (or needed) cadets to be when they graduated and were commissioned as second lieutenants were nearly constant. Lengthy lists were generated of characteristics that different constituencies considered to be essential. The cadets' response to the overwhelming diversity of demands is captured by their own cynical observation that they were becoming so well rounded so rapidly that they'd be pointless in no time. At the most basic level, an institution rests on values, and General Hosmer recognized that educational progress depended on developing and articulating a clear set of values. Starting with his immediate staff, he initiated a process to clarify and prioritize the institution's values. It was a process that would involve nearly all the academy's faculty, staff, and students over the next two years.

Both product and process were critical to future developments. A willingness by senior officers to take the time to listen to and understand inputs from across the academy exceeded expectations. Facilitated by focus groups and respectful but frank discussion, authentic conversation led to the gradual emergence of 17 syllables that many felt captured the essence of the institutional message: "Integrity first, service before self, excellence in all we do." Several years later, Sheila Widnall, secretary of the Air Force, undertook a similar process to develop a statement of core values for the entire Air Force. After reviewing many extensive formulations and elaborations, she selected the words that had been developed at the academy.

Another part of the transformation process at the academy involved a comprehensive initiative to assess educational outcomes (Porter & Eisenhut, 1996). Over the course of several years, similarly extensive and inclusive processes of developing and articulating a vision and mission further instantiated progressive ideals. This provided the foundation for developing specific educational outcomes and then initiating a process to assess their attainment by cadets. Under the leadership of the dean of faculty, Brigadier Ruben Cubero, who had been a key participant in General Hosmer's development of the core values, the academy measured for one year the contributions of each core course to students' basic knowledge, critical thinking skills, and intellectual curiosity. The institution then used the results of this study to educate faculty and staff and increase the effectiveness of educational programs and processes throughout the system (Porter, 1998).

Recognition and accolades from the Princeton Review, the North Central Association, and the AAC&U corroborated the many successes of the progressive educational transformation that had occurred. Although these reforms were rather progressive, the institution itself and the majority of its faculty, staff, and students remained quite conservative politically. However, some of the progress made in the 1990s, as well as public confidence in the institution and its leadership, was to erode in the new millennium.

With the presidential election in 2000 and the new administration's apparent consideration of ideology and affiliation as selection criteria (Branigin, 2006), senior military administration became increasingly homogenous. It is not unreasonable to suspect that the political administration's expectation of political and philosophical fealty from the most senior military officers (Eaton, 2006) also affected the academy's policies, personnel, and processes. Pervasive changes in the academy's culture and climate—including scandals involving the treatment of female cadets and religious minorities and a high rate of turnover among senior leaders, and the ensuing insecurity created by this turmoil—may well have contributed to a loss of appreciation for a diversity of perspective, increasingly centralized academic decision-making, and renewed emphasis on command and control. As a consequence, the return to more traditional hierarchical paradigms and perspectives in education and organization appears to have eroded some of the progressive advances the academy had made in the 1990s.

Western Governors University

Western Governors University (WGU) was chartered in 1996 by the governors of 19 western states and incorporated the following year. It enrolled its first students in 1999 and had its first graduate a year later. WGU is a private, nonprofit, online university that, as of the summer of 2006, had enrolled 5,000 students, graduated more than 1,000 individuals, and was growing at a rate between 40%–50% annually. Its most popular programs are in information technology, business, and education. Because of its unique competency-based approach to education, it received very close scrutiny from regional and national accrediting organizations. In fact, a special interregional accrediting committee, composed of the executive directors of four regional accrediting organizations, was established to preside over WGU's initial accreditation. After two years of rigorous review, WGU received its initial regional accreditation, which is now maintained with the Northwest Commission of Colleges and Universities. Similar scrutiny by the Distance Education and Training Council and the National Council for Accreditation of Teacher Education yielded similarly strong endorsement and accreditation. Despite its marked divergence from traditional programs, external examiners consistently praised WGU's progressive competency-based approach to education. In addition to the support WGU continues to receive from its founding governors, it receives support from 23 leading corporations and foundations as well.

Central to WGU's success is its promise to help students achieve their dreams for a degree and career success by providing a personal, flexible, and affordable education based on real-world competencies. WGU's mission of improving educational quality while expanding access led to a reconsideration of traditional educational roles, structures, and processes. The traditional process of education by course accretion was replaced by one based on student learning and demonstrated competency. Traditional hierarchical structures were disassembled and replaced by new roles for faculty and staff. Much of the education of WGU students is facilitated by a large cadre of mentors, individuals with expertise in their fields and dedicated to providing one-on-one support to each enrolled student. Mentors ensure that students are aware of what competencies will be required within each of the domains in each degree or certification program and work with students to plan how they will gain the necessary skills and knowledge using a variety of online resources. Proctored examinations, observed performance, and submitted projects and portfolios are all used to assess a student's mastery of required competencies. What is distinctive about the WGU approach is that assessment is distinguished from the processes of planning and learning. Unlike the course structure, in which a faculty member takes responsibility for teaching and assessing students, these functions are separate in a competency-based model.

From the beginning, outside experts from academic and professional realms were organized into "councils" that played a critical role in the development of WGU's progressive competency-based approach. In addition to program councils that oversaw the operations of general studies (liberal arts) as well as each of the major degree programs, WGU formed an assessment council with general responsibility for the development, effectiveness, and integrity of the assessment system that was to be so vital to the university's structure. National assessment experts such as Tom Angelo, Peter Ewell, Ed Morante, and Barbara Walvoord were among the initial cadre of this critical council. What was remarkable about these councils in general, and the assessment council in particular, was how well they were integrated into the institution. President Bob Mendenhall, Provost Chip Johnstone, and Assessment Director Alec Testa shared challenges openly and listened carefully and respectfully for the ideas council members generated at their quarterly meetings.

The administration consistently took the best ideas and found ways to turn them into viable programs and policies. The organization that developed and nurtured this uniquely progressive alternative approach to higher education was itself marked by flexibility and ingenuity. Operational decisions were consistently pushed outward through the institution as new ideas and adaptive adjustments were generated within the organization. The best thinking—not only from within the organization but from across higher education—was consistently brought to bear on the greatest institutional challenges.

WGU is a clear example of the positive impact of progressive perspectives on creating new and unique opportunities for student success. Admittedly, the WGU approach is not for everyone—the average age of WGU students is nearly 40—but for those individuals with high motivation, solid skills, and relevant experience, competency-based education can be a far more affordable and accessible alternative to achieving success.

Berea College

In the two cases just described, individuals in senior administrative positions played critical roles in enhancing opportunities for student success. At the Air Force Academy, it was enlightened and progressive general officers; at WGU it was skilled and flexible senior administrators who had a knack for listening to good advice and turning it into innovative and highly effective educational programs. Berea College—an institution at which we have all served and shared in a progressive transformation—provides an example where grassroots commitment to the college's mission significantly enhanced student success within a relatively traditional hierarchical institution.

Berea College, established in 1855, was the first school south of the Mason-Dixon Line to educate men and women, black and white, together. Despite the fact that the college was forced to segregate by Kentucky's infamous Day Law (which criminalized interracial education) for most of the first half of the 20th century, it maintained a progressive educational mission. When prevented from pursuing interracial education, Berea dedicated itself to serving Appalachian youth by offering opportunities to students of limited economic means. Rather than providing education to only those who could afford it, Berea offered education to those, and only those, who could *not* afford it. Berea established a cap on family resources, which required that all those admitted to the college were from families with limited incomes and little or no savings.

In some respects, Berea College resembles other traditional, private, residential, liberal arts colleges, with 93% of its students under 25 years of age. What is unusual about Berea's student body is the relatively high number of students who come from single-parent families and families in which neither parent graduated from college. Nearly all of Berea's domestic students are eligible to receive Pell Grants. In many of the Appalachian counties from which Berea's students come, less than 5% of the population has earned a college degree. Having rediscovered its commitment to interracial education, Berea College's student body currently includes nearly 20% African American students and another 7% international students. All students work at least 10 hours per week as a part of their scholarship, but a billion-dollar endowment, coupled with annual private donations and state and federal grants and scholarships, covers the full $22,300 cost of education for every student each year. Despite the many challenges inherent in Berea's unique mission, *U.S. News & World Report* has consistently rated the college as the best regional comprehensive college in the south.

Ten years ago Berea College was somewhat less effective in supporting student learning and success. Although the college had reaffirmed its commitment to interracial education in the early 1950s, enrollment of African American students in the mid-1990s dipped as low as 6%. A visit by the Southern Association of Colleges and Schools (SACS) in 1995 left the college with nearly 50 recommendations that needed to be addressed immediately to ensure continued accreditation. About half of the entering students required developmental mathematics. Once-beautiful historic buildings across campus were in serious disrepair. Applications for admissions had declined by 7% from 1995 to 1998. Retention rates had fallen below 70%, and graduation rates were below 50% for several consecutive years. Berea College seemed to be on a slippery slope descending toward educational mediocrity.

In contrast to these difficult years, the most recent institutional data reveal that things have improved: The institution now supports the success of its unique student body more effectively than ever. The sesquicentennial capital campaign that concluded in 2005 surpassed its goal of adding $150 million to the endowment. College finances are on a much firmer foundation, and tens of millions of dollars have been raised and invested in making necessary repairs and renovations to campus structures and systems. Perhaps even more important, the number of applicants has increased about 5% per year since 1999; freshman-to-sophomore retention rates, which averaged 69% in 1995–1997, averaged 81% in 2002–2005. Graduation rates (within five years of matriculation) have improved from a three-year average of 48% in the mid-1990s to an average of just over 60% in 2003–2005.

Over this same period, African American enrollment increased from its nadir of 6% of the class entering in 1996 to an average of 19% in 2003–2005, with graduation rates for African Americans indistinguishable from those of other domestic students. Also, increased attention to students' economic needs and the end of most exceptions to the financial cap is allowing the college to serve students with even greater economic needs. Unlike students at many other colleges and universities (see Keeling, 2004), Berea's students rate their learning within their general studies courses and cocurricular activities nearly as positively as courses within their disciplinary majors. The 2005 accreditation reaffirmation visit by SACS resulted in only a single formal recommendation. The college's role in supporting student success has been much greater for the past several years than it was only a short time ago. We believe progressive paradigms and perspectives were essential to this improvement.

Admissions. Berea College does not have a succinct statement of its mission. Instead, it has a sprawling document that lists the college's eight Great Commitments, which express the institution's aspirations toward an array of progressive social, educational, economic, and spiritual goals. Over the years and under different administrations, the spotlight was shifted from one set of commitments to another. The ambiguity created by so many commitments and so much shifting created challenges for admissions policies and programs. The Great Commitments require the admissions office to select classes of students with a very specific profile: primarily from Appalachia, gender and racially balanced, and composed entirely of students with significant economic need who possess great academic potential and a commitment to community service.

Previous administrations emphasized Berea's commitment to serve the poorest of the poor. Some faculty and administrators supported the notion that the college was fulfilling its commitment to support the Appalachian region simply by enrolling students regardless of their academic success. They saw the *selection* of only the right students to graduate as being of greater importance than a commitment to *develop* all students. At times, Berea College's commitment to provide a rigorous academic program based on a traditional liberal arts curriculum seemed incompatible with the college's other commitments. The college faculty attempted to review and revise the general education program, but this process consumed nearly a decade, including formal rejections of two separate proposals before a new general education program passed by a single vote in 2005.

The traditional instructional paradigm focuses on input variables—in particular, the academic qualifications of entering students. As Merrow (2006) suggests, admissions offices often support presidents in their quest for prestige by dedicating aid and recruiting efforts to acquiring candidates with the highest standardized test scores. The initial administrative response to the college's academic difficulties in the mid-1990s was to shift the emphasis from serving full-need students to serving those who met financial requirements but whose academic records indicated that they had the greatest potential to succeed academically. In 1998 the proportion of students admitted to the college with ACT scores of 20 or below was cut from approximately 40% to 20%, and the number of students needing remediation in mathematics fell from 47% to 23%. However, as a subsequent analysis published in 2002 in the student paper showed, the proportion of full-need students also dropped precipitously, and the median family income of students admitted to the college was increasing at over twice the rate of inflation. Thus, the institution's initial response to an academic challenge was to shift the focus from one commitment (serving the neediest students) to another commitment (serving those with the greatest academic potential). A better approach wasa needed.

In contrast to the instructional paradigm, the learning paradigm requires educators to expand their focus beyond simple trade-offs and integrate factors to consider the consequences of policy changes and develop more inclusive and enduring approaches. Based on phrases buried within the preamble to Berea's Great Commitments, an informal consensus among many faculty and staff emerged that a reasonable statement of Berea's mission was "to educate and inspire service-oriented leaders for Appalachia and beyond." This mission helped shape a collective understanding of admissions priorities. We realized that the characteristics of the class itself deserved attention—not just the qualifications of individuals within the class. As Richard Light's (2001) decade of student interviews has shown, diversity of opinion and perspective—as well as race, gender, and national origin—are among the most valuable aspects of students' college experience. Revised admissions policies and processes proved effective in recruiting and selecting classes that were more diverse in terms of race, gender, and national origin and individuals who had a greater potential to complete Berea College's rigorous educational programs. Individual interviews and students' expressed commitment toward service to community helped identify students with academic potential greater than their ACT scores might predict.

We found that looking at the many factors reflecting the whole person helped achieve a level of diversity that met the college's commitments to interracial and gender-balanced education and also facilitated student learning. From this process of engagement and synthesis, admissions staff and administrators learned that the financial cap on Berea's admissions could be lowered by approximately 20% to allow the college to concentrate its resources on the students who most need the unique educational opportunities Berea College offers. However, there was much more to the story of Berea's recapture of educational quality than just learning to recruit students who were more diverse and more likely to succeed academically. There were also many changes required in the support provided after students' matriculation.

The student services center. Sustaining the improvements realized by enhanced admissions policies required a commitment to providing the support services necessary to help students meet all the challenges that confronted them. Substantial effort was invested in understanding student satisfaction with virtually every program and service at the college. The Noel-Levitz Student Satisfaction Inventory (2006) was administered and used to identify the largest gaps between a program's importance to students and their relative satisfaction concerning its quality.

The Committee on Student Experience was chartered to investigate student dissatisfaction. Administrative runarounds and insufficient financial aid to cover expenses beyond tuition (such as room and board, fees, books, supplies, and personal expenses) were two of our students' greatest disappointments. A protracted and frustrating five-year discussion ensued. Unfortunately, a traditional hierarchical bureaucracy thwarted sincere efforts to clarify processes and identify causes. Assumed competition among departments as well as poor communication created the impression that these problems were truly intractable; the more administrators poked and prodded, the more resolution seemed to recede. Later we realized it was the system itself that was the problem.

Key personnel changes created the opportunity for a fresh start. This administrative function was reorganized with a clear focus on supporting students; new staff members consolidated and streamlined processes. Fresh perspectives and a willingness to listen to one another allowed the three new directors of academic services, student accounts, and student financial aid to plan and implement an integrated student services center in less than a year. This included an innovative layout; a new, less hierarchical organization;

streamlined processes; and specially developed training. In addition, a collaborative approach to leadership—something that had seemed impossible the previous year—provided a basis for the next challenge: offering more timely and effective financial aid.

The college offers some of the most generous financial aid packages anywhere; Berea's support guarantees that no student (or his or her family) will need to contribute toward the annual cost of education. But tuition is only one component of students' enrollment costs, and our student survey showed that aid to cover the costs of room, board, and fees was insufficient. Some administrators were inclined to point out the extensive aid already provided and criticize the ingratitude reflected by student complaints. However, withdrawal from the college (a major impediment to student success) was often due to personal rather than academic reasons.

We asked students to help us understand their challenges and soon discovered that there was merit in the concerns they expressed. Few of us were aware of a senior administrative committee's decision several years earlier to increase room and board charges at a rate of 5% annually to help retire the debt for residence hall renovations. Although our students benefited from the improved accommodations, they had no funds to pay the increasing costs and no additional financial aid had been provided to assist them. The gap between these collateral costs and the amount of aid provided had grown from about $100 to more than $700 in just a few years. Full-need students, in particular, had been canceling their reservations to attend the college due to the extra cost. Once this issue was examined, there was nearly unanimous support for finding ways to use institutional funds to close the gap that had been created inadvertently and grown unnoticed. Layers of bureaucracy and a lack of careful listening were the culprits that needed to be removed so more students could graduate.

A progressive intervention. The functions and services discussed thus far do not depend directly on faculty members, but many other functions do. Before describing these initiatives, it is worth pausing briefly to provide a little more history. Understanding the context in which challenges develop is essential to constructing effective remedies. One might expect good salaries, excellent working conditions, and an inspiring educational mission to be sufficient to ensure high faculty morale. Unfortunately, this has not been the case; national comparisons have indicated considerable dissatisfaction among the teaching faculty. In the spring of 2001, controversial tenure decisions followed by isolated but egregious behavior (Thomas, 2004) left many faculty members outraged. Although traditional, strong, centralized executive leadership had been effective to the institution's financial recovery and deserved credit for substantial improvements to the physical plant and fiscal processes, overreliance on this corporate style had also generated resentment among many faculty members. In the fall of 2002, the faculty's vehement rejection of a strategic initiative based on the learning paradigm reflected many faculty members' dissatisfaction with what they perceived to be heavy-handed administration.

This rejection created an opportunity for the academic administration to ask the college faculty to evaluate the administration's effectiveness in supporting student learning. In preparing a faculty satisfaction survey, each of 12 offices and functions within the academic division developed mission statements that identified its key contribution to the college's overall mission of educating and inspiring service-oriented leaders. After reading these brief departmental mission statements, faculty survey respondents rated each office or function on three dimensions: its importance, its responsiveness, and the quality of support it provided. The 70% response rate showed that many faculty members were eager to voice their opinions. As might be anticipated, the survey yielded mixed results. However, these results provided a basis for authentic engagement between faculty members and academic administrators concerning how to provide the most effective support for student learning.

Faculty advising. Academic advising is an essential educational function, perhaps the single most important academic activity in ensuring student success. We know that developing a positive relationship with a staff or faculty member is a strong predictor of retention and eventual graduation (Frost, 1991; Kuh et al., 2005; Light, 2001). For faculty and staff, engagement in academic advising can be both informative and rewarding. Done well, academic advising requires advisors to see the system through students' eyes. At Berea College we recognize that academic advising is crucial for overall student success. Our advising process involves primarily teaching faculty. Although national surveys have offered evidence that students have given high ratings to several aspects of our program, we also acknowledge the opportunity for substantive improvements.

The first-year experience is critical to students' eventual success. Typically, half the students in any given class who will leave an institution without graduating do so during their first year. Advisors can play a crucial role in reducing losses, particularly those that are due to misunderstanding or miscommunication. Because of their lack of familiarity with college expectations, first-year students can be quite demanding of faculty advisors' time and energy. One of the most critical roles the academic advisor plays during the first two years is helping students find the right academic major. It is important that the faculty advisor be able to provide accurate and reliable information. Advisors should appreciate that although there are no bad majors, there certainly can be bad matches. The value of their advice depends on how well they know each of their advisees and how well they understand the college's academic programs. The institution must continue to seek increasingly effective ways to engage entering students in an exploration of career opportunities and their life's work. It is equally important that the advising program provide a framework for entering students to accept responsibility for using the advice that is given, asking questions, and learning how to learn.

The designation of an associate provost for advising and academic success in 2002 brought greater administrative attention and integration to this critical function. This new position, filled by an experienced faculty educator on a three-year rotation, provided a catalyst for institutional improvement and brought new thinking and new perspectives to academic administration. Administrative inconsistencies and gaps in coverage were recognized as a result of this increased attention. We learned that faculty members need to be educated about student development as well as trained in negotiating various aspects of the academic administration system. We found that progressive models such as servant leadership or Theory Y provide a much better basis for establishing positive relationships with students than approaches that rely on power assertion. We learned that serving as an advisor provides faculty members with a new perspective on designing and conducting their courses. Further, it became apparent that we lacked a consistent process for assessing the effectiveness of the advising program and individual advisors. An additional critical challenge was how to achieve equity in advising loads across academic departments.

As we continue to develop strategies for improvement, it will be critical to identify and integrate best practices within our advising program. We hope to enhance our understanding of advising as a complement to teaching—for its potential to provide greater curricular integration, as a vehicle to develop interpersonal skills, and as a means to prompt students to reflect on the influence their own beliefs have on their ability to persist and succeed (Downing, 2005; Frost, 1991; Gordon, Habley, & Associates 2000; Kuh et al., 2005; Pascarella & Terenzini, 2005; Porter, 1991). Our goal is to develop an institutional culture that recognizes advising as an integral part of the educational system (Frost, 1991; Gordon & et al., 2000). During August 2006 the current associate provost for advising and academic success drafted an advising action plan designed to support more effective student learning. This action plan describes a process for developing a mission statement, which reflects a conceptual, informational, and relational framework (Brown, 2006) and will provide a solid foundation for future student and parent orientation sessions; faculty, staff, and administrative training; and assessment of our advising program.

The Center for Learning, Teaching, Communication, and Research. Changes made within Berea's learning center provide examples of how aspects of the progressive paradigm (such as emphasis on decentralization and develop-ment) improved support for student success. The creation of centers had become a somewhat contentious issue between faculty and administration. Many senior faculty members suspected that the administration was prima-rily interested in the potential prestige associated with centers and the faculty resented the drain on scarce academic resources. Therefore, it was not a sur-prise when the faculty survey showed dissatisfaction with the new learning center, especially among males and tenured faculty members. The learning center's mission was to "provide support for students to enhance their com-munication and other essential academic abilities within and across majors." Many respondents indicated that this was not very important, suggesting that this was a job academic departments could manage on their own.

As a result of this survey and other feedback from faculty, staff, students, and administrators, the provost and the associate provost for advising and academic success, in collaboration with the director and associate director of the learning center, agreed to begin the transition from a hierarchical model to a more flexible and inclusive one. The new model replaced the director with a coordinator but continued to use faculty and staff associates to support individual faculty members, departments, tutors, staff, and students who wanted to expand their teaching and learning abilities. Subsequently, the notion of having this role filled by a tenure-track faculty member on a three-year rotation was adopted to better integrate the learning center and the rest of the faculty.

In addition, the college formed a steering committee that included well-respected senior faculty representatives from each academic division, the library director, the associate dean of faculty, and the chief information offi-cer. This group was co-chaired by an associate provost and the learning cen-ter coordinator. The learning center's new mission reflected increased interdependence: "To provide leadership in identifying goals and program priorities in order to fully integrate the center's activities with the strategic planning initiative to create a continuous learning community." The steering committee became a cohesive and productive group, assisting in setting pri-orities and asking tough questions about the effectiveness of various learning center programs and activities.

The learning center became one of the primary levers for helping students and faculty develop the knowledge and skills necessary to support a gradual transition to the learning paradigm across the campus. Given the characteristics of Berea's student body, many students needed additional attention and support (especially in developing their writing and study skills). Highly motivated and well-trained students can be invaluable assistants to faculty members, but they must first be developed. To better prepare peer consultants and teaching assistants to support other students in learning effective communication and study skills, the center offered interactive workshops with sessions led by learning center staff and other faculty members. These workshops, combined with the learning center's comprehensive certification process, prepared peer consultants to address a wide range of student needs.

Ernest Boyer's (1990) famous axiom "Good teaching means that faculty, as scholars, are also learners" (p. 24) became the cornerstone of the center's services for faculty. The steering committee recognized that faculty also had development needs, and by identifying and prioritizing these collectively, resources were allocated more strategically. This approach echoed one of the action steps advocated in *Greater Expectations*, that "centers of teaching and learning . . . make available significant resources to support faculty members as they assume responsibilities of learning-centered education" (AAC&U, 2002, p. 36).

Building on programs like teaching/learning luncheons that were already popular allowed greater opportunities to share knowledge, prioritize needs, and develop common ground concerning a variety of issues relating to teaching and learning. Besides these highly interactive luncheons, colloquiums enabled faculty and staff to present ongoing research. In addition, faculty associates and learning center staff facilitated new faculty seminars, one-on-one faculty development, tenure review workshops, sabbatical-planning workshops, and course development collaborations with librarians. As a consequence of turning over key administrative decisions to the faculty steering committee and learning center associates and emphasizing the development of programs to address prioritized institutional needs, programs became more diverse but also more focused on priorities. This transition is far from complete, but the process has already increased faculty involvement and support for this crucial center.

A new student success course. In the fall of 2003, the academic services office reviewed academic probation policies and their effects on students. This review was prompted by an observation that for most of the past century approximately 50% of students had not graduated despite the institution's belief that nearly all students admitted to the college were capable of achieving success. There was hope that the college could do better if it understood the causes of the observed attrition. We discovered that each year about 10% of all enrolled students were placed on academic probation. Slightly more than half continued their enrollment for the next term. However, about 70% of the students who had been placed on academic probation at some time did not graduate.

Discussions with faculty, students, and administrators about these patterns elicited broad support for a program that would focus on students whose academic performance had placed them on probation. After a review by appropriate faculty committees, a proposal for the course General Studies 101: Strategies for Academic Success, was approved by the college faculty in the spring of 2004. This course was offered to all students placed on academic probation, and over the next two years, approximately two-thirds chose (or were persuaded) to take the course. All students enrolled in the course are required to purchase Skip Downing's text *On Course* (2005), but there is considerable variability in how the text is used. Sections have been kept small, with an average size of about five students. Of the 150 students completing the course, more than 60% have graduated or are still enrolled in the college. Of approximately 90 students who declined to enroll in the course, only 25% were retained or graduated. A survey of students before and after their enrollment in the course showed that there was a dramatic increase in students' willingness to attribute their academic outcomes (both successes and failures) to their own choices rather than to external sources.

It is noteworthy that the course was initially taught entirely by volunteer staff and faculty. Subsequently, a small stipend or course credit was granted to faculty, but staff members continue to be involved on a voluntary basis. Faculty members who teach the course indicate that the experience has benefited their construction and teaching of other courses. An increased awareness of student needs and recognition of the importance of early intervention with struggling students are often cited by faculty as lessons learned from their experience teaching this course. Progressive perspectives and the learning paradigm provided the essential conceptual framework for the creation and development of this novel course.

Periodic meetings and forums. Progressive approaches helped shift administrative emphasis from telling to listening. The word *alignment,* a favorite of both progressive and traditional administrators, helps illustrate this point. Those who adhere to a traditional Theory X, hierarchical perspective use the word *align* as a transitive verb. The traditional assumption is that administrators must set subordinates straight by making the specific goals clear (as well as the consequences for failing to attain them). In contrast, from the perspective of progressive paradigms, *alignment* is intransitive. It happens when people are listened to and understood. As trust develops, individuals seek new ways to contribute to goals that they understand because they helped develop those goals. This approach to having meetings dedicated to listening was manifested in several ways.

After the mixed results from the first faculty survey, small groups of center directors met to better understand and respond to faculty concerns. These evolved into biweekly meetings. These meetings included both the provost and associate provost for advising and academic success, but most of the agenda was dedicated to having the various center directors share what they were doing. In general, centers were asked to report on their most notable successes, the current challenges they faced, and what support from administration, faculty, or other centers might be helpful. As it turned out, many of the things that were working well in one center could be adapted to other centers. Similarly, the particular challenges that were shared sometimes reflected systemic problems that could be dealt with more effectively collectively.

A second example was the development of Meet the Provosts lunches held in the student dining facility once a month. Although the numbers of students attending never exceeded a dozen, the information these meetings provided was invaluable. Sometimes students' questions reflected profound miscommunication and complete misunderstanding—these instances were relatively easy to clear up. At other times, however, students provided evidence and examples of places where the system was failing them. The provosts remained for as long as there were students with questions or concerns, but typically these meeting lasted about 90 minutes. Although relatively few students participated directly, resolution of the issues identified benefited everyone.

CONCLUSION

This chapter described differences between traditional hierarchical institutions and progressive institutions and reported ways in which progressive paradigms and perspectives have affected actual practice. At the Air Force Academy, visionary commanders introduced progressive conversations about mission, vision, and values and made way for the comprehensive assessment of student learning outcomes. Although military commanders serve in their roles for only short terms, these initiatives had an extended effect. Western

Governors University is itself a highly progressive educational institution that has explored implications of the learning paradigm that lie beyond the comfort zone of many educators—even some who consider themselves to be quite progressive. Rapid growth has required this organization to remain flexible and responsive. Finally, most of the latter portion of the chapter was devoted to providing a more detailed account of various aspects of support for student success at Berea College. We discussed a variety of areas in which we believe progressive perspectives and the learning paradigm enhanced student success and contributed to increases in student retention, graduation, and learning. However, we would all hasten to add that there are many other examples from across our campus that also contributed to the many improved outcomes at Berea College.

Our experiences, both individual and collective, have helped us recognize the value of reflection and consideration of our own perspectives and paradigms in our efforts to contribute to our college's mission. There is a difference between rhetoric and reality, and it is important that we share responsibility for identifying the gaps between the two whenever they occur. Reducing such gaps is one of academic administrators' most important roles. We agree that the kind of leadership that matters most is not a person or a position but a process that is widely shared. We recognize that there is much work that remains to be done, but we have learned that when we are willing to give up the pretense of perfection, we find many opportunities, often individually small and incremental but collectively powerful, to enhance student success.

REFERENCES

Angelo, T. A., & Cross, K. P. (1993). *Classroom assessment techniques: A handbook for college teachers* (2nd ed.). San Francisco, CA: Jossey-Bass.

Argyris, C., & Schön, D. A. (1974). *Theory in practice: Increasing professional effectiveness.* San Francisco, CA: Jossey-Bass.

Association of American Colleges and Universities. (2002). *Greater expectations: A new vision for learning as a nation goes to college.* Washington, DC: Author.

Barr, R. B., & Tagg, J. (1995, November/December). From teaching to learning—A new paradigm for undergraduate education. *Change, 27*(6), 12–25.

Baxter Magolda, M. B. (1992). *Knowing and reasoning in college: Gender-related patterns in students' intellectual development.* San Francisco, CA: Jossey-Bass.

Baxter Magolda, M. B. (2006, May/June). Intellectual development in the college years. *Change, 38*(3), 50–54.

Belenky, M. F., Clinchy, B. M., Goldberger, N. R., & Tarule, J. M. (1986). *Women's ways of knowing: The development of self, voice, and mind.* New York, NY: Basic Books.

Bennis, W. G., & Nanus, B. (1985). *Leaders: The strategies for taking charge.* New York, NY: Harper & Row.

Berne, E. (1996). *Games people play: The basic handbook of transactional analysis* (Reissue ed.). New York, NY: Ballantine Books.

Boyer, E. L. (1990). *Scholarship reconsidered: Priorities of the professoriate.* Princeton, NJ: The Carnegie Foundation for the Advancement of Teaching.

Branigin, W. (2006, September 25). Three retired officers demand Rumsfeld's resignation [Electronic version]. *Washington Post.* Retrieved June 30, 2007, from www.washingtonpost.com/wp-dyn/content/article/2006/09/25/AR2006092500731.html

Brown, T. E. (2006, July). *Creating excellence in academic advising: Advisor training and development.* Workshop presented at the NACADA Academic Advising Summer Institute, Madison, WI.

Downing, S. (2005). *On course: Strategies for creating success in college and in life* (4th ed.). Boston, MA: Houghton Mifflin.

Eaton, P. D. (2006, March 19). A top-down review for the Pentagon [Op-ed, electronic version]. *New York Times.* Retrieved June 30, 2007, from www.nytimes.com/2006/03/19/opinion/19eaton.html?ex=1300424400&en=84baf801cea4e5d6&ei=5088&partner=rssnyt&emc=rss

Fischer, K. W., & Bidell, T. R. (1998). Dynamic development of psychological structures in action and thought. In W. Damon & R. Lerner (Eds.), *Handbook of child psychology, Vol. 1: Theoretical models of human development* (pp. 467–561). New York, NY: Wiley.

Freire, P. (1997). *Pedagogy of the oppressed* (Rev. ed., M. R. Ramos, Trans.). New York, NY: Continuum.

Frost, S. H. (1991). *Academic advising for student success: A system of shared responsibility* (ASHE-ERIC Higher Education Report No. 3). Washington, DC: The George Washington University, School of Education and Human Development.

Gardner, H. (1999). *Intelligence reframed: Multiple intelligences for the 21st century.* New York, NY: Basic Books.

Gladwell, M. (2002, July 22). The talent myth: Are smart people overrated? *The New Yorker,* 28–33.

Gordon, V. N., Habley, W. R., & Associates. (2000). *Academic advising: A comprehensive handbook.* San Francisco, CA: Jossey-Bass.

Greenleaf, R. K. (1970). *The servant leader.* Newton Center, MA: Robert K. Greenleaf Center.

Greenleaf, R. K. (1977). *Servant leadership: A journey into the nature of legitimate power and greatness.* Mahwah, NJ: Paulist Press.

Greenleaf, R. K. (2004). Who is the servant-leader? In L. C. Spears & M. Lawrence (Eds.), *Practicing servant leadership: Succeeding through trust, bravery, and forgiveness* (pp. 1–8). San Francisco, CA: Jossey-Bass.

Hughes, R. L., Ginnett, R. C., & Curphy, G. J. (1999). *Leadership: Enhancing the lessons of experience.* New York, NY: McGraw-Hill.

Janis, I. L. (1982). *Groupthink* (2nd ed.). Boston, MA: Houghton Mifflin.

Keeling, R. P. (Ed.). (2004). *Learning reconsidered 1: A campus-wide focus on the student experience.* Washington, DC: American College Personnel Association & National Association of Student Personnel Administrators.

King, P. M., & Kitchener, K. S. (1994). *Developing reflective judgment.* San Francisco, CA: Jossey-Bass.

Kohlberg, L. (1963). The development of children's orientations toward moral order: I. Sequence in the development of moral thought. *Human Development, 6*(11), 11–33.

Kohn, A. (1992). *No contest: The case against competition* (Rev. ed.). Boston, MA: Houghton Mifflin.

Kuh, G. D., Kinzie, J., Schuh, J. H., Whitt, E. J., & Associates (2005). *Student success in college: Creating conditions that matter.* San Francisco, CA: Jossey-Bass.

Light, R. J. (2001). *Making the most of college: Students speak their minds.* Cambridge, MA: Harvard University Press.

Lipman-Blumen, J. (1996). *The connective edge: Leading in an interdependent world.* San Francisco, CA: Jossey-Bass.

McGregor, D. (1966). *Leadership and motivation.* Cambridge, MA: MIT Press.

Merrow, J. (2006, May/June). My college education: Looking at the whole elephant. *Change, 38*(3), 8–16.

Noel-Levitz. (2006). *Student success and retention services.* Retrieved June 22, 2007, from https://www.noellevitz.com/Our+Services/Retention/

Pascarella, E. T., & Terenzini, P. T. (2005). *How college affects students: A third decade of research.* San Francisco, CA: Jossey-Bass.

Perry, W. G., Jr. (1970). *Forms of intellectual and ethical development in the college years: A scheme.* Troy, MO: Holt, Rinehart, & Winston.

Piaget, J. (1926). *The language and thought of the child.* New York, NY: Meridian Books.

Porter, D. B. (1991). A perspective on college learning. *Journal of College Reading and Learning, 24*(1), 1–15.

Porter, D. B. (1998). Educational outcomes assessment: The good, the bad, and the ugly. *Adult Assessment Forum: Journal of Quality Management in Adult-Centered Education, 8*(3), 11–14.

Porter, D. B., & Eisenhut, S. M. (1996). An integrated approach to educational outcomes assessment. *Journal of Adult Assessment, 6*(2), 1–12.

Porter, D. B., & Sergel, D. G. (1998). Institutional assessment: The indispensability of diversity. In *Proceedings: Sixteenth Applied Behavioral Sciences Symposium* (USAFA-TR Publication No. 98–1, pp. 86–90). Colorado Springs, CO: United States Air Force Academy.

Powell, C. (2000). *Leadership primer* [PowerPoint slide presentation]. Washington, DC: Department of the Army.

Stogdill, R. M. (1974). *Handbook of leadership: A survey of theory and research.* New York, NY: The Free Press.

Tagg, J. (2003). *The learning paradigm college.* Bolton, MA: Anker.

Tavris, C., & Aronson, E. (2007). *Mistakes were made (but not by me): Why we justify foolish beliefs, bad decisions, and hurtful acts.* Orlando, FL: Harcourt.

Thomas, M. (2004, March). Trauma in academia. *Journal of Safe Management of Disruptive and Assaultive Behavior, 8*(1), 17–21.

Walvoord, B. E., & Anderson, V. J. (1998). *Effective grading: A tool for learning and assessment.* San Francisco, CA: Jossey-Bass.

14 PREPARING SERVICE PROVIDERS TO FOSTER STUDENT SUCCESS

TOM BROWN AND LEE WARD

Evidence continues to mount that students' experiences beyond the classroom are as critical to their development, learning, and success as the work done in classrooms, libraries, and laboratories. Many college and university personnel who engage students outside the classroom have as much impact on student development and learning as do those who teach them in the classroom. Although faculty must master disciplinary knowledge and teaching skills to be most effective at their craft, so too must residence hall educators, career counselors, leadership programmers, academic advisors, and others develop a full complement of attitudes, skills, and knowledge to maximize their effect on student learning and foster student success on campus. Both faculty and their out-of-class counterparts are expected to develop relevant competencies before plying their trade; however, many key competencies are developed only *after* the educator arrives on campus. Therefore, colleges and universities must assume the responsibility for teaching and developing their own educators to enhance student learning inside and outside the classroom by providing structured professional development programs.

Developing educators who are able to envision, design, implement, administer, and evaluate productive out-of-class learning experiences for students is a key ingredient in the effectiveness of the modern college or university. It has become increasingly critical that our institutions enhance students' development along a variety of factors and stimulate academic and personal achievement that leads to persistence and graduation. Although we all might agree on this admirable goal, we also must understand the degree of intentionality required on the part of educators to make this goal a reality. The presence of skilled and knowledgeable shapers of students' out-of-class experiences and, ultimately, evidence that desired learning and development has occurred depend on the kinds of interventions and perspectives described in this chapter.

THE CONTEXT FOR OUT-OF-CLASS LEARNING

Tinto (1993) used the phrase "academic and social integration" to suggest that the quality of students' experiences inside and outside the classroom distinguish those who persist toward graduation from the nearly 50% of students who do not persist and leave college before graduating. Tinto concluded that institutions that consciously reach out to form personal bonds between students, faculty, and staff and that emphasize frequent and rewarding contact beyond the classroom are the most successful in promoting student persistence.

In researching programs for students of color and other at-risk cohorts, Levin and Levin (1991) supported the earlier work of Astin (1985) in observing that quality interaction with faculty is more important than any other single factor in determining minority student persistence and success. When Light (2001) studied students over 10 years, he assumed they would indicate that the most memorable learning goes on in the classroom. Instead, when students were asked to think of a critical incident or moment that changed them profoundly, 80% chose a situation or event outside the classroom.

Crookston (1972) observed that, although faculty are formally designated as teachers, there are many times in the lives of students when others in the campus community are also teachers. This view holds that teaching and significant learning can take place outside the classroom—in faculty offices during advising sessions, in counseling and career centers, in residence halls, and in student unions. Pascarella and Terenzini (1991, 2005) concluded that student learning, achievement, and engagement are greatly influenced by what happens to students during the 80%–90% of their time that they spend outside their classes.

Lovett (2006) referred to "the rise of professional silos" in higher education that transformed and "unintentionally Balkanized" higher education communities during the second half of the 20th century. Lovett suggested that one byproduct of the Balkanization of colleges and universities was the organizational and psychological separation between academic life and student life. As higher education became increasingly specialized, faculty were determined to be responsible for the academic lives of students, and student affairs professionals were responsible for students' extracurricular lives. Students, however, rarely have well-defined boundaries that separate their lives neatly into the kinds of academic and student affairs dimensions that characterize many college and university organization charts.

Today it is more accurate and appropriate to use the term *instructional faculty* to describe those whose primary work with students takes place in a classroom (whether on campus or online), a laboratory, or a library and the term *administrative faculty* for those whose impact on student learning and development occurs in venues beyond the classroom. In validating the importance of the work of administrative faculty, Lovett (2006) declared, "It is time we recognized student-affairs administrators for what they do and what they can be: full partners in the daily processes of teaching and learning" (p. B11).

In their report of findings from the Documenting Effective Educational Practice (DEEP) project, Kuh, Kinzie, Schuh, Whitt, and Associates (2005) indicated that a key factor in creating the conditions that matter for student success is the presence on campus of "the right people doing the right things" (p. 309). They reported that exemplary colleges and universities are uniquely effective because of the characteristics, behaviors, and impact of those who shape the out-of-class experience at those institutions.

In the following sections, we outline the elements that should be included in programs designed to prepare service providers who shape the educational experience beyond the classroom. We then delineate the content and techniques that should be employed for pre-service and in-service initiatives for preparing instructional faculty to engage and support their students through academic advising.

PREPARING SERVICE PROVIDERS

Service providers (referred to on some campuses as "administrative faculty") who shape out-of-class learning experiences include, but are not limited to, those working in areas such as career development, leadership programs, service-learning and volunteer experiences, residence life, counseling services, health services, judicial affairs, student organizations and activities, student unions, multicultural and international student programs, orientation and first-year experience programs, learning support programs, and disability services. The impact of these institutional programs on student learning transcends the typical divisional lines we see at most institutions. Whether those functions and the administrative faculty who fulfill them are organizationally housed within a student affairs division, an academic affairs division, or elsewhere, they all have an impact on student learning. Thus, when we refer to "administrative faculty," we are not limiting our discussion to traditional student affairs practitioners but are speaking more broadly to any campus function that has an intentional impact on desired student learning and development outcomes.

Obviously, each campus function enjoys a degree of specialization according to which the competencies of administrative faculty are delineated. Administrative faculty, as we describe them, have additional global responsibilities for student learning and success and therefore require an additional basket of global competencies. The DEEP project (Kuh et al., 2005) studied 20 colleges and universities that are exceptional at creating conditions necessary for student success and identified the specific strategies those institutions used to promote student success. Aside from general conclusions regarding institutional resources and how they are allocated, institutional structure and leadership, and institutional culture and the policies that stem from it, the project focused on more specific actions taken by the administrative faculty who are responsible for designing, delivering, managing, and evaluating student learning environments. The researchers found that at these colleges and universities, it is the instructional and administrative faculty who do the work of creating campus environments that promote student success. Therefore, it is critical to understand the attitudes, skills, and knowledge that individual administrative faculty must possess to be effective. In Table 14.1, we have expanded on the competencies identified by the DEEP project to illustrate behaviors in which each competency might be manifest.

The process of putting students first—or designing effective learning environments—can be challenging for administrative faculty, but it can be achieved once they understand how and where learning occurs (Ward & Mitchell, 1997). Given the need to fill competency gaps, we recommend four avenues for preparing administrative faculty (followed by examples of good practice for each):

- Orient administrative faculty on the mission, philosophy, and culture of the institution and the divisions/departments they will be working in or with, focusing on understanding and internalizing what the institution expects of them as educators and of students as learners

- Develop administrative faculty through the use of coordinated training programs and support mechanisms that focus on desired attitudes, skills, and knowledge

- Mentor and coach administrative faculty so that they have the opportunity to observe desired practices, test assumptions, and take risks

Table 14.1   **Competencies for Administrative Faculty that Shape Out-of-Class Learning Opportunities**

Competency Type	Specfic Competency	Example Behavior
Attitude	Personal commitment to student learning as a guiding principle for decision-making	Reallocating resources at one's disposal to learning-oriented programs and services
Attitude	Valuing the interaction of students with faculty and staff in out-of-class settings	Initiating informal contact with students where they live and learn
Attitude	Personal willingness to collaborate with other educators across divisional, functional, and disciplinary lines	Creating freshman learning communities that weave curricular elements, residential experiences, orientation programs, academic advising efforts, and assessment strategies
Skill	The ability to provide constructive and developmental feedback to students during their learning experiences	Having academic advisors of freshmen talk with advisees about reconciling the advisees' anticipatory socialization with the actual collegiate environments they encountered
Skill	Use of pedagogies and program development strategies that are shaped to fit students' individual learning styles and prior knowledge	Building programs that help students decide on a major using identity development theories as a basis for exploration and decision-making
Skill	Ability to assess learning and development and use results to shape future efforts to enhance learning	Developing a protocol for measuring students' career decisiveness
Skill	Ability to effectively engage underengaged students in educationally purposeful activities	Using structured reflection strategies to bring out reluctant student voices
Knowledge	Understanding the campus culture and its impact on student behavior	Using orientation, advising, and freshman seminar programs to help students value general education courses
Knowledge	Understanding the characteristics of the students at one's institution	Using data from the National Survey of Student Engagement to shape creation of a service-learning program
Knowledge	Understanding the intersections between academic and student affairs and the potential of those intersections for rich learning experiences	Establishing a cross-divisional team to forge a comprehensive freshman orientation program

- Involve administrative faculty in the work of professional associations or other institutions—conferences, symposia, journals, research reports, listservs, and knowledge communities—as well as in self-paced exploration of relevant literature, educational models, and other descriptions of best practices

Orienting Administrative Faculty

At James Madison University (JMU) the Division of Student Affairs and University Planning created a process for orienting new staff to the unique ethos of the division and institution. This process prepares participants to create, administer, and evaluate effective environments and programs that fulfill the division's mission to "prepare educated and enlightened citizens who will lead productive and meaningful lives" (JMU, 2007). The program—Value U—is the result of a lengthy process in which staff identified the values of the division as well as the gaps between those stated values and actual practices. Value U provides an objective-based curriculum in which new staff members are exposed to the values of the division, discuss those values, and learn to apply those values to everyday situations in their work. As a result, all staff in the division are expected to understand what the university expects of them as shapers of out-of-class environments.

On-Campus Staff Development

Most colleges and universities offer in-service professional development opportunities to administrative faculty, whether through a centralized training and development office or through coordinated efforts in each division, department, or unit. In their study of institutional excellence in the first year of college, Cutright and Swing (2005) illustrated the potential impact of staff development programs by highlighting the outstanding work being done at the Community College of Denver (CCD). CCD developed its highly regarded learning communities program partially by investing time and energy in structured development programs for staff and faculty. CCD intentionally identified and addressed those competencies early on so that staff would be in a position to be more effective in their work. Likewise, Northern Virginia Community College, which is composed of six campuses, has a professional development committee and a faculty professional development subcommittee, which offers an annual cross-campus development program that is followed up with professional development activities on the individual campuses throughout the academic year.

Professional development also takes the shape of structured periodic workshops or symposia and may include occasions for engaging outside experts who can teach selected objectives to targeted groups of staff. For example, we have provided such instruction and consulting at many institutions (e.g., the University of Wisconsin–Whitewater, Tacoma Community College, Ithaca College, the University of Connecticut, and DePauw University). At Whitewater, campus leaders have used workshops presented by external experts to shape staff perspectives and competencies related to student learning, resulting in new and highly successful approaches to student leadership development and the integration of other out-of-class experiences.

Mentoring and Coaching

Supervision remains one of the key elements of any concerted effort to develop and enhance the competencies and perspectives of those who shape student learning environments, especially new administrative faculty (Ignelzi & Whitely, 2004). The value of supervising administrative faculty lies not in directing them to perform concrete tasks or comply with policy but in nurturing and coaching them to understand and value student success and effectively apply the principles of student success to their everyday work. Winston and Creamer (1997) present a model of "synergistic supervision" in which the relationship between supervisor and supervisee is defined by a growth orientation and a holistic manner of viewing the development of individual competencies. In such a model supervision is developmental; it is about teaching and learning; it is where "new skills and knowledge needed by staff are identified and can be addressed" (p. 217); it is where the individual attitudes that form the foundation of an institutional commitment to student learning are nurtured.

At the University of Wisconsin–La Crosse, administrative faculty in areas related to enrollment services, academic advising, and career development have explored how to better integrate those areas and enhance student learning. During interviews with administrative faculty there, many staff spoke positively about the relationship between themselves and senior leaders in their departments. One staff member unwittingly illustrated the value of synergistic supervision when describing the role that her supervisor plays:

> [My supervisor] is really good at letting us know individually what is expected of us, but she is even better at helping us grow by learn-

ing new ways to fulfill those expectations. We are able to do so many good things [for students] because she helps us understand what doing good things is going to take.

Synergistic supervision is critical in the creation and administration of effective learning environments, especially considering that we typically inherit our staff and rarely can hire others who are, according to Kegan (1994), self-authored or completed professionals. If, as Kegan suggests, it is unrealistic to expect to hire administrative staff who already understand and can apply the principles and practices of learning environments, then it remains to supervisors to develop synergistic, developmental relationships with staff so that those principles and practices can be introduced and subsequent performance can be coached.

Off-Campus Professional Development

Most colleges and universities provide some level of funding for administrative faculty to attend conferences and other learning opportunities off campus. For example, at JMU administrative faculty who shape out-of-class learning environments are able to hone their competencies because the institution expects them to do so, provides resources for them to do so, and holds them accountable for results. Each professional staff member in the student affairs and university planning division must have an annual professional development plan that outlines attitudes, skills, and knowledge that the individual and his or her supervisor agree are critical for individual and unit effectiveness. Each department in the division provides financial resources for these persons to join professional associations, take on leadership roles in those associations, and participate in professional development opportunities provided by these associations and other entities. Additionally, many of these departments also provide similar funding for instructional faculty partners to attend conferences that address out-of-class learning environments and experiences. JMU's Office of Training and Development also provides financial support for student affairs staff who wish to attend such events; staff must apply for these funds and, in doing so, clearly indicate the learning objectives associated with attending as well as the subsequent educational benefits to the institution and its students.

Sending teams to visit other campuses is another valuable practice in higher education. Though the practice sometimes leads to institutional isomorphism, at their best these site visits can help administrative faculty share and discover innovative approaches to creating learning environments that enhance student success. Saint Mary's College of California, Santa Clara University, the University of the Pacific, Stanford University, and the University of San Francisco once rotated annual meetings on their campuses that combined formal and informal meetings and discussions between providers working in various campus areas.

When JMU embarked on an initiative to create a student success center, one of the first questions asked by project leaders was "What other schools are doing good work in this area?" That led them to consult with and eventually visit colleagues at Kennesaw State University, where an effective student success program was already established. Kennesaw president Betty Siegel extended the odyssey by explaining that she and her senior staff happily appropriated their student success ideas from others while on their own site visits. This led JMU project leaders to visit those institutions as well. When administrative faculty participate in such site visits, they are engaged in a cost-effective, intense means of gleaning key attitudes, skills, and knowledge needed to create new approaches to the work of student learning.

A recent trend is for institutes and symposia to design their offerings explicitly for teams of administrative faculty (often accompanied by instructional faculty). The advantage of team attendance—as found at such events as the Student Learning Institute, the NACADA Advising Administrators Institute, and the Uncovering the Heart of Higher Education conference—is that teams can engage in "dialogue between members of a working educational community" (California Institute of Integral Studies, 2006) and return to their campus armed with not only a collective knowledge but a collective will to initiate institutional change.

PREPARING INSTRUCTIONAL FACULTY

Instructional faculty frequently interact with students in their role as academic advisors. The sixth National Survey of Academic Advising (Habley, 2004) found that instructional faculty continue to be the primary deliverers of academic advising. Although 80% of respondents indicated that instructional faculty served as academic advisors in all departments, advisor development was reported to be one of the least effective aspects of academic advising programs. Brown (2005) surveyed participants who registered for the 2005 Teaching Professor Conference, most of whom were instructional faculty and/or directors of centers intended to enhance teaching and learning. Only 15% of respondents agreed that they received adequate preparation and training when they first began to advise students.

Tinto (1993) suggested that faculty development and staff training are essential elements of programs intended to increase long-term student persistence. Gordon (2003) observed that effective academic advising requires more extensive, ongoing training activities, which should be viewed as rites of renewal. Again, however, the National Survey on Academic Advising (Habley, 2004) found that the majority of institutions do not require advisor development programs and that when such programs are available, they typically take less than half a day. During general orientation presentations for new faculty, it is not unusual to find discussions of academic advising relegated to a few minutes. We should not expect that effective academic advisors are going to emerge without structured programs designed to develop or enhance critical attitudes and skills.

Pre-service and in-service development programs should be required for all those who advise students. Preparation for these programs should focus on three primary areas:

- *Content:* What will be included in the program?

- *Audience:* Who will participate, what is their level of experience, and how motivated are they to engage in these activities?

- *Techniques:* How will the program be delivered, and who will participate in planning and facilitating training/development activities?

Although the methods and means for structuring development programs will depend on the audience, effectiveness will depend on the quality and scope of program content.

Content

After nearly 20 years of presentations at the annual Academic Advising Summer Institute, Brown (2006) suggested that the training/development of academic advisors—whether teaching or administrative faculty—involves conceptual, relational, and informational elements (Habley, 1986; Higginson, 2000). Conceptual elements include issues that those who advise need to understand about the students they serve, as well as the nature, scope, and content of their work. Relational elements are the skills and attitudes needed to engage students effectively. Informational elements are specific details regarding institutional policies, procedures, and programs that advisors need to know to provide timely and accurate advice to students.

Although informational elements are most frequently included in advisor development programs, greater emphasis needs to be placed on conceptual and relational elements. This approach is especially important if faculty, institutional leaders, and others are to understand and value academic advising as more than simply giving students information to help them choose and schedule classes. (See Chapter 15 in this volume for a discussion on engaging faculty to foster student development.)

Figure 14.1 combines four models of shared responsibility for students at four-year institutions that can easily be adapted to two-year colleges. Creamer (2000) suggested that students' needs in advising change during their college years. As students "move in" (Schlossberg, Lynch, & Chickering, 1989), they have a high need for information from their advisors. As they "move through" and prepare to "move on" from college, the advising relationship shifts, and students become more inclined to seek consultation and feedback about plans and decisions they have shaped for themselves. Brown and Rivas (1994) offered that advisors may need to be more prescriptive at the outset of their relationships with some students (e.g., with first-generation, underprepared, or multicultural students). Students take on more responsibility as they are supported and encouraged to do so. Brown (2005) illustrates these models with the institution (represented by a capital or lowercase I, depending on its level of involvement in the relationship) assuming primary responsibility at the outset of the advising relationship, with planning and decision-making becoming shared, and with that planning and decision-making finally being borne by the student (who is represented by a capital or lowercase S).

Versions of Brown's model shape student success initiatives for Valencia Community College and Quinsigamond Community College. At JMU the student success unit includes career and academic planning, orientation and first-year experience, community service-learning, and learning resources. That unit's mission is to help students successfully complete transitions into, through, and out of the university.

The success of development programs for instructional faculty depends on the integration of appropriate techniques with the faculty's experience, skill level, and motivation to participate. For example, internal presenters might be more effective with faculty who have little experience; experienced faculty, however, often respond more positively to external presenters who can place their institution and the faculty member's work into a broader context. Brainstorming issues followed by brown-bag discussions of provider-identified issues also works well for new and experienced advisors. Well-developed case studies and simulation exercises can also enhance awareness of the

Figure 14.1   **Four Models of Shared Responsibility**

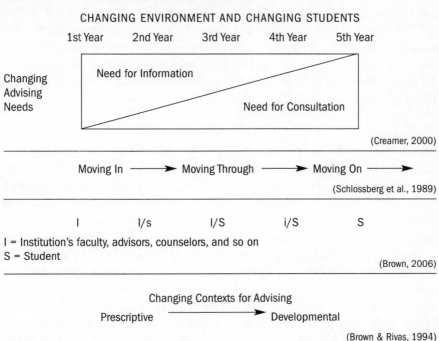

CHANGING ENVIRONMENT AND CHANGING STUDENTS

1st Year   2nd Year   3rd Year   4th Year   5th Year

Changing
Advising
Needs

Need for Information

Need for Consultation

(Creamer, 2000)

Moving In ⟶ Moving Through ⟶ Moving On ⟶

(Schlossberg et al., 1989)

I   I/s   I/S   i/S   S

I = Institution's faculty, advisors, counselors, and so on
S = Student

(Brown, 2006)

Changing Contexts for Advising

Prescriptive ⟶ Developmental

(Brown & Rivas, 1994)

importance of and commitment to working with students beyond the classroom and help faculty develop the skills needed to do that effectively.

Increasingly, campus offices created to improve the quality and scope of teaching and learning offer development programs for faculty and staff who advise students. Excellent examples include a colloquium series sponsored by the College of Arts, Letters, and Social Sciences at California State University–East Bay; presentations offered through the Center for Teaching Excellence at Prairie View A&M University; and an annual faculty professional development day sponsored by the Center for the Enrichment of Learning and Teaching at Middlesex County College.

Obtaining Participation and Support

An important part of securing provider support is determining what faculty understand to be pressing issues, challenges, or areas for development. This inventory can be done by forming a planning group or conducting a needs assessment. If this aspect of the instructional faculty's work is a part of performance reviews, the results of such reviews might highlight areas where students experience a gap between their needs and expectations and the service they receive. Planners should seek the involvement of experienced faculty and include them in the program (e.g., faculty teaching first-year seminars, serving as advisors to learning communities, or working with at-risk cohorts). Multiple sessions should be provided, including web-based programs such as those offered at the Ohio State University.

Exemplary Academic Advisor Development Programs

California State University–Chico offers an annual series of development activities and programs for faculty through its Center for Excellence in Teaching and Learning. The two- to three-day series includes a general session and small group presentations by internal and external presenters. The program culminates with a campus-wide luncheon celebrating the advisor of the year, with the selected faculty member delivering a lecture on his or her work in advising. Similarly, the University of Washington has a comprehensive curriculum for academic advisors that includes a series of workshops, readings, and colloquiums that lead to certification. And notably, Rochester Institute of Technology offers the Faculty Institute on Teaching and Learning (FITL), in which academic advising has been a major focus for the past several years. The FITL includes internal and external presenters and is scheduled each fall and spring.

Finally, the Virginia Community College System offered a drive-in workshop highlighting academic advising as an integral part of efforts to increase student persistence and success. Subsequently, a number of Virginia campuses—including the Danville, Lord Fairfax, Patrick Henry, and Northern Virginia community colleges—offered workshops for faculty and others who advise students.

CONCLUSION

Students spend most of their collegiate lives outside the classroom. Although teaching and learning in the classroom are at the center of their experiences, what happens to students outside class continues to be linked to their development, satisfaction, and persistence. Students' relationships with instructional and administrative faculty play a critical role in creating environments that lead to student success. Therefore, it is critical to offer pre-service and in-service development programs for those who shape environments that put students first.

Although efforts are increasingly being made to implement pre-service and in-service development programs, greater attention needs to be devoted to identifying intentional outcomes based on institutional missions, visions, and values. Development programs must go beyond simply reviewing information about policies, programs, and procedures. These programs must ensure that the instructional and administrative faculty who shape the experiences of students are provided with structured opportunities to develop and expand their understanding of student needs and institutional expectations. Such programs must clearly delineate shared roles and responsibilities and seek to enhance the skills needed for providers to be effective in their work with students. Because institutional values are reflected in recognition and reward systems, such as promotion and tenure, greater efforts should also be made to link provider effectiveness to evaluation, recognition, and reward.

Finally, although the development of knowledge and skills is important, those who are responsible for creating effective campus environments must possess and demonstrate the belief that student learning and development must always come first.

REFERENCES

Astin, A. W. (1985). *Achieving educational excellence: A critical assessment of priorities and practices in higher education.* San Francisco, CA: Jossey-Bass.

Brown, T. E. (2005, May). *Teaching beyond the classroom: The critical role of faculty and academic advising in promoting student learning, achievement, and success.* Keynote address at the 2nd annual Teaching Professor Conference, Schaumburg, IL.

Brown, T. E. (2006). Designing advisor training/development programs. In *NACADA academic advising summer institute session guide.* Manhattan, KS: National Academic Advising Association.

Brown, T. E., & Rivas, M. (1994, Fall). The prescriptive relationship in academic advising as an appropriate developmental intervention with multicultural populations. *NACADA Journal, 14*(2), 108–111.

California Institute of Integral Studies. (2006). *Conference purpose.* Retrieved June 27, 2007, from www.heartofeducation.org/purpose/

Creamer, D. G. (2000). Use of theory in academic advising. In V. N. Gordon, W. R. Habley, & Associates, *Academic advising: A comprehensive handbook* (pp. 18–34). San Francisco, CA: Jossey-Bass.

Crookston, B. B. (1972, January). A developmental view of academic advising as teaching. *Journal of College Student Personnel, 13*(1), 12–17.

Cutright, M., & Swing, R. L. (2005). The Community College of Denver: A second family for the first-year student. In B. O. Barefoot, J. N. Gardner, M. Cutright, L. V. Morris, C. C. Schroeder, S. W. Schwartz, et al., *Achieving and sustaining institutional excellence for the first year of college* (pp. 35–58). San Francisco, CA: Jossey-Bass.

Gordon, V. N. (2003). Advisor training and the future. In *Advisor training: Exemplary practices in the development of academic advisors* (pp. 115–119). Manhattan, KS: National Academic Advising Association.

Habley, W. R. (1986). *Advisor training: Whatever happened to instructional design?* ACT workshop presentation, Iowa City, IA.

Habley, W. R. (Ed.). (2004). *The status of academic advising: Findings from the ACT sixth national survey.* Manhattan, KS: National Academic Advising Association.

Higginson, L. C. (2000). A framework for training program content. In V. N. Gordon, W. R. Habley, & Associates, *Academic advising: a comprehensive handbook* (pp. 298–307). San Francisco, CA: Jossey-Bass.

Ignelzi, M. G., & Whitely, P. A. (2004). Supportive supervision for new professionals. In P. M. Magolda & J. E. Carnaghi (Eds.), *Job one: Experiences of new professionals in student affairs* (pp. 115–136). Washington, DC: American College Personnel Association.

James Madison University. (2007). *Division of Student Affairs and University Planning.* Retrieved June 26, 2007, from www.jmu.edu/stuaffairs/

Kegan, R. (1994). *In over our heads: The mental demands of modern life.* Cambridge, MA: Harvard University Press.

Kuh, G. D., Kinzie, J., Schuh, J. H., Whitt, E. J., & Associates (2005). *Student success in college: Creating conditions that matter.* San Francisco, CA: Jossey-Bass.

Levin, M. E., & Levin, J. R. (1991, July). A critical examination of academic retention programs for at-risk minority college students. *Journal of College Student Development, 32*(4), 323–334.

Light, R. J. (2001). *Making the most of college: Students speak their minds.* Cambridge, MA: Harvard University Press.

Lovett, C. M. (2006, March 16). Alternatives to the smorgasbord: Linking student affairs with learning. *The Chronicle of Higher Education,* pp. B9–B11.

Pascarella, E. T., & Terenzini, P. T. (1991). *How college affects students: Findings and insights from twenty years of research.* San Francisco, CA: Jossey-Bass.

Pascarella, E. T., & Terenzini, P. T. (2005). *How college affects students: A third decade of research.* San Francisco, CA: Jossey-Bass.

Schlossberg, N. K., Lynch, A. Q., & Chickering, A. W. (1989). *Improving higher education environments for adults.* San Francisco, CA: Jossey-Bass.

Tinto, V. (1993). *Leaving college: Rethinking the causes and cures of student attrition* (2nd ed.). Chicago, IL: University of Chicago Press.

Ward, W. L., & Mitchell, R. L. (1997). Being in the play: Student employment and learning. In A. Devaney (Ed.), *Developing leadership through student employment* (pp. 63–84). Bloomington, IN: Association of College Unions International.

Winston, R. B., Jr., & Creamer, D. G. (1997). *Improving staffing practices in student affairs.* San Francisco, CA: Jossey-Bass.

15 | ENGAGING FACULTY TO FOSTER STUDENT DEVELOPMENT

FAYE VOWELL

Higher education today is in a state of dynamic change. Institutions face new and growing demands from every direction. National and state governments have increased expectations for accountability in fiscal terms as well as in student persistence and graduation rates. The economy is in flux, with some institutions facing budget cuts and falling numbers of high school graduates and others seeing enrollments increase with no commensurate growth in budget. For-profit and totally online institutions have changed the competitive face of recruitment. Demographic projections forecast an increasingly diverse population of students to serve without an increasing number of diverse faculty as role models. As our institutions change, so must the roles of faculty and staff.

Gone are the days when faculty members could expect to focus only on teaching their classes and doing their research. Now faculty are expected to take a larger role in recruitment and retention efforts, supporting the long-range viability of the institution (Kramer, 1984). They are more active in shared governance, in strategic planning, and in marketing efforts. So too is the role of advising and engaging students outside class assuming greater importance in faculty life.

National data reveal that most students in higher education are advised by faculty: 0% of four-year institutions, 50% of public two-year institutions, and 80% of private two-year institutions use faculty to advise (Habley, 2004). But few institutions have a comprehensive advisor development program, and even fewer reward quality advising in a substantial way. Many faculty members in these institutions define advising as class scheduling, ignoring the deeper and more lasting contribution to student development inherent in a quality advisor-advisee relationship. Advising, more broadly defined, is any faculty-student contact that fosters students' growth and engagement with their education.

FACULTY ENGAGEMENT WITH STUDENTS

In his book *Making the Most of College,* Richard Light (2001) states that good advising may be the most underestimated characteristic of a successful college experience. For the past 20 years, the research documenting the positive impact of faculty advising and other out-of-class interaction on retention has been substantial (Backhus, 1989; Creamer, 1980; Fuller, 1983; Habley, 1981; Habley & McClanahan, 2004; King, 1993; Kramer, 2003). In addition to increased retention, faculty-student interaction has a strong correlation with increased intellectual and personal development, higher academic aspirations, and higher motivation (Chickering & Gamson, 1987; Pascarella & Terenzini, 1991); more positive attitudes toward college (Appleby, 2001b); and general cognitive development (Pascarella & Terenzini, 2005). Several studies have shown that these positive effects persist even when students enter college with different ability levels and different demographic profiles and attend schools with different rates of selectivity (Astin, 1993b; Pascarella & Terenzini, 2005).

Faculty-student interaction also positively impacts racial understanding and attitudes toward diverse racial and ethnic groups (Astin, 1993a, 1993b; Milem, 1994; Pascarella & Terenzini, 2005). Frost (1991) looked at the impact of faculty advising on female student performance on the Watson-Glaser Critical Thinking Appraisal and found significant positive impact on the recognition-of-assumptions scale and the deductions scale. Kitchner, Wood, and Jensen (1999) found a positive correlation between student-faculty interactions outside class and increased scores on two dimensions of critical thinking.

The quality of student-faculty interaction is crucial. Students want faculty to demonstrate a "caring attitude and person regard" for them (Kramer, Tanner, & Peterson, 1995; Pascarella & Terenzini, 2005). However, some studies suggest that the perception that faculty members are caring and accessible may be enough to impact retention (Halpin, 1990; Johnson, 1994; Mallette & Cabrera, 1991; Pascarella & Terenzini, 2005). Astin (1993b) found that academic advising positively correlates with a higher GPA, degree attainment, graduation with honors, and enrollment in graduate or professional school (Pascarella & Terenzini, 2005). Such correlations amply demonstrate the importance of quality faculty advising and interaction with students outside class.

But attrition, the negative side of retention, is also worth mentioning. As Swail (2006) notes, each student who doesn't persist loses valuable "life" time, probably loses his or her initial financial investment, and may incur significant loan debt. The institution also loses money in terms of tuition and fees, books, services, housing, and long-term alumni contributions. It must also recruit a student to replace each one it loses.

Motivating Faculty to Engage with Students

Given the importance of faculty members to student growth and persistence, what strategies can be applied to help motivate them to participate at higher levels in advising and one-on-one contact with students? An understanding of motivation is perhaps the place to begin.

At the most basic level, motivation can be classified as either extrinsic or intrinsic. Extrinsic rewards for advising and other faculty-student interaction can include stipends, released time, reassigned time, additional help (such as a graduate assistant or work study), additional travel or equipment money, and recognition (such as a local or national advising award or the consideration of good advising in retention, tenure, and promotion decisions).

Expectancy theory offers one valuable approach for influencing faculty motivation. "Expectancy theory states that people are purposeful beings who behave in accordance with their expectations and who believe that their efforts will result in outcomes they value" (Hancock, 1996, p. 11). Faculty members are motivated to take on a task based on their estimation of success, their estimation that their efforts will have certain outcomes, and the positive or negative values produced by these outcomes. Each of these areas can be influenced by advising administrators. Administrators can provide advising training and development to enhance a faculty member's expertise, they can make advising expectations clear, and they can create clear rewards for good advising.

For example, if advising is rewarded as an aspect of retention, tenure, and promotion, it would be helpful to provide a description of the expectations of what advisors must know, do, and understand at each rank. These expectations will vary according to several factors, including the mission of the institution; its size; whether it is a community college, a comprehensive institution, a research university, a church-related school, or a liberal arts college; and its history. In smaller institutions a faculty member may be the only advisor with whom a student comes into contact. In larger universities professional advisors may work with students in several advising-related activities, and faculty members may be engaged with students primarily as mentors, in advising student organizations, or in involving students in research or service-learning activities. Still, clear expectations for faculty engagement with students need to be made available to faculty (see Vowell & Farren, 2003, for sample expectations for faculty tenure and promotion to different ranks at a comprehensive university).

Advising expectations should deepen and broaden with each rank. If expectations are clearly and specifically articulated, faculty will be aware of the knowledge and expertise they need to acquire to reach the next level. They will know what the institution values. The institution has the obligation to offer a comprehensive advisor development and training program to enable faculty to attain these skills. It needs to implement a systematic advising assessment plan to give faculty the student feedback they need to improve their advising. Finally, the institution needs to reward good advising in the recognition, promotion, and tenure process. With these pieces in place, advising administrators can apply expectancy theory with confidence in positive outcomes.

ADVISING AS TEACHING

The belief that advising is a form of teaching has become increasingly accepted. The literature on this topic includes Appleby (2001c); Koring, Killian, Owen, and Todd (2004); Kramer (2003); Mann (1999); Mathie (1993); Ryan (1992); and Wade and Yoder (1995). Appleby presents a comprehensive comparison of the similarities of effective advisors and teachers by using Carol Ryan's synthesis and adding seven characteristics of his own. Table 15.1 is adapted from Appleby's comparison.

Crookston (1972) equates developmental advising with teaching and contrasts what he describes as prescriptive advising with developmental advising. Appleby (2001a) comments that "the major thread that runs through these differences is that developmental advisors gradually shift the responsibility of the relationship to their advisees." To do that, developmental advisors work with advisees on problem-solving and decision-making skills, developing higher order thought processes, and gaining clearer insight into their personal goals and how those fit into the goals of higher education. Appleby (2001a) presents Crookston's dimensions and adds several of his own, an adapted version of which appears in Table 15.2. As the juxtaposed dimensions illustrate, developmental advising contributes more to student engagement. The student is an equal partner in the advising relationship.

Table 15.1 **A Comparison of the Knowledge, Skills, and Characteristics of Effective Teachers and Advisors**

Effective Teachers	Effective Advisors
Master their subject matter	Possess accurate information about the policies, procedures, resources, and programs of their departments and institutions
Plan, organize, and prepare materials for classroom presentation	Are well prepared for advising sessions
Engage students actively in the learning process	Enable advisees to actively participate in the advising process by challenging them with new, more demanding learning tasks involving alternative ideas or choices and encouraging them to ask questions to clarify these ideas and explore these choices
Provide regular feedback, reinforcement, and encouragement to students	Provide timely feedback, reinforce learning that has taken place, and applaud student successes
Create an environment conducive to learning	Create a good learning climate within advising sessions
Stimulate student interest in the subject at hand by teaching it enthusiastically	Project enthusiasm for their area of academic expertise and their advisory duties
Help students learn independently	Encourage advisees to become self-directed learners
Teach students how to evaluate information	Help advisees evaluate and reevaluate their progress toward personal, educational, and career goals
Act as co-learners during the learning process	Set performance goals for themselves and their advisees
Serve as a resource to students	Provide materials to advisees and refer them to others when referral is an appropriate response
Relate course content to students' experiences	Assist students in the consideration of their life goals by helping them relate their experiences, interests, skills, and values to career paths and the nature and purpose of higher education
Provide problem-solving tasks to students	Provide tasks to be completed before the next advising meeting that will require the advisee to use information-gathering, decision-making, and problem-solving skills
Personalize the learning process	Help students gain self-understanding and self-acceptance

Effective Teachers	Effective Advisors
Deliver information clearly and understandably	Communicate in a clear and unambiguous manner with advisees
Exhibit good questioning skills	Serve as catalysts by asking questions and initiating discussions
Exhibit good listening skills	Listen carefully and constructively to advisees' messages
Exhibit positive regard, concern, and respect for students	Provide a caring and personal relationship by exhibiting a positive attitude toward students, their goals, and their ability to learn
Are approachable outside the classroom	Provide accessible and responsive advising services
Present themselves to students in an open and genuine manner	Provide a climate of trust in which advisees feel free to ask questions, express concerns, revise ideas, make decisions, and share personal experiences and knowledge
Serve as role models who can help students understand the mission, values, and expectations of the institution	Model the tenets of the university and demonstrate enthusiasm and knowledge about the goals and purposes of higher education
"Promote effective learning climates that are supportive of diversity" (Puente, 1993, p. 82)	Respect diverse points of view by demonstrating sensitivity to differences in culture and gender
Use outcomes assessment to "make data-based suggestions for improving teaching and learning" (Halpern, 1993, p. 44)	Make changes or add to advising knowledge and skills by assessing the advising process
"Stimulate learning at higher cognitive levels" (Mathie, 1993, p. 185)	Help students move beyond rote memorization or recall (Grites, 1994); help advisees test the validity of their ideas (Hagen, 1994); and "challenge students to confront their attitudes, beliefs, and assumptions" (Laff, 1994, p. 47)
Help students "choose careers that best suit their aptitudes and interests" (Brewer, 1993, p. 171)	Help students explore career goals and choose programs, courses, and cocurricular activities that support these goals
Use interactive computer software that promotes active learning (Mathie, 1993)	Use institutional technology (e.g., degree-audit reports) to augment advising; recommend interactive software (e.g., SIGI PLUS) that can help advisees clarify goals and identify career options (Rooney, 1994); and communicate with advisees via email

Table 15.2   **Contrasting Dimensions of Prescriptive and Developmental Approaches to Advising**

	Prescriptive Advising	**Developmental Advising**
Crookston's Dimensions		
Abilities	Focus is on limitations (i.e., the advisor uses students' past performance to predict future	Focus is on potentialities (i.e., the advisor uses past performance and current aspirations to anticipate potential).
Motivation	Students are viewed as passive, lazy, irresponsible, and in need of help and prodding.	Students are viewed as competent, striving, and active seekers of information.
Rewards	Students are motivated by grades, credit, income, and parental threats.	Students are motivated by mastery, achievement, recognition, status, and fulfillment.
Maturity	Students are immature and irresponsible, and they must be closely supervised.	Students are responsible, maturing, and capable of self-direction.
Initiative	Advisor takes initiative on fulfilling requirements; any additional advising is initiated by the student.	Either the advisor or the advisee can initiate advising.
Control	Advisor is the authority and is in control.	Control is shared and negotiated.
Responsibility	Advisor's responsibility is to provide advice, and the advisee's responsibility is to act on that advice.	Responsibility is negotiated and/or shared.
Learning Output	Student learns from the advisor.	Both the student and the advisor learn and develop.
Evaluation	Advisor evaluates the advisee's progress.	Evaluation is an advisor-student collaboration.
Relationship	A formal relationship exists between the advisor (authority) and student (dependent), and it's based on status, strategies, games, and a low level of trust.	The advisor-student relationship is informal, flexible, situational, and based on a high level of trust.
Appleby's Dimensions		
Purpose	To deliver accurate information to as many students as possible in as efficient a manner as possible.	To develop mentoring relationships with students that will enable them to continue to develop personally, academically, and professionally after the formal advisor-advisee relationship has ended.

	Prescriptive Advising	Developmental Advising
Ultimate Goal	The ultimate goal of advising is to enable students to earn diplomas and graduate "on time."	The ultimate goal of advising is to enable students to clarify their future goals and to plan strategies to accomplish those goals.
Location	In the advisor's office.	Anywhere (e.g., in the advisor's office, in the hall, on a campus bench, at a basketball game, or in the student union or cafeteria).
Future	"The future" refers to next semester.	"The future" refers to post-baccalaureate opportunities.
Course Rationale	Courses are taken to "get them out of the way."	Courses are taken to develop knowledge, skills, and characteristics.
Curricular/ Cocurricular Emphasis	Emphasis is on curricular activities (i.e., classes).	Emphasis is on both curricular and cocurricular activities (e.g., membership in organizations and volunteer activities).
Strength/ Weakness Emphasis	Emphasis is on hiding weaknesses and using strengths to bolster GPA.	Emphasis is on recognizing what skills will be necessary to accomplish future goals, strengthening those that are weak, and continuing to build those that are strong.
Questions Addressed	What courses do I have to take? Who is teaching them? When are they offered? How difficult are they? Do you have to write a paper? Is there a lot of reading?	What can I do with a degree in psychology? Why are statistics and experimental psychology important classes? What classes can I take after English composition to strengthen my writing skills?
Culpability	The advisee assumes that the advisor is responsible for negative consequences if errors in advising occur.	The advisee understands that the advisee is ultimately responsible for negative consequences if errors in advising occur.
Delivery System(s)	Single delivery system (one-on-one meeting in the advisor's office).	Multiple delivery systems (e.g., email, telephone, classes, seminars, workshops, group sessions, alumni panels, handbooks, and peer advisors/mentors).
Curricular Understanding	Students "understand" the curriculum when they know what classes they must take and when to take them.	Students "understand" the curriculum when they realize how they will change as a result of completing classes and how those changes will enable them to accomplish their post-baccalaureate goals.

continued

continued

	Prescriptive Advising	Developmental Advising
Stability/ Change	The advising process remains constant as the student progresses from freshman to senior.	The advising process changes in response to the student's developmental needs as the student progresses from freshman to senior (e.g., different questions are addressed).
Thinking Skills Involved	Retention (e.g., what courses to take, the sequence of courses, and the number of credit hours for graduation).	Comprehension (e.g., Why do I have to take physiological psychology? I want to be a counselor, not a biopsychologist). Application (e.g., How can I graduate if I have three semesters of classes to go and only two semesters of financial aid left?). Analysis (e.g., How can I satisfy the requirements of general education, and how do all the requirements fit together?). Synthesis (e.g., What electives should I take to help me work with unwed pregnant teenagers?). Evaluation (e.g., Is clinical psychology an attainable career for me?).
View of Electives	Electives are courses that are easy, fun, can raise students' GPA, and are offered at convenient times.	Electives are courses that enable students to expand on the knowledge they gain in their required courses and to "construct" themselves as unique individuals who are different from other undergraduates with the same degree.
Rule Orientation	The advisor attempts to make sure that advisees follow all rules and procedures to the letter.	The advisor will attempt to bend rules and procedures if such accommodations are in the best educational interest of the student.
Appropriate Topics	The advisor sticks to academic advising and avoids giving personal or career advice.	Many topics can be broached and discussed during advising sessions, as long as they fall within the competence of the advisor.
Skill Development	Emphasis is on passing skill courses (such as statistics) to "get them out of the way" rather than on actually acquiring and retaining the skills they teach.	The development of skills is stressed in a way that allows advisees to understand the value of the skills they will acquire and how the sequence of the curriculum will require them to build on these skills.

	Prescriptive Advising	**Developmental Advising**
Personal Insight	Not stressed after an advisee has decided on a major.	Personal insight is a driving force during all advising sessions (e.g., asking, "Do you still want to be a clinical psychologist?").
Curricular Rationale	It is unnecessary for advisors to explain to advisees why they must take certain classes, other than that these courses are required for graduation. (Assumption: Advisees are interested only in what classes they should take, not why they should take them or how they will be changed as a result of taking them).	One of an advisor's most important roles is to enable advisees to comprehend the rationale behind classes they will take and the way these classes are sequenced. (Assumption: Advisees are more likely to involve themselves in classes they know will enable them to accomplish their goals and will attempt to retain and strengthen the skills these goals require.)

Appleby (2001a, 2001b), Koring et al. (2004), and Mathie (1993) make the connection between developmental advising, developmental teaching, and active learning. As Appleby (2001b) notes:

According to Mathie (1993), active learning takes place when students

- participate dynamically in the learning process;
- are stimulated to learn at higher cognitive levels; and
- understand the relevance of learning activities to the specific subject matter being taught, to other contents of the course, and to the events in their own lives.

Mann (1999) emphasizes that developmental advising and active learning are concerned with facilitating a student's problem-solving, decision-making, and evaluation skills. Koring et al. (2004) describe a comment at an advising roundtable that compared teaching students to navigate college to teaching them to write a research paper because both activities require analytical, organizational, and research skills and abilities.

Both advising and classroom teaching help create human capital in students. This concept is important in a variety of institutions—from those with a vocational or career focus to those with a liberal arts focus. Shaffer (1997) defined human capital as "transferable skills that can be applied in many settings and that can inform many different occupations" (p. 6). These skills include knowing how to learn; proficiency in reading, writing, and computation; listening and oral communication; creative thinking and problem solving; goal setting; interpersonal skills; and leadership (Appleby, 2001b; Carnevale, Gainer, & Meltzer, 1988). King's College, a Catholic liberal arts college, has defined eight transferable skills of liberal learning: critical thinking, effective writing, effective oral communication, library and information literacy, computer competence, creative thinking and problem solving, quantitative reasoning, and moral reasoning (Tagg, 2003).

CHARACTERISTICS OF A QUALITY FACULTY ADVISING PROGRAM

This chapter has discussed why faculty should engage students outside class and has presented some guidelines for advising administrators to follow in motivating faculty to advise well; giving them the necessary skills and knowledge through a comprehensive, individualized professional development program; assessing their performance; and then rewarding that good performance. Best practices or characteristics of a quality advising program that engages faculty with students include the following:

- Educating faculty about the changing roles of faculty in higher education today and the relationship of advising and engagement with students to the mission of the institution as a whole

- Developing a campus advising mission statement that is based on a broad definition of advising

- Clarifying expectations for faculty advisors

- Offering appropriate faculty training and development that acknowledges individual faculty development and the faculty life cycle

- Encouraging faculty to build meaningful relationships with students through advising and mentoring, including such activities as undergraduate research and service-learning

- Encouraging collaboration by integrating faculty advisors into the campus advising community

- Promoting the concept of shared responsibility through advising as teaching

- Promoting the use of an advising syllabus

- Encouraging faculty to participate in the scholarship of advising using Boyer's (1990) expanded definition of scholarship

- Appropriately rewarding faculty for their contribution to advising and student engagement

- Assessing the success of faculty advising and student engagement

- Understanding the culture of advising at the institution and planning strategically to enhance that culture

Where Are Best Practices Working?

To find out where these best practices are being implemented and the impact that they are having, faculty advisors across the country were surveyed using the instrument in Table 15.3.

Responses to the survey reveal that these best practices are being used well. At Clarke College, a small private liberal arts college with a faculty-only advising model, Elizabeth KimJin Traver reports that the advising mission, values, and goals statement was developed by an advising committee and approved by the faculty senate. It is posted on the college web site under "Resources for Faculty" and included in the catalog. New faculty members are introduced to advising through sessions during new faculty orientation. The college culture and climate encourage meaningful relationships with students. Faculty members are given tools and opportunities that support the creation and sustaining of ongoing meaningful relationships with students. These tools include an initial interview guide with questions that assist advisors in getting to know new advisees. The college also encourages faculty-student meals and get-togethers. Finally, advisors maintain ongoing communication and meet more than once a semester. In terms of evaluation, all faculty members must include and address their role and development in advising as part of the annual peer review process.

At Concordia University, Rosie Braun reports that the advising mission statement is published in the university's advising handbook. Tenured faculty members' contracts state that advising is expected. Advisor evaluations and workload are also a part of the advancement-in-rank procedures. Advisors get workload credit for every 15–20 students they advise. In terms of development, Concordia faculty members work to have at least a 10-minute session on the subject in each department's faculty meeting. Faculty encourage out-of-classroom, off-campus activities with all incoming freshmen. As students

Table 15.3   **Faculty Advising Survey**

Name:

Department:

Institution:

1. How has your role as an advisor changed over the past 10 years?

2. Does your campus/department have an advising mission statement? How are faculty made aware of it?

3. Are expectations for faculty advisors clearly stated? How are they communicated?

4. Please describe the kinds of faculty advising development opportunities that are available. Are the sessions designed for faculty at different ranks or stages of their career?

5. Do those opportunities provide development in informational (what advisors need to know), relational (what advisors need to do), and conceptual (what advisors need to understand) topics equally; or do they focus on one exclusively?

6. How are faculty encouraged to build meaningful relationships with students? Please give an example of activities you use to accomplish this.

7. What is the scope of faculty advising? Does it include advising in regard to students' personal growth and development and career planning as well as academic matters?

8. How are faculty advisors integrated into the campus advising community?

9. Do you view advising as a form of teaching? If so, please explain.

10. Do you use any form of an advising syllabus (which functions like a course syllabus) with your advisees? If yes, what does it contain?

11. How is advising rewarded in the retention, promotion, and tenure processes?

12. Do you do research in the area of advising? Is this research rewarded in the retention, promotion, and tenure processes?

13. In what other ways are faculty rewarded for their contribution to advising? Are these rewards effective?

14. Is faculty advising successful on your campus? Why do you think so? How is that success measured or assessed?

15. Please share the metaphor that best describes the faculty advising culture on your campus.

get further into their disciplines, many advisors host students at an event, either on or off campus. Some hold group advising sessions. Concordia believes that advising is a form of teaching, that it is an opportunity for the advisor to teach one on one and often at a very teachable moment, when advisees have come to faculty offices for some reason or concern.

At Kent State University, Jessie Carduner from modern and classical language studies states that her department has had mandatory advising in place since 2001. Before then, advising was haphazard and informal; students sought advising from whomever. Now they have specific advisor-advisee assignments. The university also moved from paper advising to a managed database when it implemented mandatory advising. Carduner is a member of the Kent Academic Support and Advising Association (KASADA). As a leader in this association, she has become involved in training faculty advisors and in activities related to the professional development of all advisors on Kent State's campuses as well as in the assessment of academic advising. KASADA, in collaboration with the College of Undergraduate Studies, conducts a five-session faculty advisor workshop series. Faculty members are nominated by chairs and colleagues to participate. Between 25 and 30 faculty participate each academic year. Faculty of any rank or length of employment can participate. Typically, nontenure-track faculty and assistant professors are the ones who get nominated. Faculty members who complete the workshops receive $300 to spend on further professional development of their choice. There is also the annual Outstanding Faculty Advisor Award. This award comes with $1,000–$1,300 to be spent on professional development in advising. KASADA and Undergraduate Studies also put on a fall advising forum (a three-quarter-day program); a spring conference (a full-day, off-location event); Academic Advising Jumpstart (two half-day in-services); and monthly meetings for updates. Faculty advisors are invited to become members of KASADA and to attend these events. KASADA, in collaboration with the Faculty Professional Development Center, has also initiated two to three brown-bag sessions per academic year on advising matters in an effort to reach more faculty advisors. KASADA has a listserv and a web site with a handbook and resource section for faculty advisors; it also has a subcommittee specifically concerned with the interests of faculty advisors. Each of Kent State's college offices is actively working on developing an advising syllabus. KASADA has given each college a template so that there will be common elements; the template was approved by the executive board and will be distributed to the membership.

At the University of Wisconsin–Stevens Point, Rhonda Sprague from the Division of Communication reports that there is both a campus and a department advising mission statement. The department mission statement is displayed on a series of advising web pages. Faculty job descriptions include advising as a job requirement, and faculty members are also expected to evaluate their advising as part of their teaching responsibilities for merit.

Syracuse University has focused energy on creating a quality educational experience for its undergraduates. Its faculty advising program is exemplary. Not only is advising rewarded in the promotion and tenure process, but the provost has returned applications that do not address the applicant's advising. That kind of support for advising from central administration is rare.

Western New Mexico University, a comprehensive, open-enrollment public institution, has a campus advising mission statement that was developed by the faculty and is shared in the advising handbook. Advising expectations for promotion and tenure are articulated in a workshop for faculty each fall and are available in a manual that guides faculty in preparing for promotion and tenure. Faculty advising training and development are offered in weekly in-service sessions that are specifically for faculty advisors in the Academic Support Center, a centralized advising center for freshmen and undeclared students, and in monthly sessions that are open to the entire campus. Advising is rewarded in the promotion and tenure process in the delivery of one-on-one advising, in advising student organizations, and in the mentoring that accompanies faculty-student contact outside class. The scholarship of advising—including presenting papers at advising conferences and publishing on the topic of advising—is considered important in the promotion and tenure process. Advising as a form of teaching is accepted broadly on campus, and the Academic Support Center has begun to use a freshman advising syllabus.

In general, few responses indicated that a comprehensive advising assessment system was in place. There were few advisor development programs that addressed the informational, relational, and conceptual aspects of advising. More institutions are beginning to integrate advising into the promotion and tenure processes and to understand the connection between advising and teaching. Some schools are using an advising syllabus. The list of metaphors describing the campus advising culture also indicated progress in some areas but not in others. Responses included the following: a sheep wandering in the darkness, looking for an escape route; the idea that it takes a village to raise a student; a potluck dinner (there's some good dishes and some awful ones, and the decision to prepare a dish and contribute is voluntary); a necessary chore to endure; and faculty advising as the glue that holds the university community together.

A review of the literature on institutions that are working to increase faculty-student engagement outside the classroom includes a number of examples of best practices. In *The Learning Paradigm College,* John Tagg (2003) contrasts the characteristics of learning paradigm colleges with instructional paradigm colleges. Institutions that subscribe to a learning paradigm often focus on faculty-student engagement outside the classroom. Valencia Community College—a comprehensive community college with 40,000 students, 90% of whom require developmental reading, writing, or math classes—has instituted a program called LifeMap. Because the college is open admission and many developmental students come without a lot of reflection on life goals and a good sense of the larger purposes of education, the college is attempting to link students' goals to their educational program from the beginning of their college experience. Students are encouraged to meet with faculty members to discuss their educational background and goals as well as complete assessment measures and meet with advisors to develop an education plan. To support the implementation of LifeMap, Valencia's leaders have "begun to assess their faculty development programs on the basis of student outcomes. . . . They have looked at the retention rates and other indices of success in courses taught by faculty who have been through the professional development program compared with those who have not" (Tagg, 2003, p. 152). The college's professional development seminar focused on four pedagogical issues: critical thinking, diversity, developmental advising, and assessment.

The University of Michigan–Ann Arbor has set a goal of involving every undergraduate student in at least one direct, intensive experience in research, scholarship, or creative activity before graduation (Tagg, 2003). This goal gets faculty involved with students in a way that fits well with the mission of a large university and can be rewarded in the faculty recognition process. Inver Hills Community College, a comprehensive community college in a suburb of Minneapolis–St. Paul, has a liberal studies/professional skills program composed of 10 essential skills (Tagg, 2003). Faculty members assess students in these skills at one of five levels of mastery. These assessments are collected in an interactive database that tracks student achievement across time. This database guides faculty and student conversations about student growth.

Indiana University–Purdue University Indianapolis has established an extensive service-learning program and an undergraduate research program (Tagg, 2003). The Gemstone Program at the University of Maryland is an interdisciplinary undergraduate research program spanning all four years of a student's undergraduate experience. Students collaboratively formulate their research question and explore it with the help of a senior faculty member, a librarian, and an upper division student (Tagg, 2003). This fosters the creation of an ongoing learning community. Wagner College, a private liberal arts college in Staten Island, New York, has a curriculum focused around three required learning community experiences. The freshman learning community is more highly structured than the others, with writing-intensive tutors; the instructor in the reflective tutorial class also serves as the advisor for students in the learning community (Tagg, 2003). The second learning community does not have the reflective tutorial class. In the senior year the learning community is the capstone course with a required minimum of 100 hours of internship or a research project. This experience not only engages the students with each other; it offers ample time to interact with faculty and members of the local community.

In *Putting Students First: How Colleges Develop Students Purposefully*, Braskamp, Trautvetter, and Ward (2006) discuss 10 church-related colleges that do an exemplary job in educating students holistically: Bethune-Cookman College, Creighton University, Hamline University, Hope College, Pacific Lutheran University, the College of Wooster, Union University, the University of Dayton, Villanova University, and Whitworth College. These schools embody three characteristics necessary to significantly involve faculty in educating students holistically: "Mission is reality, not rhetoric; learning and development are integrated; and the campus community fosters support and challenge" (Braskamp et al., 2006, p. 193). The 4C's of culture, curriculum, cocurriculum, and community both on and off campus are included in each characteristic. At these institutions all stakeholders make "a concerted effort to respect the personhood of everyone, simultaneously advocating unity of purpose and diversity of viewpoints, perspectives, and people" (p. 207).

In *Student Success in College: Creating Conditions That Matter* (Kuh, Kinzie, Schuh, Whitt, & Associates, 2005), the authors discuss several baccalaureate institutions that scored higher than predicted on the five areas of the National Survey of Student Engagement: level of academic challenge, active and collaborative learning, student interactions with faculty members, enriching educational experiences, and supportive campus environment. Topics in the section dealing with student interactions with faculty members include the following:

Discussing grades or assignments with an instructor; talking about career plans with a faculty member or advisor; discussing ideas from reading or classes with faculty members outside of class; working with faculty members on activities other than coursework (committees, orientation, student-life activities, and so forth); getting prompt feedback on academic performance, and working with a faculty member on a research project. (p. 12)

The schools are diverse in mission, selectivity, size, control, location, and student characteristics (Kuh et al., 2005), but they outperform their peers in the area of student engagement.

CONCLUSION

In summary, several institutions offer models of best practices in engaging faculty with students to increase student engagement, growth, and persistence to graduation. If institutions are motivated to engage their faculty more fully with students after reading this chapter, next steps would include the following:

- Assessing the extent to which the institution embodies the characteristics of a quality faculty advising program

- Identifying the gaps that exist

- Setting goals for addressing those gaps in consultation with faculty leadership

- Formulating a plan that includes a timeline and action steps

- Creating measurements that will inform the institution in regard to progress toward meeting the goals

- Sharing the plan and the measurements broadly across the institution

- Regularly updating the campus on the progress toward meeting the goals

Engaging faculty is a challenging undertaking for any institution today, but the resulting impact on student learning, growth, and persistence is worth the effort.

REFERENCES

Appleby, D. (2001a, March 19). The teaching-advising connection: Part III. *The Mentor: An Academic Advising Journal.* Retrieved June 27, 2007, from www.psu.edu/dus/mentor/appleby3.htm

Appleby, D. (2001b, April 9). The teaching-advising connection: Part IV. *The Mentor: An Academic Advising Journal.* Retrieved June 27, 2007, from www.psu.edu/dus/mentor/appleby4.htm

Appleby, D. (2001c, April 30). The teaching-advising connection: Part V. *The Mentor: An Academic Advising Journal.* Retrieved June 27, 2007, from www.psu.edu/dus/mentor/appleby5.htm

Astin, A. W. (1993a, March/April). Diversity and multiculturalism on campus: How are students affected? *Change, 25*(2), 44–49.

Astin, A. W. (1993b). *What matters in college? Four critical years revisited.* San Francisco, CA: Jossey-Bass.

Backhus, D. (1989). Centralized intrusive advising and undergraduate retention. *NACADA Journal, 9,* 39–45.

Boyer, E. L. (1990). *Scholarship reconsidered: Priorities of the professorate.* Princeton, NJ: The Carnegie Foundation for the Advancement of Teaching.

Braskamp, L. A., Trautvetter, L. C., & Ward, K. (2006). *Putting students first: How colleges develop students purposefully.* Bolton, MA: Anker.

Brewer, C. L. (1993). Curriculum. In T. V. McGovern (Ed.), *Handbook for enhancing undergraduate education in psychology* (pp. 161–182). Washington, DC: American Psychological Association.

Carnevale, A. P., Gainer, L. J., & Meltzer, A. S. (1988). *Workplace basics: The skills employers want.* Washington, DC: U.S. Department of Labor and the American Society for Training and Development.

Chickering, A. W., & Gamson, Z. F. (1987, June). Seven principles for good practice in undergraduate education. *AAHE Bulletin, 39*(7), 3–7.

Creamer, D. G. (1980, Spring). Educational advising for student retention: An institutional perspective. *Community College Review, 7*(4), 11–18.

Crookston, B. B. (1972, January). A developmental view of academic advising as teaching. *Journal of College Student Personnel, 13*(1), 12–17.

Frost, S. H. (1991, July). Fostering the critical thinking of college women through academic advising and faculty contact. *Journal of College Student Development, 32*(4), 359–366.

Fuller, A. G. (1983, March). A strategy to improve retention. *NACADA Journal, 3*(1), 65–72.

Grites, T. J. (1994, Fall). From principle to practice: Pain or gain? *NACADA Journal, 14*(2), 80–84.

Habley, W. R. (1981, Spring). Academic advisement: The critical link in student retention. *NASPA Journal, 18*(4), 45–50.

Habley, W. R. (Ed.). (2004). *The status of academic advising: Findings from the ACT sixth national survey.* Manhattan, KS: National Academic Advising Association.

Habley, W. R., & McClanahan, R. (2004). *What works in student retention: Four-year colleges.* Iowa City, IA: ACT.

Hagen, P. L. (1994, Fall). Academic advising dialectic. *NACADA Journal, 14*(2), 85–88.

Halpern, D. F. (1993). Targeting outcomes: Covering your assessment concerns and needs. In T. V. McGovern (Ed.), *Handbook for enhancing undergraduate education in psychology* (pp. 23–46). Washington, DC: American Psychological Association.

Halpin, R. (1990, Spring). An application of the Tinto model to the analysis of freshman persistence in a community college. *Community College Review, 17*(4), 22–32.

Hancock, D. R. (1996, Fall). Enhancing faculty motivation to advise students: An application of expectancy theory. *NACADA Journal, 16*(2), 11–15.

Johnson, G. M. (1994, September). Undergraduate student attrition: A comparison of the characteristics of students who withdraw and students who persist. *Alberta Journal of Educational Research, 40*(3), 337–353.

King, M. C. (Ed.). (1993). *New directions for community colleges: No. 82. Academic advising: Organizing and delivering services for student success.* San Francisco, CA: Jossey-Bass.

Kitchner, K. S., Wood, P. K., & Jensen, L. (1999, August). *Curricular, co-curricular, and institutional influence on real-world problem solving.* Paper presented at the annual meeting of the American Psychological Association, Boston, MA.

Koring, H., Killian, E., Owen, J. L., & Todd, C. (2004, July 28). Advising and teaching: Synergistic praxis for student and faculty development. *The Mentor: An Academic Advising Journal.* Retrieved June 27, 2007, from www.psu.edu/dus/mentor/040728hk.htm

Kramer, G. L. (Ed.). (2003). *Faculty advising examined: Enhancing the potential of college faculty as advisors.* Bolton, MA: Anker.

Kramer, G. L., Tanner, J. S., & Peterson, E. D. (1995). Faculty mentoring: A key to first-year student success. In M. L. Upcraft & G. L. Kramer (Eds.), *First-year academic advising: Patterns in the present, pathways to the future* (pp. 63–67). Columbia, SC: University of South Carolina, National Resource Center for The Freshmen Year Experience and Students in Transition.

Kramer, H. C. (1984, October). Advising for the advisor. *NACADA Journal, 4*(2), 41–51.

Kuh, G. D., Kinzie, J., Schuh, J. H., Whitt, E. J., & Associates (2005). *Student success in college: Creating conditions that matter.* San Francisco, CA: Jossey-Bass.

Laff, N. S. (1994, Fall). Reconsidering the developmental view of advising: Have we come a long way? *NACADA Journal, 14*(2), 46–49.

Light, R. J. (2001). *Making the most of college: Students speak their minds.* Cambridge, MA: Harvard University Press.

Mallette, B. I., & Cabrera, A. F. (1991, April). Determinants of withdrawal behavior: An exploratory study. *Research in Higher Education, 32*(2), 179–194.

Mann, K. (1999, October 18). Incorporating active-learning strategies in academic advising. *The Mentor: An Academic Advising Journal.* Retrieved June 27, 2007, from www.psu.edu/dus/mentor/991018km.htm

Mathie, V. A. (1993). Promoting active learning in psychology classes. In T. V. McGovern (Ed.), *Handbook for enhancing undergraduate education in psychology* (pp. 183–214). Washington, DC: American Psychological Association.

Milem, J. E. (1994, Winter). College, students, and racial understanding. *Thought and Action, 9*(2), 51–92.

Pascarella, E. T., & Terenzini, P. T. (1991). *How college affects students: Findings and insights from twenty years of research.* San Francisco, CA: Jossey-Bass.

Pascarella, E. T., & Terenzini, P. T. (2005). *How college affects students: A third decade of research.* San Francisco, CA: Jossey-Bass.

Puente, A. E. (1993). Toward a psychology of variance: Increasing the presence and understanding of ethnic minorities in psychology. In T. V. McGovern (Ed.), *Handbook for enhancing undergraduate education in psychology* (pp. 71–92). Washington, DC: American Psychological Association.

Rooney, M. (1994, Fall). Back to the future: Crookston and O'Banion revisited. *NACADA Journal, 14*(2), 35–38.

Ryan, C. C. (1992, Spring). Advising as teaching. *NACADA Journal, 12*(1), 4–8.

Shaffer, L. S. (1997, Spring). A human capital approach to academic advising. *NACADA Journal, 17*(1), 5–12.

Swail, W. S. (2006, January). Seven guiding questions for student retention. *Student Success.* Retrieved June 27, 2007, from www.studentretention.org/pdf/0601_Success.pdf

Tagg, J. (2003). *The learning paradigm college.* Bolton, MA: Anker.

Vowell, F., & Farren, P. J. (2003). Expectations and training of faculty advisors. In G. L. Kramer (Ed.), *Faculty advising examined: Enhancing the potential of college faculty as advisors* (pp. 55–87). Bolton, MA: Anker.

Wade, B. K., & Yoder, E. P. (1995). The professional status of teachers and academic advisers: It matters. In A. G. Reinarz & E. R. White (Eds.), *New directions for teaching and learning: No. 62. Teaching through academic advising: A faculty perspective* (pp. 97–102). San Francisco, CA: Jossey-Bass.

PART IV

ACHIEVING SUCCESS

Part IV addresses common themes that impact student success and next steps for campuses to consider in fostering student success in the campus community. The chapters focus on intervening to retain students and on achieving success in the first year of college and in the two-year college. The final two chapters establish a framework and provide further examples of putting students first on the campus. In particular, Part IV summarizes from chapters throughout the book the common themes that are associated with successful student-centered practices.

16 | INTERVENING TO RETAIN STUDENTS

Wesley R. Habley and John H. Schuh

Few individuals would argue with the contention that college student retention and degree completion have risen to the forefront of major issues in American higher education. Until the middle of the 19th century, higher education was provided by private colleges and was seen as a privilege afforded to the affluent and the intellectual elite. Although some students did not complete degrees, the personal and societal impact of noncompletion went largely unnoticed. With the passage of the Morrill Act in 1862, higher education became more accessible to citizens through a series of publicly funded land-grant colleges. Yet a college degree was still viewed as a privilege available to a small percentage of the populace, and because a college degree was not a prerequisite to personal and economic success, the consequences of student attrition continued to be a nonissue.

Higher education enrollments grew slowly until the middle of the 20th century, when enrollments (fed by returning soldiers) and educational opportunity (provided through the growing community college movement) expanded rapidly. This expansion also accounted for a shift in attitudes about the value of a college degree. What was once seen as a privilege for the elite became a right for the common person. And what was seen as a nicety became an economic necessity and a ticket to upward mobility. Before the 1950s retention and degree completion were of little more than passing interest to educational researchers. But increasing enrollments and attitudinal shifts, when coupled with the significant numbers of students who entered but did not complete college, spawned intellectual curiosity about retention and degree completion and why some students dropped out of college.

This chapter attempts to synthesize the voluminous information on retention and degree completion that has accumulated over the past 50 years. Several assertions guide this chapter. The first assertion is that, in spite of all we have learned about students, institutions, and successful retention interventions, retention and degree completion rates remain flat. Second, all that we have learned may not be useful to us because the educational landscape is changing dramatically. Demographics, enrollment patterns, and pathways through college are far different from what they were even 10 years ago. The third assertion is that we must extend the existing institutionally focused retention/degree completion paradigm to a paradigm that broadens the definition of student success. The final section of this chapter provides a blueprint for the student success paradigm, outlining the interventions that institutions and policymakers should consider to put the paradigm into practice.

WHAT WE HAVE LEARNED ABOUT STUDENT RETENTION

We have indeed learned a great deal about student retention over the past several decades. We have learned that, although retention is difficult to define, significant personal and societal benefits can be attributed to a college degree. We have also learned about student and institutional characteristics that contribute to retention. And we have learned that, in spite of all we know, retention and degree completion rates remain static.

Retention Is Difficult to Define

A review of the literature on student retention since the 1950s suggests that the lack of an accepted operational definition of retention is a constant theme. Summerskill (1962) observed that retention was variously defined as the percentage of students lost to a particular division within a college, lost to the college as a whole, or lost to higher education as a whole. He articulated similar concerns about the differing definitions of dropouts. Through the years, a variation on that theme has been cited by, among several others, Astin (1975), Braxton (2000), Cope (1978), Cowart (1987), Pantages and Creedon (1978), and Tinto (1975, 1987).

Hagedorn (2005) believes that determining the correct formula for the measure of college student retention is one of the two most vexing issues in higher education research. (The other issue is the inability to obtain true transfer rates.)

The most simplistic and nondebatable definition of a persister is an individual who enrolls in college and remains enrolled until the completion of a degree. Yet in reality, the completion of a college degree for many students varies greatly from the linear path suggested by this definition. Although there are probably far more examples, Hagedorn (2005) describes 11 nonlinear pathways to degree completion. These pathways are characterized by multiple institutions of attendance (sometimes simultaneously), variations in full- or part-time student status, interruptions by intervening life variables, distance learning, and periods of nonenrollment. Hagedorn goes on to state that because of the difficulty in defining retention or persistence, "higher education researchers will likely never reach consensus on the 'correct' or 'best' way to measure this very important outcome" (p. 89).

Degree Completion Leads to Significant Personal and Societal Benefits

The benefits of student success accrue both to the degree holder and to the larger society. It is important to emphasize that a college education in this case is defined as completing a baccalaureate degree program, not just attending an institution of higher education for a period of time (although certain benefits may result from college attendance). In some respects it is difficult to differentiate who benefits from a college education. An illustration of this is the effect that educational attainment has on cigarette smoking (Pascarella & Terenzini, 2005) because college graduates are less likely to smoke. Not smoking is a personal benefit, but individuals who do not smoke provide a benefit to the larger society as well. The cost of cigarette smoking was approximately $157 billion annually from 1995–1999 according to the Centers for Disease Control (Fellows, Trosclair, Adams, & Rivera, 2002). If fewer people smoked, the costs of smoking to society would decline. The direct costs of cigarette smoking include hospitalization, prescription drugs, and nursing home care, so cessation of smoking leads to individual benefits in terms of a healthier lifestyle but also to benefits to the larger society in lower health care costs, less work time lost to illness and absenteeism, and reduced negative consequences from secondhand smoke. In this section of the chapter we will review selected individual and societal benefits that result from individuals' holding a bachelor's degree. The taxonomy that will be used to describe these benefits was originally published by Dickeson (2004) and will focus on public and private economic and social benefits.

The economic benefits of a college education are widely recognized. For example, Pascarella and Terenzini (2005) have concluded, "Earnings in the United States are strongly related to level of formal schooling or educational attainment" (p. 452). Individuals with a bachelor's degree are less likely to be unemployed than those without a bachelor's degree and tend to earn more money than those with lower levels of educational achievement. As an illustration, the National Center for Education Statistics (NCES) reported that in 2004 holders of at least a bachelor's degree—regardless of gender or race—experienced an unemployment rate of 2.7% compared with 5% for those who had completed high school but had no college experience (Snyder & Tan, 2005).

Moreover, people with a bachelor's degree earn more money than those without one. According to NCES, the median annual income of males with a bachelor's degree in 2003 was $56,502, compared with $35,412 for males with a high school diploma (Snyder & Tan, 2005). Similarly, women college graduates had a median annual income of $41,327, compared with $26,074 for women with a high school diploma. In addition to these economic benefits, "Having a college education tends to have a positive indirect effect on job satisfaction through its impact on such factors as job prestige and earnings, job autonomy, and nonroutine work" (Pascarella & Terenzini, 2005, p. 451).

Greater earnings translate into other differences between those with and those without college degrees. According to the U.S. Census Bureau (2006), householders who are college graduates are less likely to live below the poverty line than those with less education. They also are more likely to have secured a variety of assets than those without college educations, including having interest-earning assets at financial institutions, stocks and mutual fund shares, motor vehicles, homes, rental property, IRA or Keogh accounts, and 401(k) or thrift savings plans. They are also more likely to own their own business or engage in professional activity.

In addition to the individual benefits of higher income and more secure financial circumstances, the larger society also benefits economically from individuals who hold bachelor's degrees. According to Dickeson (2004), the economic benefits of higher education include increased tax revenue, greater productivity, and increased workforce flexibility. Individuals with college degrees spend more money on reading and education, and they make larger annual cash donations than persons without college degrees. On the other hand, they spend less on tobacco products and smoking supplies (Bureau of Labor Statistics, 2006). Hamrick, Evans, and Schuh (2002) indicate that individuals with a bachelor's degree are less likely to participate in public assistance programs such as Aid to Families with Dependent Children or Supplemental Security Income.

Several social benefits accrue to people who complete a bachelor's degree, according to Pascarella and Terenzini (2005), including some related to health. In addition to the effect that holding a bachelor's degree has on smoking, they cited one study that concluded that college graduates have a "significantly lower risk for coronary heart disease and cancer" (p. 556). Hamrick et al. (2002) also indicated that women with a college degree were less likely to have borne children during their teenage years and were more likely to receive prenatal care when pregnant.

Individuals with college degrees are more likely to be active in their community than those without college degrees. For example, according to the U.S. Census Bureau (2006), persons with college degrees are more likely to attend jazz and classical music performances, musical and nonmusical plays, and the ballet; visit historical parks; and read literature than those without college educations. In addition, they are more likely to play classical music; engage in dancing, drawing, photography, and creative writing; buy artwork; and sing in groups. They are more likely to go to the movies, sporting events, and amusement parks. And they are more likely to participate in exercise programs, play sports, and engage in home improvement and gardening activities.

The larger society also benefits from people who have college degrees. College graduates are more likely to participate in charity work than people without college degrees (U.S. Census Bureau, 2006) and to spend more time per day on organizational, civic, and religious activities (Bureau of Labor Statistics, 2005).

Finally, people with college degrees are less likely to be incarcerated. According to the U.S. Department of Justice, college graduates made up just 2.9% of jail inmates in 2002 (a decline from 3.2% in 1996) and a smaller percentage of those incarcerated than people without a college degree (James, 2004).

The data presented in this section clearly indicate that student success in college provides significant personal and societal benefits. With that in mind, student success in college must become a public policy priority.

Identifiable Student and Institutional Characteristics Contribute to Retention

Perhaps no topic has been the focus of more research in higher education in the past five decades than student characteristics that increase the likelihood of persistence to a degree. We will not attempt to share a complete summary of the research because it is both voluminous and, more than occasionally, contradictory. Astin and Oseguera (2005) suggest that a significant proportion of this research has focused on the development and testing of empirical models that either predict a student's likelihood of degree completion or identify the optimal conditions that will yield the best chance of completing a degree.

In a review of more than 150 empirical tests of 13 propositions based on Tinto's (1987) theory, Braxton and Lee (2005) concluded that only three of the propositions constituted reliable knowledge about student success at residential colleges and universities. Those propositions were 1) the greater the degree of social integration, the greater the level of subsequent commitment to the institution; 2) the initial level of commitment affects the student's subsequent level of commitment; and 3) subsequent commitment positively affects the likelihood of student persistence. None of the propositions constituted reliable knowledge about two-year colleges.

Astin and Oseguera (2005) reported the results of a comprehensive regression study of four-year and six-year completion rates at four-year colleges. The study was organized into three clusters: pre-college student characteristics, institutional characteristics, and environmental contingencies. A small subset of the more than 100 pre-college characteristics and attitudes was found to have a positive impact on degree completion. Those factors were the level of the father's education, mother's education, and parental income; whether students were women; whether they were Roman Catholic or Jewish; their self-rated emotional health; the time they spent in clubs or groups; and their plans to participate in community service projects. The single institutional characteristic with a positive effect on degree completion was the level of admissions selectivity. The environmental contingency showing the strongest positive effect was living in a residence hall during freshman year. Two additional positive effects related to student finances: savings from summer work and parental contributions to help cover college costs.

Identifiable Institutional Interventions Contribute to Retention

In addition to this research, other studies have focused on identifying institutional interventions that foster persistence. Pantages and Creedon (1978) strongly supported the "college fit" theory, which stressed the importance of the interaction between student and institutional characteristics and its effect on persistence. They suggested that admissions policies and counseling programs (broadly defined) were key institutional factors contributing to persistence. Noel (1978) agreed that admissions management was critical, but he further defined counseling interventions to include both academic advising and career planning as essential retention interventions.

In the first of three *What Works in Student Retention* (WWISR) surveys conducted by ACT and the National Center for Higher Education Management Systems, Beal and Noel (1980) identified several institutional characteristics and interventions that supported retention efforts. These were faculty and staff attitude, academic advising, adequate financial aid, curriculum revisions, counseling support, academic support, and career planning. The second WWISR study (Cowart, 1987) affirmed the interventions identified in the Beal-Noel study and expanded the list of characteristics and interventions to include high-quality teaching, student involvement, admissions management, a counseling program, and an early-warning system. Parallel conclusions were drawn by Hossler, Bean, and Associates (1990). The most recent ACT study (Habley & McClanahan, 2004) identified 82 interventions and sorted those interventions into 12 clusters. Although many of the interventions had a positive impact on persistence, the clusters of interventions that were seen as having the greatest impact were transition programs, academic advising, learning support, and assessment. And, in its 2005 study of four-year public colleges, the American Association of State Colleges and Universities concluded that the institutional interventions and characteristics having the most positive impact on student success were first-year experience programs, intentional advising, coordinated and integrated student services, and specific curricular features designed to build greater student identification and engagement.

RETENTION AND DEGREE COMPLETION RATES HAVE NOT IMPROVED

The results of a review of higher education first-to-second-year retention, degree completion, and time-to-degree data from 1975 through 2005 are a cause for concern.

Stagnant First-to-Second-Year Retention Rates

Despite the methodological problems with defining retention, first-to-second-year persistence rates have remained relatively constant over time. Cope and Hannah (1975) reported that the first-to-second-year retention rate was 69.4% at four-year public colleges and 73.2% at four-year private colleges. Since 1983, ACT has reported institutional retention rates calculated from the annual collection of data through its institutional data questionnaire.

A review of these rates invites three significant observations. First, the reported rates did not change much between 1983 and 2006. In addition, these figures do not vary substantially from those reported by Cope and Hannah (1975). And although the retention rate for all institutions reached a

24-year high in 2006 (68.7%), that rate was only 2.1% higher than the lowest national retention rate recorded, in 1996.

The second observation is that the high-to-low retention ranges for each of the institutional types are remarkably narrow over time. With the exception of the two-year private college cohort, the spread between highest and lowest retention rates is less than 5% for all institutional types. Finally, the stability of these rates over time continues to support an often heard orientation exhortation: "Look to your left and look to your right. One of you won't be here a year from now."

Stagnant Degree Completion Rates

ACT has also collected and reported data on degree completion rates between 1983 and 2006. A review of them prompts two important observations. First, the lowest completion rates for all colleges have been reported since the turn of the millennium. In addition, the highest rates for all institutional types (with the exception of four-year private institutions granting B.A. and B.S. degrees) were recorded in 1990 or before.

Cope and Hannah (1975) echoed Iffert (1957) in lamenting that 40% of all students who enter higher education will not earn a baccalaureate degree. Although degree completion rates have improved somewhat in the past 30 years, a significant number of students do not complete degrees. The Education Trust (2004) reported that the six-year graduation rate for four-year colleges is 54%. And Adelman (2004) suggested that there had been virtually no significant change in the eight-year graduation rates for students entering college in 1972 (66%), 1982 (66%), and 1992 (67%). Mortenson (2005) reported that 50.6% of the 24- to 29-year-olds who have ever entered college earned a bachelor's degree and that 14.2% earned an associate's degree. Finally, the U.S. Census Bureau (2006) reported that 27% of Americans over age 25 have earned a bachelor's degree or higher.

Increasing Time to Degree

Time to degree is another concept that suggests there is a nonlinear path through college. NCES tracked the time between high school graduation and bachelor's degree completion and discovered that 33% of bachelor's degree holders completed the B.A. in four years (U.S. Department of Education, 2003). An additional 23% had completed the bachelor's degree in four to five years, but a staggering 44% of bachelor's degree recipients took five years or longer to complete their degrees. Adelman (2004) reported a gradual increase in time to degree for students entering college in 1972, 1982, and 1992. During that period, time to degree increased from 4.34 years to 4.56 years.

THE CHANGING EDUCATIONAL LANDSCAPE

Increasing numbers of students from underrepresented populations and students who are at risk provide very serious challenges to higher education. In addition, institutions are also challenged as students increasingly take variable pathways to and through college. The future successes of colleges and universities to retain and graduate students will be due, in large part, to institutions' ability to adapt to the changing composition and enrollment patterns of the student body.

College Student Demographics

As enrollments at institutions of higher education grow and diversify in the future, colleges and universities will have to adjust to several new developments. Among these will be the changing characteristics of students. According to Price, Kramer, Nelson, Singer, and Wohlford (2002), "Demographic trends show that most of the increase in the traditional college-age population will be students of color and students from low-income homes." Hussar and Bailey (2006) report that the number of African Americans, Hispanics, Native Americans, and Native Alaskans enrolled in college is expected to grow from 4.2 million students in 2004 to 5.6 million by 2015. Many of these students will come to college with several issues that will need to be resolved; central among them are completing the admissions process, actually enrolling, and managing the cost of attendance.

Encouraging students from low-income families to enroll in college is an initial problem faced by higher education leaders, policymakers, and others interested in increasing the college-bound rate in the United States. According to the Economic Policy Institute (2005), "What is less appreciated is the fact that even for academically high-performing students, income and poverty greatly affects [sic] subsequent educational attainment such as completing college." For example, children from high-income families who receive a low score on an eighth-grade test of mathematics (30%) are more likely to complete a bachelor's degree than students from low-income families who receive a high score on the same test (29%).

If low-income students apply to college and are offered admission, it is far more likely that they will not enroll immediately after high school (Horn,

Cataldi, & Sikora, 2005, p. 153). They are also more likely to focus on vocational training and short-term programs rather than baccalaureate programs (Horn et al., 2005).

In addition, students from low-income families who are dependents are more likely to enroll in two-year colleges than students from more affluent families (Horn, Peter, & Rooney, 2002). To complete a baccalaureate degree program, they have to transfer to a four-year institution. Transferring to another institution includes additional challenges that students need to address, including "the lack of articulation agreements between institutions, ineffective information systems and databases, financial aid limitations, and unsupportive transfer policies" (Aragon & Perez, 2006, p. 84).

Finally, students from low-income families face the problem of financing their education. According to one study, "Depending on the type of institution attended, 74 to 92 percent of low-income students . . . had unmet need" (Choy & Berker, 2003, p. 39). "Unmet need" is defined as the amount of money that is not covered by financial aid (including loans and work) or expected family contribution. To cover the balance of their cost of attendance, students have to rely on sources other than their financial aid package and their family. Ways of overcoming this problem include working more hours than the financial aid package projects, enrolling in fewer credit hours, taking a longer period of time to complete a degree, or using other approaches. These strategies are typically not recommended, however, because they are believed to hinder progress to degree—that is, going to college part-time, borrowing more money, and/or working long hours are not positively associated with persistence to graduation.

The following characteristics are of students at four-year institutions who after six years had not transferred or graduated (Berkner, He, & Cataldi, 2002). Compared with students who had graduated, they:

- Had lower grades in high school
- Had a lower combined SAT score
- Were less likely to be enrolled continuously
- Were more likely to be male
- Were more likely to be people of color
- Were more likely to work
- Were more likely to come from a lower income family

Students who transferred to a four-year institution were less likely to graduate than students who had never transferred (Berkner et al., 2002).

In addition to increases in enrollment of low-income students and students of color, there are other demographics that make college students today even more heterogeneous. At one time, a nontraditional undergraduate student was defined as an individual over the age of 24. NCES has expanded that definition and suggests that 75% of today's college students exhibit one or more characteristics of nontraditional students (Choy, 2002). These characteristics include being above the age of 25, delaying enrollment, attending part-time, working full-time, being financially independent, having dependents, being a single parent, and lacking a high school diploma.

Pathways to College

These demographic implications are further confounded by the burgeoning availability of alternative secondary school preparation programs and alternative means for earning college credit. Students may earn college credit while enrolled in high school or through the demonstration of academic competence in many subject areas through a variety of assessments.

Secondary school credentials. At one time, a diploma from a public or private high school was a necessary credential for entrance into college. NCES reported that in 2001 nearly 1.1 million students completed the GED program (Snyder & Tan, 2005). In another report, NCES noted that of the more than 1 million home-schooled students, 275,000 were in grades 9–12 (Princiotta & Bielick, 2006).

Earning college credit. In addition to these alternative preparation programs, it is more and more common for first-time college students to have already earned college credits; many such students have earned enough credits to enter college as sophomores or even as juniors. For the year 2002–2003, NCES reported that 57% of all high schools offered dual credit for college courses and that 813,000 students earned college credit while still in high school (Kleiner & Lewis, 2005). The College Board (2005) reported that in 2002–2003, 67% of all high schools offered advanced placement (AP) courses, with 1.2 million students taking 2.1 million AP exams. Students may also earn college credit on the basis of six competitive examinations taken through the International Baccalaureate program. There are additional routes to earning credit before students begin full-time college enrollment. These include College Level Examination Program (CLEP) exams, institutional placement exams, and portfolio evaluation.

Yet even though many students are entering with earned college credits, there is significant evidence that many students do not have the academic skills required to be successful. When responding to the WWISR survey (Habley & McClanahan, 2004), college officials reported that inadequate academic preparation was a major contributor to dropping out of college. The lack of academic preparation for the rigors of college work was underscored by NCES, which reported that 63% of first-year students at two-year colleges, 38% of students at four-year public colleges, and 17% of students at four-year private colleges need a year or more of remedial education (Parsad & Lewis, 2003). As further support for the contention that many students are unprepared for academic success in college, ACT (2005) reported that only 26% of first-year students were predicted to earn grades of C or better in English composition, college algebra, college biology, and introductory social science courses.

It is an interesting paradox that many high school students are taking courses for college credit while many college students are required to take skill-building courses in subjects that should have been mastered in high school.

Pathways Through College

Over the past few years, the concept of swirling has been applied to attendance patterns of college students. In its basic form, *swirling* is defined as achieving a higher education degree via enrollment at two or more institutions, either simultaneously or consecutively. Although swirling is very difficult to measure, Berkner et al. (2002) provide an overview of measurable swirling. Their study found that 41% of students attended more than one institution during their college career, 11% were simultaneously enrolled in more than one college, and 32% had changed colleges at least once. Undoubtedly, these figures would be far higher if these students were asked to identify other ways in which they earned college credit.

Finally, earning credit through online courses is mushrooming. NCES indicates that 56% of all colleges and universities offer courses via various distance technologies (Waits & Lewis, 2003). Although data are not available on college credits earned online, it is very likely that many college students are taking online courses in addition to a full-time course load at their college of primary enrollment. It is also possible for a student to earn a complete college degree online. Western Governors University as well as several other institutions now offer this opportunity to students.

It is clear that these routes to earning college credit before enrollment or from other institutions during enrollment are not simply passing fads. They have a profound influence on enrollment, retention, and degree completion. The linear path to a college degree is no longer applicable to many of today's students.

RECONSIDERING THE RETENTION/DEGREE COMPLETION PARADIGM

The stark reality of the retention and persistence-to-degree data is that despite the considerable energy the higher education community has expended in understanding retention and degree completion, such understanding has not resulted in a concomitant improvement in student success in college. The community can document the personal and societal benefits that accrue from a college degree. It can identify the student, institutional, and environmental factors contributing to retention. And it can pinpoint the institutional interventions that contribute to retention. Yet in spite of all that is known, little has changed over four decades. Nearly one-third of all first-year students do not return for a second year, fewer than half of all students who earn bachelor's degrees do so within five years of high school graduation, and approximately 40% of all students who enter higher education in a given fall will not earn a degree at any time in their life. With the additional factors of multiple ways that students can earn college credit and the phenomena of student swirling and increased time to degree, it is not likely that the future holds a great deal of promise for improvements in retention or degree completion based on the existing retention paradigm.

Perhaps the time has come to revisit the retention paradigm and broaden it to shift the focus from institutional retention rates to student success rates. For far too long, the issue of retention and degree completion has been characterized by the assertion that success is determined by the number of students who enter, are retained, and earn degrees at a specific institution. That characterization has two main flaws. First, it assumes a linear path and the timely completion of a degree or a certificate. As demonstrated in the previous sections of this chapter, the path to a degree is not linear. It is not time constrained. And it is no longer characterized by attendance at a single institution.

The second main flaw is that institutions are held accountable for retention and degree completion outcomes that are not under their control. Policymakers and resource allocators rely on accountability measures as the lowest common denominators: how many students are retained and how many students graduate. The reality is that not all students enroll with the goal of earning a degree or certificate. Some enroll for personal development or career enhancement. Some students enroll with the intent to transfer. Others enroll without a particular educational goal. And still others enroll because life circumstances either allow for educational exploration or mandate the development of additional skills. Simply stated, for many students, a college degree is not the immediate goal.

The student success paradigm depicted in Table 16.1 expands the existing institutionally focused retention/degree completion paradigm to one that acknowledges that student success, whether at the institution of first enrollment or at another institution, should be the dominant consideration. The paradigm for student success in no way diminishes the importance of institutional efforts to retain and graduate students. Rather, it suggests that students who are not retained or do not graduate from one institution are neither personal nor institutional failures. The paradigm presents the argument that institutions and educational policymakers have a far greater responsibility to assist students in making successful transitions to other educational experiences.

INSTITUTIONAL AND POLICY IMPLICATIONS OF THE STUDENT SUCCESS PARADIGM

The student success paradigm suggests that both institutions and policymakers must examine traditional definitions of student success, review policies that hinder student transitions, and explore systemic and systematic approaches to ensuring student success. This section presents institutional and policy implications of the student success paradigm.

Institutional Implications

Implications for institutions include extending dialogue with secondary school educators, reviewing institutional policies and requirements for transferring, providing advising and counseling for departing students, and expanding articulation agreements. Core to all of these is the need to redefine what is meant by "student success."

Engage in basic skills dialogue with secondary school teachers. College faculty members teach entry-level courses in mathematics, English, and science based on assumptions about what students know and can demonstrate in the classroom. In those same subject areas high school teachers teach the skills that they assume are needed to succeed in college courses. These assumptions

Table 16.1   **The Student Success Paradigm**

Dimension	Retention Paradigm	Expanded Paradigm
Who benefits?	· Student · Institution	· Student · Society
Path to success	· Linear path	· Discontinuous, nonlinear path
Key questions	· How can we best serve? · Why did the student leave?	· How can we best serve? · Where is the student going? · How can we help the student get there?
Desired outcome	· Student receives a degree or certificate from this institution	· Student receives a degree or certificate from any institution
Student's role	· Student's role is primary	· Multiple and variable life roles
Time to degree	· With all due speed	· At the student's speed
Relationship to other education providers	· Friendly but competitive · Opaque · Discrete · Unsystematic	· Transparent · Collaborative · Systematic
Important transitions	· Into this institution · Through this institution · Graduation from this institution	· Into this institution · Transition to another institution
Measure of effectiveness	· Institutional retention rate · Degree completion rate	· Student's success

are not always accurate. Rather than place blame for this disconnect, secondary and postsecondary educators should seek solutions. The gaps between the two sets of assumptions will be closed only through dialogue.

Review policies and requirements. It is recommended that each institution examine those policies and requirements that have a bearing on students transferring into, moving within, and leaving the institution. Although such policies and requirements have been established to ensure the academic integrity of a degree, the unintended consequence of many of them is that students transitioning into, within, or out of the institution may be disserved. As reported in *Student Success in State Colleges and Universities* (American Association of State Colleges and Universities, 2005), researchers found that several of the colleges in the study ensured that students did not lose credits in transitions into and within the institution. The following are several policy-related issues that should be examined:

- The number of transfer credits that can be applied to a degree
- The number of hours for graduation (or for the major) that must be taken on campus
- Department- or major-based general education requirements
- Prerequisite strings that include multiple courses
- Provisions for students who are in good academic standing but have not been admitted to programs with limited admissions
- Provisions for students who are in good academic standing but have been excluded from majors in which they were enrolled
- Prior approval for courses taken at other institutions
- Application of credits earned at other colleges while students are on academic suspension
- Clarity of catalog statements on the evaluation of transfer credits
- Consistency across departments on the application of transfer credits

Provide transition advising and counseling services for departing students. Over the past several decades there has been significant improvement in the level of advising and counseling services provided to students before and during enrollment. Yet there is little evidence that colleges provide the same care and nurturing to students who intend to, or eventually will, pursue their educational goals at another institution. As noted earlier, more than 40% of bachelor's degree holders reported attendance at two or more institutions, and 10% of that group was co-enrolled at some point in their academic careers. Although it is not possible to anticipate all student departures, success in the new institution will be greatly enhanced if transition advising and counseling services are provided at the previous institution.

Expand the structure of articulation agreements. More often than not, an articulation agreement is primarily an understanding that delineates the application of credits between institutions. Some articulation agreements are arranged between two or more institutions; others involve a statewide policy on the transfer of courses between public two-year and four-year colleges.

Still another example of an articulation agreement was implemented by the League for Innovation in the Community College (2001). Member schools in the league partnered with eight four-year colleges to facilitate the transfer of students between partner colleges.

Although it is clear that the applicability of credit is a primary issue in successful student transition, institutions should also consider broadening institutional connections to ensure successful student transitions. As an example, the 2 Plus 2 program is an agreement between the University of Iowa and community colleges. The program features (University of Iowa, 2006):

- Guaranteed early registration for the first semester at the University of Iowa

- Contact with admissions counselors and academic advisors

- A university ID card, email account, and electronic access to student records

- Use of the career center

- Use of the university library

- Student-priced discounts on tickets to university events

Redefine the measures of student success. The time has come for institutions to examine the simplistic, linear, and time-constrained measures of student success. Simply stated, the current measures of institutional success are the percentage of students who enroll, the percentage who stay, and the percentage who subsequently graduate. The assumptions supporting these measures are flawed. Not every student enrolls in a specific college with the intent of earning a degree at that college. Although many students do enroll with that intent, others enroll with the plan to transfer or to upgrade employability skills. Still others enroll because intervening life experiences either require or provide the opportunity for additional education. Under current measures of retention and degree completion, students in these categories could achieve their educational goals only to be counted as dropouts. And from the perspective of these traditional measures, institutions that serve such students do not fare very well.

In addition, not every student who enters with the intent of completing a degree completes that degree on a traditional timetable. Some students earn degrees on a part-time basis while meeting obligations of their workplace or family. Others do not enroll continuously—that is, they stop out of college for a variety of reasons, either planned or unplanned. Yet these students are also counted as dropouts. Again, applying the traditional measures of retention and degree completion, institutions that meet the needs of these students do not fare very well.

In reality, there are multiple definitions of student success, and higher education's current institution-based approaches to measuring student success have become too narrow and counterproductive. These measures have muffled the institutional dialogue that must take place on campus so that more students realize their educational goals.

Implications for Policymakers

Although the student success paradigm presents important implications for institutions, the role of higher education policymakers is even more critical. The term *policymaker* is meant to be broadly inclusive and encompasses state departments of education and legislative bodies at both the federal and state levels. It includes accrediting associations, higher education system heads, and professional associations. Several of the implications for policymakers are discussed in the following sections.

Adopt broader measures of student success. The drive for accountability in higher education has led to wide acceptance that institutional success can be effectively measured in the retention and degree completion rates of an institution's students. Although knowledge of such rates is informative, earlier sections of this chapter suggest that this is both an unrealistic metric and a dramatic oversimplification of a very complex process. Unfortunately, these quantitative retention and degree completion data are being used as measures of quality, shaping policy decisions and the allocation of resources. In many ways institutions are judged on a production model, which simply measures the output against the input.

The time has come for policymakers to redefine the meaning of student success in metrics that focus on the percentage of students who enter higher education at any institution, the percentage of students who are retained in higher education, and the percentage of students who complete degrees at *any* institution. Although several formulas for measuring student success have been suggested, one provides for broad applicability at institutional, system, state, and even federal levels. It accounts for multiple institutions of enrollment and variable attendance patterns. This formula considers the ratio of first-time, full-time degree-seeking students divided into the number of graduates six years later. As an example, an institution with a first-time, full-time, degree-seeking enrollment of 1,000 that graduates 800 students six years later would have a student success ratio of 0.8. The ratio reflects not only the retention and degree completion rates of students who entered the institution six years earlier, but it also takes into account those individuals who transferred into the institution as well as those who may have stopped out of the institution for a period of time. Although this formula is not a panacea, it does provide a measure that focuses on student, rather than institutional, success.

Build integrated educational systems. Policymakers in 31 states (Education Commission of the States [ECS], 2006) have come to the realization that dramatic demographic shifts and the lack of alignment of the constituent parts of the educational system require a critical reexamination of how education is delivered. The result of this realization is the establishment of statewide efforts, variously identified as K–16, P–16, or P–20 initiatives. Although all levels of education are included in these initiatives, ECS suggests that education beyond high school is a "multi-layered nonsystem . . . [whose institutions have] difficulty working together and [are] largely disconnected from the K–12 system whose success is so vital to its own efforts" (Van de Water & Rainwater, 2001, p. 5).

Although these initiatives vary widely from state to state, State Higher Education Executive Officers (2003) suggests that efforts to align the educational system include five essential components: early outreach, curriculum and assessment systems, high-quality teaching, student financial assistance, and data and accountability systems.

Use a common course numbering system. A common course numbering system for colleges and universities would greatly assist student transitions from institution to institution. Common course numbering systems are in place in several states. Florida provides a common course numbering system of articulation that includes all public vocational-technical centers, community colleges, and universities, as well as participating nonpublic institutions (http://scns.fldoe.org/scns). The Texas Common Course Numbering System (www.tccns.org) is a voluntary, cooperative effort by community colleges and universities. And the state of Colorado (www.cccs.edu/cccns) has initiated a system that articulates coursework at all community colleges and area vocational schools. Although these efforts are laudable, each has limitations. Participation in Florida's system includes only those nonpublic institutions that choose to participate. The Texas system is voluntary, and Colorado's system includes only two-year colleges. Even though the real challenge comes from the articulation of course content and course rigor, a common course numbering system would ease student transition from institution to institution. An effective statewide common course numbering system should include all institutions at all levels of postsecondary education.

Implement a course applicability system. Students' decisions to enroll are often predicated on the availability of courses and the acceptance and application of credits earned at other institutions. Yet at many institutions decisions about the applicability of prior credit takes place immediately before or, in some cases, after a student has enrolled. What is called for is a broad-based system that enables prospective students to search institutions to ascertain the availability of courses and the applicability of credits already earned. One example of such a system is the Course Applicability System (CAS; http://oh.transfer.org/cas). CAS is an electronic advising system intended primarily for potential transfer students. The system provides information on courses, course equivalencies, and program requirements at participating institutions. Students who become CAS members receive information on how their specific coursework will transfer and apply toward a degree at a participating institution. Although CAS is currently operational in only 11 states, it shows great promise as a tool that will assist students in making smoother transitions from one institution to another. AcademyOne (www.academyone.com) is another example of a course applicability system that provides information on how transfer credits will be applied at participating institutions. Although CAS, AcademyOne, and similar systems provide useful services to students and show great promise, the number of participating institutions represents only a fraction of higher education institutions in the nation. The implications of implementing a course applicability system on a far broader scale should become a matter of public policy.

Minimize the complexity and expand the breadth of articulation agreements. Higher education is rife with articulation agreements. There are articulation agreements that include two institutions and those made by one institution with many other institutions. There are articulation agreements between all two-year and four-year public colleges within a state. However, the multiplicity of articulation agreements creates a complex, unsystemic, and unsystematic web of relationships that serve institutional purposes while they disserve student transitions. The current system of institution-based articulation agreements is fraught with gaps. Some colleges participate in multiple agreements, and other colleges participate in no agreements. Unless policymakers focus attention on expanding, streamlining, and simplifying these agreements, students will continue to fall through the cracks, which minimizes their potential for success.

In addition, articulation agreements should include more than systems for course applicability and common course numbering. Services such as advising and counseling, access to library resources, shared transcripts, and participation in cocurricular programs increase the likelihood of transitions that lead to student success.

Establish a student postsecondary education clearinghouse. Although redefining student success and such efforts as common course numbering, articulation agreements, course applicability systems, and P–20 approaches show great promise for increasing student success, these efforts are situational—that is, they apply only to some institutions, to some situations, or to some jurisdictions. These efforts are also fragmented; each approach is useful but provides only a single piece of the student success puzzle. What is lacking is the integration of these approaches into a coherent national system—a clearinghouse—that facilitates student transitions and in turn enhances student success. The clearinghouse would be a repository for pertinent assessment data (such as admissions tests, placement tests, AP, and CLEP), dual-enrollment credits, college transcripts, and other information that supports the transition process. All input data would be supplied with the permission of the student and would be stored in a student-owned and student-controlled portfolio. At the core of the clearinghouse would be an extensive course equivalency database. Although development of the course equivalency database could be a complex and long-term undertaking, initial equivalency tables could be constructed from existing articulation agreements and course applicability systems.

The student portfolio would serve two critical functions. First, it would provide a secure, official, and accessible record of a student's cumulative postsecondary history. The portfolio could be requested by the student or, at the student's request, sent directly to an institution as part of the admissions process. The inclusion of the course equivalency database in the clearinghouse would provide additional functionality. No matter how many transcripts were included in the portfolio, the student could query the equivalency tables to see how credit from multiple institutions would apply to academic programs at institutions of interest.

The postsecondary education clearinghouse would also benefit institutions in two major ways. First, the clearinghouse would eliminate much (but not all) of the work associated with transfer credit evaluation. As the system grew, more and more course equivalencies would be articulated. The second major benefit of the clearinghouse would be the availability of timely and accurate information during academic advising and registration.

CONCLUSION

This chapter examined the critical issue of student retention and degree completion, taking the position that if more students are to succeed in college, institutional leaders and educational policymakers must expand the retention/degree completion paradigm, which has guided their decisions over the past five decades. Although intervention efforts that focus on retention and graduation from the institutions where students first enroll must continue, it does not seem likely that institutional retention/graduation rates will improve in the foreseeable future. The expanded paradigm for student success urges institutional leaders and educational policymakers to recognize that the path to a college degree is not linear. It is not constrained by time; it is characterized by alternative means of earning college credit and multiple institutions of attendance. The expanded paradigm calls for institutional introspection and for greater inter-institutional collaboration and cooperation. Finally, if more students are to succeed in earning college degrees, the paradigm urges educational policymakers to recognize that student success is a systemic issue that must be addressed in a systematic manner.

REFERENCES

ACT. (2005). *Crisis at the core: Preparing all students for college and work.* Iowa City, IA: ACT.

Adelman, C. (2004). *Principal indicators of student academic histories in post-secondary education, 1972–2000.* Washington, DC: U.S. Department of Education, Institute of Education Sciences.

American Association of State Colleges and Universities. (2005). *Student success in state colleges and universities: A matter of leadership and culture.* Washington, DC: Author.

Aragon, S. R., & Perez, M. R. (2006). Increasing retention and success of students of color at research-intensive universities. In F. S. Laanan (Ed.), *New directions for student services: No. 114. Understanding students in transition: Trends and issues* (pp. 81–91). San Francisco, CA: Jossey-Bass.

Astin, A. W. (1975). *Preventing students from dropping out.* San Francisco, CA: Jossey-Bass.

Astin, A. W., & Oseguera, L. (2005). Pre-college and institutional influences on degree attainment. In A. Seidman (Ed.), *College student retention: A formula for student success* (pp. 245–276). Greenwich, CT: Praeger.

Beal, P. E., & Noel, L. (1980). *What works in student retention: Report of a joint project of the American College Testing Program and the National Center for Higher Education Management Systems.* Iowa City, IA: ACT.

Berkner, L., He, S., & Cataldi, E. F. (2002). *Descriptive summary of 1995–96 beginning postsecondary students: Six years later* (NCES Publication No. 2003–151). Washington, DC: U.S. Department of Education, National Center for Education Statistics.

Braxton, J. M. (Ed.). (2000). *Reworking the student departure puzzle.* Nashville, TN: Vanderbilt University Press.

Braxton, J. M., & Lee, S. D. (2005). Toward reliable knowledge about college student departure. In A. Seidman (Ed.), *College student retention: A formula for student success* (pp. 107–128). Greenwich, CT: Praeger.

Bureau of Labor Statistics. (2005). *American time use survey* (USDL Publication No. 05–1766). Washington, DC: U.S. Department of Labor.

Bureau of Labor Statistics. (2006). *Consumer expenditures in 2004* (Report No. 992). Washington, DC: U.S. Department of Labor.

Choy, S. (2002). *Nontraditional undergraduates* (NCES Publication No. 2002–012). Washington, DC: Department of Education, National Center for Education Statistics.

Choy, S. P., & Berker, A. M. (2003). *How families of low- and middle-income undergraduates pay for college: Full-time dependent students in 1999–2000* (NCES Publication No. 2003–162). Washington, DC: U.S. Department of Education, National Center for Education Statistics.

College Board. (2005, September 19). *College Board honors AP® community on program's 50th anniversary* [Press release]. Retrieved June 28, 2007, from www.collegeboard.com/press/releases/47343.html

Cope, R. G. (1978). Why students stay, why they leave. In L. Noel (Ed.), *New directions for student services: No. 3. Reducing the dropout rate* (pp. 1–12). San Francisco, CA: Jossey-Bass.

Cope, R. G., & Hannah, W. (1975). *Revolving college doors: The causes and consequences of dropping out, stopping out, and transferring.* New York, NY: Wiley.

Cowart, S. C. (1987). *What works in student retention in state colleges and universities.* Iowa City, IA: ACT.

Dickeson, R. C. (2004). *Collision course: Rising college costs threaten America's future and require shared solutions.* Indianapolis, IN: Lumina Foundation.

Economic Policy Institute. (2005). *Low income hinders college attendance for even the highest achieving students.* Retrieved June 28, 2007, from www.epi.org/content.cfm/webfeatures_snapshots_20051012

Education Commission of the States. (2006). *P–16 collaboration in the states.* Denver, CO: Author.

The Education Trust. (2004). *EdWatch Online 2004 state summary reports.* Washington, DC: Author.

Fellows, J. L., Trosclair, A., Adams, E. K., & Rivera, C. C. (2002, April). Annual smoking-attributable mortality, years of potential life lost, and economic costs—United States 1995–1999. *MMWR Weekly, 51*(14). Retrieved June 28, 2007, from www.cdc.gov/mmwr/preview/mmwrhtml/mm5114a2.htm

Habley, W. R., & McClanahan, R. (2004). *What works in student retention: Four-year colleges.* Iowa City, IA: ACT.

Hagedorn, L. S. (2005). How to define retention: A new look at an old problem. In A. Seidman (Ed.), *College student retention: A formula for student success* (pp. 89–106). Greenwich, CT: Praeger.

Hamrick, F. A., Evans, N. J., & Schuh, J. H. (2002). *Foundations of student affairs practice: How philosophy, theory and research strengthen educational outcomes.* San Francisco, CA: Jossey-Bass.

Horn, L., Cataldi, E. F., & Sikora, A. (2005). Waiting to attend college: Undergraduates who delay their postsecondary enrollment. *Education Statistics Quarterly, 7*(1&2). Retrieved June 28, 2007, from http://nces.ed.gov/programs/quarterly/vol_7/1_2/5_1.asp

Horn, L., Peter, K., & Rooney, K. (2002). *Profile of undergraduates in U.S. postsecondary institutions: 1999–2000* (NCES Publication No. 2002–168). Washington, DC: U.S. Department of Education, National Center for Education Statistics.

Hossler, D., Bean, J. P., & Associates. (1990). *The strategic management of college enrollments.* San Francisco, CA: Jossey-Bass.

Hussar, W. J., & Bailey, T. M. (2006). *Projections of education statistics to 2015* (NCES Publication No. 2006–084). U.S. Department of Education, National Center for Education Statistics. Washington, DC: U.S. Government Printing Office.

Iffert, R. E. (1957). *Retention and withdrawal of college students* (U.S. Department of Health, Education, and Welfare Bulletin No. 1). Washington, DC: U.S. Government Printing Office.

James, D. J. (2004). *Profile of jail inmates, 2002.* Washington, DC: U.S. Department of Justice.

Kleiner, B., & Lewis, L. (2005). *Dual enrollment of high school students at postsecondary institutions: 2002–03* (NCES 2005–008). U.S. Department of Education. Washington, DC: National Center for Education Statistics.

League for Innovation in the Community College. (2001). *League for Innovation announces articulation agreements.* Retrieved June 28, 2007, from www.league.org/league/about/press/articulation_agreements.htm

Mortenson, T. G. (2005). Measurements of persistence. In A. Seidman (Ed.), *College student retention: A formula for student success* (pp. 31–60). Greenwich, CT: Praeger.

Noel, L. (Ed.). (1978). *New directions for student services: No. 3. Reducing the dropout rate.* San Francisco, CA: Jossey-Bass.

Pantages, T. J., & Creedon, C. F. (1978, Winter). Studies of college attrition, 1950–1975. *Review of Educational Research, 48*(1), 49–101.

Parsad, B., & Lewis, L. (2003). *Remedial education at degree-granting postsecondary institutions in fall 2000* (NCES Publication No. 2004–010). Washington, DC: U.S. Department of Education, National Center for Education Statistics.

Pascarella, E. T., & Terenzini, P. T. (2005). *How college affects students: A third decade of research.* San Francisco, CA: Jossey-Bass.

Price, D., Kramer, J., Nelson, J., Singer, J., & Wohlford, J. (2002). *What we know about access and success in postsecondary education: Informing Lumina Foundation's strategic direction.* Retrieved June 27, 2007, from www.luminafoundation.org/research/what_we_know

Princiotta, D., & Bielick, S. (2006). *Homeschooling in the United States: 2003* (NCES Publication No. 2006–042). Washington, DC: U.S. Department of Education, National Center for Education Statistics.

Snyder, T. D., & Tan, A. G. (2005). *Digest of education statistics, 2004* (NCES Publication No. 2006–005). U.S. Department of Education, National Center for Education Statistics. Washington, DC: U.S. Government Printing Office.

State Higher Education Executive Officers. (2003). *Student success: Statewide P–16 systems.* Boulder, CO: Author.

Summerskill, J. (1962). Dropouts from college. In N. Sanford (Ed.), *The American college: A psychological and social interpretation of the higher learning* (pp. 627–657). New York, NY: Wiley.

Tinto, V. (1975, Winter). Dropout from higher education: A theoretical synthesis of recent research. *Review of Educational Research, 45*(1), 89–125.

Tinto, V. (1987). *Leaving college: Rethinking the causes and cures of student attrition.* Chicago, IL: University of Chicago Press.

University of Iowa. (2006). *2 plus 2.* Retrieved June 28, 2007, from www.uiowa.edu/2plus2/how_plan_works

U.S. Census Bureau. (2006). *Statistical abstract of the United States.* Washington, DC: Author.

U.S. Department of Education, National Center for Education Statistics. (2003). *The condition of education 2003* (NCES Publication No. 2003–067). Washington, DC: U.S. Government Printing Office.

Van de Water, G., & Rainwater, T. (2001). *What is P–16 education? A primer for legislators.* Denver, CO: Education Commission of the States.

Waits, T., & Lewis, L. (2003). *Distance education at degree-granting postsecondary institutions: 2000–2001* (NCES Publication No. 2003–017). Washington, DC: U.S. Department of Education, National Center for Education Statistics.

17 | ACHIEVING STUDENT SUCCESS IN THE FIRST YEAR OF COLLEGE

RANDY L. SWING AND TRACY L. SKIPPER

The preceding chapters have built a powerful case for the value of putting students first in the planning and delivery of higher education. This chapter will apply that argument to first-year students—a group that has historically experienced high rates of low achievement or failure. One of the most common indicators of student failure is attrition. Nationally, one-third of first-year college students will not complete their first college year—a statistic that has been remarkably stable over the past two decades (ACT, 2006a, 2006b). We have yet to develop a comprehensive system to track what happens to students who do not return for the sophomore year. Research on enrollment trends suggests that students may attend several different institutions while earning a college degree. Thus, a drop out from one institution may not indicate a drop out from higher education altogether. Nonetheless, such statistics pose both a financial and ethical challenge for institutions. Calls for increasing accountability have rightly or wrongly focused attention on college retention and graduation rates. Institutions that fail to retain students feel the drain of lost revenue, but they may also face decreasing support from the public sector and private donors. However, institutions must acknowledge and respond to the commitment they make to the students they admit—to ensure that the entrance to the campus does not become a revolving door.

First-year students also face several developmental challenges that may make them more vulnerable for failure. For example, traditional-age college students are frequently addressing issues related to identity, autonomy, and purpose as they enter higher education. Nontraditional first-year students who may be trying to reconstruct identity or find new purpose after years in the workforce or the home share these challenges. In both cases, questions of identity and purpose have profound implications for institutional fit and academic performance. New students may also struggle with feelings of incompetence. Pascarella and Terenzini (2005) note that academic self-confidence may decline for some students from the end of high school to the beginning of the sophomore year. First-year students are also reporting higher levels of stress and depression than in the past, and one study suggests that stress and depression increase over the course of the first year for some students (Keup & Stolzenberg, 2004).

The struggles of new students in higher education are not, of course, breaking news to faculty or college administrators. Yet understanding and, even better, predicting which students are at high risk of failure have resulted in a rich literature base on the subject and an array of programmatic interventions.

FOUR LENSES FOR EXPLORING STUDENT SUCCESS (OR FAILURE)

At various times over the past five decades, researchers have tended to focus attention on a limited set of variables. These research "lenses" can be broadly summarized in four areas: entering student characteristics, external influences, what students do, and what institutions do.

Focus on Entering Student Characteristics

Alexander Astin's groundbreaking survey of entering students began in 1966 (Higher Education Research Institute, n.d.) and continues to be the world's largest database of characteristics of new college students. Relying on this database of entering student characteristics and institutional data, researchers have shown that it is possible to identify cohorts of students who are likely to have higher or lower rates of success in college based on readily knowable demographic or prior experience variables. Such research has helped institutions understand how shifting admissions patterns provide new institutional opportunities and challenges and has helped the nation understand the impact of broadening access to higher education.

Although it is highly important in advancing new knowledge, a focus on fixed variables (such as gender, high school grades, and family background) is limited in its ability to explain the exceptions—those students who either overperform or underperform based on their entry characteristics. Every educator knows students who entered college with the deck stacked against them by virtue of being first generation, low income, marginally prepared, or employed full-time and nonetheless overcame the odds to become college success stories. Likewise, we know students who arrived at college from well-educated, affluent, and highly encouraging families—the kinds of backgrounds that usually foretell success in college—and have watched as they failed to parlay those advantages into collegiate success.

In an effort to improve their ability to predict outcomes for individual students, some institutions have begun to rely on a wider array of entering student characteristics, using sophisticated algorithms to create a profile for student success. However, even these more sophisticated methods do not adequately control for all the variables that contribute to new student success. An inspirational family member who provides extraordinary support, an above-average willingness to delay gratification, and personal motivations are examples of mitigating variables that may not be captured through traditional measures.

Unfortunately, understanding how entering characteristics correlate with outcomes has too often been used simply to increase student screening in the admissions process. Such efforts have worked best at institutions that have more applicants than they can admit. Other institutions, including open-admissions colleges and those that accept a very high percentage of applicants, have too often cited entering student characteristics as an excuse for low levels of student success. Overemphasis on entering student characteristics can be tantamount to simply blaming students and their families, high schools, and communities for low levels of success in college.

Focus on External Influences

Colleges, whether public or private, are part of a social and political web that, at times, shape students' experiences in ways the institution cannot control. Some external events create extraordinary impact on the experiences of college students. The sharp decline of male enrollment during world wars interrupted degree attainment for some students and changed the daily life on campus for thousands more. National financial aid policies, such as the introduction of Pell Grants in 1972 and the shift toward merit-based rather than need-based aid, are other examples of influences that are largely out of institutions' control and that shape students' experiences on campus.

External influences need not be national in scope. Regional differences in social norms, patterns of in- and out-migration, or regional economies, for example, are also useful in explaining differences in student success across geographic areas. Likewise, local conditions can have enormous impact on a single campus. Hurricane Katrina in 2005 disrupted the lives of thousands of students and drastically reshaped their college experience. A campus fire, the closing of a nearby manufacturing plant or military base, or other local events have singularly affected other campuses.

A large body of literature highlights the impact of national policy and, to a lesser degree, regional events that shape the college experience. Although such studies contribute to the knowledge base, it can be exceedingly difficult or, in the case of natural disasters, impossible to control these external influences.

Focus on What Students Do

Robert Pace's (1979, 1990) work on student engagement showed that how students spend their time is highly correlated with the level of their ultimate learning and success. The construct of student engagement underpins the research work of George Kuh and Kay McClenney, authors of survey instruments that measure how students engage (or fail to engage) with the college environment. (Information about these instruments, the National Survey of Student Engagement and the Community College Survey of Student Engagement can be found at http://nsse.iub.edu/index.cfm and www.ccsse .org/index.cfm, respectively.) These efforts are solidly based on research that suggests that the amount of time students spend in educationally meaningful activities is a predictor of their ultimate success in college.

One of the strengths of the student engagement focus is the practice of asking students how they spend their time and how they elect, individually, to engage with the campus. Such evidence has shown wide variability in student engagement on any given campus, making it unclear to what degree engagement is a product of entering student characteristics, peer influence, and institutional policies. Certainly, it is difficult to explain how some students can be marginally engaged in the intellectual life of a campus while making above-average grades and maintaining progress toward degree completion. Other students may find that overinvolvement in certain types of activities can become a detriment to their overall learning and success. Thus, the quality of engagement matters, and, as Kuh and Kinzie argue elsewhere in this volume, institutional expectations for student experiences are an important factor in shaping engagement.

Focus on What Institutions Do

The fourth lens is used to understand the role that institutional policies, structures, and values play in shaping student success. Here the focus is on conditions that are under the direct control of the institution and that could be changed if the institution wished to do so. This lens is truly about putting students at the center of all institutional decisions. It incorporates the lenses described earlier in that the focus is on institutional decisions and actions that document the degree to which an institution accepts the challenges and leverages the opportunities associated with entering student characteristics, external influences, and levels of engagement. An institution's policies, established practices, inventory of programmatic responses, and even the way it organizes itself to address student needs may be the best marker of institutional excellence in putting students first. This focus does not unduly reward institutions that manage simply to recruit the "best" students; rather, it acknowledges the role institutional decisions play in shaping the way students experience college and, to a large extent, how they engage with the institution.

Thus, we argue that this lens provides the best opportunity for transforming the first college year and ensuring student success. As such, this chapter focuses on four areas of institutional effort or control: values and goals, organizing structures, undergraduate teaching, and cocurricular experiences. When institutions make decisions to put students at the center by focusing their energies and efforts in these areas, we believe they have an almost unbeatable formula for student success.

A PHILOSOPHY STATEMENT TO GUIDE INSTITUTIONAL DESIGN OF THE FIRST YEAR

"Historically, the dominant culture of higher education has been to hold students primarily, if not exclusively, responsible for sinking or swimming" (Barefoot et al., 2005, p. 381) especially in the first year of college. In contrast, the first decade of the 21st century has thus far been marked by greater institutional accountability for student success. A growing chorus of national reports and research-based books has called for intentional planning and delivery of the first college year. The 1984 report *Involvement in Learning* by the Study Group on Conditions of Excellence in American Higher Education called for "frontloading" first-year courses with senior faculty to ensure that new students were intentionally given access to an institution's finest professors who otherwise might teach only upper division or graduate courses. The impact of institutional decisions concerning programs, policies, and practices was found to significantly explain student success in a select group of colleges and universities (Kuh, Schuh, Whitt, & Associates, 1991). A similar study, focused on the first year of college (Barefoot et al., 2005), identified 12 core findings revolving around a central idea—that institutions of excellence are intentional about and accept a significant share of the responsibility for the success of new students.

One way to demonstrate that intentionality is to articulate a philosophy or values statement for the first college year. In collaboration with more than 300 colleges and universities, the Policy Center on the First Year of College established an aspirational model for the first year based on nine foundational dimensions. The philosophy is explicit, easily understood, consistent with the institutional mission, and widely disseminated; and, as appropriate, it reflects a consensus of campus constituencies. Further, the philosophy is the basis for first-year organizational policies, practices, structures, leadership, department/unit philosophies, and resource allocation (Policy Center on the First Year of College, 2007).

To date, few institutions have a written, formally approved, and widely disseminated statement of philosophy for the first year. Whereas campuses have established goals for graduates or even goals for the core curriculum, few have established benchmarks for formative assessment—or guidelines for how much progress students are expected to make during the first year of college. In the absence of a clearly established philosophy for the first year, it is difficult for institutions to ensure that their efforts support intended outcomes and to communicate the philosophy to faculty, staff, and students (Swing, 2006).

Because there are few model statements to emulate, the following rubric is proposed as a guide to the key elements that a campus-specific philosophy statement might address. A philosophy statement for the first college year:

- Is intentionally aligned with, and supportive of, the campus mission statement.

- Clearly articulates campus beliefs about the purpose of the first year of college. These purposes might be expressed as hopes, goals, values, or a grand design for student learning and growth during the first year. This is the core message in the philosophy statement and should be written in language that can be easily understood by students and their families, external constituents, and all members of the institution. The philosophy statement covers all aspects of the first year and is not limited to a single program or initiative.

- Focuses on what the institution controls—its design for the first year of college. The purpose of the statement is to articulate the institution's commitment to the desired outcomes of all aspects of the first year—both in and out of the classroom. As such, the philosophy statement "speaks for" the institution rather than for students or others.

- Clearly states why the institution values the purposes made explicit in the philosophy statement—why the stated purposes are a priority for the institution and how they affect its role in society.

- Acknowledges the process of endorsement by the institution and the date of last revision, either in the body or a footnote.

A first-year philosophy statement is not simply the overall campus mission statement that captures the goals of the entire collegiate experience. It is not a list of programs or program goals, a statement of what students will do, an institution's honor code, or the mission statement of a single campus unit, department, or program (Policy Center on the First Year of College, 2007). Rather, it serves as a public declaration and guidepost for institutional decision-making.

Developing a Philosophy Statement for the First College Year

Ideally, a philosophy statement for the first year of college would be developed through open dialogue that involves all stakeholders. There is no single methodology because the development process will reflect differences in campus cultures and organizational structures. No matter what the beginning point is, it is highly unlikely that a small group working in isolation will produce a philosophy statement that will ultimately be widely embraced. Vetting the statement through the institution's formal governance system is a necessary step to ensure wide acceptance for the philosophy statement. Thus, it will be useful to establish the path to final approval (such as votes by disciplinary departments, divisional units, senior campus administrators, committees, and even external governing boards) early in the process.

The development process should also identify specific dissemination strategies. The initial launch of the philosophy statement should probably be greeted with some fanfare—the focus of a campus-wide event or a special publication. However, disseminating the philosophy statement is work that is never finished; it must be communicated each time new students or new employees enter the institution. In addition, to maximize impact, it must be disseminated repeatedly in annual publications, incorporated into the campus strategic plan, and aligned with quality assurance initiatives.

FIRST-YEAR ORGANIZING STRUCTURES

In the literal sense, every new college student has a first-year experience, and every college that enrolls new students delivers a first-year experience. Because it is common knowledge that the first year of college is the time when students are most at risk of failure, it is a rare postsecondary institution that has yet to develop an array of initiatives to improve the success of new students. First-year seminars, orientation programs, and other support services for new students are necessary but insufficient to put students first. Many colleges and universities appear to have collected student support structures through incremental acquisitions that did not include the development of a central coordinating structure. In such an environment there can be considerable redundancy, large numbers of students who are not served, and a great deal of student confusion about how to find help when needed.

The Policy Center on the First Year of College (2005) has proposed that one of the markers of institutional excellence is the effectiveness of a college's first-year organizing structure (FYOS) in weaving together the array of initiatives into a seamless first college year:

> [Such institutions] create organizational structures and policies that provide a comprehensive, integrated, and coordinated approach to the first year. These structures and policies provide oversight and alignment of all first-year efforts. A coherent first-year experience is realized and maintained through effective partnerships among academic affairs, student affairs, and other administrative units and is enhanced by ongoing faculty and staff development activities and appropriate budgetary arrangements.

This statement is clear in describing the intended outcomes of an intentional organizational structure, but it is not specific about the form it should, or could, take. Certainly, no one form of FYOS would fit all sizes and varieties of institutions of higher education. Rather than focus on the design of the structure, the aspirational statement provided by the Policy Center on the First Year of College focuses on the desired outcomes:

- A structure that encourages a comprehensive approach rather than one that focuses on a single problem area or serves only specific populations (e.g., developmental education, persistence, and students from underserved backgrounds)

- An integrated approach that is part of the college's standard operating procedures and not simply added on as an extra layer of administration

- An approach that includes coordinated planning and purposeful communication between all stakeholders

Typology of Organizing Structures

What follows is a typology of FYOS that identifies the major ways that institutions organize and manage the components of their first year of college. Although five levels are presented, in reality, these levels rarely exist as "pure" forms in American higher education. Rather, the reader may wish to think of them as a continuum, with most institutions having some elements across several levels of the typology.

Comprehensive single unit/administrative structure. There is no one name for comprehensive organizing structures, but some are known as "university college," "undergraduate studies division," and "general college." The key feature is not the name but that these administrative units provide campus-wide oversight and alignment of first-year efforts. Such structures may serve students beyond the first year. Some will have responsibilities for general education, interdisciplinary majors, and other services to all undergraduate students. The key distinguishing feature is that a majority of the unit's efforts are focused on most or all of the policies, practices, and programs that define the first year of college. As such, a chief academic affairs officer or chief student affairs office with broad responsibility for all undergraduates would not meet this criterion. To fully meet this defined type, the unit will do the following:

- Appear on the campus's organizational chart as an ongoing, named administrative unit

- Have a chief administrative officer (e.g., a director, dean, or associate vice president) with line authority for the unit's personnel and functions

- Be responsible for one or more components of both the curriculum and cocurriculum (it may have faculty lines or may coordinate curriculum matters without its own faculty)

- Have a recurring operational budget

Single unit/administrative structure. A single unit/administrative structure meeting some but not all of these conditions may exist but have a more limited scope. Centers variously named Office of the Dean of Freshmen, Office of the Dean of Undergraduate Studies, or Center for First-Year Students may describe administrative structures that focus exclusively on academic affairs or student affairs functions or otherwise fail to be comprehensive in scope.

Formal coordinating body. A standing committee with campus-wide institutional authority for oversight of a broad range of first-year initiatives is an example of a formal coordinating body used as the FYOS. These committees may be appointed by senior campus leaders or through a faculty governance structure. They may be freestanding committees or a subcommittee of a larger governance structure. The distinguishing feature is that they have institutional authority, not just an advisory role, to oversee elements of the first year. Most do not provide daily administrative leadership for any component of the first year. A single-focus committee, such as a "retention committee" or "advising committee," would not meet this criterion.

Multiple administrative structures. In the absence of a single coordinating structure, two or more units may work together to provide comprehensive oversight of the first year. Through voluntary cooperation, these units—each with sole responsibility for one or more elements of the first year (policies, practices, or programs)—provide a coordinated approach to the first college year. Key to this configuration is the existence of an effective structure for the multiple administrative units to regularly communicate. Through communication and strategic planning, the net effort of the individual units is greater than what would be realized by the units working independently.

Discrete structures. The lowest level of FYOS is the use of discrete structures that individually provide oversight for distinct aspects of the first year (such as retention, orientation, advising, and first-year seminars) with little or no coordination between them. Although each may be highly effective at managing one or more elements of the first year as an independent unit, there is no formal structure for communication and cooperation between the units. Nonetheless, discrete structures may provide an effective FYOS, but such arrangements are more frequently noted for being distracted by competition for resources and disagreements about the scope of each unit's authority. Although such a scenario is clearly not an ideal arrangement, it remains a common institutional response for organizing the first college year.

Putting Students First Includes Attention to Organizational Structures

On some campuses the formal or informal name of the first-year seminar is the First-Year Experience course. It is unfortunate that some educators have come to think of the first-year experience as a single course rather than to develop a more expansive view of the entire new student experience—ranging from recruiting to admissions to orientation and continuing both in and out of the classroom until a student has earned standing as a sophomore. Certainly one's understanding of the scope and complexity of the first year would shape opinion about the need for a coordinated FYOS.

When one views first-year approaches broadly, as we have, the advantages arising from institutional investment in both direct services to students and administrative structures to manage and coordinate the institution's vision for the first year are easily seen. Plainly stated, investing in services for first-year students signals an institution's commitment to student success, but investing in both services and institutional coordination for all services that affect the growth and learning of new students is the gold standard for putting students first.

INSTITUTIONAL SUPPORT FOR IMPROVED UNDERGRADUATE TEACHING

Although students spend comparatively little of their time in the classroom, the quality of teaching and learning that takes place within higher education settings is a critical factor in student success. Moreover, the delivery of high-quality teaching and learning experiences is one aspect of the first-year experience that is completely within the institution's control. Whether or not it is fully articulated, the issue of undergraduate instruction should be a central component of an institution's first-year philosophy.

As noted earlier, the increasing focus on the first year stems from several reports released in the mid-1980s that underscored the need for greater student involvement in learning, more coherence in the undergraduate curriculum, and increased assessment of student learning. In response to these reports, Chickering and Gamson (1987) articulated the now classic "Seven Principles for Good Practice in Undergraduate Education," which emphasized, among other things, increased contact between students and teachers, opportunities for active learning, prompt feedback, and increased time on task. Since that time, institutions have explored and adopted a number of initiatives, particularly in the first college year, that respond to the criticisms of undergraduate education and enact many of the principles espoused by Chickering and Gamson. Learning communities and first-year seminars are discussed in greater depth in this section because they represent two surprisingly flexible and effective strategies for improving the quality of undergraduate instruction that emerged in response to these calls for reform.

Learning Communities

Barefoot (2002) reports that learning communities have become fairly common on college campuses, with 62% of institutions offering some type of learning community. These curricular structures "link together courses or course work so that students find greater coherence in what they are learning as well as increased intellectual interaction with faculty and fellow students" (Gabelnick, MacGregor, Matthews, & Smith, 1990, p. 5). As such, these communities can take a variety of forms, from loose configurations of classes that enroll common cohorts of students to fully integrated and team-taught thematic course clusters. Goodsell Love and Tokuno (1999) identify five dimensions that are necessary for a successful learning community: student collaboration, faculty collaboration, curriculum coordination, shared setting, and interactive pedagogy. These factors exist along a continuum in individual learning communities, but the authors suggest that the benefits to students increase as learning communities become more developed along each of these dimensions. At the same time, more complex learning community structures demand greater institutional and individual resources in terms of scheduling, course planning and development, and knowledge of engaging pedagogies.

Students who participate in learning communities accrue several benefits, most notably improved retention rates and academic performance. By bringing small groups of students together with one or two faculty members, learning communities also offer new students social supports that help them make a successful transition to college. For example, Crissman (2001) found that first-year students participating in clustered courses experienced greater peer support, had more contact with faculty outside class, and were more satisfied with their faculty contacts than students in nonclustered courses. Participation in learning communities may also help students develop skills essential to academic success. Walker's (2003) research on first-year learning communities suggests that participation in clustered courses has a significant and positive impact on four cognitive outcomes: critical thinking, problem solving, reading skills, and writing skills.

Although the benefits of learning communities for students are clear, some institutions experience difficulty recruiting faculty for and retaining faculty in learning community courses, especially when the institution expects a high level of curricular integration or interactive pedagogy. Integration and team teaching simply take more time than traditional course preparation, and some faculty may be uncomfortable with a course design that requires them to teach content outside their discipline. Yet once faculty work through this initial resistance, they may find learning community work to be an invigorating teaching experience. Faculty at Indiana University–Purdue University Indianapolis expressed enthusiasm for participating in thematic learning communities (TLCs), enjoyed interacting with faculty outside their disciplines, and appreciated having the opportunity to get to know students better (MacKinnon, 2006). Still, they acknowledged that "time [was] needed to develop the common theme, to foster the interdisciplinary dialogue that enriches the TLCs, and to interact in one another's classes" (MacKinnon, 2006, p. 11). To meet these additional demands, institutions should offer faculty added compensation in the form of a stipend, course credit, or release time.

The nature of a learning community demands a different approach to teaching. Although some learning community courses may include lectures, overall they emphasize more interactive and student-centered pedagogies. Faculty may need additional training or support to learn and adopt new teaching strategies and to design a course plan that maximizes these strategies. Training and planning workshops can happen outside the term in which the learning community is offered, but faculty members also need a centrally identified source of support for challenges and issues that may arise after the training. So in addition to annual or semiannual workshops, institutions need to investigate and offer a variety of programs designed to support innovative pedagogies.

Finally, we need to remember that sustained learning community efforts do not arise from faculty initiatives. Although an interested and committed group of faculty may develop and participate in learning community pilots, learning communities cannot ultimately be sustained by faculty alone because they span academic departments and institutional units. Institutions must intentionally design structures to support learning community initiatives. A centralized unit for faculty development is one such structure. Other structures may require making changes to the master schedule of courses to allow for learning community courses to be cross-listed in multiple departments or to allow for extended blocks of class time for learning community courses. Similarly, the registrar's office may need to modify computerized registration processes to allow students to register for a learning community rather than individual courses. Additional and different kinds of classroom space may also be needed to accommodate learning community programs. For example, large theater-style classrooms with rows of fixed seating may not be conducive to the kinds of engaging pedagogies practiced in learning communities. Institutions with highly formalized FYOS may be better equipped to respond to these issues.

First-Year Seminars

Although courses designed to acclimate students to the first college year are more than a century old, the modern seminar emerged in response to student protests at the University of South Carolina in the early 1970s. Early assessment of the course demonstrated its effectiveness in retaining students, improving academic performance, and increasing persistence to graduation (Fidler, 1991; Shanley & Witten, 1990). In the mid-1980s, as campuses looked for ways to improve the undergraduate experience in general and the first college year in particular, they began to adopt the first-year seminar model. In 2002, Barefoot reported that nearly all campuses (94.1%) had some type of first-year seminar course. Like learning communities, first-year seminars encompass several different approaches. Since 1991, the National Resource Center for The First-Year Experience and Students in Transition has attempted to identify the prevalence of the different types of seminars on American campuses. Clearly, the extended orientation seminar (a college survival or success course that focuses on an introduction to campus resources, time management, academic and career planning, learning strategies, and student development issues) has been the most commonly reported type by respondents to surveys from 1991 to 2003, with nearly two-thirds of campuses offering this type of course (Tobolowsky, 2005). During that same time period, the number of institutions reporting that they offer academic seminars (interdisciplinary or theme-based courses focusing on a theme or disciplinary knowledge and the development of academic skills such as critical thinking and expository writing) increased from 19.1% of respondents of the 1991 survey to 51.4% of respondents of the 2003 survey (Tobolowsky, 2005).

The three most frequently reported goals for first-year seminars for all institutions are developing academic skills, orienting students to campus resources and services, and encouraging self-exploration and personal development. Extended orientation courses most frequently report as course goals orientation to campus resources and services, development of academic skills, and development of a support network; whereas academic seminars report developing academic skills, creating a common experience for first-year students, and increasing student-faculty interaction as the most important course goals (Tobolowsky, 2005). First-year seminars have been linked to a wide range of outcomes, including improved academic performance and retention, increased persistence to graduation, greater satisfaction with the college or university experience, greater feelings of academic and social integration, and increased feelings of academic competence (Barefoot, 1993; Barefoot, Warnock, Dickinson, Richardson, & Roberts, 1998; Davis, 1992; Fidler, 1991; Fidler & Moore, 1996; Shanley & Witten, 1990; Tobolowsky, Cox, & Wagner, 2005).

The nature of the seminar makes it a unique setting for learning. For example, most seminars enroll no more than 20 students per section, allowing for more interactive pedagogies. Further, although many first-year seminars have specific disciplinary or thematic content (i.e., a learning product), all seminars also focus on learning process as evidenced by the most commonly reported course topics: study skills, campus resources, time management, academic planning/advising, and critical thinking (Tobolowsky, 2005). This focus on process outcomes in addition to (or in some cases, instead of) product outcomes may create a more dynamic learning environment for students. It certainly demands a different approach to teaching the course. These process outcomes, particularly as they relate to academic planning and development, are also highly personal, meaning that the curriculum of the first-year seminar seems more relevant to students than what they are studying in other courses. Academic-themed seminars give faculty the opportunity to develop courses that explore areas of interest in the discipline that may not fit neatly into other departmental offerings or programs of studies. In other words, the first-year seminar may give faculty a space for experimentation and innovation that offers students a highly engaging learning experience early in their careers.

Although the process goals of the seminar may make it more appealing to students, faculty may resist teaching the seminar for this very reason. The lack of a "true" curriculum or disciplinary focus may be troubling to them. This may be particularly problematic if faculty are reluctant volunteers to fill a departmental obligation to the course or if teaching in the seminar will not figure favorably in tenure and promotion decisions. Yet several studies have demonstrated the potential benefits for faculty who teach in first-year seminars, including changes in teaching approaches in other courses and better attitudes toward and understanding of first-year students, suggesting that faculty who have taught first-year seminars may be better and more willing advisors and mentors to students outside the classroom. Also, faculty report feelings of enhanced collegiality, often associated with participation in training workshops that expose them to other colleagues on campus who share similar research interests and concerns (Fidler, Neururer-Rotholz, & Richardson, 1999; Wanca-Thibault, Shepherd, & Staley, 2002).

What These Structures Tell Us About All Undergraduate Instruction

Learning communities and first-year seminars work for several reasons, and institutions can draw from them important lessons that can be applied to the whole of undergraduate instruction.

Size matters. First-year seminars and learning communities bring students together in smaller groups that allow for greater interaction between students and between faculty members and students. Tutorials and discussion groups attached to large lecture courses can perform a similar function, increasing students' level of engagement in what might otherwise be an anonymous learning environment.

Process learning goals are important. We no longer have the luxury of assuming that all college graduates—or even all students majoring in a particular discipline—will have been exposed to, and to some extent mastered, a discrete body of knowledge. Knowledge is changing and expanding too rapidly for specific content goals to have meaning. What has become increasingly important is helping students master processes—for finding and synthesizing information, evaluating claims, and applying concepts to real-world problems. Such process-oriented goals demand interdisciplinary and integrated learning environments, much like those we see in certain kinds of first-year seminars and in thematic learning communities.

Good teachers develop within a community of colleagues. Like learning communities, the first-year seminar is team taught on many campuses. Team-teaching structures expose faculty members to new strategies and ways of thinking about classroom instruction. Faculty may also be energized by looking at their own areas of interest through the lens of another discipline. Although team teaching may not be feasible for all courses, institutions can encourage collegiality by promoting cross-departmental peer observations, offering opportunities for informal discussions about teaching strategies (such as monthly brown-bag luncheons), or developing a campus-wide newsletter focused on promising classroom practices.

Good teaching is intentional; it doesn't just happen. Institutions cannot expect faculty members who have been trained as researchers and content specialists to automatically know and adopt active learning strategies in their classrooms. Because the structure of first-year seminars and learning communities demands engaging pedagogies (rather than more passive strategies, as lectures do), coordinators of these programs frequently offer training workshops and ongoing support for their faculty. Similarly, if institutions expect faculty to adopt and master innovative pedagogies, they must provide opportunities for faculty to be exposed to, practice, and evaluate the effectiveness of such strategies. Finally, institutions are more likely to excel in areas of high value because these areas receive attention, resources, and support. If institutions hope to excel in undergraduate instruction, that instruction must be highly valued not only in terms of funding but in terms of the faculty rewards structure.

OPPORTUNITIES FOR OUT-OF-CLASS LEARNING

Students spend little time in the physical space of the classroom and engaged in activities connected to the formal curriculum. If institutions want to truly maximize learning and success, they need to structure opportunities for learning that are aligned with, but sometimes outside, these spaces. Moreover, faculty expectations for the amount of time students will spend studying and preparing for class are frequently out of step with the reality of most students' actual work habits. In part, the disparity between faculty expectations and student performance may reflect a disconnect between faculty and student perceptions of what it takes to succeed in college. However, many students may simply be unable to devote two to three hours per week for every in-class hour because of employment or family obligations. Thus, if students are to increase their time on task in regard to learning outcomes, institutions need to intentionally create opportunities beyond required readings, problem sets, and essays connected to the traditional curriculum.

Traditional extracurricular activities (e.g., membership in Greek organizations or other student groups and leadership in student government) have often been seen as distractions to an institution's learning mission. Yet Whipple (1996) suggests the primary objectives of traditional cocurricular programs are "to enhance learning outside the classroom, provide for relationship and community building . . . and promote a value-based developmental experience" (p. 303). As such, involvement in cocurricular activities increases students' satisfaction with their overall academic experience, leads to greater academic success, and increases persistence (Berger & Milem, 1999; Peltier, Laden, & Matranga, 1999). In the mid-1990s involvement in these more traditional activities began to decline, and students became more engaged in academic clubs, service experiences, undergraduate research, and internship and co-op experiences (Kuh, Douglas, Lund, & Ramin-Gyurnek, 1994). The shift in student involvement patterns provides institutions with an opportunity to intentionally design cocurricular experiences that more clearly support student learning.

Yet extending learning opportunities beyond the classroom calls into question traditional definitions of teaching and learning. For example, in *Learning Reconsidered*, Keeling (2004) suggests that "educational practice has . . . emphasized information transfer without a great deal of thought given to the meaning, pertinence, or application of the information to students' lives" (p. 9). Rather, he argues that our approach to education can no longer look at learning and psychosocial development as separate and distinct processes. We must broaden our definition of learning to account for how learning and development interact and "shape each other" (p. 8). When we expand our current definition of learning, we move beyond a notion of mastery of a core set of concepts or disciplinary knowledge to encompass outcomes such as cognitive complexity, knowledge acquisition, integration and application, humanitarianism, civic engagement, interpersonal and intrapersonal competence, and practical competence. Although certain kinds of classroom-based experiences may increase cognitive complexity, these other outcomes are more frequently achieved outside the classroom. For example, involvement in living-learning communities (which may or may not include connections to the formal curriculum) leads to increases in cognitive complexity and knowledge acquisition and application. Service-learning experiences lead to gains in knowledge acquisition and application, humanitarianism, and civic engagement (Keeling, 2004).

Expanding our definition of learning may also necessitate redefining what we mean by teaching and who the teachers are on our campuses. Institutions need to empower a wide range of community members, including other students, to be educators. Although such a redefinition might lead to classroom-based instructional teams that link faculty, advisors, librarians, and students, it would also acknowledge the educational potential of staff in the financial aid office, cafeteria workers, and housekeepers in the residence halls. More formally, it vests responsibility for education with advisors to student organizations, residence hall coordinators, and students. By recognizing the potential of all members of the campus community to be teachers, educational opportunities are necessarily extended beyond the physical space of the classroom. The upshot is that institutions must be intentional about designing cocurricular learning environments rather than relying on students to make the "right" decisions about how to spend their time outside class.

Some opportunities for out-of-class learning can and should be grounded in the curriculum. Service-learning and undergraduate research opportunities are two examples of such structures. In a pilot study of the Your First College Year Survey (Vogelgesang, Ikeda, Gilmartin, & Keup, 2002), more than half the students responding indicated that they had performed some service work in their first year of college. However, less than one-quarter of students reported involvement in course-based service. Students involved in course-based service were more satisfied with their level of faculty contact, opportunities for leadership, and their sense of community with other students than those who had no service experience. In general, involvement in community service (whether or not it was related to a course) enhanced students' feelings of personal success in such areas as establishing relationships with faculty or staff, making friends, and developing effective study skills. Students who were involved in service experiences were also more likely to be retained to the sophomore year (Vogelgesang et al., 2002). Although involvement in generic service experiences accrues several benefits to students, Paul (2006) suggests that traditional service-learning pedagogy and direct service experiences frequently do not afford students the opportunity to use "higher-order academic skills . . . because they are typically unaccompanied by faculty . . . [and] miss the benefit of direct faculty role-modeling and engagement" (p. 13). Faculty should assume lead teaching roles in such settings, but they aren't the only teachers. Community partners and those served by local agencies are also powerful educators as students attempt to apply neat classroom concepts to messy social problems.

Similarly, undergraduate research teams led by faculty mentors would work together to design methodologies and test theories, educating each other about the research question and methods in the process. Although many institutions are beginning to explore the concept of undergraduate research experiences, these efforts most frequently involve upper level students and are likely to be capstone experiences for the major. First-year students may be less cognitively ready than upper level students to take on the demands of scholarly research. But with the assistance of a faculty member, who helps the student not only see but also inhabit the process of knowledge construction, students may be able to move beyond more dualistic ways of thinking. Such experiences would need to be carefully designed, but undergraduate research projects in some form could appear across all disciplines and at all stages of the undergraduate experience. They need not be reserved as a capstone experience.

CONCLUSION

In this chapter we have focused on putting first-year students first—not because sophomores, juniors, and seniors deserve any less attention, but because the foundation of the entire undergraduate experience is built from each student's early collegiate experiences. Simply put, institutional decisions and actions are critically important in shaping student expectations about college and that in turn significantly shapes the way students approach higher education. Research has shown, for example, that the allotment of time students give to studying is established in the first year and remains amazingly stable across the undergraduate years (Schilling & Schilling, 1999). Other research has established that most of the gain in critical thinking skills occurs in the first year of college (Pascarella & Terenzini, 2005). The evidence is clear that the first year of college is foundational to the achievement of many of the goals colleges and universities hold for their graduates.

We hope readers have recognized the central theme of this chapter: It matters what institutions do. Perhaps the greatest achievement of the first-year movement, begun at the University of South Carolina, is to increase institutional accountability for student success. Over the past three decades, institutional quality has increasingly been measured by the amount students learn and grow during the college years. Pride in student success has replaced the misguided notion that student failure is a marker of institutional quality. Focusing on new students has shown that wide access to higher education does not necessitate lowering standards or reducing our expectations for what graduates know and can do.

There is no shortage of proven strategies for increasing the success of college students. Certainly, undergraduate pedagogies, first-year seminars, learning communities, out-of-class learning opportunities, institutional policies and practices, and other initiatives that support student success will continue to evolve. The greatest challenge in putting first-year students first is not designing new educational arrangements but rather in intentionally aligning and coordinating institutional decisions with what is already known about the conditions that increase student success. It is simply not enough to only "teach the best" or to rely on the principle that a nation's best students will rise to the top on their own. What matters most is the intentional alignment of institutional decisions, policies, and practices to ensure that all new students build a solid foundation for their success in college and in life after college.

REFERENCES

ACT. (2006a). *National collegiate retention and persistence to degree rates.* Retrieved June 29, 2007, from www.act.org/path/policy/pdf/retain_2006.pdf

ACT. (2006b). *Trends: 1983–2006.* Retrieved June 29, 2007, from www.act.org/path/policy/pdf/retain_trends.pdf

Barefoot, B. O. (Ed.). (1993). *Exploring the evidence: Reporting outcomes of freshman seminars* (Monograph No. 11). Columbia, SC: University of South Carolina, National Resource Center for The First-Year Experience and Students in Transition.

Barefoot, B. O. (2002). *Second national survey of first-year academic practices.* Brevard, NC: Policy Center on the First Year of College.

Barefoot, B. O., Gardner, J. N., Cutright, M., Morris, L. V., Schroeder, C. C., Schwartz, S. W., et al. (2005). *Achieving and sustaining institutional excellence for the first year of college.* San Francisco, CA: Jossey-Bass.

Barefoot, B. O., Warnock, C. L., Dickinson, M. P., Richardson, S. E., & Roberts, M. R. (Eds.). (1998). *Exploring the evidence: Reporting outcomes of first-year seminars, Vol. II* (Monograph No. 25). Columbia, SC: University of South Carolina, National Resource Center for The First-Year Experience and Students in Transition.

Berger, J. B., & Milem, J. F. (1999, December). The role of student involvement and perceptions of integration in a causal model of student persistence. *Research in Higher Education, 40*(6), 641–664.

Chickering, A. W., & Gamson, Z. F. (1987, June). Seven principles for good practice in undergraduate education. *AAHE Bulletin, 39*(7), 3–7.

Crissman, J. L. (2001). Clustered and nonclustered first-year seminars: New students' first-semester experiences. *Journal of The First-Year Experience and Students in Transition, 13*(1), 69–88.

Davis, B. O., Jr. (1992). Freshman seminar: A broad spectrum of effectiveness. *Journal of The Freshman Year Experience, 4*(1), 79–94.

Fidler, P. P. (1991). Relationship of freshman orientation seminars to sophomore return rates. *Journal of The Freshman Year Experience, 3*(1), 7–38.

Fidler, P. P., & Moore, P. S. (1996). A comparison of effects of campus residence and freshman seminar attendance on freshman dropout rates. *Journal of The Freshman Year Experience and Students in Transition, 8*(2), 7–16.

Fidler, P. P., Neururer-Rotholz, J., & Richardson, S. (1999). Teaching the freshman seminar: Its effectiveness in promoting faculty development. *Journal of The First-Year Experience and Students in Transition, 11*(2), 59–74.

Gabelnick, F., MacGregor, J., Matthews, R. S., & Smith, B. L. (Eds.). (1990). *New directions for teaching and learning: No. 41. Learning communities: Creating connections among students, faculty, and disciplines.* San Francisco, CA: Jossey-Bass.

Goodsell Love, A., & Tokuno, K. A. (1999). Learning community models. In J. H. Levine (Ed.), *Learning communities: New structures, new partnerships for learning* (Monograph No. 26, pp. 9–17). Columbia, SC: University of South Carolina, National Resource Center for The First-Year Experience and Students in Transition.

Higher Education Research Institute. (n.d.). *The freshman survey.* Retrieved June 29, 2007, from www.gseis.ucla.edu/heri/freshman.html

Keeling, R. P. (Ed.). (2004). *Learning reconsidered 1: A campus-wide focus on the student experience.* Washington, DC: American College Personnel Association & National Association of Student Personnel Administrators.

Keup, J. R., & Stolzenberg, E. B. (2004). *The 2003 Your First College Year (YFCY) Survey: Exploring the academic and personal experiences of first-year students* (Monograph No. 40). Columbia, SC: University of South Carolina, National Resource Center for The First-Year Experience and Students in Transition.

Kuh, G. D., Douglas, K. B., Lund, J. P., & Ramin-Gyurnek, J. (1994). *Student learning outside the classroom: Transcending artificial boundaries* (ASHE-ERIC Higher Education Report No. 8). Washington, DC: The George Washington University, School of Education and Human Development.

Kuh, G. D., Schuh, J. H., Whitt, E. J., & Associates. (1991). *Involving colleges: Successful approaches to fostering student learning and development outside the classroom.* San Francisco, CA: Jossey-Bass.

MacKinnon, J. L. (2006, May/June). Assessment of thematic learning community pilots at Indiana University–Purdue University Indianapolis. *Assessment Update, 18*(3), 11.

Pace, C. R. (1979). *Measuring outcomes of college: Fifty years of findings and recommendations for the future.* San Francisco, CA: Jossey-Bass.

Pace, C. R. (1990). *The undergraduates: A report of their activities and progress in college in the 1980s.* Los Angeles, CA: University of California–Los Angeles, Center for the Study of Evaluation.

Pascarella, E. T., & Terenzini, P. T. (2005). *How college affects students: A third decade of research.* San Francisco, CA: Jossey-Bass.

Paul, E. L. (2006, Winter). Community-based research as scientific and civic pedagogy. *Peer Review, 8*(1), 12–15.

Peltier, G. L., Laden, R., & Matranga, M. (1999). Student persistence in college: A review of research. *Journal of College Student Retention, 1*(4), 357–375.

Policy Center on the First Year of College. (2005). *Foundations of excellence.* Retrieved June 29, 2007, from www.fyfoundations.org/4year.aspx

Policy Center on the First Year of College. (2007). *Campus philosophy statement about the first year of college.* Retrieved June 29, 2007, from www.fyfoundations.org/doc.aspx?id=167

Schilling, K. M., & Schilling, K. L. (1999, May/June). Increasing expectations for student effort. *About Campus, 4*(2), 4–10.

Shanley, M. G., & Witten, C. H. (1990, Summer). University 101 freshman seminar course: A longitudinal study of persistence, retention, and graduation rates. *NASPA Journal, 27*(4), 344–352.

Study Group on Conditions of Excellence in American Higher Education. (1984). *Involvement in learning: Realizing the potential of American higher education.* Washington, DC: U.S. Department of Education.

Swing, R. L. (2006). Constructing a philosophy for achieving institutional excellence in the first college year. *Journal of the Liberal and General Education Society of Japan, 28*(1), 84–91.

Tobolowsky, B. F. (2005). *The 2003 national survey of first-year seminars: Continuing innovations in the collegiate curriculum* (Monograph No. 41). Columbia, SC: University of South Carolina, National Resource Center for The First-Year Experience and Students in Transition.

Tobolowsky, B. F., Cox, B. E., & Wagner, M. T. (Eds.). (2005). *Exploring the evidence, volume III: Reporting research on first-year seminars* (Monograph No. 42). Columbia, SC: University of South Carolina, National Resource Center for The First-Year Experience and Students in Transition.

Vogelgesang, L. J., Ikeda, E. K., Gilmartin, S. K., & Keup, J. R. (2002). Service-learning and the first-year experience: Outcomes related to learning and persistence. In E. Zlotkowski (Ed.), *Service-learning and the first-year experience: Preparing students for personal success and civic responsibility* (Monograph No. 34, pp. 15–26). Columbia, SC: University of South Carolina, National Resource Center for The First-Year Experience and Students in Transition.

Walker, A. A. (2003). Learning communities and their effect on students' cognitive abilities. *Journal of The First-Year Experience and Students in Transition, 15*(2), 11–33.

Wanca-Thibault, M., Shepherd, M., & Staley, C. (2002). Personal, professional, and political effects of teaching a first-year seminar: A faculty census. *Journal of The First-Year Experience and Students in Transition, 14*(1), 23–40.

Whipple, E. G. (1996). Student activities. In A. L. Rentz & Associates (Eds.), *Student affairs practice in higher education* (2nd. ed., pp. 298–333). Springfield, IL: Charles C. Thomas.

18 | ACHIEVING STUDENT SUCCESS IN TWO-YEAR COLLEGES

Margaret C. King and Rusty N. Fox

Putting students first certainly seems like a respectable goal. Who could possibly be opposed to designing, defining, and aligning campus services with students as the first priority in mind? We have all participated in campus conversations that touch on this issue. However, many of us have only begun to focus on this issue on our own campuses. Why is that? If we value the concept of putting students first, why is the practice not more widespread in our daily interactions with students? This question serves as a catalyst to assist us in the exploration of this issue of putting students first in two-year colleges and the impact this practice has on student services.

KNOWING OUR STUDENTS

Putting students first at the community college requires knowing our students well. This includes understanding their needs and their goals.

Today's Community College Students

The circumstances and decisions that lead students to community colleges today are not necessarily the same as those that brought them in the past. Soaring tuition rates and other financial increases at universities have caused students who typically might have gone away to college to instead choose to stay near home and attend their local community college. However, an increasing number of students are attending community colleges and still "going away," traveling a few hours from home for the college experience. Cheryl Sparks (2006), president of Howard College, has suggested that often such students are seeking a university-style experience. But community colleges often lack the needed facilities, personnel, programming, and resources to fully address students' needs. For example, many rural community colleges are facing housing shortages as well as the need for more social events and more education for students about successful life on a college campus. Many urban community colleges face a growing traditional-age population that looks to the community college to provide social interaction and even entertainment. Such challenges have caused community colleges to band together to explore resources, ideas, and solutions. Organizations like the Rural Community College Alliance (www.ruralcommunitycolleges.org) show the usefulness of collaboration. The group's Rural Community College Initiative explores issues of economic development and access. These organizations address the challenges that colleges face when local economies decline.

Unlike the student bodies of most four-year institutions, a cohort of community college students may include students from several generations. Lancaster and Stillman (2002) define the four generations likely to be found on a community college campus: traditionalists (born 1934–1945); baby boomers (born 1946–1964); Generation Xers (born 1965–1980); and Generation Y/millennials (born 1981–2000). Each generation brings its own set of values, beliefs, life experiences, expectations, and attitudes to college.

There are other developments in community colleges: Women now outnumber men, more students attend part-time, the student body is more diverse, many more students commute to college, and approximately 6% of students have some kind of disability. Family stability is decreasing, with more students coming from families characterized by physical violence, sexual abuse, and alcohol and drug abuse. Students may have relationship problems, low self-esteem, physical ailments such as eating disorders and substance abuse, and psychological illnesses. More of today's students require remediation in reading, writing, and math (Upcraft & Stephens, 2000). The Community College Survey of Student Engagement (CCSSE, 2003a) found that out of a typical community college class of 100 students, almost 64 are part-time students with full lives outside college, approximately 59 are women, and about 61 are listed as white. Community college students increasingly come from single-parent homes, are first-generation Americans, and are first-generation college students.

Understanding Community College Students' Needs and Goals

Nearly half of all students who begin their education at a community college fail to earn a degree from *any* higher education institution within a six-year period. The reasons vary: some students don't have the motivation for college-level work; some students have too many competing responsibilities; in some cases, the institution may not be providing sufficient academic and social support services for certain students to achieve their goal. A recent report from MDRC (Gardenhire-Crooks, Collado, & Ray, 2006) questions who needs what services and notes:

> Subgroups, such as parents, full-time workers, older returning students, or younger students coming directly from high school, likely engage in college in ways different from one another. This suggests that there is no one recipe for success. Students need different sets of services at different points in their lives. (p. 40)

A CCSSE (2003b) survey considers some of the risk factors that impact retention and undergraduate success. These include academic underpreparedness (such as not having graduated from high school or needing remedial education), status as a single parent, financial independence (i.e., students who do not receive assistance for educational costs), child care responsibilities, employment in excess of 30 hours per week, status as a first-generation college student, and part-time student status.

The four guiding tenets of the 2003 educational reauthorization congressional committee meetings—accessibility, accountability, affordability, and quality—illustrate the broad range of needs that educational institutions, and community colleges in particular, are asked to address (Committee on Education and the Workforce, 2003). Consider just the first two: accessibility and accountability. Community colleges face the challenge of trying to ensure one and yet not interfere with the other in the process. For example, open-door admissions policies and nationwide initiatives to leave no student behind mean that community colleges are working with more underprepared students than ever. At the same time, accrediting bodies and taxpayers alike are requiring increased accountability, applicability of learning, and measurable outcomes. Community colleges are attempting to address greater needs in greater numbers, with the expectation they will demonstrate greater outcomes while doing so.

IMPROVING STUDENT SERVICES

Once an institution understands its students' characteristics, needs, and expectations, it may find it necessary to alter student services in a way that will put students first and engage students more in their learning. For many institutions, the overall organization of those services is being reviewed. According to Sandeen and Barr (2006):

> How student affairs is organized on the campus is an important issue facing the student affairs profession in 2006, as competition for resources becomes more intense, as expectations from students for service increase, as greater public scrutiny is given to what students are actually learning, and as technology continues to change the way education is delivered. The issue is important as well because the effectiveness of the student affairs organization on the campus affects the quality of students' educational experiences. (p. 30)

In focusing on the organization of student services, Kramer (2003) stresses the importance of an "interconnected, collaborative system of services that support student development and success" (p. xi) and notes that student academic services are directly connected to the academic purposes of the institution. Kramer (pp. xiv–xv) poses several questions institutions can consider as they look to improve their student services:

1. How prepared are students for learning, and what academic support and services do they need?

2. How should students' readiness needs be addressed within the institutional environment?

3. At what point are students vulnerable to failure, and how should student academic services rally to support student development, growth, retention, and achievement?

4. What is meant by the student-centric view (versus the department-centric view), and how can being student-centered lead to the creation of a seamless, integrated, horizontal, and collaborative student academic services environment?

5. How do we know that students are engaged in the learning process, are receiving the support they need, and are making progress?

6. What delivery model(s) work best for a given institution or mission? Where are the successful programs, and what critical success factors drive these best practices? What metrics do they employ?

7. What is meant by managing and ensuring a collaborative student academic services enterprise?

8. Are standards for student services clearly defined? Who sets them, what should they be, and do they map to the campus culture?

9. How should existing and natural connections be managed among the various student academic services to ensure a maximally, personally, and coherently responsive system to address student needs, learning, and satisfaction?

10. What are the training issues involved in motivating and coordinating the work of service providers as they seek to deliver timely, comprehensive, and accurate academic services to students?

Student services is not necessarily a business-based concept. When dealing with placement scores, maximum hours, academic suspension, and a host of other daily issues, the "customer" is not always right. Often in the best interest of the "customer," we must present bad news or even say no. However, quality student service usually says, "No, but . . ." Our services involve action beyond the initial interaction, or "service after the sale." Those after-sale services often include centralized advising and student development services, smaller classrooms, teaching faculty, increased writing, math and science labs, additional tutoring, and faculty mentoring. Most community colleges have an enrollment services or retention office or at least have these services as goals. Brand-new freshmen, apprehensive returning adults, and discerning older adults are funneled through student-centered services designed to make students feel welcome, assess their skill levels, and address their needs.

Among other community colleges that could be cited here, Cuyamaca College consolidated more than a dozen student services and created a shopping mall experience when it implemented its one-stop center in 2003. Cuyamaca wanted students who might have been away from higher education for many years to see the services available to them. Situated in a three-building complex built around a courtyard, the center is strategically and conveniently located at the entrance to the campus; the buildings are the first ones seen by prospective students. Since the center opened, enrollment has increased 20%. New class offerings and improved educational programs have contributed to the increase in enrollment, but the one-stop center is considered to be partly responsible for the growth (Klein, 2006).

Anne Arundel Community College (AACC) has also experienced significant growth in recent years as well as improvements in its retention rate.

AACC has implemented a new student system, created a one-stop portal, and developed a one-stop center, which is located in a $9 million student center featuring an inviting 60-foot atrium. Students use the portal for self-service transactions and take advantage of e-advising to communicate with their advisors and develop an education plan. When they want personal service, they can go to the convenient one-stop center, where staff can access all the information necessary to provide students with immediate and accurate responses. Approximately 80% of students enroll online, and 20% enroll in person. AACC credits the one-stop center for contributing to its enrollment growth and improved retention rate (Klein, 2006).

The commitment of Estrella Mountain Community College (EMCC) is evidenced by its service motto: "Your Success Is Our Success." The Arizona college's student services office has its own mission statement: "Student Services delivers comprehensive services to all students and provides a caring environment that supports academic and personal success" (EMCC, 2007).

Through their one-stop student services, EMCC student services staff members carry out this mission by performing the following functions:

- Assisting prospective and current students by evaluating transfer credit, interpreting placement test scores, scheduling and sequencing classes, providing educational planning for certificate and degree requirements, assisting with financial aid, and providing veteran services

- Helping students create their educational plans and goals and revisiting these plans on an ongoing basis to keep students on track

- Helping students navigate print and online materials by serving as a resource about institutional policies, procedures, programs, and resources

- Recommending changes to institutional policy and practice based on what they see and hear from students

The EMCC web site includes an email link to contact a member of the one-stop student services staff and the direct telephone number for each member of the staff. With technology embedded throughout the college for teaching and learning and for the administrative infrastructure, students have come to expect that technology will support their college experience (Oblinger, 2006).

Conceptual Changes

A study of six community colleges in Florida by the Community College Research Center (Jenkins, 2006) focused on institutional effectiveness and examined community college management practices that promote student success. Results showed that institutions that focused on student retention and outcomes, not just on enrollment, were far more successful. According to the study:

> [The most effective institution] established a standing retention committee, increased its research on student outcomes, and launched its own student success services program that uses the colleges' student information system to identify students who are struggling academically and then direct them to services that will help them stay in school. (p. 23)

The study also noted that the institution provided services that were well aligned, with staff working together with each other and with faculty to help students make progress toward achieving their goals. This was all founded on a strong conceptual approach.

Collaboration to provide services and engage students in their learning is also critical, particularly between academic units and student affairs. Schuh (2003) notes that "students are served best when services, programs, and learning opportunities are linked so that they can be accessed easily and build on one another, resulting in a robust learning environment for students" (p. 57). Learning communities and service-learning provide excellent opportunities for such partnerships and for engaging students. Ardaiolo, Bender, and Roberts (2005) suggest that students also often overlook valuable opportunities to learn outside of class: "Students need to embrace the ethos that a college education is more than just attending classes, and institutional practices need to stimulate that understanding" (p. 91).

Redesign and Integration

For many institutions focused on redesigning and integrating student services, a starting point should be to identify student needs and to look at situations where there are inconsistencies in service. A review of existing policies and procedures should follow. If bringing related services together requires restructuring, cross-training for staff can help reduce the runaround students often experience. Many institutions have moved to a one-stop center, bringing together such offices as admissions, registration, financial aid, bursar, and academic advising. Similarly, many institutions have integrated their information systems.

Johnson County Community College (JCCC) is an excellent example of an institution that has done just that. JCCC serves more than 16,000 credit students and 17,000 noncredit students per semester. Dealing with increasing enrollments, expansion of degree programs offered, and changes in the diversity and needs of the student population, student feedback indicated that processes were becoming increasingly fragmented, with students being sent from one office to another or facing long waits in line. Recognizing that students would be more likely to succeed if they had clear educational and career goals, felt a personal connection to the institution, and were engaged in the educational process, JCCC transitioned to a new student services model. The Student Success Center became a natural first stop for new and prospective students. Staffed by trained, knowledgeable, and accessible generalists, the center has goals

> to assist students with the first- and second-level questions they typically bring on their first visit, to assist them in gathering the information needed as part of their planning process, and to direct them to the appropriate specialist for individual assistance. (Ramos & Vallandingham, 1999, p. 116)

The center uses technology to get information to students and to allow students to access the student information system. Instead of focusing on enrollment, the college now focuses on where students are heading and how staff members can help them get started. This allows the institution to concentrate on how to facilitate the growth and development of each student and how to encourage student learning and achievement of individual goals. Collaboration between student services staff, faculty, and students was a key to the model's successful implementation.

Changes to the organizational structure often require corresponding changes in the staffing model. The new model should detail the responsibilities of each individual in the new organization. Some staff will need additional training to get started, and ongoing training and support are critical. In moving toward a one-stop model, an institution may create generalist positions, in which staff armed with basic information about a wide variety of services respond to many different questions on the front line. Such staff should be able to work well with people, have a broad base of knowledge, and know how to use the relevant technologies (Burnett & Oblinger, 2003). With the move to more online services for distance learners, it is important that those responding to questions from such learners have the same training and expertise as those at the service desk. All interactions should focus on providing a positive experience and creating a relationship.

EXEMPLARY PRACTICES THAT FOCUS ON STUDENT SUCCESS

In her article "Benchmarking Best Practices in the Learning College," Kay McClenney (2003) looks to the League for Innovation in the Community College and its 12 Vanguard Learning Colleges (see www.league.org/league/projects/lcp/vanguard.htm) to explore examples of strong institutions that are focusing more intensely on student learning to become even better. The article lists Cascadia Community College and the Community College of Denver as examples of institutions whose very organizational structure is designed to support student learning. It also mentions Kirkwood College's Student Success Council, which has been successful at seeing several initiatives through to implementation. Likewise, it mentions resource manuals developed at Humber College that define generic skills, writing across the curriculum, and a variety of other personal and thinking skills. It also mentions the teacher-formation program at Richland College, a faculty development and appraisal system based on *The Courage to Teach* (1998), by Parker Palmer.

The following section describes several other community colleges that have organized their student services in a way that puts students first. Three of these institutions, through the CCSSE, have been identified as MetLife Foundation Best-Practice Colleges. Another is an exemplary practice that has been developed in conjunction with the MDRC Opening Doors research project. Finally, one exemplary practice was recognized in the research of Barefoot et al. (2005), which identified "institutions of excellence in the first college year."

Valencia Community College

In the 1980s the leaders of Valencia Community College, a multicampus urban college, became concerned about student completion rates. Since then, they have worked steadily to increase student success. Using a team approach, a focus on student learning, and a focus on the student experience at the college, Valencia took advantage of several Title III grants to concentrate on student retention initiatives and to become more learning centered. Over a 15-year period, those initiatives have grown into "sustained, integrated systems that shape the Valencia student experience" (CCSSE, 2005b, p. 1). Those initiatives included the following:

- A sustained program of professional development opportunities on such topics as diverse students, learning technologies, developmental advising, and other programs that emphasize active and collaborative learning. Valencia's Teaching and Learning Academy provides professional development for full-time faculty and also offers a similar program for adjuncts. Since implementation of this program, the college has seen significant improvements in degree completion, retention, and grades.

- Creation of a developmental advising program called LifeMap, "a five-stage student progression model that encompasses a student's plan of action for using Valencia resources to achieve career and educational goals, a guide to help students determine where they are going and identify easy step-by-step directions for getting there, and a planning process through which students define and achieve their educational goals" (CCSSE, 2005b, p. 1). The system integrates developmental advising with the curriculum, business practices and procedures, and publications.

- A focus on "start right" strategies that include changes in procedures, processes, and student/staff interactions throughout the enrollment process. Some of these changes include an application deadline two weeks before the start of a term, not allowing a student to add a class once it has met, and an automated prerequisite-checking system that blocks students from classes for which they have not taken the prerequisites.

- Implementation of a three-credit student success course.

- Assessment that has shown a 3% increase in fall-to-fall retention from 2002–2003, an increase in the number of credit hours attempted by students, and improved completion rates for students enrolled in developmental courses (CCSSE, 2005b).

Housatonic Community College

Also recognized as a MetLife Foundation Best-Practice College, Housatonic Community College, an urban community college of 4,700 students, faced issues related to a significant enrollment increase that included many more ethnically diverse, academically underprepared, and financially disadvantaged students. Many students had extensive family obligations. The college recognized the need to address the challenges of these at-risk students. As a result, the entire college community looked at approaches to help students succeed. The college gathered information through student surveys, faculty-staff collaboration, and identifying best practices. The strategies that were implemented included:

- Requiring academic advising for students who are new, returning after a break, transfers, or changing their major (the college also holds special advising days to encourage student use of advising)

- Offering 24/7 online tutoring (in addition to regular individual and group tutoring)

- Creating a college-wide early-warning and referral system that makes a personal connection early in the semester and encourages use of tutoring, advising, and counseling services

- Focusing on ESL students and English skills through an individual assessment that includes a personal interview and ensures correct placement in courses

Ongoing assessment has shown an increase in graduation rates, an increase in students who enroll in their sophomore year, and an increase in students transferring to four-year institutions (CCSSE, 2005a).

Sinclair Community College

Sinclair Community College (see CCSSE, 2006), another MetLife Foundation Best-Practice College, created a holistic student success program designed to increase retention and graduation rates for high-risk students. Responding to statistics that showed Sinclair had significantly lower retention and graduation rates than other Ohio community colleges, Sinclair's leaders made a commitment to improving student success. They reviewed the literature, researched best practices, and looked at their own successful programs.

Sinclair's student success program uses a case management approach, counseling, and a web-based support system to monitor and help students in creating and implementing their individual learning plans (ILPs). Staff had to cross traditional work boundaries to become a fully functioning team and were trained in five different areas. Case management notes are maintained online so everyone has access to the same information and can deliver consistent information and advice. The program is mandatory for approximately one-third of Sinclair's entering students (based on specific criteria, such as needing two developmental courses, being undecided, and working full time), but currently enrolled at-risk students are referred to the program as well.

Data are collected quarterly to evaluate the program's effectiveness. Results have shown an improvement in retention to the next term and an increase in retention of the ILP students compared to non-ILP high-risk students. And for the first time there is no significant difference between the retention of minority students and nonminority students.

Kingsborough Community College

Kingsborough Community College volunteered to participate in MDRC's Opening Doors research project. MDRC was created in 1974 to learn about what works in social policy and has conducted extensive evaluations of policies and programs for economically disadvantaged people. Recognizing that community colleges are a key resource for low-income individuals, MDRC has researched initiatives designed to help students be successful.

Kingsborough Community College is testing the Opening Doors Learning Communities program, which has served 750 freshmen whose test scores indicated that they needed developmental coursework in reading, writing, or math. In the program students are placed into learning communities of up to 25 students. The learning communities take three courses together: English (or developmental reading or writing), an academic course, and a one-credit freshman orientation course taught by a counselor. The instructors work as a team to integrate the courses, review student progress, and devise strategies to enhance student success. The counselor works with students struggling with obstacles to attendance and success. Students also receive extra tutoring and a voucher to purchase books. Early results show that Opening Doors students achieved higher course pass rates than those in the control groups and that after one year they were more likely to have completed their remedial English requirements.

Other Opening Doors colleges are focusing on the importance of mandatory intrusive academic advising and the importance of providing additional financial support.

The Community College of Denver

The Community College of Denver, whose demographic profile is generally not associated with strong student success rates, was named an "institution of excellence in the first college year" (Barefoot et al., 2005). One of the factors in that recognition was its three-tiered advising program implemented to enhance student success. Level 1 is called Red Carpet Days, where entering students come to campus for assessment, orientation, advising, registration, and campus tours. Level 2 is targeted advising for special programs. One aspect of level 2 is the First Generation Student Success Program, which "includes a combination of strategies to increase student learning and retention, including educational case management, peer mentoring, learning communities, computerized instruction, and a focus on skills development, academic tracking and intervention" (Barefoot et al., 2005, p. 41). Level 3 is for students with at least 30 academic credits. At this level the educational case management is housed in four academic centers. Educational case management is described as a model for holistic student success in which "case managers maintain one-to-one relationships with a cohort of students and manage a comprehensive portfolio of student support services" (Barefoot et al., 2005, p. 43). Case managers actively monitor student progress and intervene whenever necessary. Technology plays a key role in the educational case management.

CONCLUSION

There are numerous exemplary student services practices that put students first. Institutions implementing those practices have pulled together faculty and staff from both student and academic affairs to consider their student population, evaluate student needs and expectations, compare the match between existing services and student needs, and then develop concepts for what new or altered services should look like. Once the concepts are in place, these institutions could then look at facilities, staffing, technology, and assessment. The exemplary practices are interconnected, they view the student holistically, and they focus on engaging and creating positive experiences for the student.

REFERENCES

Ardaiolo, F. P., Bender, B. E., & Roberts, G. (2005). Campus services: What do students expect? In T. E. Miller, B. E. Bender, J. H. Schuh, & Associates, *Promoting reasonable expectations: Aligning student and institutional views of the college experience* (pp. 84–101). San Francisco, CA: Jossey-Bass.

Barefoot, B. O., Gardner, J. N., Cutright, M., Morris, L. V., Schroeder, C. C., Schwartz, S. W., et al. (2005). *Achieving and sustaining institutional excellence for the first year of college.* San Francisco, CA: Jossey-Bass.

Burnett, D., & Oblinger, D. G. (2003). Student academic services: Models, current practices, and trends. In G. L. Kramer & Associates, *Student academic services: An integrated approach* (pp. 27–52). San Francisco, CA: Jossey-Bass.

Committee on Education and the Workforce. (2003). *State of American higher education: What are parents, students, and tax payers getting for their money?* Washington, DC: U.S. Government Printing Office.

Community College Survey of Student Engagement. (2003a). *CCSSE national student characteristics.* Retrieved June, 30, 2007, from www.ccsse.org/survey/national2.html

Community College Survey of Student Engagement. (2003b). *Closing the gaps: A look at high-risk students.* Retrieved June 30, 2007, from www.ccsse.org/survey/nr_closing.html

Community College Survey of Student Engagement. (2005a, February). *CCSSE Highlights, 4*(4), 1–2.

Community College Survey of Student Engagement. (2005b, May). *CCSSE Highlights, 4*(8), 1–2.

Community College Survey of Student Engagement. (2006, May). *CCSSE Highlights, 5*(7), 1–2.

Estrella Mountain Community College. (2007). *Student services.* Retrieved July 2, 2007, from www.emc.maricopa.edu/studentservices/

Gardenhire-Crooks, A., Collado, H., & Ray, B. (2006). *A whole 'nother world: Students navigating community college.* New York, NY: MDRC.

Jenkins, D. (2006). *What community college management practices are effective in promoting student success? A study of high- and low-impact institutions.* New York, NY: Community College Research Center.

Klein, A. (2006, March). One-stop wonders. *University Business, 9*(3), 56–60.

Kramer, G. L. (2003). Preface. In G. L. Kramer & Associates, *Student academic services: An integrated approach* (pp. xi–xxiii). San Francisco, CA: Jossey-Bass.

Lancaster, L. C., & Stillman, D. (2002). *When generations collide: Who they are. Why they clash. How to solve the generational puzzle at work.* New York, NY: HarperCollins.

McClenney, K. M. (2003, April). Benchmarking best practices in the learning college. *Learning Abstracts, 6*(4), 1–4.

Oblinger, D. G. (2006, January/February). Radical flexibility and student success: An interview with Homero Lopez. *EDUCAUSE Review, 41*(1), 44–55.

Palmer, P. J. (1998). *The courage to teach: Exploring the inner landscape of a teacher's life.* San Francisco, CA: Jossey-Bass.

Ramos, B., & Vallandingham, D. (1999). Student development model as the core to student success. In M. Beede & D. Burnett (Eds.), *Planning for student services: Best practices for the 21st century* (pp. 113–118). Ann Arbor, MI: Society for College and University Planning.

Sandeen, A., & Barr, M. J. (2006). *Critical issues for student affairs: Challenges and opportunities.* San Francisco, CA: Jossey-Bass.

Schuh, J. H. (2003). The interrelationship of student academic services. In G. L. Kramer & Associates, *Student academic services: An integrated approach* (pp. 53–77). San Francisco, CA: Jossey-Bass.

Sparks, C. T. (2006). *Opening session address.* Proceedings from the Texas Association of Community College Chief Student Affairs Administrators Fall Meeting, Hurst, TX.

Upcraft, M. L., & Stephens, P. S. (2000). Academic advising and today's changing students. In V. N. Gordon, W. R. Habley, & Associates, *Academic advising: A comprehensive handbook* (pp. 73–83). San Francisco, CA: Jossey-Bass.

19 PUTTING STUDENTS FIRST IN THE CAMPUS COMMUNITY

GARY L. KRAMER

(WITH THOMAS J. GRITES, ERIC R. WHITE, MICHAEL A. HAYNES, VIRGINIA N. GORDON, MICHAEL MCCAULEY, WESLEY R. HABLEY, AND MARGARET C. KING)

The need to improve student support services has never been greater, particularly as higher education enrollments continue to rise to new levels (Hussar, 2005). As this volume attests, student success continues to be a topic of keen interest on college and university campuses. Fortunately, creating an environment that supports student success is especially attainable today. A large body of research directs campus leaders and policymakers to make adjustments and commit to addressing the needs and circumstances of today's and tomorrow's students. The characteristics of these students, as described in Chapter 1 in this volume, bring unique challenges that require those who work in higher education to rethink and modify their educational and cultural environments.

Furthermore, although the United States has fallen behind as a world leader in higher education (slipping on measures including college participation, access to college, and degree completion; see Hebel, 2006), during the past decade higher education has sought to become more student centered. A landmark example is the work by Kuh, Kinzie, Schuh, Whitt, and Associates (2005) on the Documenting Effective Educational Practice project. Using the National Survey of Student Engagement as the base research tool, these authors have established benchmarks for student success. In addition, they have identified effective educational practices across the institutional spectrum for other institutions to follow.

The manifestation of one-stop student services centers has also addressed critical service needs of students from admission to graduation. In Chapter 7 of this volume, Louise Lonabocker and James Wager note the benefits of one-stop organizations in meeting the expectations of today's students. Such centers underscore the importance of staff collaboration and shared partnerships in offering better, more convenient services to students. However, not all campuses have the means to organize a physically central-ized center for student services. Cost and other factors may hamper such undertakings. The authors suggest bypassing extensive remodeling, adminis-trative reorganization, and cross-training by concentrating on creating a vir-tual student services center. The virtual approach provides a richer opportunity to integrate services and allows the campus to provide services at any time and from any place. But as pointed out in Chapter 7, virtual one-stop services require a strong information technology (IT) infrastructure, which not all campuses have.

The expectations of today's students for services are high and rising. They expect improved, responsive, and comprehensive services from the academy, which has an escalating array of technological solutions to choose from. The effective use of such technologies requires a strong partnership between advi-sors, service providers, academic departments, and technologists. These groups have boundless opportunities to work together as a team and to respond to—and even exceed—students' expectations.

CHAPTER FOCUS

Chapter 9 in this volume, by Wesley Habley and Jennifer Bloom, effectively set the stage for this chapter, especially the use of the Council for the Advancement of Standards in Higher Education (CAS) as a framework to respond to students' expectations and their need for comprehensive services from the campus academic advising community. Academic advising is an essential element of a student's collegiate experience. It is one of the very few institutional functions that connect all students to the institution. In fact, many leaders of advising, including the author-contributors of this chapter, have noted that advising is the only structured activity on campus in which all students have the opportunity for ongoing, one-on-one interaction with a concerned representative of the institution. According to CAS (2006a):

> Advising evolves from the institution's culture, values, and practices
> and is delivered in accordance with these factors. In recent years,
> increasing political, social and economic demands, along with newly
> developed technologies, have spurred changes in educational deliv-
> ery systems, student access, and faculty roles. As a result of these
> changes, more specialized student support opportunities have
> emerged, including adaptations in academic advising. (p. 28)

Why Is Academic Advising Pivotal to Putting Students First?

In *Making the Most of College* (2001), Richard Light concludes that good advising may be the most underestimated characteristic of a successful college experience. Similarly, Habley and Bloom state in Chapter 9 that quality academic advising has the power to positively influence individuals as well as the campus community as a whole. Perhaps no other program on the campus bridges the teaching-learning roles of faculty and the academic department with campus student services support programs as does academic advising, especially in helping students achieve their academic goals. When there is commitment and broad vision, academic advising can be interwoven throughout the campus tapestry of services and academic departments.

When institutions effectively and consistently assess and adjust their advising program goals to the goals that students set for themselves, good results occur. Specifically, a well-coordinated and collaborative campus advising program can positively influence students' academic success, satisfaction with faculty and the college experience, retention, academic skill development, career decision-making, lifelong education, persistence to graduation, campus involvement, effective use of time, and meaningful relationships with faculty. To achieve student success, there is no need as pressing as the development of collaboration or shared partnerships. This is especially noted in *Powerful Partnerships: A Shared Responsibility for Learning* (1998), a joint report of the American Association for Higher Education (AAHE), American College Personnel Association (ACPA), and National Association of Student Personnel Administrators (NASPA), which contains 10 principles about learning and collaboration. As Fuller and Haugabrook (2001) describe, "Much of the actual work of collaboration boils down to team building and attending to the individual relationships behind the larger partnerships" (p. 85).

At its best, academic advising serves as the campus hub of academic services from students' point of entry to graduation. Advisors have a broad vision of the institution and, therefore, play an important interpretive role with students, administrators, and faculty in helping them further understand students' academic and personal development needs (see Chapter 15 in this volume; Kramer, 2003a, 2004a, 2004b). Because academic advising cuts across all dimensions of campus student services and its success is inextricably tied to the success of all other campus services, it is important that there be institutional shared partnerships that focus on fostering student success on the campus. Thus, to advance student learning and success, an institution needs a shared philosophy of how best to achieve student success.

The Council for the Advancement of Standards in Higher Education

Gary L. Kramer, Thomas J. Grites, and Eric R. White

To increase student success and learning on the campus, researchers, national organizations, and associations have focused on quality educational practices, standards, principles, and imperatives and overall greater collaboration among professionals on the campus. Examples include *The Student Learning Imperative* (ACPA; 1996); *Good Practice in Student Affairs* (Blimling, Whitt, & Associates, 1999); *Powerful Partnerships* (AAHE, ACPA, & NASPA, 1998); the Baldrige National Quality Program; the Academic Quality Improvement Project; the American Productivity and Quality Center; Sandeen and Barr's (2006) critical issues to achieve success on the campus; and Kuh, Kinzie, Schuh, and Whitt's (2005) conditions for a student-centered culture.

However, perhaps the most comprehensive set of standards and assessment guidelines for directing student success programs, evaluating current programs, advocating for new initiatives, and establishing professional development come from CAS. Founded in 1979 to promulgate and promote standards for various enterprises in higher education, CAS fosters student learning and development, quality assurance, student success, and professional integrity.

Over the years these standards have served as a reference point for colleges and universities as they examine the nature of their academic advising and related student services programs. In instances where no program existed, institutions have looked to the standards as a beginning point to delineate the basic components of any advising program. Using the CAS (2006a) standards and guidelines for academic advising as a foundation for the initial development and subsequent improvement of campus advising can help institutions achieve their goal of student success. The CAS standards assume that such improvement is more readily achievable when it is self-directed rather than externally mandated. Likewise, a hallmark of any profession is its commitment to self-assessment and monitoring the behaviors of its members.

In other cases colleges and universities have used the standards, along with the companion *Self-Assessment Guides* (CAS, 2006b), to make improvements in their programs through a rigorous process of self-examination. Some institutions have used the standards when regional accreditation, state or local evaluation, or discipline-based accreditation has been required.

The *Self-Assessment Guides* translate the standards and guidelines into a format that can be used for assessing one's own advising program or unit. Through this approach, the strengths and deficiencies of an academic advising program can be identified. In addition, the self-assessment approach provides a formal action plan for making improvements. As a self-regulatory approach, the *Self-Assessment Guides* are a tool with profession-wide endorsement for examining an academic advising program in relation to the most currently accepted standards of practice. Thus, there is no need to proceed with assessment in an ad hoc manner because those who conduct assessment are assured that the instrument has been thoroughly tested.

To further support the CAS standards and the work of academic advisors, the National Academic Advising Association (NACADA; 2004) provides the "Statement of Core Values of Academic Advising." This document serves as a framework to assist those who practice academic advising in understanding their roles and responsibilities to the students with whom they work, to the institution where they are employed, to higher education and society in general, and to themselves.

In addition, the most recent document that should be used in the development or improvement of academic advising programs is the NACADA (2006) "Concept of Academic Advising" statement. This document provides a framework from which an institution can develop its own definition of what academic advising is on that campus. The concept is grounded in the teaching and learning mission of higher education and offers a fundamental curriculum (the what), a pedagogy (the how), and sample student learning outcomes (the result) of academic advising.

The following sections consider academic advising in terms of themes from the CAS standards and guidelines and from other models mentioned earlier. These sections emphasize six pathways to achieving student success on the campus. Each pathway presents the standard, its context and importance for implementation, and its application. Using the CAS standards and guidelines, the NACADA "Statement of Core Values of Academic Advising," and the NACADA "Concept of Academic Advising" statement, we will argue that effective academic advising is key to providing a student-centered culture and, ultimately, helping students achieve success.

PATHWAY ONE: ESTABLISHING A LIVING MISSION

Michael A. Haynes

The CAS standards and guidelines for academic advising and the NACADA "Statement of Core Values of Academic Advising" both stress the importance of having a strong mission statement for all academic advising programs. The CAS standards are very direct: "The institution must have a clearly written mission statement pertaining to academic advising that must include program goals and expectations of advisors and advisees" (CAS, 2006a, p. 29). The

NACADA statement is less direct, but in its emphasis on academic advisors' operating in the context of higher education, their institutions, and their educational community, the efficacy of a clear, accessible written mission statement for academic advising is most evident.

Context

A mission statement that places academic advising firmly in the context of the goals of higher education and the particular institution, that is recorded and disseminated, and that is regularly reviewed is a living mission statement. It's a statement that educates internal and external audiences about the primacy of effective academic advising at the institution and that challenges professional and faculty advisors and students to work effectively together toward meeting sound educational goals.

The institutional mission statement and, perhaps, its strategic plan are the starting points for developing a living mission statement for academic advising. The CAS (2006a) standards assert that the primary purpose of academic advising "is to assist students in the development of meaningful educational plans" and that a mission statement for an advising program "must incorporate student learning and student development" (p. 29). Going beyond the basics and crafting a mission statement that reflects the unique qualities of advising within the particular institution is part of making a living statement.

Application

The University of Akron states in its strategic plan that student success is essential to an Akron educational experience: "This means that we have an environment conducive to opportunity and one where students acquire the skills, knowledge, and disposition with which they can capture and experience success" (University of Akron, n.d.). The Academic Advisement Center at Akron reflects this emphasis on student success: "Our mission is to educate, counsel, and empower students to make effective academic decisions as they work to fulfill their education, career, and life goals" (University of Akron, 2006).

The "Statement on Academic Advising" for Syracuse University (n.d.) is easily found on its web site. In the statement, the Syracuse leadership clearly states the importance of advising at the institution, describing it as an "essential component of a Syracuse University education" and emphasizing that it involves a "shared commitment." The statement continues:

Students are responsible for scheduling, preparing for, and keeping advising appointments; for seeking out contacts and information; and for knowing the basic requirements of their individual degree programs. Students bear the final responsibility for making their own decisions based on the best information and advice available and, ultimately, on their own judgment.

Advisors at Syracuse "will be available to students on a regular basis, monitor their advisees' progress, assist in considering career options, and make appropriate referrals to other campus offices."

In Ball State University's advising handbook, given to students and families at orientation and also available on its web site, the university affirms its commitment to provide students with "academic support services to assist [them] in making progress toward [their] academic goals" (Ball State University, 2007). The statement also lists 10 student responsibilities that range from general expectations about being knowledgeable about institutional academic policies and regulations to very specific expectations, like keeping a current address on file with the university and checking institutional email regularly. Since Ball State uses professional advisors for all freshmen and faculty advisors for students with sophomore standing or above and a declared major, responsibilities for both types of advisors are clearly delineated alongside the student responsibilities.

As an assessable measure of success for its advising program, the University of Akron (2006) publicly states learning outcomes for its students, including the expectations that Akron students "understand the university's general education and pertinent degree-related requirements" and "will develop an educational plan consistent with life goals." Syracuse University (n.d.) pledges "to help faculty and staff develop effective advising skills, to evaluate its system of academic advising and support services, and to make improvements where necessary."

Summary

The living mission statement is the starting point for articulating to audiences both inside and outside the institution the vision of a program that is committed to student learning and development, respectful of the institutional vision, and responsive to student and advisor needs as reflected in ongoing assessment practices. A sound living mission statement will challenge—even inspire—advisors and students and be a guide to consistent, effective advising practice at the institution for many years.

PATHWAY TWO: CONNECTING ACADEMIC AND CAREER PLANNING

Virginia N. Gordon

According to the CAS standards for academic advising, the fundamental purpose of academic advising is to help students create educational plans that will allow them to accomplish their goals in life. The CAS standards for career services provide a similar focus: Career services exist to help students "in all phases of their career development" (CAS, 2006b, p. 6). The similarity of goals for these two CAS standards emphasizes the importance of integrating academic and career advising.

Context

Today's college students are facing a fast-paced, ever-changing work world. To be prepared to enter this diverse and competitive workplace, it will take not only careful educational planning but the acquisition of knowledge and skills essential to entering and managing a productive and satisfying career. The role of the academic advisor is to assist students in making choices about their major and potential career areas by helping forge the connections between in-class and out-of-class educational experiences. Career services is often the designated on-campus entity that assists students in finding potential job opportunities and career paths. This is done through assessing how and what students learn, suggesting new ways of implementing the learning process, and determining how that process can be applied to students who are transitioning into the full-time workforce. Both services are enhanced through improved information, resources, and evaluation of all outcomes.

This important pathway for connecting academic and career planning parallels most students' expectations because students typically equate their educational decisions with career choices. Many students and their parents assume that it is the institution's responsibility to provide career exploration, planning, and assistance with job placement. Academic and career decisions can have lifelong consequences, so it is important for students to receive the highest level of assistance in this area.

According to the CAS standards and guidelines, career services should not only help students clarify their values, interests, and abilities but also help them identify the academic and career-related skills they possess and provide opportunities to acquire those they don't. Students must also be able to document knowledge, skills, and accomplishments resulting from both in-class and out-of-class learning; articulate their preferred work environment; and initiate a job search that includes constructing a job résumé with clear career objectives. Some students may need assistance in exploring their interests in graduate or professional education. Career services also needs to develop positive relationships with employers and external constituencies.

Application

The CAS standards for academic advising and career services provide guideposts for defining exemplary practices and implementing specific methods and techniques for these important functions. Several effective practices from the CAS standards are described in the following sections.

Career advising and counseling. Career exploration and decision-making must start with a realistic assessment of the student's strengths, talents, and limitations. Resources for helping students understand their interests, abilities, and values can range, for example, from seeking information on the Internet to matriculating in career courses to completing computerized or written self-assessments in a career center. This process can help students become aware of how past associations and experiences have influenced their academic and career decisions. Careful self-assessment will suggest additional experiences that can fill in any gaps students may have as they prepare for the careers they are considering. Many skills can be acquired through coursework, volunteer opportunities, or work experiences. Campus resources that help students with internships, volunteer opportunities, study abroad, community service, and other work-related experiences are vital for students entering today's competitive and demanding workplace.

As students make academic and career decisions, they should be able to articulate clearly why the choices were made. Students should be able to recognize how their academic major does and does not relate to occupational possibilities. They should be able to describe the type of environment in which they prefer to work and why its attributes are desirable. Academic and career advisors and career placement professionals can help students make the connections between classroom learning and the work world. Providing professional assistance in job search techniques and job placement can be a revealing teaching tool.

Information resources. The CAS standards for both academic advising and career services emphasize the need to help students identify and access valid career information, which is critical to educational and career planning. Although the Internet tends to be the predominant source of academic and career information for students, faculty, and staff, there are many other valuable sources that should be part of a comprehensive system. Career libraries are important repositories for many types of information, including printed guides, computer-assisted career guidance systems, and audio-visual materials. It is essential to provide students with instruction on how to use any of these sources—online or off—effectively. This helps students focus and prioritize the information they are accessing. Advisors must be well versed in the campus information resources available to students and should have firsthand knowledge of their purpose and content so that relevant referrals can be made.

Experiential learning. Experiential learning programs enable students to integrate their academic studies with work experiences and career exploration. Such programs provide students with opportunities to define both their learning and career objectives and to reflect on ways they have grown through their experience. Academic departments that offer experiential learning experiences—such as coursework, service-learning, cooperative experiences, and internship opportunities—should work closely with career services so a broader approach to life and career planning can be provided.

Kent State's Collage program. An example of an institution that has successfully integrated academic and career standards is Kent State University. The university offers a web-based program, called Collage, that engages students in a variety of academic and career activities that help them identify and connect academic majors with related career fields. The Collage web site (http://career.kent.edu/home/general/whatisCollage.cfm) offers students the opportunity to create their own "collage," or career portfolio, by accumulating information about themselves and academic and career alternatives. A "Tools for Researching Careers" page offers different ways to do this, including completing SIGI PLUS, contacting alumni through the alumni association's mentor program, attending career fairs, and using resources for obtaining internships and part-time jobs related to a specific career field.

As students engage in various activities, the "My Collage" page records and summarizes their results and asks questions to help them process what they have learned. A final page called the "Junk Drawer" describes the many resources that students can draw on, such as academic planning assistance, electronic business cards (i.e., an address book), a survival kit (containing, e.g., assertiveness and procrastination tests), an emotional intelligence test, and a list of campus resources that can assist in planning.

Summary

The pathway connecting academic and career services on campus is critical to the goal of helping students reach their full potential. These services should reflect the developmental and demographic profile of the students being served. Some of the challenges students entering today's workplace will encounter are new, but most are similar to what generations of graduating students have faced in the past. Although today's students need to be technologically literate, other traits required in the workplace—flexibility, collaboration, the willingness to learn, and the ability to communicate well—have always been hallmarks of a college education.

PATHWAY THREE: OUTCOMES ASSESSMENT

Thomas J. Grites

It is no accident that the final CAS standard, standard 13, has to do with assessment and evaluation. This standard is the true test of whether all the other standards have been met. This standard requires reflection on the academic advising program's mission, goals, and objectives, asking what the academic advising program is expected to accomplish. This standard calls for further reflection on the human, physical, and fiscal resources necessary to achieve the mission and program, as well as the organizational structure that is best suited to manage them. It requires institutions to consider how these factors can be combined into an educational framework and environment that maximizes conditions for institutional and student success. Finally, the standard recommends a cyclical process of review and change. A well-conceived strategy or pathway to determine the efficiency and effectiveness of these conditions ensures a quality assessment effort and product.

Context

The standard harkens to the NACADA (2004) "Statement of Core Values of Academic Advising," asking whether individual academic advisors are fulfilling the expectations of their institutions, their students, their colleagues, and their profession. This pathway to success, therefore, must be considered as an integrated approach of both macro and micro analyses of the academic advising program. In addition, the NACADA (2006) "Concept of Academic Advising" statement reinforces the need for determining what student learning outcomes result from academic advisement.

With the outcomes identified, the institution can undertake a systematic review of processes, materials, resources, programs, events, and activities to determine whether they are being achieved. Such a review is often conducted in the form of a self-study, similar to an accreditation process. This review is really an audit of the overall academic advising program. The CAS standards and guidelines provide an excellent framework for conducting such an audit, and the corollary *Self-Assessment Guides* (CAS, 2006b) provides the mechanism to do so.

Another excellent tool for conducting a programmatic assessment review is the compact disc *Guide to Assessment of Academic Advising* (Campbell, Nutt, Robbins, Kirk-Kuwaye, & Higa, 2005). Opportunities to learn specific applications of this guide are also available through the annual NACADA Assessment of Academic Advising Institute.

Once an assessment plan is in place, how the results will be distributed and used become important considerations. Will they be used to compare advising units across campus, or will they be used simply to measure a unit's own standards? Will they be used to determine the overall role and function of academic advisors in the unit or across the campus? Of course, such questions should be predetermined as part of creation of the assessment plan. Clearly, the best use of the data is to provide a basis for identifying the strengths and weaknesses of the advising program and how it might be improved to benefit all constituencies.

Application

The following are examples of institutions that have followed this pathway to student success by determining the outcomes of their academic advising processes.

The University of Southern Maine. According to Elizabeth Higgins, executive director of the advising and academic resources at the University of Southern Maine (USM), Advising Services has academic advising responsibility for students who are undeclared, who are admitted through USM's conditional acceptance program, or who are not matriculated into any undergraduate or graduate degree program. The department has developed an outcomes-based assessment plan that complements the university's mission and supports its student success initiatives.

College of DuPage. Jocelyn Harney, dean of student services at the College of DuPage, a community college serving 32,000 students, says that academic advising is provided by counseling faculty, instructional faculty, and professional advisors. Each group includes full- and part-time faculty. Consequently, advising is housed in both the academic and student affairs divisions. In an effort to unify and improve the advising function, advising has been linked to the accreditation process, which has resulted in a close, institution-wide examination of advising.

Advising outcomes were identified, improvements were implemented, and an assessment plan was designed. An advisory committee was formed to provide continued monitoring and oversight of academic advising on an institution-wide basis. With the assistance of the research department, assessments were designed, piloted, implemented, and interpreted. The results of the assessments yielded recommendations for future improvements. Efforts to maintain and improve this overall process will continue.

The Richard Stockton College of New Jersey. Peter L. Hagen, director of the Center for Academic Advising at the Richard Stockton College of New Jersey, says that the academic advising program is considered an academic department and, therefore, is required to conduct a programmatic self-study every five years. The college has consistently used the CAS standards in this effort; student surveys and the ACT Academic Advising Audit instrument have also been used.

Each spring term students complete a survey with 19 items to evaluate their advisors. The survey was designed by the Office of Academic Affairs and the faculty union. Results of the survey are shared individually with each advisor, but no comparisons between individual advisors or departments are made.

Annually, a review of the functions of the Center for Academic Advising is conducted to produce a cost-benefit analysis—that is, to determine an actual fiscal value for the programs and services provided by that office.

Summary

Assessing the outcomes of the academic advising process is not an easy task, but when these outcomes are identified, fostered, and realized, student success is maximized and becomes an integral part of the total value of the higher education experience. To begin this process, an institution might consider the following steps to develop an effective pathway to student success through outcomes assessment:

- Establish a work group, team, task force, advisory council, or committee to review current practices in the assessment of academic advising as it currently functions on the campus

- Review the CAS standards, NACADA "Statement of Core Values of Academic Advising," and NACADA "Concept of Academic Advising" statement

- Consider sending a campus team to the NACADA Assessment of Academic Advising Institute, or at least review the NACADA *Guide to Assessment of Academic Advising* (Campbell et al., 2005) to develop an implementation strategy for success through outcomes assessment

PATHWAY FOUR: BLENDING TECHNOLOGY: HIGH TECH + HIGH TOUCH = HIGH EFFECT

Michael McCauley

According to the CAS standards for academic advising programs, technology that supports the advising enterprise must be "adequate" to support its defined mission (CAS, 2006a). Further, it states that the technology, as well as facilities and equipment, must be evaluated regularly and be in compliance with relevant federal, state, provincial, and local requirements on access, health, safety, and security. Also, the standards require that technology-assisted advising include appropriate mechanisms for obtaining approvals, consultations, and referrals and that servers be secure and comply with institutional policies on data stewardship. Finally, the CAS standards state that all advisors have access to computing equipment, local networks, student databases, and the Internet. In other words, these standards encourage the use of technology but say it must be evaluated regularly, comply with all known statutes, be secure, and provide the appropriate and necessary services.

Context

The CAS standards address institutions' difficulty in attracting and retaining a qualified IT workforce. Thus, a growing number of institutions have stopped internally developing systems and software and have instead purchased packaged systems and relied on external consultants to lead implementation efforts. Oftentimes, however, this results in a mismatch between the institutional practice and the technical features offered by the vendors. And costs are typically high, especially when a packaged system is customized. The question campuses must grapple with is whether institutional practice should change to align with the capabilities of the IT system or whether custom IT solutions should be developed to meet service needs. Either choice can create divisive situations on campus. Creating an IT infrastructure and technical features that match student expectations, learning environments, and institutional policies and that monitor student academic progress or academic advising is difficult at best. The good news is that today's vendors are compensating for unique campus environments by supplying provisions for flexibility. But there are limitations and cost inhibitors.

In the information age, using technology to assist in advising is a foregone conclusion. Although the delivery of student services is not about technology, it is about using technology wisely (Oblinger & Oblinger, 2005). With respect to automated advising support systems, the most common is the automated degree audit, which matches a student's completed coursework with a designated set of requirements (e.g., for a major, minor, or general education) and provides a report that clearly illustrates progress toward graduation. Effective and efficient degree-audit reports describe the various requirements and show what has been completed and what objectives need to be fulfilled for degree completion (such as courses and regulations). Further, these reports highlight grades, calculate appropriate grade averages (major, minor, upper division, honors, etc.), illustrate when specific milestones need to be addressed (e.g., filing an application for graduation), and so forth. An efficient degree audit not only monitors academic progress but also performs the final graduation audit. Thus, these activities take a minimal amount of the advisor's time when meeting with a student or conducting necessary reporting activities and gives the advisor adequate time to discuss important issues with advisees.

Communicating with advising clients in an efficient and effective manner is of paramount concern to academic advisors. Large advising caseloads, an increased complexity of degree and program requirements, and changes to key university policies necessitate frequent communication between the advisor and the advisee. Notification of advising appointments, cocurricular activities, and important advising activity dates are also vital. Thus, providing an efficient system of communication lends itself to improved advising and better informed students. Particularly important for students who attend multiple campuses is an automated transfer evaluation system (see the next section for a further description of this technology innovation, particularly Ball State's Automated Course Transfer System).

Application

Because managing and communicating academic information is so important, some institutions have developed technologies that facilitate these components of advising that contribute to student success. In Florida, for example, the Florida Department of Education has created the Florida Academic Counseling and Tracking for Students (FACTS) web site (www.facts.org). High school students, college students, parents, and even counselors can use the services provided on this web site to help plan and track educational progress in Florida. This system provides online services to assist students in doing the following: determining career objectives, evaluating high school progress, seeing a summary of high school coursework and grades, learning about higher education opportunities in Florida, applying to college online, choosing a major, accessing college transcripts and grades, and tracking progress toward college graduation. In addition, FACTS provides assistance to community college students who are contemplating a transfer to a four-year institution within the state. This system has been highly successful in Florida and could serve as a model for other states.

Another example of a well-constructed advising support system is found at Ball State University. Ball State's Automated Course Transfer System (ACTS) allows prospective transfer students to load their transcript data (completed and in-progress coursework) to determine what courses would be accepted by Ball State. Further, ACTS shows how the accepted courses would apply to the student's intended major at Ball State. In addition, ACTS suggests equivalent courses at the student's current institution that would apply to remaining requirements for the desired major at Ball State. Thus, a community college student can select courses to complete an associate's degree and see how those courses will apply to the intended major at Ball State. This leads to decreased time spent at the four-year institution and a higher likelihood of a timely graduation. The same principles are being applied to a statewide transfer system in Indiana, which will ultimately include all public and private institutions that choose to participate.

Perhaps the most comprehensive automated advising support system in the United States is the one used at Brigham Young University. On the web-based, locally developed Academic Information Management (AIM) system, students can not only monitor their progress toward graduation but also see all their evaluated transfer credits, receive assistance with career planning, register for classes, and engage in financial planning for their entire educational career. This system, developed in the 1990s and subsequently released as an integrated web-based and comprehensive student information system, is unique in higher education today because it encompasses every aspect of student academic support.

Summary

The CAS standards related to technology in academic advising support the notion that technology is an integral part of the enterprise. Technological solutions present the most efficient way to collect, manipulate, and disseminate information vital to the success of students. Ideally, custom information technology solutions should be developed to meet the needs of an institution's unique advising needs. If technology adequately supports advising, then advisors will have the time to relate to their students in a meaningful manner, and this relationship will produce satisfied and successful students.

PATHWAY FIVE: REWARD AND RECOGNITION

Wesley R. Habley

Few individuals would argue with the contention that the three most critical and interrelated components of effective performance in any field are training, evaluation, and reward and recognition. Without training, there are no assurances that the appropriate tasks will be accomplished. Without evaluation, there are no assurances that the tasks are being done well. Finally, without reward and recognition, there are no assurances that the tasks will continue to be done well. The CAS standards for academic advising (CAS, 2006a) underscore the interrelatedness of training, evaluation, and reward and recognition. Part 5 (human resources) of the standards delineates the importance of training and professional development as well as the expectation that the academic advising program include routine staff evaluation. Part 13 connects recognition and reward to assessment of the advising program and advisors. The criterion measure (13.4) that addresses the importance of recognition and reward appears in the *Self-Assessment Guides* (CAS, 2006b). It states, "Results of these evaluations are used to revise and improve the program and to recognize staff performance" (p. 28).

Context

During past few decades, research on advising has resulted in greater clarity on both training and assessment practices. At the same time, however, best practices in reward and recognition remain somewhat of an enigma. In the most recent survey of advising practices, Habley and McClanahan (2004) conclude that reward and recognition remain the weakest link in the advising effectiveness chain. A literature review provides little guidance on the topic, offering not much more than the assertion that reward and recognition are critical components of quality advising.

Kerr (2000) suggests that there are two roadblocks to the implementation of effective reward and recognition strategies. First, he suggests that there is no consensus on an appropriate level of reward. Kerr also contends that the competition for scarce resources confounds the situation. Adding to these roadblocks is the complexity created by the broad range of individuals who deliver advising on campus. Advisors may be full-time staff members who have a primary (and sometimes sole) responsibility to deliver advising services. Or they may be faculty members for whom advising is but one of several responsibilities. These factors help explain the absence of detail on advisor recognition and reward included in the CAS *Self-Assessment Guide* (2006b).

Application

Although the design of an effective reward and recognition system for advising is indeed a complex and dynamic process, it is incumbent on institutional leaders to orchestrate a set of rewards, incentives, and recognitions—both tangible and intangible—that encourages advisors to deliver quality advising services.

The often cited management principle "what gets rewarded is what gets done" applies to those who serve as academic advisors. A tangible reward is an external validation to which a value may be assigned. The most obvious form of tangible reward comes in some form of compensation—that is, the result of exemplary performance as an advisor leads to an increase in remuneration. For staff advisors, this reward often comes in the form of merit salary increases. Or it may result from movement to a higher pay grade based on advancement on a career ladder. Because of the competition for scarce resources, however, salary increments for advising (other than cost-of-living adjustments) are not typically implemented. For faculty advisors, tangible rewards may come in the form of promotion or tenure decisions, which in turn lead to salary increases. An additional example of a tangible reward is a monetary award earned as a result of being selected as an outstanding advisor. There is considerable evidence that campus advising awards (compensated or uncompensated) are growing in popularity. A Google search for "academic advising awards" yields more than 100 examples of such awards.

The paucity of tangible rewards for advising makes the intangible recognition that much more important. In fact, although management experts underscore the importance of tangible rewards, many surveys of employees indicate that the intangibles are extremely critical to workplace satisfaction. An intangible reward, then, is one of unquantifiable and intrinsic value to the advisor. Thus, advisor satisfaction with the advising role and the workplace environment are, in and of themselves, rewards. Although there may be other examples of intangible recognition and reward, all of them have one thing in common: Each of the strategies underscores the notion that academic advising and the work of advisors are valued by the institution.

Summary

It is neither desirable nor possible to delineate a program of advisor recognition and reward that applies to all institutional settings, but it is possible to provide recommendations for readers interested in an extension of those provided in the CAS Standard 13 and in Criterion Measure 13.4. In that spirit, the following additional criterion measures are suggested:

- Exemplary performance as an advisor leads to tangible rewards.

- Exemplary performance as an advisor leads to tangible incentives.

- Exemplary performance as an advisor leads to intangible recognition.

- The recognition and reward system is based on assessment.

- The recognition and reward system is viewed as fair and equitable by those who advise.

- The recognition and reward system takes into account the needs and values of individual advisors.

- Institutional leaders publicly affirm the role of advisors and support the rewards, incentives, and recognition afforded to academic advisors.

- Those who supervise advisors demonstrate through application an understanding of the importance of the intangibles.

In reality, the development of an appropriate and valued recognition and reward program for advisors may be more of an art than it is a science. And perhaps that is why there are few models that are both effective and transferable. An effective program of advisor recognition and reward must include not only intangible recognition but also external validation through tangible rewards and incentives. Advising is far too important to be left solely to those who intrinsically cherish it.

PATHWAY SIX: DELIVERABLES AND ACCOUNTABILITIES

Margaret C. King

Part 2 of the CAS standards and guidelines focuses on the advising program itself and stresses the importance of identifying "relevant and desirable student learning and development outcomes" (CAS, 2006b, p. 4) and providing an advising program that encourages the achievement of those outcomes. The outcomes include

> intellectual growth, effective communication, realistic self-appraisal, enhanced self-esteem, clarified values, career choices, leadership development, healthy behaviors, meaningful interpersonal relations, independence, collaboration, social responsibility, satisfying and productive lifestyles, appreciation of diversity, spiritual awareness, and achievement of personal and educational goals. (p. 29)

Context

The CAS standards state that the academic advising program must be guided by written goals and objectives that tie in with the program mission statement. Examples of those goals include assisting students in assessing their interests and abilities; helping them clarify their educational, career, and life goals; advising on course selection and other educational experiences; directing them to other resources on campus when needed; and evaluating and monitoring their progress toward achieving their goals. Program assessment is critical in determining whether these goals are achieved.

How do institutions ensure that they are providing adequate opportunities for students to achieve these outcomes and goals? First, they must look at the organizational structure of academic advising. There must be a clear organization of advising services. Habley (1983, 1988) identified seven organizational models for advising services that can be classified as decentralized, centralized, and shared (Pardee, 2000). Whatever model is used, advising programs need strong leadership—someone must be in charge. The program also needs to provide appropriate training that addresses informational, conceptual, and relational content. The advising program needs to be regularly assessed and should provide appropriate recognition and reward for those who do advising well.

Application

The following examples focus on how institutions have organized advising services, prepared their advisors to work with students, prepared students to work toward the identified outcomes and goals, and determined whether the efforts have been successful. The examples are taken from the NACADA award winners described at www.nacada.ksu.edu/Awards/OP_Recipients.htm.

The University of Central Florida was recognized for its advisor enhancement program. This collaborative program encompasses academic affairs, student development, and enrollment services and provides opportunities for networking, professional development, and improved communication. The monthly advising enhancement program includes presentations facilitated by selected university officials and advising offices. Working with the Faculty Center for Teaching and Learning, new faculty advisors attend workshops at the new faculty orientation. The University Academic Advising Council provides an online advising web site, an advising handbook, a variety of training materials, and a communication network that provides regular email updates.

The University College Advising Center at Indiana University–Purdue University Indianapolis developed an ongoing professional development series for faculty and staff who serve as advisors. The series uses a variety of formats and includes several components: a standardized advisor training program, professional portfolios for advisors, an annual campus-wide advising symposium, a graduate-level seminar in academic advising, and a campus-wide listserv for advisors.

Enhancing the academic success of first-year students was the goal of Virginia Commonwealth University when it created an early-intervention program. Each October the university collects early semester grades from faculty teaching 100- and 200-level courses and then, through an intrusive advising program, notifies and contacts those students receiving D or F grades. In a meeting with the students, the advisor addresses the specific academic difficulties the student is experiencing, recommends general study strategies, and provides specific study tips from the instructor. The program increased the number of A, B, and C grades earned; decreased the number of students placed on academic warning; and increased the first-to-second-semester retention rate.

Through a collaborative effort between student and academic services, Monroe Community College created the Liberal Arts Mentor Program, a dynamic program that allows faculty and students to develop ongoing connections in and out of the classroom. It begins with a classroom connection and leads to the faculty assisting their assigned students in long-range career planning, having social and intellectual discussions with other mentors and mentees, and engaging in basic advising for course selection. The program provides programming opportunities, additional training, newsletters, a database for student contact information, and guidance and support from the two program coordinators (one a faculty member and the other a professional academic advisor).

Summary

Institutions that have made significant improvements to their academic advising programs have been intentional, collaborative, and focused on student learning and development outcomes. They provide students with opportunities designed to encourage achievement of the identified outcomes and provide assessment to demonstrate that the outcomes have been achieved. They recognize that students and advisors share responsibility for the advising process, they provide offerings that are designed to meet the developmental needs of relevant student populations and communities, and they assist students in making the best academic decisions.

CONCLUSION

Like other student-oriented services, advising is most effective and makes the largest difference in students' lives when it is based on the premise of student growth and success. No single activity can do more to set the academic tone of the college experience and establish a comprehensive approach to student success than quality advising. However, even with standards and guidelines in place like those from CAS, campus leaders will not be able to assure all stakeholders involved that such standards contribute to student learning, are administered effectively, and are consistently aligned with institutional and student expectations unless there is a strong assessment of student and program outcomes (see Chapter 3 in this volume as well as Pathway Five in this chapter for more on assessment). As most accrediting bodies insist, the quality of programs must be regularly assessed, and data about student progress must be known. Successful advising programs put students first by knowing their needs and goals and then consistently evaluating and aligning student progress and program objectives. It cannot be a peripheral activity; rather, it must be central to the work of advising.

Putting students first in the campus community, however, involves the goodwill of the institution. Certainly, a living mission, broad visionary leadership, a clear and straightforward program strategy, and measures of learning outcomes are extremely important. However, just as important, if not more so, are the attitude, culture, and commitment of the campus to make a difference in the lives of students. This should be most evident in the advising arena, the gatekeeper for the institution's academic progress and the vehicle for the delivery of student services.

You might ask, as we did at the beginning of this volume, what the defining moment or experience during your sojourn in higher education was. Probably, long after you have forgotten the information, learning objectives, and advice given, you remember most the gift of time and attention. Researchers in higher education have long advocated that the people who are most influential in the lives of students are those who build relationships with students that are tailored to each student's unique situation (Astin & Astin, 2000; Bailey, 2006; Braxton, 2006; Hearn, 2006; Kuh, Kinzie, Buckley, Bridges, & Hayek, 2006; Kuh, Kinzie, Schuh, & Whitt, 2005; Light, 2001; Pascarella & Terenzini, 2005; Perna & Thomas, 2006; Tinto, 2000; Tinto & Pusser, 2006). On the other hand, for important outcomes to occur, including satisfaction with college and with academic and personal achievement of goals, students must also adjust expectations, take initiative, and share responsibility for learning through preparation. An important purpose of a campus advising program is to increase students' capacity to take charge or what Piper and Mills (see Chapter 11 in this volume) identify as "self-authorship."

The theme for the 2002 Winter Olympics was "Light the Fire Within." Audience and participants alike expected and looked for the best. In a similar way students, faculty, staff, and campus leaders expect the best from each other. And there is evidence (cited in this chapter and throughout this volume) that these expectations are being met. Still, it is obvious that we can do more to improve campus efforts, especially in the advising context, as we all seek to better understand student needs, monitor their progress, and put them first in the campus community. Although advising is not a panacea for the ills of higher education, advisors can be bellwethers for students because of their close and lasting relationship with them. It is in the advisor's office that the institution and the student meet face to face. Thus, guided by the CAS standards and the six pathways to achieving student success discussed in this chapter, advisors have the opportunity to represent and align the best of the institution to the student and the best of the student to the institution (Kramer, 2003b). Furthermore, using the CAS standards to clearly and consistently define the roles of academic advising on the campus has the potential not only to put students first but also to create pathways that will more thoughtfully integrate and humanize the processes of services to students.

REFERENCES

American Association for Higher Education, American College Personnel Association, & National Association of Student Personnel Administrators. (1998). *Powerful partnerships: A shared responsibility for learning.* Washington, DC: American College Personnel Association.

American College Personnel Association. (1996). *The student learning imperative: Implications for student affairs.* Washington, DC: Author.

Astin, A. W., & Astin, H. S. (2000). *Leadership reconsidered: Engaging higher education in social change.* Battle Creek, MI: W. K. Kellogg Foundation.

Bailey, T. R. (2006, November). *Research on institution level practice for post-secondary student success.* Paper presented at the National Symposium on Postsecondary Student Success, Washington, DC.

Ball State University. (2007). *Academic advising.* Retrieved July 1, 2007, from www.bsu.edu/advising/

Blimling, G. S., Whitt, E. J., & Associates. (1999). *Good practice in student affairs: Principles to foster student learning.* San Francisco, CA: Jossey-Bass.

Braxton, J. M. (2006, November). *Faculty professional choices in teaching that foster student success.* Paper presented at the National Symposium on Postsecondary Student Success, Washington, DC.

Campbell, S., Nutt, C., Robbins, R., Kirk-Kuwaye, M., & Higa, L. (2005). *Guide to assessment of academic advising* [Compact disc]. Manhattan, KS: National Academic Advising Association.

Council for the Advancement of Standards in Higher Education. (2006a). *CAS professional standards for higher education* (6th ed.). Washington, DC: Author.

Council for the Advancement of Standards in Higher Education. (2006b). *Self-assessment guides* [Compact disc]. Washington, DC: Author.

Fuller, T. M. A., & Haugabrook, A. K. (2001). Facilitative strategies in action. In A. Kezar, D. J. Hirsch, & C. Burack (Eds.), *New directions for higher education: No. 116. Understanding the role of academic and student affairs collaboration in creating a successful learning environment* (pp. 75–88). San Francisco, CA: Jossey-Bass.

Habley, W. R. (1983, November). Organizational structures for academic advising: Models and implications. *Journal of College Student Personnel, 24*(6), 535–540.

Habley, W. R. (Ed.). (1988). *The status and future of academic advising: Problems and promise.* Iowa City, IA: ACT.

Habley, W. R., & McClanahan, R. (2004). *What works in student retention: Four-year colleges.* Iowa City, IA: ACT.

Hearn, J. C. (2006, November). *Student success: What research suggests for policy and practice.* Paper presented at the National Symposium on Postsecondary Student Success, Washington, DC.

Hebel, S. (2006, September 15). Report card on colleges finds U.S. is slipping. *The Chronicle of Higher Education,* p. A1.

Hussar, W. J. (2005). *Projections of education statistics to 2014* (NCES Publication No. 2005–074). U.S. Department of Education, National Center for Education Statistics. Washington, DC: U.S. Government Printing Office.

Kerr, T. (2000). Recognition and reward for excellence in advising. In V. N. Gordon, W. R. Habley, & Associates, *Academic advising: A comprehensive handbook* (pp. 349–362). San Francisco, CA: Jossey-Bass.

Kramer, G. L. (Ed.). (2003a). *Faculty advising examined: Enhancing the potential of college faculty as advisors.* Bolton, MA: Anker.

Kramer, G. L. (2003b). The light within us: Advising with heart and mind. *NACADA Journal, 21*(1&2), 5–7.

Kramer, G. L. (2004a, June). A baker's dozen for enhancing first year commuter student advising. *Journal of Metropolitan Universities: An International Forum, 15*(2), 31–53.

Kramer, G. L. (2004b, Spring). Core principles of a qualitative faculty advising program. *The Department Chair, 14*(4), 21–23.

Kuh, G. D., Kinzie, J., Buckley, J. A., Bridges, B. K., & Hayek, J. C. (2006). *What matters to student success: A review of the literature.* Paper presented at the National Symposium on Postsecondary Student Success, Washington, DC.

Kuh, G. D., Kinzie, J., Schuh, J. H., & Whitt, E. J. (2005). *Assessing conditions to enhance educational effectiveness: The inventory for student engagement and success.* San Francisco, CA: Jossey-Bass.

Kuh, G. D., Kinzie, J., Schuh, J. H., Whitt, E. J., & Associates (2005). *Student success in college: Creating conditions that matter.* San Francisco, CA: Jossey-Bass.

Light, R. J. (2001). *Making the most of college: Students speak their minds.* Cambridge, MA: Harvard University Press.

National Academic Advising Association. (2004). *NACADA statement of core values of academic advising.* Retrieved July 1, 2007, from www.nacada.ksu.edu/clearinghouse/AdvisingIssues/Core-Values.htm

National Academic Advising Association. (2006). *NACADA concept of academic advising*. Retrieved July 1, 2007, from www.nacada.ksu.edu/Clearinghouse/AdvisingIssues/Concept-advising-introduction.htm

Oblinger, D. G., & Oblinger, J. L. (Eds.). (2005). *Educating the net generation*. Boulder, CO: EDUCAUSE.

Pardee, C. (2000). Organizational models for academic advising. In V. N. Gordon, W. R. Habley, & Associates, *Academic advising: A comprehensive handbook* (pp. 192–209). San Francisco, CA: Jossey-Bass.

Pascarella, E. T., & Terenzini, P. T. (2005). *How college affects students: A third decade of research*. San Francisco, CA: Jossey-Bass.

Perna, L. W., & Thomas, S. L. (2006, November). *A framework for reducing the college success gap and promoting success for all*. Paper presented at the National Symposium on Postsecondary Student Success, Washington, DC.

Sandeen, A., & Barr, M. J. (2006). *Critical issues for student affairs: Challenges and opportunities*. San Francisco, CA: Jossey-Bass.

Syracuse University. (n.d.). *Academic Advising and Counseling Services*. Retrieved July 1, 2007, from www-hl.syr.edu/cas-pages/AcademicAdvCounselServ.htm

Tinto, V. (2000). Learning better together: The impact of learning communities on student success in higher education. *Journal of Institutional Research, 9*(1), 48–53

Tinto, V., & Pusser, B. (2006, November). *Moving from theory to action: Building a model of institutional action for student success*. Paper presented at the National Symposium on Postsecondary Student Success, Washington, DC.

University of Akron. (2006). *2006–2007 undergraduate bulletin*. Retrieved July 1, 2007, from www.uakron.edu/academics/docs/ugrad.pdf

University of Akron. (n.d.). *Enabling competencies*. Retrieved July 1, 2007, from www.uakron.edu/president/chart/enable.html

20 | FOSTERING STUDENT SUCCESS: WHAT REALLY MATTERS?

Gary L. Kramer

This volume's chapter contributors have offered a myriad of suggestions to assist higher education policymakers, campus leaders, faculty, and practitioners in establishing a student-centered culture. They have defined student success as more than just timely graduation, identified foundational conditions that foster student success on the campus, aligned student success research with effective educational practices, and suggested qualitative next steps for institutions to consider.

This concluding chapter will first address the questions about the concept of student success raised in the preface. The sections that follow then summarize important points from the book's chapters: 1) common themes or factors that contribute to effective educational practices (or what colleges do to create an environment for student success); 2) services that matter to students (or effective educational practices); and 3) next steps for campuses to consider in fostering student success in the campus community.

THE CONCEPT OF STUDENT SUCCESS

Student success as presented in this volume takes on a variety of forms and is related to a multitude of characteristics, conditions, indicators, outcomes, and institution-specific factors. This book does not claim that these are the only critical issues that must be resolved by higher education or that answers are readily available and transferable across the higher education spectrum. However, the issues identified in this volume are matters higher education must consider. And policymakers and campus leaders must commit to student success research, especially longitudinal research and strong programs of assessment and evaluation of foundational practices. Otherwise, the concept of student success will continue to be rhetorical, isolated, debatable, and

Figure 20.1   **Visual Ambiguity**

something that depends on the eye of the beholder—much like Joseph Jastrow's famous image in Figure 20.1. Which is it—a rabbit or a duck?

However, unlike that image, student success as presented in this volume is not necessarily left to perception only. Although it may vary from campus to campus, there are common threads or themes of effective educational practices that suggest promise for a campus-wide student-centered culture.

The inherent problem with the image is that it leads the viewer to believe that the first-seen possibility is the only way to understand the picture; alternative understandings are not explored (Love & Estanek, 2004). In the context of student success, if graduation is the only variable institutions look for in achieving success, they may not see other ways to successfully develop students. Thus, the challenge that the authors of this volume extend is to think differently about what student success means on the campus and reconsider how faculty, campus leaders, and service providers can be more fully engaged to systemically foster student success.

Although there will always be institutional constraints, the campus commitment and will to believe and see students as first are unrestrained. The ideas attributed to Harold Hodgkinson and John Gardner in the Preface of this volume—the necessity of knowing students' needs and expectations and the importance of caring about whether they achieve success on the campus— are more cultural than they are related to resources. The challenge for each campus community is to define student success so that the outcome can be more systematically fostered and monitored.

In Consideration of Influencing Student Success

It can be argued that the emphases of this book—aligning expectations, connecting services, fostering student development, and achieving success—are very difficult assignments for campus leaders, policymakers, service providers, faculty, and staff to advance on today's campus. This is especially true in light of changing student, faculty, and staff roles and characteristics (see Chapter 1). The very concept of student learning (where, when, and how) and institutional adaptations required to be effective are in constant flux. Serving students of the millennial generation (Coomes & DeBard, 2004)—or as Oblinger and Oblinger (2005) term them, "the Net generation"—compounds matters because many students shift from institution to institution and even attend more than one institution at the same time. Millennials tend to struggle to meet institutional expectations of the traditional classroom and campus environment. Lovett (2006) observed that such students often must hold more than one job to support family and thus are not always involved or engaged on campus. And, at times, they resist institutional pressures to participate in social, recreational, or cocurricular activities. Thus, Lovett points out that it is often difficult for the campus to build a sense of community and to measure student success in the traditional ways of retention or time-to-graduation studies. Institutions are often left to find alternative ways to enrich student learning and success.

Another factor to consider in the equation of defining and fostering student success is aligning reasonable institutional and student expectations around learning, development, and success. Miller and Reyes (see Chapter 3) examine student expectations and compare them with the realities of the student experience. These authors determine that considerable effort goes into notifying students of the institution's expectations but much less energy goes into determining what students expect of institutions. Student expectations about the classroom, student services, and campus life are not always factored in with institutional expectations and definitions of student development, learning, and success. Student success begins with a good student-institution fit. Institutions need to be what they claim to be, and they need to claim to be only what they are, state Miller and Reyes. An institution has a duty to discuss with students how college can help them succeed and to dispel false expectations from outside sources (Miller, Bender, Schuh, & Associates, 2005; for further discussion, see Chapters 2, 3, 6, 11, and 16 in this volume). Engaging faculty and preparing service providers are also essential parts of communicating and effectively aligning institutional and student expectations (see Chapters 14 and 15 in this volume).

In addition, of particular importance is the role of assessment and evaluation to gather data and link measures of student success to approaches to teaching, class size, student services, and college organizations (Perna & Thomas, 2006). Without ongoing student outcomes assessment or continuous monitoring of student progress, how will the institution know whether institutional and student learning outcomes are obtained? Knowing students and how they are progressing in the higher education system is fundamental to the discussions presented in this volume (see, e.g., Chapters 8, 9, and 10). This is particularly important in light of increasing pressure for higher education to provide evidence of student learning outcomes and overall student success. These indicators of success will vary and become more difficult to assess because of the characteristics and changing roles of the millennial generation (see, e.g., Chapters 4 and 5 in this volume).

The Preface raised the following three questions: 1) What does higher education research tell us about student success on the campus? 2) What services matter to students? 3) What should the campus consider as next steps to foster student success? Thus, based on findings from the chapters in this volume, the next section summarizes common themes found across effective student-centered educational practices in a variety of higher education institutions. Also highlighted are key factors or conditions for campuses to consider as they seek to develop and implement student success programs.

WHAT CAN COLLEGES DO TO CREATE AN ENVIRONMENT THAT FOSTERS STUDENT SUCCESS?

What then are the common threads that weave research findings and principles into a rich tapestry of practice leading to student success? Building on the success of the National Survey of Student Engagement (NSSE), Kuh, Kinzie, Schuh, Whitt, and Associates (2005) have identified several common themes and conditions at high-performing institutions. Themes from their work include the following: 1) a living mission and a lived educational philosophy, 2) an unshakeable focus on student learning, 3) environments adapted for educational enrichment, 4) clearly marked pathways to student success, 5) an ethos of improvement/outcomes, and 6) shared responsibility for educational quality and student success. Furthermore, in this regard, this chapter and book would be remiss if it did not recognize another outstanding work by Kuh and his fellow researchers (Kuh, Kinzie, Buckley, Bridges, & Hayek, 2006) on achieving student success on the campus, which offers a comprehensive and evidence-based review of the factors that facilitate and inhibit student success.

Fundamental to this volume and many other scholarly works is the question of effectively defining and measuring student success. Bailey (2006) points out that graduation with a desired degree is an appropriate indicator of student success and of the institution's performance. He goes on to emphasize that although graduation is on the minds of policymakers, leaders, and students themselves, each institution's students differ in their ability to do college work. A focus on graduation rates alone runs the risk of embellishing the reputations of selective schools while tarnishing the perceptions of those serving a wider range of students. Therefore, institutions must look at other indicators of student success. Examples include students' being prepared for jobs, entering jobs serving society's needs, finding employment after attendance, achieving financial literacy, becoming civically engaged, gaining basic general education understandings, acquiring appropriate certification or licensure for employment, and pursuing lifelong learning (Bailey, 2006). Relying solely on graduation rate data—and thereby implicitly assuming that students not graduating from an institution represent a failure on the institution's part—is a narrow definition of student success (Bailey, 2006). Graduation from college, albeit an important indicator of student success, is not the only factor for student success. Indeed, as presented throughout the chapters, there are many other factors or threads that define student success, which Table 20.1 summarizes as indicators or themes common to promoting student success on the campus.

SERVICES MATTER TO STUDENTS: EFFECTIVE EDUCATIONAL PRACTICES

Although this volume provides a theoretical framework for student success in higher education, it also considers institutions where research has been applied effectively. Though there is still much to learn, we already have a good sense of what works. Where we fail is not so much in knowing what to do but in being serious about building effective partnerships between institutions and policymakers on behalf of the students we serve. Researchers in higher education have proposed frameworks, benchmarks, principles, standards, conditions, and expectations to guide institutions in the delivery of effective and improved services that matter the most to students. For example, Braskamp, Trautvetter, and Ward (2006) identified several student-centered considerations for action based on an in-depth study of 10 colleges and universities; Blimling, Whitt, and Associates (1999) centered their contribution to achieving student success on the campus on 7 principles of good practices; Sandeen

Table 20.1   **Common Themes Among Institutions that Foster Student Success**

1. Promoting student success through a clearly stated mission.
   · Educated decisions are based on the mission.
   · The mission reflects the core values of the institution.
   · Campus leadership is committed to and focused on student success.
   · The mission is focused on learning environments.
   · The mission reflects an intentional institutional commitment to student success.

2. Integrating educational and social support networks that complement the institution's mission.
   · The institution supports shared partnerships and collaboration within the campus community.
   · The institution creates human-friendly environments in which students can easily interact with each other and faculty.

3. Assessing institutional practices in accordance with student success and expectations.
   · Institutions establish accountability through continuous assessment.
   · A culture exists in which data drive decisions.
   · Institutions align outcome measures with educational practices.

4. Maintaining a focus on students and their success through assessment.
   · Assessment mirrors what other institutions are doing to succeed.
   · Assessment monitors the advisors who help students grow and succeed.
   · Assessment promotes individual self-awareness.
   · Assessment makes students accountable.

5. Knowing who the institution's students are.
   · Screening tools help define student characteristics.
   · The institution reaches out to incoming students and preparatory institutions to prepare future students.
   · The institution anticipates and aligns student and institutional expectations.

6. Engaging students in meaningful ways.
   · Out-of-class learning experiences are promoted.
   · Seminars (such as freshman or senior seminars) and learning communities support students.
   · The institution assists students in becoming self-authored before leaving college (through such things as out-of-class learning and multicultural and ethnic experiences).

7. Creating friendly environments that encourage student, staff, and faculty interactions.
   · Student-centric buildings and facilities provide students with easier access to services.
   · Students can be referred to a specialist after a single contact with student services.
   · The institution offers integrated offices of academic and student services.

8. Developing collaborative working relationships (i.e., shared partnerships) between student and academic affairs.
   · Institutional services are integrated to offer seamless delivery.
   · Staff are developed through ongoing training.

9. Fostering an atmosphere of success through student services.
   · Student services providers are cross-trained.

10. Using technology to promote student success and learning.
    · Technology makes information easily and readily accessible.
    · Technology allows students to change personal information, view test scores, and perform other important functions.
    · Portals allow students to promote their own success.
    · E-portfolios help measure student success and promote student abilities.
    · Emerging technologies are used to better assist students in achieving their academic goals and aims.
    · Technology is adapted to the classroom to improve student learning and satisfaction.

---

and Barr (2006) focused on decades of experience in putting students first on 12 critical issues; Barefoot et al. (2005) based their research on several case studies of institutions that are known for their effectiveness in addressing student needs; Jillian Kinzie and George Kuh in this volume (Chapter 2) and in other scholarly works (Kuh et al., 2006; Kuh, Kinzie, Schuh, & Whitt, 2005; Kuh, Kinzie, Schuh, Whit, & Associates, 2005) extended findings from the NSSE to 20 effective educational practices and 12 common themes or indicators for student success; and Dalton offered his 12 principles and practices for strengthening student moral and spiritual growth (Chickering, Dalton, & Stamm, 2006). Similarly, Chapters 17 and 18 in this volume focus specifically on achieving success in the first-year experience and in the two-year college, and Chapter 19 identifies and expands on the CAS standards as a framework to deliver programs that influence student success.

In Chapter 5 Earl Potter notes that the term *benchmarking* is often used as a synonym for best practice research and that it is the process of finding comparison data for a set of measures. Once again, drawing from the chapters in this volume, Table 20.2 lists practices that align with the common themes discussed in the previous section. However, there is no claim here that the effective educational practices cited are the best or are the most effective educational practices on fostering student success.

NEXT STEPS TO FOSTERING STUDENT SUCCESS

Certainly, it is the intent of all colleges to purposefully engage and help students succeed on the campus. They invest in students with purpose and intentionally apply their resources, talents, and time to foster student success. However, the changing roles of faculty, students, technology, campus organizational structures, the globalization of higher education, and other factors

Table 20.2   **Educational Practices that Foster Student Success**

Model	Concept (Emphasis)	Institutions Cited in Chapters
Living mission statement	Institutions that put students first in education and focus on student learning through student-centered work areas	Alverno College; California State University–Monterey Bay; Coker College; Luther College; Sweet Briar College; University of Maine at Farmington; University of Michigan; University of Texas at El Paso; Ursinus College; Wabash College
	Institutions with student success practices based on their mission statements	The Evergreen State College; Fayetteville State University; George Mason University; University of Kansas; University of Maine at Farmington, University of the South (Sewanee); Winston-Salem State University; Wofford College
	Institutions that clarify academic advising roles and use CAS standards to help students achieve success	Ball State University; Boise State University; Brooklyn College; Clemson University, College of DuPage; Hamilton University, Indiana University–Purdue University Indianapolis; Kent State University; Monroe Community College, Oregon State University; Pennsylvania State University; Richard Stockton College of New Jersey; Syracuse University; University of Akron, University of Central Florida; University of Southern Maine; Virginia Commonwealth University
	Institutions that have education practices designed to challenge students in and out of the classroom	Alverno College; California State University–Monterey Bay; The Evergreen State College; Fayetteville State University; George Mason University; Gonzaga University; Longwood University; Macalester College; Sweet Briar College; University of Kansas; University of Maine at Farmington; University of Michigan; University of the South (Sewanee); University of Texas at El Paso; Ursinus College; Wabash College; Wheaton College; Winston-Salem State College; Wofford College
Assessment	Institutions that use continual assessment to improve services and retention of students	Alverno College; California State University–Monterey Bay; George Mason University; Miami University; University of Kansas
	Tools for researching and aligning student and institutional expectations	Academic Quality Improvement Program (Purdue University Calumet); College Student Expectations Questionnaire; College Student Experiences Questionnaire; Cooperative Institutional Research Program; Malcolm Baldrige National Quality Award (University of Northern Colorado)

Model	Concept (Emphasis)	Institutions Cited in Chapters
	Institutions that use benchmarking to identify best practices and improve organizational performance	Metro College; Mountain Top Community College; South Central College
	Institutions that have a well-conceived strategy to determine the accomplishment of program expectations	College of DuPage; Oregon State University; Richard Stockton College of New Jersey; University of Southern Maine
One-stop student services (physical)	Institutions that use innovative methods to improve students' access to vital student services	Anne Arudel Community College; Boston College; Brigham Young University; Carnegie Mellon University; Cuyamaca College, Estrella Mountain Community College; New York Institute of Technology; Northeastern University's School of Professional and Continuing Studies; Seton Hall University; University of Connecticut; University of Delaware; University of Minnesota; University of Pennsylvania
One-stop student services (virtual)	The use of technology to assist and empower students	Brigham Young University; Cuyamac College; Pennsylvania State University; University of Maryland; University of Michigan; University of Minnesota; University of Texas at El Paso
Learning technologies that serve students	Institutions that have employed technological innovations to enhance the student learning process and assist in student services	College of William and Mary; Community College of Denver; Duke University; Massachusetts Institute of Technology; Metropolitan State College of Denver; Nottingham University; Pennsylvania State University; Purdue University; University of Arizona; University of Colorado–Denver; University of Southern California; Wake Forest University
Academic and career planning	Institutions whose service groups collaborate to enhance students' educational process from enrollment through graduation	Florida State University; George Mason University; James Madison University; Kent State University, University of Illinois at Urbana-Champaign; University of Maryland, University of Northern Iowa; University of Wyoming

continued

continued

Model	Concept (Emphasis)	Institutions Cited in Chapters
Developing students for success	Institutions that create processes to put students first in their personal search for meaning and purpose within the campus community and in their personal lives	Bethune-Cookman College; Bowling Bethune-Cookman College; Bowling Green State University; California State University–Northridge; College of Wooster; Colorado College; Creighton University; Hamline University; Hope College; Northwestern University; Pacific Lutheran University; Pennsylvania State University; Princeton University; Swarthmore College; Union University; University of California–San Diego; University of Dayton; University of Nevada–Las Vegas; University of South Carolina; University of Wisconsin; Villanova University; Whitworth College; Williams College
Engaging faculty in advising students	Institutions that use faculty and trained professionals to assist students in achieving success in educational goals	Clarke College; Concordia University; Kent State University; University of Wisconsin–Stevens Point
Enhancing the first-year experience	Institutions that have programs to help students successfully complete their first year of college	Clarke College; Concordia University; Indiana University–Purdue University Indianapolis; Inver Hills Community College; Kent State University; Syracuse University; University of Maryland; University of Michigan–Ann Arbor; University of Wisconsin–Stevens Point; Valencia University; Wagner College; Western New Mexico University
Enhancing the two-year college experience	Two-year institutions whose institutional structure is designed to support student learning, provide clear educational and career goals, and foster a personal connection to the institution	Cascadia Community College; Housatonic Community College; Humber College; Johnson County Community College; Kingsborough Community College; Kirkwood Community College; Richland College, Sinclair Community College; Valencia Community College

have created significant challenges for institutions to maintain consistency, let alone provide for continuous improvement on all educational fronts.

Table 20.3 identifies next steps to help institutions of higher education stay the course. Based on recommendations from this volume's authors, this list collates important action items, or next steps, for colleges to consider, especially as they seek to improve on existing student services and create a campus-wide, student-centered environment.

Table 20.3   **Next Steps to Fostering Student Success**

1. Colleges and universities should review institutional data about their students.
   - Institutions can use a cultural lens to systematically discover and examine aspects of institutional life that encourage student success.
   - Trustees need to be better informed about national recruiting concerns and be proactive in requesting reports that fully disclose recruitment practices.
   - Institutions should not consider social and academic life separately because much learning takes place in the social context of a student's life.
   - Institutions should ask themselves how the technology that students use influences their personal learning styles and social inclinations.
   - Institutions need to do a better job of understanding the expectations of students before their academic experience begins.
   - Institutions should use assessment on a continuous basis to identify learning outcomes and to adjust educational practices.

2. Institutions should put students first on the campus.
   - Institutions should reevaluate instructional techniques to ensure that students' needs are being met.
   - Institutions should review system-wide policy to ensure that current policies serve all students.
   - Institutions need to remember that students are individuals and make that fact the basic tenet of working with them.
   - Institutions must be willing to challenge the expectations and assumptions of faculty and administrators in the institution.
   - Institutions should periodically review and evaluate institutional policies and practices with an eye on student success.
   - Student-centered institutions create and sustain campus cultures that challenge and support all students to high levels of achievement.
   - Institutions should compare incoming students' expectations with the realities of student life to understand students' specific needs.
   - Institutions should regularly invite students to suggest services and comment on existing services.
   - Institutions should foster an atmosphere in which students can safely challenge, test, and identify personal values along with their academic pursuits.
   - Institutions should base advising on the premise of student growth and success.

3. Institutions should make students responsible for their own performance.
   - Institutions should communicate the importance of students' becoming involved in different dimensions of the college experience and encourage students to share responsibility for their performance and for that of their peers inside and outside the classroom.
   - Institutions should value and support student success.
   - Institutions should understand incoming students' expectations about their life and what they believe it will take to be successful.
   - Institutions should encourage all students to participate in learning activities.
   - Institutions should use such tools as learning partnerships as a map toward self-authorship.
   - Institutions should prepare students to examine and develop purpose for their lives.

continued

continued

4. To create a student-centered culture, institutions should develop widespread support in which everyone is pulling in the same direction.
   - Institutions should intentionally design their services in ways that reinforce effective educational practices.
   - Institutions should establish a continuing assessment program for all programs, services, and student learning experiences.
   - Institutions should support the retention of first- and second-year students as well as persistence to completion through quality advising.
   - Institutions should foster collegial relationships between faculty and other professionals by encouraging qualities like integrity, perseverance, and courage.
   - Institutions should create a living mission, broad leadership, a clear and straightforward program strategy, and measures of learning outcomes.
   - Institutions should encourage service providers and advisors to build relationships with students that are tailored to students' unique situations.
   - Institutions should improve performance through intentionally designed approaches.

5. Institutions should seize opportunities to spark cultural change.
   - Student services leaders should seek to develop effective partnerships with campus colleagues.
   - Campus leaders should define new expectations and hire to those expectations.
   - Executives and senior administration officials should yield traditional organizational chart territories for new configurations that meet current student expectations and needs.
   - Institutions should make creating a campus environment in which students succeed their highest priority.
   - Institutions should understand that success is systematic and must be addressed systematically.

6. Successful institutions should stay the course.
   - University presidents should hire student services leaders as much for their courage and insight as for their experience in an array of roles.
   - Institutions should make known their educational philosophy to all.
   - Institutions should pay more attention to identifying intentional outcomes based on institutional mission, vision, and values.

7. Institutions should remember that today's students are consumer driven and expect institutions to meet their needs.
   - Institutions should be prepared to provide support for the technologies that students bring to school.
   - Institutions should be aware of students' desire to conduct business on campus through self-service portals.
   - Institutions should move toward web-based solutions and personal services.
   - Institutions must decide whether the institutional practice should change to align with the information technology system or whether custom IT solutions should be developed to meet their specific needs.
   - Institutions should regularly invite students to comment on existing services and to suggest new approaches.

8. Institutions should use one-stop service centers
   - Institutions should avoid organizational silos.
   - Institutions should cater to students and families by integrating and centralizing services.
   - Institutions should minimize overhead by consolidating services, thereby reducing the staff and amount of equipment required.
   - Institutions should use technology to allow students to control the place, time, and medium of the campus services they receive.

9. Institutions should realize that advising, when properly supported, adds value to the student experience.
   - Institutions should know about current technologies that are being used to advise students.
   - Institutions should ensure that their staff is thoroughly trained.
   - Institutions should encourage students to develop relationships with faculty to create a stronger learning environment.
   - Institutions should use advising as a way to increase students' capacity to take charge.
   - Institutions should use the CAS standards to clearly and consistently define the roles of academic advising on the campus.

10. Institutions should offer first-year seminars, transition programs, and learning support as strategies to improve retention rates.
   - Undergraduate programs should incorporate first-year seminars, learning communities, out-of-class learning opportunities, and institutional policies and practices to improve retention.

CONCLUSION

McDonald (2002) attributes the concept of a campus community to Ernest Boyer, a highly respected and influential higher education scholar. Over his career, Boyer, former president of The Carnegie Foundation for the Advancement of Teaching, consistently advocated that all parts of campus life—from the recruitment of students to teaching—contribute to students' sense of "wholeness." He advocated that the "true calling" for higher education is to create a community that includes everyone on the campus and to foster the success and dignity of each person. In this context, then, what matters to student success, and what needs to be factored in as the campus creates a student-centered culture? Bailey (2006) suggests the following:

- The trajectory for academic success in college is established long before students matriculate.

- Family and community are indispensable to a student's raising educational aspirations, becoming college prepared, and persisting in college.

- The right amount and kind of money matter to student success (i.e., too little can make it impossible for students to pay college bills; too much loan debt can discourage students from persisting).

- Most students—especially those who start college with two or more characteristics associated with premature departure—benefit from early interventions and sustained attention at various transition points in their educational journey.

- Students who find something or someone worthwhile to connect with in the postsecondary environment are more likely to engage in educationally purposeful activities during college, persist, and achieve their educational objectives.

- Institutions that focus on student success and create a student-centered culture are better positioned to help their students attain their educational objectives.

- Because we value what we measure, institutions should focus assessment and accountability efforts on what matters to student success—institutional effectiveness and student success will not improve without valid, reliable information to guide change efforts and monitor performance.

At the beginning of this chapter was a picture of a duck or a rabbit, depending on the perspective of the viewer. The point of the image is that the viewer can see both animals, just not at the same time. Seeing more in regard to enriching student success on the campus is a dominant theme of this book. To see student success, the viewer must also see assessment as integral to knowing when success has been achieved. Attempting to see more leads us to act differently as we seek to put students first in our work. If institutional leaders in higher education are serious about promoting a culture that is sensitive to student needs and dedicated to the development of student success, they will strive to align institutional and student expectations, connect services that are valuable to students, enrich students' development through viable learning opportunities, and monitor student achievement of goals through assessment of learning outcomes, which allows them to see how what they do contributes to the overriding goal of student success. Indeed, if colleges are to be successful in fostering student success, it must be everyone's business. Or, applying Csikszentmihalyi's (1990) definition of the "optimal experience," student success is something we *make* happen.

REFERENCES

Bailey, T. R. (2006, November). *Research on institution level practice for post-secondary student success.* Paper presented at the National Symposium on Postsecondary Student Success, Washington, DC.

Barefoot, B. O., Gardner, J. N., Cutright, M., Morris, L. V., Schroeder, C. C., Schwartz, S. W., et al. (2005). *Achieving and sustaining institutional excellence for the first year of college.* San Francisco, CA: Jossey-Bass.

Blimling, G. S., Whitt, E. J., & Associates. (1999). *Good practice in student affairs: Principles to foster student learning.* San Francisco, CA: Jossey-Bass.

Braskamp, L. A., Trautvetter, L. C., & Ward, K. (2006). *Putting students first: How colleges develop students purposefully.* Bolton, MA: Anker.

Chickering, A. W., Dalton, J. C., & Stamm, L. (2006). *Encouraging authenticity and spirituality in higher education.* San Francisco, CA: Jossey-Bass.

Coomes, M. D., & DeBard, R. (Eds.). (2004). *New directions for student services: No. 106. Serving the millennial generation.* San Francisco, CA: Jossey-Bass.

Csikszentmihalyi, M. (1990). *Flow: The psychology of optimal experience.* New York, NY: Harper & Row.

Kuh, G. D., Kinzie, J., Buckley, J. A., Bridges, B. K., & Hayek, J. C. (2006). *What matters to student success: A review of the literature.* Paper presented at the National Symposium on Postsecondary Student Success, Washington, DC.

Kuh, G. D., Kinzie, J., Schuh, J. H., & Whitt, E. J. (2005). *Assessing conditions to enhance educational effectiveness: The inventory for student engagement and success.* San Francisco, CA: Jossey-Bass.

Kuh, G. D., Kinzie, J., Schuh, J. H., Whitt, E. J., & Associates (2005). *Student success in college: Creating conditions that matter.* San Francisco, CA: Jossey-Bass.

Love, P. G., & Estanek, S. M. (2004). *Rethinking student affairs practice.* San Francisco, CA: Jossey-Bass.

Lovett, C. M. (2006, March 16). Alternatives to the smorgasbord: Linking student affairs with learning. *The Chronicle of Higher Education,* pp. B9–B11.

McDonald, W. M. (Ed.). (2002). *Creating campus community: In search of Ernest Boyer's legacy.* San Francisco, CA: Jossey-Bass.

Miller, T. E., Bender, B. E., Schuh, J. H., & Associates. (2005). *Promoting reasonable expectations: Aligning student and institutional views of the college experience.* San Francisco, CA: Jossey-Bass.

Oblinger, D. G., & Oblinger, J. L. (Eds.). (2005). *Educating the net generation.* Boulder, CO: EDUCAUSE.

Perna, L. W., & Thomas, S. L. (2006, November). *A framework for reducing the college success gap and promoting success for all.* Paper presented at the National Symposium on Postsecondary Student Success, Washington, DC.

Sandeen, A., & Barr, M. J. (2006). *Critical issues for student affairs: Challenges and opportunities.* San Francisco, CA: Jossey-Bass.

NAME INDEX

SUBJECT INDEX